REPRINTS OF ECONOMIC CLASSICS

THE AGE OF THE CHARTISTS
1832-1854

Also Published In

REPRINTS OF ECONOMIC CLASSICS

By J. L. & Barbara Hammond

The Village Labourer 1760-1832. A Study in the Government of England before the Reform Bill [1913]

The Town Labourer 1760-1832. The New Civilization [1917]

The Skilled Labourer 1760-1832. [1919]

THE AGE
OF THE CHARTISTS

1832-1854

A Study of Discontent

BY

J. L. HAMMOND AND BARBARA HAMMOND

REPRINTS OF ECONOMIC CLASSICS

AUGUSTUS M. KELLEY · PUBLISHERS
NEW YORK · 1967

First Edition 1930

(London: Longmans, Green & Co., 1930)

Reprinted 1967 by

AUGUSTUS M. KELLEY · PUBLISHERS

by arrangement with LONGMANS, GREEN & Co. LTD.

LIBRARY OF CONGRESS CATALOGUE CARD NUMBER

66 - 22625

PRINTED IN THE UNITED STATES OF AMERICA
by SENTRY PRESS, NEW YORK, N. Y. 10019

TO THE MEMORY OF

DIGHTON AND MARGARET POLLOCK

PREFACE

In two earlier works, *The Town Labourer* and *The Skilled Labourer*, the writers made a study of the life of those parts of England that were affected most directly by the first Industrial Revolution. Those books ended at 1832. *The Age of the Chartists* treats the social life of the same districts for the period between the passing of the Reform Bill and the outbreak of the Crimean War. The title might suggest a wider scope, for the Chartist movement was not, of course, confined to the North and the Midlands, or indeed to England. But this book is not, in any sense, a history of the Chartist movement. That movement, so long neglected by historians, has been treated in three excellent books, all published in the last twenty years ; one by a French writer, M. Édouard Dolléans, the others by young English writers, Mr. Mark Hovell and Mr. Julius West, whose early deaths were a calamity to English scholarship. In this book the writers are attempting to describe the society that was brought to life by the great changes of the time ; the spirit of that society ; the first efforts to regulate its life, and the discontent that distinguished this phase of English history. If the same period were discussed with special reference to the ideas that guided its constructive efforts, it might be called the Age of Bentham ; if with special reference to the liberal and sanguine outlook of the time, the Age of Cobden ; if, again, with special reference to the dominating figure in its politics, the Age of Peel. But if it is examined with special reference to the unrest of the time, and the relation of that unrest to the life of this new society, it is convenient to take the name that symbolises that unrest. The title has therefore been chosen because it calls attention to this discontent and provides a background for the study of the social life of the time in various aspects.

The writers have to thank a number of friends for suggestions and criticisms; among them Mr. T. S. Ashton, Sir Lawrence Chubb, Mr. C. H. Driver, Mr. H. M. F. Hammond, Mr. Michael Heseltine, C.B., Professor H. J. Laski, Mr. C. M. Lloyd, Professor N. Micklem, Mrs. Ida O'Malley, and Mr. R. H. Tawney. They are under special obligations to Mr. R. J. G. Mayor, C.B., Professor Gilbert Murray, and Mr. Arnold Toynbee for help and advice in their attempt to compare the spirit of the new industrial age with that of classical civilisation. Mr. A. P. Wadsworth has been kind enough to read the book in proof.

They are indebted for guidance in their researches into local history to the Town Clerks of Birkenhead, Blackburn, and Gateshead; to Mr. Ernest Axon, Mr. J. D. Chambers, Mr. T. W. Hanson, Mr. John Helliwell, Mr. Alfred Mattison, Mr. Thomas Midgley, Mr. Skillington, Mr. Charles Smith, and Mr. and Mrs. A. P. Wadsworth.

HEMEL HEMPSTED, *July* 1930.

CONTENTS

CHAPTER I

INTRODUCTORY

DISCONTENT

IF any one were asked to give the causes of the Gordon Riots he would not hesitate long about his answer. He might turn to the pages of *Barnaby Rudge* for a graphic picture of the nightmares that religious terror could excite in an ignorant and credulous populace. He might quote the letter in which Burke, who had risked his life in the riots, appealed to the Government to be moderate in the hour of punishment, on the ground that the guilt of the rioters was shared by the nation, since the law till lately had lent its sanction to intolerance, and the heads of the Church and Dissenting communities had wilfully encouraged it. He might describe the scene in a street in Newgate where a chimney-sweeper held a Bible upside down as he pretended to read it, while a mob searched the house of the trembling merchant. He would point to the weakness of a discredited Government, to the negligence of the City magistrates, to the want of a police force, in order to explain how lawlessness gained the upper hand and London fell for some days into the wild power of rage and plunder.

> "When the rude rabble's watchword was 'destroy'
> And blazing London seem'd a second Troy."

If the same person were asked to give the causes of the Chartist movement, he would be much less ready with an explanation. For he would see at once that no such simple analysis would account for the facts; that this agitation was connected with others, each of them significant of active and conscious discontent; that violence, the most important fact in the Gordon Riots, was the least important fact in the Chartist demonstrations; that unlike the mob, drawn by a strong passion which spent its inarticulate fury in burning Newgate prison to

the ground, the men and women who kept the Chartist movement alive had a steady and responsible quarrel with the conditions of their lives, which gave a unity to efforts that look
distracted and confused. The London mob shouting for Wilkes,
for Gordon, for Queen Caroline, obeyed a simple emotion; the
silent crowds tramping to Newcastle Moor or leaving the
factories of Bradford or Halifax to climb the overlooking hills
for a Chartist meeting, obeyed a deeper and more complex
sense of wrong.

There was a good deal of lawlessness in eighteenth-century
England; particular grievances, like Enclosure Bills, or dear
food, or new machines, excited riots in one place or another.
This kind of violence continued in the next century: the riots
against the raising of prices for the Covent Garden Theatre
lasted several days, and succeeded in their object; there were
savage attacks on the Irish quarter in more than one Northern
town; in 1816 mobs were moving about in East Anglia with
banners inscribed "Bread or blood"; the enclosure of Otmoor
provoked small farmers and labourers to a kind of guerilla
struggle. But any one who throws his mind over the succession of popular movements on a larger and less local scale in
the nineteenth century will see that working-class discontent
assumed in that century a more serious character and significance. The Luddite rising in the Midlands and the North in
1811 and 1812; the agrarian revolt in the southern counties in
1830; the passionate movement inspired by Owen which
collected the energy and enthusiasm of the working classes
throughout England for a great constructive idea in 1833; the
Chartist agitation, in its several forms in the thirties and forties
—all these are expressions of a spirit of which there is little
trace in eighteenth-century England: the resentment of men
convinced that there is something false and degrading in the
arrangement and the justice of their world.

When this discontent appeared, sensible and public-spirited
writers pointed out to the poor that they were much better off
than their fathers and grandfathers. Invention had made com-
modities cheaper; food and clothing were more abundant; the
mills increased family incomes; the poorest people wore stock-
ings; and in other respects the humblest person enjoyed
advantages that had been out of the reach of the lords and squires

of other ages. These contentions have been repeated by recent writers who think that historians have been apt to draw the life of this time in colours too sombre for the truth. Statisticians tell us that when they have put in order such data as they can find, they are satisfied that earnings increased and that most men and women were less poor when this discontent was loud and active than they were when the eighteenth century was beginning to grow old in a silence like that of autumn. The evidence of course is scanty, and its interpretation not too simple, but this general view is probably more or less correct. If, then, there is for the first time systematic and widespread discontent, the explanation must be sought outside the sphere of strictly economic conditions. The rebels, though they included men and women who found it difficult to keep the wolf from the door, were not composed altogether of starving handloom weavers, or unemployed mill-workers. There were other elements in the anger and the envy of the times, and to understand what those elements were it is necessary to look a little more closely into the character of this new society and the general colour of its life.

It is obvious that when men are wandering over the steppes in search of food their pursuits and interests are too narrow in range to make the term civilisation suitable to describe their manner of life. Civilisation implies some degree of independence ; it implies that man has learnt how to mould his surroundings to his own purposes ; that he is not in complete subjection to nature or even just holding his own in a stern struggle.[1] If, then, we are comparing the life of Manchester with the life of the steppes or the tropical forest, we think chiefly of this difference in material power. That is the distinguishing difference. But when we compare two ages or two societies, both of them in a later stage of development, both of them able to follow a settled life and to express their character, their tastes, and ideas in complicated and deliberate institutions, we do not merely compare their material circumstances. If we compare Western civilisation with that of China, or the civilisation of modern Lancashire with that of Rome under Augustus, we do not merely count the material advantages that one possesses and the other lacks—railways, cotton mills, a stock exchange, other

---

[1] See Toynbee, chapter on " History " in *The Legacy of Greece.*

signs and products of economic wealth. We survey the whole of their social life, their religion, their art, their literature, their methods of government and justice, the several institutions in which their public life finds form and expression, the relationships and the sentiments of classes to each other. We recognise, that is, that such a society has to satisfy a wider range of needs than the needs that the nomad is trying to satisfy on the steppes or the tropical man in the depths of the forest. To understand discontent we must keep this range in mind.

For discontent comes from the imagination. "Human sorrow springeth of man's thought."[1] Poverty may produce such a state of the imagination; injustice may produce it; inequality may produce it; but we may find a society enduring great poverty, suffering what seems to us gross injustice, living under conditions so unequal as to look as if they were deliberately designed to provoke envy, in which discontent is unknown. We know that some men like St. Francis find happiness in poverty just because their imagination finds in renunciation and hardship a field for the sublime in thought and action.[2] To thinkers who held, as most Radicals held a century ago, that justice demanded that every adult man should have a vote for Parliament and that any other political arrangement was vicious, it seemed difficult to believe that social life had been happy or successful when government had been despotism, despotism it may be with a kind face, but still despotism. Yet as we look back over history we see that almost every sort of government has been made tolerable to human nature, and that men and women have lived with equanimity under political systems which left them not merely without political rights, but without any pretence of personal liberty. In such cases it is clear that in some way or by some device these excluded men and women were given the sense of sharing in the life of this society; their imagination and their emotions were satisfied, some would say deceived, by its dispositions or its illusions. For if men and women are to be attached to a society, they must look on it as

---

[1] Bridges, *Testament of Beauty*, i. 179.

[2] " Thus tho' 'twas otherwise than on Plato's ladder
　　That Francis climb'd—rather his gentle soul had learn'd
　　From taste of vanity and by malease of the flesh—
　　He abjured as worthless ev'n what good men will call good."
　　　　　　　　　　　　　　Testament of Beauty, i. 229.

something in which they have a part; a world in which what we may call the common mind finds in some degree, or by some means, scope, peace, comfort, and self-respect; in which distinctions of class and fortune, however hardly and sternly drawn, do not forbid all ties of sympathy, all unity of sentiment.

Professor Graham Wallas, describing the difference between the reactions produced by human and non-human obstruction to our impulses, points out that when Shakespeare sets out the ills that drive men to suicide he gives

> " The oppressor's wrong, the proud man's contumely,
> The pangs of despised love, the law's delay,
> The insolence of office, and the spurns
> That patient merit of the unworthy takes,"

and does not mention the want of food and clothing from which he must himself have suffered during his first wanderings from Stratford.[1] So Wordsworth draws a poor man holding dispute

> " With his own mind, unable to subdue
> Impatience through inaptness to perceive
> General distress in his particular lot;
> Or cherishing resentment, or in vain
> Struggling against it; with a soul perplexed,
> And finding in herself no steady power
> To draw the line of comfort that divides
> Calamity, the chastisement of Heaven,
> From the injustice of our brother man." [2]

Neither Shakespeare nor Wordsworth would have doubted that a man might be less poor and less uncomfortable than his grandfather, and yet have in his consciousness a more wounding sense of baulked instincts, more of the sting of defeat, more of that impatience of calamity which springs from a belief that it is injustice. It is the aim of these pages to inquire what it was in the conditions and setting of English social life in the first half of the nineteenth century that created this sense of wrong.

---

[1] *Our Social Heritage*, p. 157.   [2] *Excursion*, book ii. lines 70, etc.

CHAPTER II

THE REMEDY OF THE ANCIENT WORLD

COMMON ENJOYMENT

THE art of government may be described in one aspect as the art of making men and women think that the world they inhabit obeys in some degree their own ideas of justice. Cavour's often-quoted saying that any one can govern in a state of siege meant, of course, that when you are released from this task and government becomes naked force, statesmanship, a rare quality, ceases to be needed, and firmness, which is more common, takes its place. Peoples, great and small, have often been ruled against their will by firmness. But clearly, if we wish to understand the discontent of the nineteenth century, we shall learn less from ages and places where government was of this character than from those in which rulers sought to justify their authority, and societies sought to satisfy their self-respect. Bacon pointed out that when Virgil attributed to Augustus the best of human honours he made this the mark of his rule :—

> " Victorque volentes
> Per populos dat jura."

Bacon used this verse to illustrate his argument that " it was ever holden that honours in free monarchies and commonwealths had a sweetness more than in tyrannies, because the commandment extendeth more over the wills of men, and not only over their deeds and services." [1] It may help us to understand the discontent of Manchester amid all the improvements and new knowledge that the Industrial Revolution brought, if we ask ourselves in what sense Virgil's boast was true, and what there was in Roman civilisation which gave it the appearance of a voluntary or consenting society.

[1] *Advancement of Learning*, edited by Wright, p. 70.

As we look back over the history of Graeco-Roman civilisation we find every variety of political government, but through all those varieties we see that a definite effort was made to command the wills of men, and not merely their deeds and services. Elaborate care was taken to produce a stable society creating a sense of fellowship, by satisfying the imagination of the ruled, whether their political rights were considerable or insignificant. And as that civilisation reflects the experience of the most capable peoples in Europe, whose society endured over a long space of time, it is worth while to consider what methods were used to make men and women think that the world in which they lived obeyed their own ideas of justice.

On this aspect of ancient history we have learnt a great deal in recent years from the discovery and interpretation of inscriptions. We see that what was most important in the civilisation of classical Greece or the Hellenised East or the Roman Empire was the quality of its city life ; the character of the institutions and customs which inspired or sought to inspire a common pride and common emotion in populations tempted into strife by savage inequalities of fortune and sharp antipathies of history and race. To appreciate the importance of those institutions it is necessary to remember what difficulties these societies had to overcome.

The struggles of rich and poor in ancient Greece, of city and city, were bitter and incessant. Greek literature is full of this strife ; the fear of revolution is constant ; Isocrates said that Greeks feared their fellow-citizens more than they feared a foreign enemy. The reason is partly that the Greeks were intelligent and contentious above their neighbours, pursuing ambitions greater and nobler (it has been well said that their great achievement was bringing freedom and civilisation into union),[1] partly that they lived in an atmosphere of fierce economic competition, and trade routes and commercial openings had an exceptional importance for peoples whose livelihood depended upon them.[2]

It is not surprising, then, that Greek history is full of strife, and that it seems to end in political failure. Yet the history of

[1] Bevan, *House of Seleucus*, p. 3.
[2] On Greek Poverty, see Zimmern, *Greek Commonwealth*, part iii. chap. i. Compare Cornford's *Thucydides Mythistoricus*, and Lucian, *The Wisdom of Nigrinus* : " Philosophy and Poverty have ever been foster brothers."

the world has been largely moulded by the achievements of this small and distracted people : the new spirit they brought into politics ; the beauty of art, life, and manners that fascinated first Macedon, then Rome ; the literature and science that made them the teachers of Europe until the Roman Empire was lost in the Dark Ages, and again so soon as the Renaissance summoned the ghost of Greece from libraries and monasteries, where it had slept through the storm. A people apparently given up to war and conflict left these riches to mankind. What is the explanation ? It is to be found in the power of disinterested emotion to lighten the dark misery that man suffers when shut up within the narrow circle of selfish aims and cares. The class struggle was veiled or softened by the moral influence of common possessions ;[1] the practice of social fellowship was stimulated by the spectacle of beautiful buildings, and the common enjoyment of the arts and culture of the time. If the many and the few, the rich and poor, had pursued their quarrels in a world untouched by this gentle and mysterious spirit, a State like Athens could not have lived long enough to lay her spell upon the world.

When we turn to the history of the East under Alexander's successors, we come on perpetual wars in which brothers contend with brothers and every king has a rival of his own blood, so that these rulers, proud as they were of their civilised traditions, seem to differ little in fact from the oriental despots whose culture they despised. Of the poverty and hardships of life among their subjects modern scholars draw a melancholy picture.[2] In the island of Rhodes, which takes the place of Athens as a pioneer, elaborate provision was made for the relief of the poor, but over most of the Hellenised East the poor were becoming poorer as prices rose and wages fell. There was all the material for revolution, and Naxos and other islands were the scenes of violent class struggles. The treaties made between Alexander and the states of the League of Corinth in 335 B.C. contained some significant provisions. Both sides agreed to

---

[1] Cf. the appeal of the democrats after the battle with the Thirty in 404 B.C., when the two parties were mingling whilst the dead were being given back. " We never did you any harm, but we have shared with you in the most solemn rites and sacrifices and the most splendid festivals. We have been companions in the dance and schoolmates and comrades in war."—Xenophon, *Hellenica*, II. iv. 20.

[2] Tarn, *The Hellenistic Age*, pp. 128 *seq.*

take precautions to prevent any state from proceeding to the confiscation of personal property, the division of land, the cancellation of debt, or the liberation of slaves for the purposes of revolution. The same kind of Holy Alliance reappears in Demetrius's League in 303 B.C. In the third century there was a revolution in Sparta which only failed because Cleomenes, who organised it and carried it at first to success, mixed plans for foreign conquest with his social schemes. Yet we find in the midst of all this strife of class and of fratricidal war between rivals for Alexander's empire, a brilliant city life, where the arts flourish and beauty and grace are admired. The Seleucid kings made deliberate efforts to foster and develop that life as the means to progress and unity, as an educating influence over the indigenous races brought into contact with Greek ideas. The saying that Arrian put into the mouth of Alexander is significant: " My father led you down from the mountains to the plains ; when you lived in scattered places he made you dwellers in cities, and he equipped you with institutions adapted to your changed mode of life." [1] The last sentence sums up the task of a developing civilisation, and it has a special importance in the history of the people that first made town planning an art.

The Roman Empire succeeded where Greece and the Hellen-ised East failed, for it established long spells of peace over a great part of the world. The Romans gained their Empire by their military prowess and their political genius, but for the purposes of this comparison military success is the least im-portant thing about that Empire. It was not on that ground that St. Augustine bade the citizens of the City of God look to Rome for lessons and inspiration.[2] The secret of its power was its ability to satisfy and attach the races and classes that came under its rule. Of the evils and perils that this civilisation over-came and survived, Roman history is full. We have only to recall some of the pictures given in Dr. Heitland's *Agricola*, Mommsen's saying that the sum of negro slavery was a drop in the bucket compared with the misery inflicted by the slave trade of Delos, the slave wars almost as horrible as the struggle between Carthage and her mercenary army after the first Punic

---

[1] Reid, *The Municipalities of the Roman Empire*, p. 391.
[2] See *De Civitate Dei*, v. 16 : " De mercede sanctorum civium civitatis aeternae quibus utilia sunt Romanorum exempla virtutum."

War described by Flaubert in *Salammbô*, the brutalising atmosphere of the amphitheatre,[1] the Social War, the civil strife that so nearly put out the light of this civilisation in the closing days of the Republic, to realise how remarkable an achievement it was for this social life to hold the Empire together during the centuries necessary to fix its foundations deep in the habits and mind of Europe.[2]   We know from such books as those of Dill, Reid, and Professor Rostovtzeff how stimulating and various an enjoyment of life was organised in the cities of the Empire ; how great an importance was given to public beauty ; how lavishly the rich, and even the middle classes, spent their money on theatres, baths, libraries, and temples; how widely, as Greenidge put it, the supply to the poor of what we call luxuries was deemed an obligation of wealth.   The civilisation of that Empire is known as Graeco-Roman just because it kept this Greek tradition and spread it under different forms all over the Western world.

How persistent was this tradition, even though the rulers of the State might differ as sharply as Augustus differed from Pericles, or the spirit of politics as sharply as those of fifth-century Athens and those of the Antonines, we can see when we remind ourselves that a man visiting Athens in the fifth century B.C., Rhodes in the second century B.C., and a Roman town in Africa or Spain in the second century A.D., would have noted that certain characteristics were common to all of them.   First he would see that public beauty held a sovereign place in the ambitions and esteem of the time.   The boast made by Smyrna when she claimed the title of " First City of Asia by beauty and importance, most brilliant and glory of Ionia," named the distinctions that every city, Greek, Hellenist, or Graeco-Roman, put first.[3]   The beauty of which cities were proud was not beauty hidden away in private houses, but beauty that the whole world could see and admire.   An observation by a Greek sophist, Archytas of Tarentum, which Cicero quotes in his

---

[1] Lecky says this was the reason why the Romans never developed tragedy.

[2] " One of the most telling points in the history of Roman conquest is that a nation once conquered hardly ever afterwards struck a signal blow for liberty, even when the conqueror was deep in difficulty elsewhere."—Reid, *op. cit.* p. 168.

[3] Reid, *op. cit.* p. 380.   " Every ancient city was ambitious that its public buildings, with costly artistic decorations, should rival those of other cities which came into comparison with it, and resources were not uncommonly strained in the competition. The remains on ancient sites impress this fact on the beholder."—*ibid.* p. 459.

treatise on Friendship, throws some light on their feeling about it : " Si quis in coelum ascendisset naturamque mundi et pulchritudinem siderum perspexisset, insuavem illam admirationem ei fore, quae jucundissima fuisset, si aliquem cui narraret habuisset."[1] A hungry man coming on food in a desert island would not say that he could not enjoy that food because he was alone ; Robinson Crusoe was glad enough to eat before he had the company of Friday. The sophist held then that the enjoyment of beauty is not, like the enjoyment of food, an individual satisfaction ; that it is connected in some way with man's social nature. He held, that is, with some modern philosophers that beauty is a reality which is perceived specially in the contact between minds. It was perhaps this conviction or this intuition that led the Greeks to realise the power that beauty has over men's sympathies and imagination,[2] and in consequence to look upon beauty as essentially for common enjoyment.[3] Demosthenes reminded the Athens of his day that Themistocles or Aristides lived in plain houses indistinguishable from those of their neighbours, and that the great buildings were to be found on the Acropolis. Alcibiades outraged public sentiment by painting his house.[4] The Greeks then regarded beauty as a spiritual power that could influence politics, helping to make men generous and public-spirited, able to forget in a common loyalty the passions that tended to drive them and keep them apart.[5] " Even a man whose soul was utterly burdened," said Dion Chrysostom of Pheidias' statue of Zeus at Olympia, " who had drained in his life the cup of sorrow and misfortune and had not closed his eyes in sleep, will forget when he stands oppo-

[1] " If a man should climb alone into heaven and look upon the structure of the world and the beauty of the stars, he would find no pleasure in that spectacle though it would fill him with delight if he had some one to whom he could speak of it."—Cicero, *De Amicitia*, xxiii. 88.
[2] Cf. Lucian on Beauty : " no doubt something of beauty flows through the eyes into the soul."—*The Hall*, p. 4.
[3] " To spend a large fortune in acquiring things of beauty for his private gratification was a use of money of which a Greek would have been incapable."—Abbott, *History of Greece*, ii. p. 406.
[4] M. Rostovtzeff remarks that it was in the Hellenistic age that " architecture stooped to the construction of convenient and beautiful private houses."—*History of the Ancient World*, i. p. 391.
[5] Cf. Lucian on the contrast between Greeks and Persians. Speaking of Darius' golden plane, he says: " That was wonderful only on account of its cost ; there was no craftsmanship or beauty or charm or symmetry or grace wrought into the gold or combined with it. . . . The barbarians are not beauty lovers : they are money lovers."—*The Hall*, p. 6.

site this statue, all the terrors and hardships of human life." [1]

The second thing that such a visitor would have noticed was the great proportion of expenditure of wealth and labour that was devoted to things that were for common enjoyment. This was illustrated not only by the beauty and grace of the public buildings, but also by the amenities that were brought within the reach of poor people. Every town had its theatres, its baths, its public games and festivals, its great gardens and colonnades.[2] Many towns engaged public doctors, and sophists, philosophers, and grammarians were generally relieved of all public burdens. All this elaborate provision for the amusement of the mass of the population was made possible partly by the possession of common land and other common property, and partly by the fashion of private liberality for public objects. One of the first uses to which a rich man thought of putting his wealth was to adorn his city or to make an endowment that would associate his name and memory with its renown and the happiness and gratitude of its citizens ; he would build a theatre or racecourse, or he would set aside a sum of money for education or for providing baths for the poor or for the slaves. He believed with Bacon that " riches are for spending and spending for honour and good actions." [3]

The habits and tastes of the East spread to the West, and musical and literary exhibitions became common there, while gladiatorial shows and wild beast hunts penetrated to the East, not without protest from Plutarch and Lucian. Galen, the well-known medical writer, was physician to a troop of gladiators at Pergamum. There were still differences between East and West, for Greece never took whole-heartedly to the gladiatorial games, and the West never quite lost its contempt for the palaestra and the gymnasium. But in East and West alike the diversions offered to the mass of the population assumed an importance in expenditure and public life to which the modern world affords no parallel.

---

[1] Quoted, R. W. Livingstone, *Mission of Greece*, p. 135.

[2] Among the ruins brought to light at Timgad was a bath for the use apparently of the workers in a factory.—Reid, *op. cit.* p. 288.

[3] " The public spirit which they displayed can be compared only with that shown by many rich Americans to-day. But relatively the Romans gave much more money for public purposes than modern Americans."—Rostovtzeff, *Economic and Social History of the Roman Empire*, p. 522.

This truth is illustrated in the sermon on Poverty which Lucian put in the form of a dialogue between the cobbler and the cock inhabited by the soul of Pythagoras. Certain reflections are common to all the arguments by which philosophers and teachers have sought at different ages to persuade the poor that they are happier than the rich. All touch on the pleasures or comforts of the body. Horace says that a rich man cannot hold more in his stomach than a poor man ; [1] Lucian contrasts the afflictions of the rich, gout, pneumonia, and other diseases due to intemperance, with the good health of the poor, who live on sprats and a bunch of onions ; Paley reminds the poor man that if anything unusual comes his way he finds a feast, whereas the epicure dines too well every day to enjoy any novelty. At all ages again philosophers have dwelt on the cares and responsibilities of the rich and powerful. "You sleep well on a rug," said Martial to the slave, "your master lies awake on a bed of down." [2] Lucian told the poor in a lively passage that the rich have to risk their lives in the field as commanders of horse or foot, " whereas you with but a wicker shield have little to carry and nothing to impede your flight and are ready to celebrate the victory when the general offers sacrifice after winning the battle." Paley argues that the poor escaped the anxieties of the rich about their children. "All the provision which a poor man's child needs is contained in two words, industry and innocence." These arguments are used to console the poor in all ages. But we notice one important difference : whereas in the nineteenth century the argument runs that there is no capital without the rich, no production without capital, and no wages without production, Lucian put it that the rich had to toil that the poor might have baths, shows, and everything else, to their hearts' content.[3] That is, whereas the modern economist put it that the poor man is indebted to the rich for his livelihood, the ancient moralist said that he was indebted to the rich for his luxuries.

The third feature of public life that such an observer would notice was the great part played in social life by voluntary associations. This was specially noticeable in the Roman Empire, where all classes were encouraged to form clubs and colleges, for the maintenance of their corporate dignity, the

---

[1] *Satires*, I. i. 46.   [2] ix. 93.   [3] Lucian, *The Dream and the Cock*, p. 22.

celebration of a patron or festival, the organisation of common pleasure or thrift, or to secure for the poorest and humblest person such a funeral as would not leave him an outcast in death. If the highest class had its group in the Curiales and the men who rose to wealth from the freedman class had their group in the Augustales, the lower classes of freedmen, artisáns, and slaves, marched under their own flags in great processions to their special places at the games, and kept festivals and ceremonies at which, if only for a passing hour, the common life of the city seemed more important than all the inequalities of fortune. In such a group it might even happen that a slave would preside in a company with freedmen present.[1]

The Roman Empire depended on its power to satisfy the social imagination of its subjects, and it lasted as long as that power lasted. Montesquieu said that the Romans received slaves from all parts of the world and returned them as Romans. This, of course, is a picturesque exaggeration, but the phrase describes the Roman genius at its best, the kind of spirit that distinguishes and explains its success. It is not so much ironical as significant that the man who had to repeat Terence's famous declaration, " Homo sum ; humani nihil a me alienum puto," was a slave, acting in a play composed by a man who had first set foot in Rome as a slave. Compared with the Greeks the Romans were a brutal people, but they devised the political system by which the Greek tradition of humane, beautiful, and comforting life was kept alive and spread over Europe. Nothing in M. Rostovtzeff's pages is more interesting than his description of the efforts of the later Emperors to combat the dangers that threatened and finally extinguished the Empire, by creating new centres of city culture whence this gentle light might be cast over the passions of fierce neighbours and races that were still untamed. The history of the Empire, from a certain point of view, is the history of an euthanasia, the decay of a civilising power, of which this municipal life had been the most conspicuous expression. If we

---

[1] " Some colleges were confined to free men, others to freedmen and slaves, others to slaves alone ; but it is possible to find all classes blended together : wherever slaves are to be found in the same colleges as free men, they suffer no disability : in a college election their vote is of equal worth and they rise to office, frequently taking precedence over free men. They serve as magistri and ministri, as curatores, decuriones and prefecti, and so on."—Barrow, *Slavery in the Roman Empire*, p. 165. Cf. Dill, *Roman Society from Nero to Marcus Aurelius*, p. 281.

may vary a phrase of Bacon's, we may say that the Romans had devised a plan under which men could be ruled by a despotism without putting off the generosity of their minds. Pelham said that this eager stirring city life was a substitute for politics. But there came a time when freedom and civilisation were no longer united in fact or in illusion. A change passed over the life of the Empire. Diocletian's reorganisation marked a stage in a decline. The cities lost their self-government ; compulsory services supplied the needs of the State ; the bureaucracy became all-powerful, and the Empire sought to satisfy the social imagination of the ruled by the pomp of its ceremonies and the sheer magnificence of its ruler.

No attempt has been made in these few pages to estimate the happiness and misery of the poor under Greek or Roman government ; to calculate how far social amenities compensated for the privations and the cruelties to which they were exposed ; to consider all the evils that a society suffers and inflicts if its basis is slavery. That is a task for scholars. The aim of this survey is different and more modest. It is to see what light we can draw from well-known facts about ancient history for our inquiry into the causes of social discontent in the nineteenth century. In the history of Graeco-Roman civilisation we are watching the government, not of docile or acquiescent races, or of primitive and unsophisticated tribes, but of societies conspicuously intelligent, critical, and high-spirited. Or we may put it that we are watching experiments in group life which have a special value for all time, because we possess rich and illuminating records of the active and interesting peoples that were engaged in making them, and a literature in which those experiments are discussed, explained, and criticised, by acute and penetrating minds. In such a world the problem of making a stable society is not a problem set to force, but a problem set to wisdom ; it is not an essay in terrorism, but an essay in statesmanship. The same problem was set to nineteenth-century England, for the English people were no more docile and acquiescent than the communities for whose satisfaction this elaborate city life was devised. And the Industrial Revolution which had spread far and wide the improvements that the economists describe, had put to that statesmanship problems not less subtle and difficult than the problems put to Augustus or the Antonines in the government of a Roman province.

CHAPTER III

THE NEW PROBLEM

THERE have been long ages in the history of the world when social life has been languid and impoverished, and yet there has been no revolt of which literature gives any record. Custom will reconcile men and women to conditions that they would find intolerable if they came fresh to them. For custom has a magic that takes the sting out of injustice, making it seem rather the decree of heaven than the sin of man. Thus the spell that custom casts on the imagination is the greatest conservative force in the world, a force so strong that it will keep life in institutions which have long ceased to serve, or even to remember, the purpose that brought them into use. As life follows its circle of unbroken routine no fierce questions are asked about facts and conditions that seem part of everyday experience, the face of a familiar world. When, therefore, society is passing through changes that destroy the life of custom, the statesman who seeks, in Bacon's words, to command man's will and not merely his deeds and services, has a specially difficult task, for those changes bring into men's minds the dreaded questions that have been sleeping beneath the surface of habit.

England at this time was passing through such changes. Some critics argue that the Industrial Revolution described by Toynbee has been pushed into a false importance. It is true that that revolution was a phase in a series of changes reaching far back into history. Some may put the beginning of the revolution on the day when Columbus set sail in his cockle shell to cross the Atlantic ; others when Godfrey de Bouillon led crusaders and merchants to the Holy Land, bringing the West with its needs and energy once more into touch with the resources of the East ; others will go back to the time when Cretan and Phoenician first learned how rich a basin holds the Mediterranean

16

Sea.   The student may take his choice.   But whatever the date
and whatever the cradle we name for this great event, it remains
true that the England of this time was an England in movement,
that speculation was in the air, that the indolent influence of
habit was shaken, and that the statesman could no longer hope
that half his work would be done for him by custom.

Another aspect of this age must be kept in mind.   It was an
age of energy and power, in which man eclipsed, in his new
authority over nature, the spectacular triumphs of the architects
and engineers of Rome.   We can dig up to-day the bones of
strong cities, which had once a vigorous and brilliant life in the
waste of the African desert, desert when the Romans went there,
desert to-day.   Those buried columns speak of a miracle, but
of a miracle less astonishing than the creation of the railway
power that conquered distance, the obstacle that had so long
arrested the development of Europe ; less astonishing than the
creation of the Lancashire cotton industry, its raw material
brought across the Atlantic Ocean, its finished products carried
round the Cape to India and the China Seas.   There was no
question here of a society drawing its ebbing breath under some
stroke of disease or destiny.   Man's power stared the new world
in the face.   In such an age the inequalities of life are apt to
look less like calamities from the hand of heaven and more like
injustices from the hand of man.

Upon the society in whose manner of life and sense of power
this change was taking place, there had fallen the shock of the
French Revolution.   We can measure the effect of that shock
if we compare the world of ideas within which Wordsworth or
Coleridge or Southey or Mill were moving when they reflected
on the future of society, with that in which Gibbon was moving
when he asked himself in a famous passage whether the
civilised world might ever suffer again a calamity like the fall
of the Western Empire.   The dangers and the dreams that haunt
the nineteenth-century thinkers never appear on his horizon.
He looks out from a world composed and untroubled about
its basis ; they belonged to a world where the moral foundations of society, and the justice and the power of the bonds
that unite its members, are the subject of vehement and incessant
debate between hope and fear.   No disappointment, however
cold, could make the world after 1789 exactly what it was before,

for intimations strange and alien to the eighteenth-century mind linger in the senses, although a blight had fallen on the first promise of " the greatest and best thing that had ever happened in the history of man." Between Gibbon and Wordsworth fear and hope had both passed through a revolution.

This was an atmosphere to excite thinkers and dreamers, and we know how quickly the active minds, philosophers and poets, turned to new problems in this crisis of our history. The atmosphere that produced Bentham and Godwin, Southey and Coleridge, Ricardo and Malthus, Shelley and Wordsworth, Mill and Carlyle, was certain to produce some intellectual movement in the working-class world. We see the result in the appearance of thinkers and writers representing revolt in different aspects, Paine, Spence, Carlile, Hone, Hetherington, Cobbett who idealised the past the peasant was losing, and Lovett who idealised the future that he saw in the workman's grasp. It has been said that when the licence enjoyed by Gibbon was claimed by Carlile a new world had taken to infidelity; so when Cobbett's " Twopenny trash " succeeded to the Letters of Junius a new world had taken to politics. The characteristic of this age was the cheap pamphlet or paper written for the working man. At first this literature found its audience chiefly among London shoemakers, small tradesmen, and artisans, but in time it spread to the miners and the mill workers ; Lancashire was for Church and King in 1793, but for radical reform in 1819. It was said in the exaggeration of panic of *The Black Dwarf*, published by Wooler the Yorkshire printer who migrated to London, that in one northern district in 1819 it was to be found in the crown of the hat of almost every pitman you met.[1] Ten years later the mills used to turn out when the London coach brought Cobbett's *Register* to the Lancashire towns. The first paper was published in London, but the provincial towns soon followed. Manchester had a *Wardle's Manchester Observer* ; Birmingham, *Edwards' Weekly Register* ; Coventry its *Recorder*; Dudley its *Patient*. In addition to the better-known papers, like Carlile's *Gauntlet*, Detroisier's *Cosmopolitan*, the Spencean paper *Man*, the Owenite paper *The Crisis*, the *Working Man's Friend*, there were several unstamped papers in the country, especially in Manchester, Leeds, Bradford, and such towns,

[1] Wickwar, *The Struggle for the Freedom of the Press*, p. 57.

taking their tone from the *Poor Man's Guardian*, owned by
Hetherington and edited by Bronterre O'Brien. The *Pioneer*
was the organ of the Builders' movement in the early thirties;
Doherty ran *The Voice of the People* and the *Poor Man's
Advocate*; and in 1837 Feargus O'Connor started the most
successful of all the democratic papers, the *Northern Star*.[1]

The propagandist newspaper was scarcely more important
than the cheap book or cheap pamphlet for the distribution
of which publishers made elaborate arrangements. A good
example was "The Cottage Library," established by William
Milner, a Halifax grocer, who sold his cheap books at fairs and
markets all over England.[2] Milner published a cheap edition of
Fielden's *Curse of the Factory System*. Politicians saw the advantages of this method of propaganda, and Roebuck used to publish
weekly pamphlets airing his views on contemporary questions.

To understand what forces were ready to gather behind these
rebel or these building minds, we must remember that the new
towns were drawing into factory and slum men and women who
had themselves passed through a revolution. Mr. Redford says
that the census returns for 1851 show that in almost all the great
towns the migrants from elsewhere outnumbered the people
born in the town.[3] Now the industrial towns were growing at
a great pace. We can get an idea of the pace if we take the
census figures for three years, 1801, 1831, and 1851, for some of
the towns of Lancashire and the West Riding. The figures for
Manchester and Salford are roughly 90,000, 237,000, 400,000;
for Leeds, 53,000, 123,000, 172,000; for Sheffield, 46,000,
92,000, 135,000; for Bradford, 13,000, 44,000, 104,000; for Oldham, 22,000, 51,000, 72,000; for Bolton, 18,000, 42,000, 61,000;
for Blackburn, 12,000, 27,000, 65,000; for Halifax, 12,000,
22,000, 34,000. In all these towns and in many others a great

---

[1] For the wild hopes about this new force that inspired democrats at the time, see
the concluding verse of Ebenezer Elliott's poem, *The Press*:

> "' The Press ' all lands shall sing,
> The Press, the Press we bring,
> All lands to bless !
> O pallid want ! O labour stark,
> Behold we bring the second ark,
> The Press, the Press, the Press."

[2] Hanson, *The Story of Old Halifax*, p. 254.

[3] *Labour Migration in England, 1800–1850*, by Arthur Redford (1926). Dr. Redford's book is the chief authority on this subject.

proportion of the inhabitants had changed their home, their occupation, and their surroundings. Now the Industrial Revolution seen in the perspective of the life of the world may seem a gradual process, so gradual that economists find fault with the phrase as inexact. But as an experience in the individual and family lives of the men and women drawn into Manchester or Bradford, the Industrial Revolution was sudden and its consequences sweeping.[1] The revolution that had given them a new home and a new manner of life would not have lost its sharp taste if the economist had explained to them that large-scale production was known in the ancient world, and that specialised industry had once enriched Babylon and Damascus just as it was then enriching Manchester and Bradford. The towns had now large populations of men and women who had passed from the life of the village to the life of the slum ; from the occupations of the peasant to those of the urban worker.

Where did these immigrants come from ? Mr. Redford has shown that most of the migration was short-distance migration; that the great majority of the people who migrated to the Lancashire towns came from Lancashire and Cheshire, that most of those who migrated into the Yorkshire towns came from Yorkshire, and that, contrary to usual belief, when the textile industries declined in East Anglia and the South-West, the workers in those industries did not follow the industry in its movement northwards. This is true of the spontaneous movements of population. There were, however, two methods by which migration had been organised. A number of children were sent from the South by the system of apprenticing workhouse children to the textile mills, which was in force till 1816, when Bootle's Act made it illegal to apprentice London children more than forty miles from London, and in 1835 an experiment was made by the Poor Law authorities, who thought that as there were too many labourers in the eastern and southern counties arrangements might be made for moving some of them to the industrial districts. It was at this time that schemes for encouraging emigration from these counties were under discussion,

---

[1] Dr. Scoresby, the Vicar of Bradford, started a society for befriending the women workers in the mills of that town. He found that from 1000 to 2000 of them were single women living in lodgings, some of them in disorderly houses.—*Leeds Intelligencer*, October 10, 1846. His society started a model lodging-house as an experiment.—*Leeds Mercury*, April 3, 1847.

and it seemed natural to send labourers to the manufacturing districts. Some 5000 persons moved in this way to the manufacturing towns; half of them coming from Suffolk, nearly 600 from Norfolk, 389 from Bucks, 298 from Bedford, 175 from Kent, 134 from Essex, 154 from Cambridgeshire, and the rest mainly from Wilts, Sussex, Hampshire, and Berkshire. The great majority went to Lancashire and Yorkshire: 1785 to Lancashire and 1356 to the West Riding. The Poor Law Commission sought to avert the hardships that arose by employing two full-time agents, one in Manchester and the other in Leeds, but the scheme came to grief, partly because a depression of trade in the North upset the labour market, and partly because the association with the Poor Law and the suspicion, not altogether baseless, that the plan was meant to reduce wages brought odium upon it.[1]

The new population was mainly composed of people born and bred in the country. Wordsworth said that the invention of the steam engine had saved the countryside, for mills could now be built in the ugly towns instead of spoiling the streams and valleys. For the country people turned into slum dwellers the change was less fortunate. They had not lost their instincts and longings or their sense for beauty and peace. Some observers think that we are paying the penalty to-day for making our towns unsightly in the destruction of our landscape by a town people in whom the sense for beauty has been killed. It was feared in the thirties that if London people found themselves in a park or garden the " propensity to mischief " would assert itself with disastrous results.[2] In the North, on the other hand, where the workman's memories of his country life were still alive, observers noticed with astonishment that this propensity was kept in check. When Lord Stamford threw open his park on a Sunday the workpeople of Manchester flocked there, making the journey in many cases on foot, and the park suffered no damage at the hands of 20,000 visitors.[3] Sir Joseph Paxton told the Committee on Public Houses in 1854 that the Duke of Devonshire allowed excursionists from Birmingham, Nottingham, Leicester, and Leeds to visit Chatsworth, and that

[1] See Redford, *op. cit.* chap. vi.
[2] 1836 Committee on Arts and Principles of Design, p. 175.
[3] *Manchester Guardian*, November 20, 1844.

their behaviour was most orderly. "As many as 1000 or 1200 people go round at a time and in no instance have we found any difficulty arise. . . ." "We had only one man or perhaps two over the whole premises to look after them ; and the people behaved exceedingly well."[1] The love of nature dies hard. Faucher, a French visitor, said that one of the evils of which the poor were most conscious in Leeds was the smoke that destroyed their little window gardens.

Nor was the loss of beauty the only discomfort these immigrants suffered. Wordsworth has described the lone shepherd on a promontory,

> "Who lacking occupation looks far forth
> Into the boundless sea and rather makes
> Than finds what he beholds."[2]

Nature gives some play to the fancy of the peasant as his eye wanders slowly over field and woodland, and though we picture him with a simple mind, town life to make him happy has to find some substitute for the satisfaction that the lone shepherd found in his promontory looking far forth into the boundless sea. For the first half of the nineteenth century the industrial town was absorbing the English peasant used to an open-air life, learning from the landscape, in touch with nature, moving and thinking with its gentle rhythm, making rather than finding what he beheld.

The towns were thus receiving a large population strange to town life in habits and experience. But there was an even more disturbing element in the problem now set to governments and magistrates, to architects and engineers, to doctors, schoolmasters, and ministers of religion. If you went to Manchester or Leeds, or to the smaller towns like Oldham or Stalybridge, you would find that the immigrants were in the main either countrymen from the same or a neighbouring county, or Irishmen and Irishwomen. It was easier to reach Lancashire and Yorkshire from Ireland than from Norfolk or Dorset. A Wiltshire peasant would have to make his way North by coach or

---

[1] Select Committee on Public Houses, 1854. Compare Dickens : "It is an extraordinary thing to know of a people systematically excluded from galleries and museums for years, that their respect for such places and for themselves as visitors to them, dates without any period of transition, from the very day when their doors were freely opened."—Crotch, *Dickens as Social Reformer*, p. 171.
[2] *The Prelude*, iii. 516.

canal boat or waggon, or on foot. The labourers who were sent to Lancashire by the Poor Law authorities were taken to London, put on a boat of Pickford's at the Paddington basin of the Grand Junction Canal, and carried to Manchester in four or five days at a cost of fourteen shillings. But an Irishman could cross to Liverpool for half a crown in fourteen hours; in 1827 fierce competition brought down the price to fourpence or fivepence.[1]

Now Ireland so dangerously near to Lancashire was an uncomfortable neighbour. For the Irish peasant was the victim of unexampled misgovernment and neglect. "In no other country," said the *Times*, "have the wealth of the proprietor, the power of the magistrate and the accomplishments of the educated, been employed less for the benefit of the many, more for the gain and the pleasure of the few." [2] Consequently the Irish immigration had a special character. Sir George Cornewall Lewis pointed out that the Greeks and Phoenicians settling in the Mediterranean, the Spaniards and the English settling in the New World, went from a more to a less civilised community. The Fleming woollen weavers, the Huguenot silk weavers, the German tailors, brought to England, the English mechanics took to France, a special skill. "But the Irish emigration into Britain is an example of a less civilised population spreading themselves as a kind of substratum beneath a more civilised community." [3]

This Irish substratum composed in 1841 a tenth of the population of Manchester and a seventh of the population of Liverpool. At that time the Irish population in Lancashire was over 133,000. But after the failure of the potato in the forties, the event that precipitated the repeal of the Corn Laws and the break-up of the Conservative party, the flood became a deluge. It has been calculated that 500,000 Irish people entered Great Britain between 1841 and 1851. By the later date the Irish population in Lancashire had nearly reached 200,000, swollen by the refugees flying from the famine that destroyed nearly a million lives in Ireland. "During the last two or three months," wrote the registrar of a Manchester district, "large numbers of the poor from Ireland have crowded themselves in this district, droves of them rambling about the streets seeking

---

[1] Redford, *op. cit.* pp. 56 and 81.   [2] July 12, 1847.
[3] Report to the Poor Law Commissioners on the Irish Poor, Appendix G, 1836.

lodgings and no doubt being exposed to the severe and in-
clement weather.   Many of the poor creatures have died from
cold producing fevers and diseases." [1]   At Liverpool there were
" thousands of hungry and naked Irish perishing in our streets,"
and in South Wales they were described as " bringing pestilence
on their backs, famine in their stomachs." [2]

We have a picture of the influence of Irish habits on the life
of the industrial towns before this deluge in a Report on the
Irish Poor prepared for the Poor Law Commission in 1836.
Dr. Duncan, the well-known Liverpool doctor, said that the
" Irish seemed as contented amidst dirt and filth and close confined air as in clean and airy structures." [3]   There is evidence
in the same Report to show that Irish workpeople who were put
into better houses by their employers at Hyde and Dukinfield
discovered a taste for cleanliness and order.   But Dr. Duncan's
statement, though not universally, was widely true, for when
this poor population migrated on so considerable a scale, vast
numbers of men and women left their country not because they
were enterprising and ambitious and refused any longer to put
up with the conditions that existed there, but because exile was
the easiest and indeed the only escape from famine.   Thousands
of men and women were now living in Manchester and Liverpool who had never minded the squalor they had shared with
their pigs in the hovels of Tipperary.

This explains a characteristic of the Irish population which
struck English observers.   It was noticed that in many cases
Irish people made few changes when their circumstances
improved.   Cobbett described the difference between the
English, the Scottish, and the Irish in a famous phrase.   One
country had " meat and bread and knives and forks, the other
had oatmeal and brose and horn spoons, and the third had only
potatoes and paws."   One of the witnesses cited in the Report on
the Irish Poor said that the English were accustomed to eat meat
if not every day at least most days of the week ; that the Irish,
who lived on potatoes, ate more food but not better food when
their wages went up.   Other witnesses said that the Irish did
not improve either their food or their homes when they had more
to spend ; that they spent their extra money largely on spirits
or sometimes on improving their dress.   Thus the dirtiness and

---

[1] *Times*, February 2, 1848.   [2] Redford, *op. cit.* p. 136.   [3] Report on Irish Poor.

disorder of the squalid English town were now increased by the presence of a large body of Irish people who lived normally under conditions repugnant to their English neighbours.

This had two serious consequences. In the first place, the greatest blot on the towns where the Irish settled was the cellar-dwelling. The immigrants crowded into these cellars, and as there was no check on the speculative builder, cellars were built in great numbers with the confident expectation of finding tenants for them.[1] This was not the only evil that was prolonged and extended by the Irish immigration. The Irish immigrants in Lancashire, competing with a more skilled population, were confined as a rule to the coarser and less eligible employments. Among the occupations from which English workmen were turning away because its wages and prospects were steadily declining was that of handloom weaving. The Irish resorted to this failing industry and drew out its slow and painful death.[2]

In these ways the Irish immigration was a burden on towns where filth and poverty were already unmanageable problems. But it brought also the friction that is inevitable when immigrant labourers can underbid the natives.[3] As Irishmen were often bricklayers' labourers, and as they had been employed a good deal on roadmaking and canal-cutting, they were specially suitable for such work as railway construction. But trade depression had brought unemployment by the late thirties, when railway projects were in great favour, and there were riots in several places when attempts were made to introduce Irish labour. More than once such riots became battles, and it was often found impossible to put English and Irish to work together.[4]

---

[1] "A great part of the towns inhabited by the poor . . . has been built by persons who speculated on the existence of a population which would be content with the minimum of the comforts of life."—Kay, Report on Irish Poor, p. 60. At Warrington the rents of the poorest houses were raised by Irish immigration.—House of Lords Committee on Rating of Tenements, 1859.

[2] Redford, op. cit. chap. ix.

[3] Ebenezer Elliott on the "Miseries of the Poor" :

> " But work grew scarce, while bread grew dear,
>   And wages lessened too ;
> For Irish hordes were bidders here,
>   Our half-paid work to do."

[4] See Redford, op. cit. p. 141 ; also Halifax Express, October 13, 1838, for riots at Lancaster ; Bradford Observer, November 16, 1848, for riots at Cleckheaton.

That the Irish were used to keep down wages and to break strikes was admitted by textile employers, and Irish labour was brought over from Ireland for this purpose by a silk manufacturer at Newton Heath and by cotton spinners at Preston.[1] The employers, however, regarded Irish workmen with mixed feelings, and they spoke of them sometimes much as a Roman master used to speak of the slaves from turbulent Sardinia. "The Irish," said one employer, "are more disposed to turn out, to make unreasonable demands, to take offence at slight cause and to enforce their demands by strikes or bad language."[2] A Catholic priest said that he had noticed that the Irish were more prone than the English to take part in trade unions, and he attributed this to habits acquired under the bad laws of Ireland.[3] Whether this or the Celtic temperament was the cause, it is undoubtedly true that Ireland gave several leaders to the English workmen, the most notable of them being, of course, the celebrated John Doherty, the founder of the strongest union of the time, whose services to reform must be set against the squalor that his countrymen brought with them.

The discord due to economic friction was inflamed by religious differences. Nobody can study the papers of this time without seeing how widespread and violent were the religious quarrels of the industrial towns. There were riots on a large scale at Manchester in 1807 and 1834; at Bradford in 1847; at Stockport in 1852. Angry meetings were common. It is significant that in the late thirties Conservatives talked openly of their desire to repeal the Catholic Emancipation Act,[4] and as late as 1839 the Vicar of Halifax held a Guy Fawkes service in the parish church and preached an appropriate sermon.[5] The controversy over the grant to Maynooth College first made by Peel in 1845 was embittered by the violence of this anti-Catholic feeling in the North. A study of this discord, inflamed at times by passionate Protestant pilgrims from Ireland, who made Leeds and Bradford echo with stories of Catholic oppression, encourages respect for those statesmen like Melbourne, Peel, Russell, Gladstone, and Cobden, who held on their way, apply-

---

[1] Redford, *op. cit.* pp. 139, 140.   [2] Report on Irish Poor, p. 68.
[3] Report on Irish Poor, Appendix, p. 62.
[4] See speeches at Operative Conservative Association dinners.—*Leeds Intelligencer*, January 26, 1839.
[5] *Halifax Guardian*, November 9, 1839.

ing what remedies they thought Ireland needed, undismayed by the violence of English sectarian feeling.

The towns, then, to whom it fell to act as the civilising influence in this new society were largely inhabited by men and women who were country people by experience, taste, and habit, and in respect of great numbers, alien in history, religion, and race. But it was not only in this way that this population felt the strain of change. There was at the same time a revolution in the life and rhythm of industry. English industry before this time was unmethodical. Bouts of work and bouts of play used often to alternate, violent play following violent work. Bamford has described the Christmas festivals of his young days when beer was brewed and spice-cake baked, and the weavers, young and old, kept at work night and day to finish their tasks so that the days after Christmas might be free for feasting and revelry. Even in ordinary times whole days rather than hours in a day were given to recreation. The Sheffield journeymen were said to work only three days in the week.[1] This is probably an exaggeration, but the custom of taking days off even when work was plentiful survived in non-factory industry. Thus the framework knitters at Hinckley sat at their work for 13 to 16 hours a day, never getting into the open air till 12 on Saturday, when the work was sent to the warehouse and they stopped completely till Tuesday. Monday was market day, and the workers were fagged out.[2] In the Potteries, too, the custom survived,[3] and in the country districts round Coventry the ribbon weavers, however poor they were, were said in 1840 to " absent themselves from work nearly the whole of Saturday, Sunday, the whole of Monday and a little of Tuesday," working excessively hard for the rest of the week, including often the whole of Friday night.[4] These outbursts of work and play were uneconomical, and, where machinery was introduced, a new system of work was obviously necessary. Improved methods of production involved the training of the working

[1] ". . . As the wages given to the journeymen are very high, it is pretty generally the practice for them to work for three days in which they earn sufficient to enable them to drink and riot for the rest of the week, consequently no place can be more fit for seditious purposes."—Letter from Colonel de Lancey, June 13, 1792, *Home Office Papers*, 42. 20.
[2] 1843 Select Committee on Allotments, p. 82.
[3] See *Rise of Modern Industry*, p. 177.
[4] 1840 Health of Towns Committee, p. 71.

population in orderly and regular habits. Unfortunately the regularity was made to apply to work only, and play was left out of account. The position in the new factory areas was described by Richard Walker, member for Bury. When asked whether it was true that now, when the population was " congregated together in large manufacturies, they had less of the means of exercise than they formerly had," he answered: "They have no means; they have an hour for dinner, and a very small portion of that could be devoted to exercise, even if they had a place, and when they do take exercise they either trespass on their neighbours' lands, or play in the public streets." [1]

To people accustomed to the irregular and undisciplined atmosphere of the old industry, the system of fines in the mills seemed gross tyranny. Fines regulated every detail of conduct. The *Poor Man's Advocate* complained that some employers imposed fines for " footings," the customary treating of the workroom by a new entrant. [2] The editor disliked the custom, but he regarded the claim of the employer to interfere with the workmen's behaviour as intolerable to self-respecting men. M'Connel, one of the members of that well-known family, described a mill at Bakewell that his firm took over in 1835, with girls from 14 to 21 and overlookers carrying small switches with a discretionary power of corporal punishment. [3] By this time beating in the mills had become uncommon, but that picture helps us to understand what factory life looked like to this new population. There were, of course, great numbers of people employed outside the factories, but the new spirit of order and time-tables spread over industry in general. The machine, in this sense, governed industry where the machine itself was not in use.

Here, then, were all the elements of a difficult social problem. The towns were the homes of workmen, once artisans with scope for their instinct to express and create, who had passed into the impersonal routine of the mill; of men and women, with peasant outlook and tradition, accustomed to the peace and

---

[1] 1833 Committee on Public Walks, p. 58.

[2] January 1832. For the prevalence of drinking customs of the kind, see Dunlop, *The Philosophy of Artificial and Compulsory Drinking Usage*, 1839.

[3] Children's Employment Commission, 1843, Second Report, Appendix, part i. pp. b 63 ff.

beauty of nature, shut up in slum and alley ;[1] of immigrants from a land of deadly poverty, bringing their own habits and religion into a society struggling with dirt and torn by sectarian strife. All of these types were being drawn into new associations, creating and receiving the influence of new group atmospheres. We know to-day how subtle and powerful is the influence of what Mazzini called " collective intuitions " : how true it is that ten men acting or working or thinking or playing or praying together create a particular atmosphere, for there is a spirit in the group which affects every member, to which each member contributes something, and from which each member receives something.[2]   This spirit is not the same in the cricket club and the Church, the trade union and the regiment.   The new town had thus to satisfy the spiritual needs of men and women wrestling with the most difficult of all spiritual adjustments, forming a new social mind, disturbed by changes that had destroyed the basis of custom in their lives. The evidence of man's power in the world was impressive and ubiquitous.   The contrasts that religion had to justify, the inequalities that culture had to reconcile, were glaring and provocative.   How was this society placed for that task ?   On what did it rely to draw these various elements together in mutual sympathy and confidence ?

[1] " Nothing to see but streets, streets, streets; nothing to breathe but streets, streets, streets."—*Little Dorrit*.

[2] For an excellent discussion of this aspect, see Hobson, *Wealth and Life*, p. 27 : " The symphony, the church service, the cricket match, even the working of a steamer or a factory are not mere additions of the separate contributions of those who take part.   The unity of the plan or purpose, the harmony which they express, is the essential character of the joint activity and carries a corresponding unity of consentient feeling in the participants.   If I am told that after all this feeling is only existent in the particular participants, I shall not demur, but shall merely stress the fact that the participation produces and communicates feelings that could not be experienced otherwise than by this common organised activity."   See also Delisle Burns, *Industry and Civilisation*, on the Group Mind, and Laski, *Grammar of Politics*, pp. 22 and 23.

CHAPTER IV

THE REMEDY OF THE NEW WORLD

INDIVIDUAL OPPORTUNITY

A VISITOR coming from the ancient world to Manchester and Leeds in 1830 would have been struck by their wealth, but he would have noticed that it was wealth owned by private persons and displayed, where it was displayed, in private magnificence. For though the new Englishman was richer than the Greek or the Roman, the new English city was poorer than the Greek or Roman city: poorer in its looks, its possessions, its ambitions, and the range and dignity of its desires and enjoyments. The new town had no share in the arts or culture of the time. De Quincey said at the beginning of the century that no great city could present so repulsive an appearance as the Manchester of his day.[1] Lyon Playfair told the Health of Towns Commission in 1844 that in all Lancashire there was only one town, Preston, with a public park, and only one, Liverpool, with public baths. Popular theatres and galleries, public libraries and museums were almost unknown. It was not until 1845 that municipal authorities were given power to impose a rate to establish museums. So late as 1850 William Ewart,[2] the leader of the movement for civilising town life, told the House of Commons that large and populous towns like Sheffield and Leeds were without public libraries of any kind. There were few public spectacles, festivals, or amusements to draw classes together: the rich and well-to-do had music, theatres, and games of their own; the poor moved outside their orbit.[3] Thus the visitor

---

[1] *Collected Works*, i. p. 385.

[2] William Ewart's father was a friend of Gladstone's father, and Gladstone was named after him.

[3] The *Liverpool Examiner* remarked about the high prices of the Liverpool theatre in 1832, that a mechanic could enjoy a glass of wholesome beer every night for a week, for the cost of a single attendance in the gallery (October 2, 1832). Bradford had a theatre in 1838-39 at which the charge for the gallery was one shilling.—*Old Bradford*, p. 128.

from Greece or Rome would have found himself in a society
that employed none of the devices and the means by which
ancient states had tried to engage the imagination of their
subjects. The remedy of the ancient world was thrown
aside.

Now this society was not blind to the danger of discontent,
nor was it unaware of the reasons for expecting that discontent
to increase. De Quincey has an interesting passage in his
description of his early life at Greenheys in Manchester about
what he called personal Jacobinism. He and his brother, when
on their way to school, used to meet a number of mill boys
who called them " bucks " and pelted them with stones because
they wore Hessian boots. De Quincey adds that however
angry they were made by his aristocratic dress, the youths from
the mill had no sympathy with political Jacobinism and would
shout readily enough for Church and King. Their personal
Jacobinism, he explained, was " of that sort which is native to
the heart of man, who is by natural impulse (and not without a
root of nobility, though also of base envy) impatient of inequality,
and submits to it only through a sense of its necessity, or
under a long experience of its benefits." [1] De Quincey was
speaking of the opening years of the century. Long before
1830 it had become evident that this personal Jacobinism was
developing into political Jacobinism, and the problem of dis-
arming or repressing this political Jacobinism had become the
main care of the Governments of the time. It did not follow
because those Governments neglected the methods used for this
purpose by ancient societies that they had no methods of
their own.

To understand what those methods were it is convenient to
return to Bacon's distinction between rulers who seek to command the wills of men and those who seek only to command
their deeds and services. The distinction is roughly between
governments that seek to rule with the help of the imagination
of the ruled, and those that seek to rule without it. That distinction divides both governments and politicians. In England
in the early nineteenth century both schools were represented by
men of vigour, courage, and tenacity. Both schools had been
greatly strengthened by the French Revolution, which had con-

[1] *Collected Works*, i. p. 70.

firmed in their convictions both the school that trusted entirely to force and the school that believed in governing men by persuasion.

The school of force refused to admit that society could be made happier or more stable by attempting to create a spiritual sympathy between government and governed, between class and class. A spokesman of this school, say Castlereagh or Sidmouth, would have said, if asked to explain his philosophy, something like this : " Life for the mass of men and women must inevitably be hard, bleak, and painful. Poverty is bearable by those who are used to it. Great economic and social changes are upsetting the life of custom, which is the life of acquiescence. For that very reason let us cling more closely to custom, where it can still be preserved, custom in government, custom in religion, custom in law. After all, the mass of men have obedience in their bones. The moment you begin to reform your capital institutions you destroy the attachment of custom, and you cannot make sure that you are going to create in its place ties of affection or confidence. Keep, therefore, what you have : an unreformed Parliament, unreformed law, unreformed Church, a landed aristocracy maintained by the Corn Laws. Use these institutions to make disobedience terrible to those who are tempted into it. But keep temptation out of their way. Do not let any disturbing or stimulating influence reach this subject population. Put down the cheap press ; shut up agitators ; leave the poor ignorant, or if you must teach them give them only such an education as will put the fear of God and of the magistrates into their hearts. The more the inequalities of life increase the more essential is it to see that government rests on an adequate force of power, tradition, and the prestige that belongs to superior culture. Look to this, and do not flatter your fancy with dreams of *populi volentes*." This school, strongly represented among politicians, churchmen, and magistrates, in the first twenty years of the century, had a powerful influence on the life of the times. It sought to crush the cheap press and popular propaganda by imposing heavy stamp duties on all periodicals, it put men in prison freely for distributing pamphlets and books, and Sidmouth would have liked to suppress all reading rooms.[1] At this time, as Dr. Hook said later,

[1] Wickwar, *Struggle for the Freedom of the Press*, p. 156.

every sermon preached on behalf of a charity school had to prove that no harm would be done in educating the poor.[1]

This school survived, of course, after 1830, but no longer as a political party ; it was a die-hard faction. You would have found among landlords, manufacturers, magistrates, parsons, and other persons of influence, men who thought like Sidmouth and Castlereagh. But Peel, who led the Conservative party until he destroyed it, had nothing in common with this sentiment ; he differed from a Tory like Sidmouth more than he differed from a Radical like Hume. The Conservative party in his hands was a party of reform, not of repression. Men disagreed in the value they put on existing institutions ; on attachment to Church or squire ; on the uses of custom or the dangers of change. But none of the greater leaders of thought or of politics would have held that their society could be ruled without the help of its imagination. Wordsworth or Coleridge, Maurice or Arnold, Carlyle or Mill, Peel or Russell, Bentham or Southey, all of them in their plans for improving or regulating the world rejected the garrison system of Sidmouth and Castlereagh, and aimed at commanding the wills and not merely the deeds of the ruled. The motives of loyalty or ambition, of sympathy or reverence, these, and not the spirit of fear, were the forces to which the guiding minds looked for the salvation of their society.

This truth can be illustrated by the case of Southey. If you look at his opposition to Catholic Emancipation and the reform of Parliament, he seems to be more conservative than Wellington, who knew when to yield to circumstances. But in other aspects he was more advanced than Bright or Macaulay. For while he was in favour of many reforms that the Radicals wanted— mitigation of the criminal laws, reform of the game laws, national education—he saw further on certain questions, since he was in favour of the Ten Hours Bill from the first, and he was one of the few men of his time who grasped the grave consequences of leaving the growth of the new towns to avarice and chance.[2] What was true of Southey was true of Wordsworth. Political conflict among thinkers was not a conflict between stagnant and indolent minds on one side and active and

---

[1] *Leeds Intelligencer*, March 16, 1839.   [2] Dowden's *Southey*, p. 154.

vigilant minds on the other. On both sides there were generous and constructive ideas.

Among all these ideas one predominated in the practical life of the time. It was the belief that the Industrial Revolution had discovered the best remedy for discontent. For it offered to the poor man something to take his imagination ; something to stimulate the element of nobility in the personal Jacobinism described by De Quincey, and to discourage the base envy that embittered it. It offered to him the prospect of ceasing to be a poor man. For the Industrial Revolution had put a new ladder within the reach of diligence and worth. Never had men passed with steps so sure and swift from poverty to wealth, from obscurity to renown. To recite the names on this new roll of fame, from Brindley to Stephenson, from Davy to Arkwright, from Telford to Peel, is like reciting the names of Napoleon's field-marshals, from Hoche to Murat, from Ney to Bernadotte. Seen in this light, the cotton industry offered to the English workman the prospect that the revolutionary armies had offered to the French peasant. When did thrift, enterprise, and intelligence reap such reward ?

It is true that men had found their way in other ages from insignificance to power ; that starting within the Roman slave system a man might become a great bureaucrat, a great doctor, a great man of letters ; that inscriptions tell us of a senator and censor who began life as a clodhopper,[1] of towns adorned and paved by rich men who had once crept along their streets behind a master with power of life and death ;[2] that in the Middle Ages the Church offered an escape from the drudgery of the soil to such men as the Minister Suger, or Pope Silvester II. ; that in the sixteenth and seventeenth centuries banking and commerce could turn plain homespun material into something that would pass for the finished product of a proud and ancient line. But where in other ages there had been room for one man on this golden staircase, there was now room for a hundred. A merchant or a spinner like Gould or Cobden moved in a world where it was more likely than not that the first rich man he met had been born poor, and was, in Tiberius' phrase, his own ancestor.[3]

[1] Reid, *op. cit.* p. 319.   [2] Barrow, *Slavery in the Roman Empire*, p. 62.
[3] Cf. Peel's speech against the Ten Hours Bill in 1847 : " I would have the father

It was not only the railway king or the cotton lord who symbolised this triumphant principle for the optimists of the age. Cobden was enthusiastic about the ease with which a thrifty man could make himself independent without luck or genius. " I would then," he said in a famous letter, " advise the working classes to make themselves free of the labour market of the world, and this they can do by accumulating twenty pounds each, which will give them the command of the only market in which labour is at a higher rate than in England— I mean that of the United States. If every working man would save this sum, he might be as independent of his employer as the latter, with his great capital, is of his workmen." [1] So simple a sacrifice was all that was needed to make the man who to-day looked the slave of his circumstances, a person of standing, choosing his employment and his employer. In the great campaign for the Repeal of the Corn Laws, Cobden discovered and revealed another inspiring opportunity. The workman who saved fifty pounds and bought cottage property in a county constituency, could make himself a voter, as a forty-shilling free-holder, under the Reform Act of 1832.[2] Any artisan, then, who wished could put himself on the register. Those who cared for their freedom and dignity could obtain them if they cared to sacrifice their comforts and their leisure.

Men dominated by this excitement about the Industrial Revolution naturally held that society should arrange its institutions in such a way as to take full advantage of the new opportunities. " Remove all obstacles," they would have said, " to the spirit of initiative and enterprise. Encourage thrift ;

of a family left at liberty to imitate the example of the honourable member for Salford, and by his praiseworthy industry lay the foundation of a fortune which hundreds have acquired. Why, sir, I could name a dozen cases—and I have no doubt they are all familiar to the honourable member—of men who were once living upon 20s. or 25s. a week but who now possess fortunes of £100,000. But who is to answer for the result, if you paralyse the efforts of such men by your legislation."—*Annual Register,* 1847, p. 118.

The Member for Salford, Brotherton, was one of the leaders of the movement for the Ten Hours Bill.

It is interesting to note the comment of the *Poor Man's Guardian* on what we may call the Samuel Smiles philosophy : " For example, it is no answer to our argument to tell us how one Morison, M.P., in Fore Street has emerged from a needy pot boy to an opulent merchant worth a round million . . . it is not by his own industry but by the industry of others that Morison gets rich, and the richer he gets the greater must be the misery of those out of whose labour it comes."—June 8, 1833.

[1] Morley, *Life of Cobden,* vol. i., Appendix. Letter of October 21, 1836.
[2] *Ibid.* vol. i. p. 305.

make it easy for capital and labour to move from industry to industry, from place to place ; get rid of the Corn Laws which check the free exchange of goods ; abolish abuses in State and Church ; remove the dead-weight of custom wherever it checks man's energy and spirit ; spread education.   Then you will see what the Industrial Revolution can do to give you a rich and a happy instead of a poor and discontented people.   Give this clear field to the Industrial Revolution, and the steam engines and the railway will take care of society."

To understand how strongly this spectacle attracted the vigorous minds of the time, we must remember the history and tradition of the class that provided the leaders of thought and fashion in the new towns.   The pioneers of commerce and industry, who had been gaining wealth and position with such steady progress in the last two centuries, had acquired from their experience definite habits of mind and character.   The great commercial and industrial expansion of the seventeenth and eighteenth centuries was due largely to the energy of Nonconformists, who had been excluded or discouraged from a public career by the nature and sincerity of their religious opinions.   The pioneers who laid the foundations of the great metal industries were often men who had suffered themselves, or whose fathers had suffered, under Acts of Uniformity and other intolerant laws.   Unincorporated towns like Manchester and Birmingham offered a refuge to the uncompromising Dissenter whose conscience would make no terms with Church and State.   The vigour and initiative on which the new towns depended were largely to be found in men brought up in this atmosphere, in men, that is, who had been compelled by their circumstances to concentrate their attention on one side of life.

Mr. Tawney has shown in his classical work on *Religion and the Rise of Capitalism* how Puritan teaching came to identify application and success in business with religious worth.   This identification was not peculiar to the ethics or the philosophy of the Protestant Reformation.   At all times in the history of religion, as he shows, there has been a conflict of views on the relation of religion to the acquisition of wealth.   In Puritan England, by the seventeenth century, business and theology had accommodated those great quarrels which, in other ages, had distressed the conscience, exercised the dialectic, and shaken the peace of Christian churches.   The rich man of the Bible, who found it so difficult to enter the kingdom of heaven, was succeeded by the rich man of the Puritan revival who stepped into wealth and Paradise off the same ladder.[1]   For the rich man was no longer the idle man, who enjoyed himself while others toiled ; he was the industrious man who made others richer by his industry.   In many centuries of the world's history the man who suddenly became rich was regarded with the suspicion expressed in one of Menander's fragments : " Fellow, last year you were a beggar and a corpse, and now you are wealthy. Come, tell me, at what trade did you work ?   Why do you set us a bad example ? . . . Why do you show off injustice to us as an advantage ? "[2]   The rich man who was yesterday a beggar was now a noble figure, for in this age the acquisition of wealth was the sign of a virtue which had resisted the temptations of pleasure and pursued the serious business of life with un-interrupted devotion.   In this atmosphere success in the pursuit of wealth seemed to satisfy man's moral aspirations ; happiness and duty had been reduced to the simplest terms.

St. Augustine, when criticising the religions of Rome, argued that if you wanted moral lessons in Roman life or literature, you went not to the priests but to the philosophers and poets.   He quoted with approval as an illustration the well-known lines of Persius :

> " Discite, io miseri, et causas cognoscite rerum,
> Quid sumus, aut quidnam victuri gignimur ; ordo
> Quis datus, et metae qua mollis flexus et unde ;
> Quis modus argento, quid fas optare, quid asper
> Utile nummus habet ; patriae carisque propinquis
> Quantum elargiri deceat : quem te deus esse
> Jussit et humana qua parte locatus es in re." [3]

---

[1] Coleridge described the " distinguished and world-honoured company of Christian Mammonists " as " a drove of camels, heavily laden, yet all at full speed, and each in the confident expectation of passing through the *eye of the needle*, without stop or halt, both beast and baggage."—*Lay Sermons*, p. 386.

[2] Loeb edition, p. 387.

[3] *Satires*, iii. 66 : " Poor fools, learn wisdom and study the causes of things ; the nature of man and purpose of his birth ; the chain of circumstance ; the way gently to round life's goal ; the bounds that should be set to wealth ; the proper objects of prayer ; the little profit mere gold brings to man ; the portion of our goods we should bestow on country and dear kinsmen ; in short, what part God has bidden you play, what post in life's battle he would have you hold."

This picture of the complexity of life, this belief that you might have too much wealth for happiness and welfare, reflected ideas and scruples that were common to Roman philosophers and to early Christian teachers. But to a man brought up on Puritan principles, in the form those principles had taken it would have seemed strange to imagine a Peel or an Arkwright or a Crawshay pausing to ask himself whether it would be a good thing or a bad thing for him to become still richer. And it was natural to suppose that if you wanted to fire a poor man with noble ardour, if you wanted to set before the workman a prospect that would stimulate his ambition, you could not do better than offer him the ideal in which you had found happiness and virtue. Thus individual success took in this society the place that common enjoyment had taken in the ancient world. The business man, pointing to the triumphant career of the Lancashire cotton spinner, with " nitor in adversum " for his family motto, would have argued that there was here a more inspiring spectacle, a truer sign of human progress, than a theatre at Epidaurus, crowded with Greeks of every class listening to a chorus of the " Agamemnon."

This ideal had the glamour and freshness that belonged to a new religion, for it was associated with the great emancipating truths that the world had learnt from the French and American Revolutions. The freedom to make the most of yourself in competition with your fellow men seemed to the Englishman of the age the most important of all the personal rights that those Revolutions had proclaimed and vindicated. This right marked a great step forward in the history of mankind. As individualism dethroned feudalism, the prestige of work dethroned the prestige of idleness. Now the prestige of idleness had been one of the curses of the world. From time to time it had been shaken. The monks, building their monasteries with their own hands, had put to shame the false pride that made a Roman think it less disgraceful to depend upon a State or upon a patron than to earn his living by the labour he called sordid. But the prestige of idleness had persisted through the world's history, and eighteenth-century England maintained gentlemen of good families, living on pensions and sinecures, who thought themselves morally superior to any one who worked for his living. Herodotus explained why industrial occupations were despised in the ancient world in comparison with occupations or modes of life that fitted men and States for war. Manchester reflected the new light in which this false perspective had been destroyed:[1] war and industry had changed places. What was the history of progress but the history of man's advance from a world in which wealth and power had been seized by those who had conquered and plundered their fellows, to a world in which they had been earned by those who supplied the wants of mankind? It had been a great day in that history when the merchants of Venice and the bankers of Florence were strong enough to make themselves the rivals of feudal lords and royal princes. With the new prestige of production a still more brilliant day had dawned. When men admired the Peels and the Arkwrights, they would soon estimate at their true value the Bourbons and Napoleons, the great drones or the great pirates, who had once cast such a fatal spell on the human mind.

The Manchester merchant would have argued also that the new industrial system had given the English people a flexible society. Movement from class to class is a sign of a healthy social life. Men were rising in the world in Cobden's Manchester by hard work, prudent abstinence, shrewd sense, and inspired daring. How had men risen in other ages? What were the arts by which slave and ex-slave had made their way to independence and power in the Roman State? Listen to Juvenal or to Tacitus on the climbing freedman. When a weak Emperor was on the throne, or a strong Emperor lost his power of will, the Roman Empire slipped into the hands of favourites and had all the look of a degenerate Oriental state. Seneca has described Claudius giving an order in heaven: " You might have imagined they were all his own freedmen : so little notice did they take of him." When the worst had been said about the forces and qualities that brought a man to the front in the early scramble of the Industrial Revolution, this method of promotion was at least to be preferred to the arts by which many a

---

[1] The Manchester citizen who wrote an introduction to Faucher's book on *Manchester* put this : " The past history of our race proclaims the supremacy of force, the selfishness of empire, and the subjugation of mankind, as the prevailing aspect of society. But the rise and progress of the industrial arts, and the extension of beneficent commerce, indicate in terms too plain to be misunderstood, the real destiny of society, and the existence of a new epoch which shall substitute the ploughshare for the sword, and the loom for the battery. The cause of industry is the cause of humanity."

Roman Prefect had become a power in the government of the Roman Empire.[1]   The system which had made Peel the master of the House of Commons need not fear comparison with the system which made a Pallas the master of the Senate.

Let anybody, again, compare this industrial England with feudal England : Manchester with the villages of Dorset and Wilts.   Here men rose by their merit and by their own efforts. A man who saved a few pounds could put his best foot foremost without touching his cap to any of the powerful men on whose pleasure Crabbe, or Porson, or Clare had had to wait.   And the most active minds of the time had no liking for the historical institutions through whose doors poor men in other ages had passed to fame.   Those institutions from the Church downwards were as remarkable at this time for their abuses as their virtues, and the spirit of the age welcomed as the solution of most of the problems of life an arrangement which seemed to make the individual his own master, and to reduce in proportion the prestige and the power of the institutions that offered at once discipline and shelter to those who would step across their threshold.   The man who in other ages wished to follow in the footsteps of Wolsey had to put on the cassock of a church, but a Peel or an Arkwright could become a millionaire without the surrender of conscience or freedom to anybody's keeping.   This was the novelty that fascinated men like Cobden.   They contrasted this world in which men needed no patron, with the world where everything depended on the smile of squire or parson, much as Lucian contrasted the free life of Athens with the degrading atmosphere of Rome, where flatterers courted the rich, and spoke to them as slaves spoke to a master.

Not least, perhaps, of the advantages that the Manchester merchant would have claimed for his age would have been its success in turning aside from the frivolities of the ancient world.   For he would have regarded the social life of the Roman Empire as a warning rather than an example.   Where had that social life ended ?   Dion Chrysostom scolded the people of Alexandria for their wild excitement over horse-racing. " For cities are not only taken when men demolish their walls, kill the men, enslave the women, and burn their houses.   When there is indifference to all that is noble, and a passion for one

---

[1] See, on the whole subject, *Freedmen in the Early Roman Empire*, by A. M. Duff.

ignoble end : when men devote themselves and their time to it, dancing, mad, hitting each other, using unspeakable language, often blaspheming, gambling their possessions, and sometimes returning in beggary from the spectacle, that is the disgraceful and ignominious sack of a town." [1] Amid the orgies of the theatre at Carthage, when the Vandals were outside the walls, " confundebatur vox morientium voxque bacchantium." [2] Gibbon has drawn a graphic picture of the violence of the factions of the circus at Byzantium and the fierce and bloody contests of green and blue that distracted the politics of the Eastern Empire.   A sober merchant of Manchester would have laughed at the suggestion that his town, busy from rising to setting sun increasing the riches and comforts of the world, had anything to learn from a civilisation that had degenerated into these scenes of outrage and discord ; in which production had never been given its true importance, enjoyment had been allowed to run wild, and the men who served mankind the worst received the highest honours.   Happy the new age in which success was so clearly the reward of merit, and private wealth and public benefit were so fortunately united. [3] We have now to see what kind of town was created by these ideas ; what was its education, its religion, its culture, and its social life.

[1] Livingstone, *Mission of Greece*, p. 124.

[2] Dill, *Roman Society in the Last Century of the Western Empire*, p. 58.

[3] For the optimism of the time, see Cobden's letter to Place of July 1, 1846 (quoted Wallas, *Life of Place*, p. 396) : " You have lived through by far the most eventful seventy years in the world's history.   Nay, the fifty years during which you have been an observer of public events have been more fertile in great and enduring incidents than any five centuries I could select.   Bless yourself that you live in times when reform bills, steamboats, railroads, penny postage, and free trade, to say nothing of the ratification of civil and religious liberties, have been possible facts."

CHAPTER V

THE GOVERNMENT OF THE NEW TOWN

THE active city life, described by Mrs. Green in her picture of fifteenth-century England, had sunk into decay long before the steam engine was invented. The ritual of pageants, festivals, and dances fell into disuse as the cities lost their prestige with the growing power of the Tudor State, and the common people lost their share in the Guilds with the growing power of the richer classes. The towns so proud of their independence had come under the grasp, first of kings, then of families and politicians. The life of ceremony had not disappeared all at once. Leeds commemorated the Peace of Utrecht in 1713 with a great procession and festival.[1] Preston has preserved her Guild Festival to our own day. But it is perhaps significant of the change in city life that the wool-combers' festival in honour of St. Blaise, kept as a popular pageant down to 1825, was replaced by dances and dinners at which the respectable classes entertained each other.[2] The loss of political importance was not, of course, peculiar to the English towns, but Continental towns, though they no longer held the commanding position they had gained in the Middle Ages, had kept much more of the spirit of their rich and interesting past, and its afterglow still comforted and inspired their city life. When the Industrial Revolution collected large populations in the North and the Midlands, the genius of this common life was almost extinct, and a new society had to create its own institutions. The spirit and manner in which this task was conceived and accomplished illustrate very well the ideas described in the preceding chapter. To understand them we must first look at the arrangements

[1] Webb, *Manor and Borough*, p. 418.
[2] *Leeds Intelligencer*, January 26, 1839; *Halifax Express*, February 16, 1839; *Leeds Mercury*, February 9, 1839.

under which these towns lived before the Municipal Corporations Act of 1835.

There were, of course, wide differences in the character and method of government in different places before the revolution of that year. There was first of all the difference between incorporated and unincorporated towns. The status of towns to-day depends largely upon population. But the 246 incorporated towns before 1835 included some of the smallest places in England, such as Dunwich crumbling into the sea, described in 1816 as forty-two houses and half a church, and left out some of the largest.[1] Hence, whereas some of the towns that were leading or representative towns in the new life of England, like Leeds, Liverpool, Newcastle, Leicester, and Macclesfield, had ancient charters, others not less important, such as Manchester, Birmingham, Sheffield, Halifax, Bradford, and Huddersfield, were subject to a lord of the manor. Leeds had her mayor and aldermen ; Manchester, as Cobden put it, was governed from Rolleston Hall. At Rolleston Hall lived Sir Oswald Mosley, the lord of the manor, whose steward summoned a court leet at which the jury elected a borough reeve, as it elected constables, market lookers, ale tasters, pounders and muzzlers of mastiff dogs.

The incorporated towns differed widely among themselves. But it is roughly true that in all but a very few instances the government and patronage were in the hands of a small oligarchy, though structure, title, and powers might differ from town to town. Leeds, for example, had a mayor, twelve aldermen, and twenty-four assistants from whom the aldermen were chosen. This ruling body recruited itself by co-option from among the leading Church of England families in the towns. In Liverpool there was a close body of a mayor and two bailiffs, and thirty or forty aldermen or common council men, recruiting itself exclusively by co-option. This body had a much wider range of duties than the corresponding body in Leeds, for whereas the Leeds corporation had little to do outside the administration of justice, the supervision of the police, and the superintendence and licensing of public-houses, the Liverpool Corporation governed

---

[1] Cobbett had his own way of distinguishing borough towns : "I can tell a borough-town from another upon my entrance into it by the nasty, cunning, leering, designing look of the people ; a look between that of a bad (for *some* are good) Methodist parson and that of a pickpocket."—*Rural Rides*, November 15, 1821.

the port, controlled the markets, owned a great deal of land, and received a large revenue from dues and tolls. Mr. and Mrs. Webb, who regard Liverpool as the best governed of the populous towns, describe Leicester as the worst. Here a mayor and aldermen derived an income of £4000 a year from a fine landed estate of which they refused to publish any accounts, providing for the town nothing beyond salaries for a Recorder, Superintendents of the market-place, and one or two petty officers. There were, on the other hand, a few towns like Norwich and Morpeth with large bodies of freemen entitled to vote for the Council.[1] Berwick-on-Tweed, a town of this kind, was described by a Select Committee of the House of Commons in 1833[2] "as the most popular in its constitution, not the most faultless in its practice." The adjective chosen by the Committee would seem temperate enough to those who have read Mr. and Mrs. Webb's account of the condition of this little town.

The great mass of inhabitants shut out from these bodies had some scope and outlet for their feelings in the meetings of the parish vestries. For the vestries exercised certain civil functions, sometimes sharing in the control of the workhouse, and sometimes electing members to special bodies like street commissioners. In Leeds the corporation was entirely in the hands of Tories and Churchmen, but the Radicals and the Dissenters pressed into the parish church vestry meetings, where they soon became a dominant force. Such behaviour became general in times of excitement. The conflict in Leeds was mainly sectarian, but in Manchester it was more political, embittered by Peterloo, and the system of espionage employed by the justices. So the vestries of the Church became in Manchester the battlefield for issues that were national in their scope and interest. Mr. and Mrs. Webb have described how men like John Edward Taylor, the Potter Brothers, and Archibald Prentice used these meetings to agitate against the government of the manorial court, seeking to disallow payment made for special constables and to elect their own candidates for such offices as that of surveyor of highways. In Liverpool, on the

---

[1] There were 41 electors at Liverpool, 37 at Leeds, 36 at Newcastle, 24 at Leicester, 25 at Preston (Preston had 8000 Parliamentary voters). At Norwich, on the other hand, there were 3640; at Nottingham 2880; at Berwick-on-Tweed 1105.—Somers Vine, *English Municipal Institutions*, p. 52.   [2] See p. 49.

other hand, the vestries and the corporation worked together amicably and effectively.

We have thus two sets of institutions : the institutions connected in the incorporated towns with the corporation, and in the unincorporated towns with the manorial court on the one side, and the institutions connected with the parish on the other. There is a third set of institutions more important than either.

It was the custom in the eighteenth century when anything needed to be done to apply to Parliament for a private act, setting up a body for this special purpose. The Turnpike Trusts which built so many of our modern roads, the Enclosure Commissions which carried out the agrarian revolution, are examples of this device. The first improvements in the towns were made by this method. When a body of citizens wanted to pave streets or to provide themselves or their neighbours with water or light, they did not ask for further powers to be bestowed on the corporation or the officials of the manor : they applied to Parliament for leave to create a body of special Commissioners. A new organ of government was thus constituted. Between 1745 and 1835 almost every municipal borough in the country provided itself with Improvement Commissioners of one kind or another.[1]

How were these Commissions composed ? Most of them had an *ex officio* element, consisting of such persons as the mayor, the lord of the manor, local magistrates, or clergymen. As a rule, the other members of the Commission were named in the act, and were authorised to fill vacancies by co-option. Birmingham, Bradford, Huddersfield, Wakefield, Halifax, and Durham had Commissions constituted on this principle. In some towns, as in Leeds and Liverpool, the Commission included an elective element, the elective representatives being a small proportion of the whole body. In such cases there was a high property qualification, both for voters and for office holders. Sometimes, again, the local Act would specify as Commissioners all members of a particular class together with persons named in the Act. Preston, Rochdale, Oldham, Derby, and Stockport had Commissions of this kind. The Stockport

---

[1] " The only municipal boroughs, having in 1831 11,000 inhabitants, that had never had any separate body of Improvement Commissioners seem to have been Leicester, Nottingham, Wenlock, and Wigan."—Webb, *Statutory Authorities*, p. 242 n.

Commissioners consisted of all persons, except publicans, who occupied premises of the yearly value of £35, and of all owners of property of the yearly value of £50 who resided within three miles of the market-place.

Manchester had each kind of Commission in turn. The first Commission, set up in 1765, consisted of persons named in the Local Act who were to co-opt their successors. In 1792 the Commission was converted into a body resembling the Commission of Stockport. It consisted of the Warden and Fellows of the College of Christ in Manchester, the Borough Reeve and Constable, and all owners and occupiers of premises of a yearly rent of £30 who took the prescribed oath. The meetings of this Commission became disorderly when local quarrels were active; sometimes as many as 800 Commissioners would attend. This led to the reconstruction of the Commission in 1828; it was turned into an elected body confined to persons with a £28 qualification, elected by voters on a £16 franchise. The Commissioners were 240 in number, with two main Committees, the Gas Directors and the Improvement Committee, and four other Committees, Accounts, Finance, Watch, and "Lamp, Scavenging, Fire Engines, and Main Sewers." From speeches made in the House of Commons on the Municipal Corporations Reform Bill, we learn that there were about 3000 electors. Salford, on the other hand, had an Improvement Commission for which all ratepayers had a vote.[1]

These Commissions were the most important Local Authorities of the time, and most of the work which we associate with municipal government was in their hands.[2] They could borrow or levy rates within strict limits for special purposes.

In these arrangements there was nothing to foster a common zeal for the beauty and welfare of the town. Power, credit, interest, and duties were divided, and divided often between bodies that were mutually hostile.[3] It is generally agreed that

[1] Speech of Brotherton, June 22, 1835.

[2] "The powers granted by Local Acts of Parliament for various purposes have been from time to time conferred, not upon the municipal officers but upon trustees or Commissioners distinct from them, so that often the corporations have hardly any duties to perform. They have the nominal government of the town, but the efficient duties and the responsibility have been transferred to other hands."—Report Municipal Corporations Commission, p. 17.

[3] "At Leeds no persons are elected Commissioners of Police whose political principles are not opposed to those of the Corporation."—Municipal Corporations

the Commissioners of 1835 took too severe a view of the delinquencies of the old corporation, but nobody who wanted to make a town proud of itself, eager to raise the tone of its life or to create among its citizens a strong sense of spiritual fellowship, would take this kind of government for his model.   Nor would he put great towns like Manchester and Birmingham under the rule of the officers of the manor court.   The vestries, if they gave some outlet to discontent, were hardly an aid to social unity.   They provided a battlefield for local quarrels of religion or family or class.   They could embarrass and even thwart a ruling body, but could do little more.   The Improvement Commissioners had active duties, but their duties and their outlook were sharply limited : the first by law, the second by the circumstances of their creation.   Bodies so exclusively representative of property were not likely to take generous or ambitious views of the needs of their towns.   The Commissioners were chiefly interested in the abuses that caught the notice of a merchant as he rode to his business : the condition of the main streets.   In Manchester, where there was an active Commission, the narrow courts and the alleys and the growing workmen's quarters were completely neglected.   In Bradford the Improvement Commissioners, a self-elected body of substantial citizens qualified by an estate of £1000, made so poor an impression on the chaos and squalor of a district growing rapidly in wealth as well as in numbers, that the Health of Towns Commission described Bradford as the dirtiest and worst regulated town in the United Kingdom.   Halifax spent just £50 on cleansing the streets in six months in 1846; it is not surprising to learn that the town suffered severely in that year from an epidemic of typhus fever.[1]   A witness before the Select Committee on the Buildings Regulations Bills of 1842 stated that the Manchester Commissioners of Police employed a staff of four Inspectors of Nuisances at 25s. a week, with one superintendent at 30s. a week.   When a town is in the hands of such bodies the improvements that are made tend to widen the breach between rich and poor.

Report, p. 121. At some places such as Bristol, Coventry, and Hull, the conflict between Corporation and Commission prevented the effective maintenance of order.— Redlich and Hirst, *English Local Government*, p. 121.

[1] *Halifax Guardian Historical Almanack*, 1898. For the general character of the Commissions, see Spencer, *Municipal Origins*, p. 172.

It is easy to see, then, that as these towns were governed before 1835 there was little to encourage ambitious or imaginative ideas about the scope and purpose of town life. Historians can find individual achievements to praise, records of honesty and even of enterprise. The Leeds oligarchy was attacked fiercely in the sectarian strife that raged during the last twenty years of its life, but its integrity was never challenged. The Manchester Commissioners distinguished themselves by establishing municipal gasworks, from which they made a profit of £20,000 to £30,000 a year for town improvements.[1] But even such good rulers as those of Liverpool rejected a petition praying for the appropriation of certain open spaces for the recreation of the working classes.[2] No town was so governed as to inspire pride and affection among a new population crowding into its streets.

One other aspect of municipal government must be noted. Under two Acts passed in the reign of Charles II., the first (1661) aimed principally at the Presbyterians, the second (1673) at the Roman Catholics, nobody could be admitted to a corporate office who had not taken the Sacrament within one year before his appointment. In 1727 Parliament passed the first of a series of Acts of Indemnity to protect persons who " through ignorance of the law, absence or some unavoidable accident " had taken office without complying with the law, and after 1760 such an Act was passed every year. These Acts at the best excluded consistent Nonconformists and Roman Catholics, and apart from this they stamped municipal government with an odiously partisan character. It was not until 1828 that these Acts were repealed. When Lord John Russell carried his Bill for Repeal (1828), he said that the corporations did not include one-tenth of the Dissenters who ought to be serving on them.[3] In the new industrial districts Nonconformity was specially strong, and these injustices surviving long after they had lost all meaning, had a great effect in poisoning social life both at the time and afterwards. In the towns that were given self-government in 1835, there was from the start the disabling discord left by these memories. We must now turn to the revolution of 1835.

[1] Evidence of Chairman of Paving and Sewerage Committee of the Police Commissioners of Manchester. Committee on Buildings Regulations Bills, 1842.
[2] Touzeau, *Rise and Progress of Liverpool*, p. 823.
[3] *Annual Register*, 1828, p. 88.

One of the first acts of Lord Grey's Government was to set up a Select Committee to examine the municipal corporations of England and Wales. This Committee reported in 1833 calling attention to abuses that seemed to belong to the system : the local jealousies, the violence of party and sectarian feeling, the use of borough funds for private and party purposes, the absence of checks on the conduct of those in power, the want of confidence and of respect for authority. The Committee recommended the appointment of a Commission to inquire into the state of the different towns in detail. The Government acted on this advice, setting up a Commission consisting mainly of young barristers, one of whom was Shelley's friend, Jefferson Hogg. The chairman was Blackburne, member for Huddersfield, and the secretary, Joseph Parkes, who brought to this subject the same special knowledge and enthusiasm that Chadwick contributed to the discussion of Poor Law Reform. In March 1835, the Commissioners presented Lord Melbourne, the new Prime Minister, with four volumes, in which they described the condition of 285 towns together with a general report making recommendations. Within four weeks the Government had introduced a Bill, and after three months of struggle between the two Houses, in which some important changes were made, the Bill became law. In December of the same year elections were held for the new town councils.

In this case, as in that of Poor Law Reform, the Government could count on some measure of co-operation from the Opposition benches. The preamble of their Bill, " Whereas divers Bodies Corporate at sundry times have been constituted within the Cities, Towns and Boroughs of England and Wales to the Intent that the same might forever be and remain well and quietly governed . . ." touched at once on an aspect of the problem to which no responsible statesman could be indifferent. For nobody who remembered Manchester in 1819, or Nottingham and Bristol in 1831, could think that these great towns were " quietly governed." Peel, who had already laid the foundations of his fame as a reforming Home Secretary, put on one side all the Tory misgivings about this revolution in a single decisive sentence : " I cannot contemplate the conditions of some of the great towns of this country, and witness the frequent necessity of calling in the Military in order to maintain tranquillity without feeling desirous that the inhabitants of such towns should be habituated to obedience and order through the instrumentality of an efficient civil power and a regular and systematic enforcement of the law." [1]   So strong was Peel's interest in this reform that he withstood all the pressure of his party in the Lords and gave Russell active help in carrying the Bill.

The new Act applied to 178 incorporated towns and made provision for the incorporation of other towns after petition to Parliament.[2]   In all these towns the mayors and aldermen and other co-opted and self-elected rulers were swept aside to make way for elective town councils.   With the old oligarchies there disappeared what remained of custom and pageant in municipal life.[3]

About the new town councils there are four points to be noted.   The first is their composition.   The Government Bill as introduced imposed no property qualification and excluded no set of persons from service on the councils.   The Lords amended the Bill in both respects, introducing a property qualification and inserting a clause to shut out clergymen and ministers of religion.   The Government accepted both amendments, though not in the precise form the Lords had given them. Consequently the new town councils consisted mainly of merchants and tradesmen with a sprinkling of professional men. We can see that the old Leeds Corporation misrepresented the political feelings of Leeds when it petitioned Parliament against parliamentary reform.   The new town council, though of course on a wider basis, still represented the sentiment and outlook of particular classes.   A simple illustration will make this clear.   The people of Leeds in the forties were in favour both

---

[1] House of Commons, June 15, 1835.   It is interesting to notice the use made by Cobden of the incident of Peterloo in the famous pamphlet, *Incorporate your Borough*, which he addressed to the people of Manchester in 1835.

[2] 5 and 6 William IV. cap. 76.   Manchester was incorporated in 1838, Birmingham in 1839, Sheffield in 1843, Bradford in 1847, Halifax in 1848, Oldham in 1849, Blackburn in 1851, Rochdale in 1856, Dewsbury in 1862.   Between 1835 and 1871 only forty-six towns were incorporated.—Somers Vine, *op. cit.* p. 254.   At the time of the Royal Commission in 1869 such towns as Merthyr Tydvil (population 83,000) and Birkenhead (population 51,000) were still unincorporated.

[3] Sir Robert Inglis moved an amendment to provide that the insignia and decorations used by the old bodies should be retained by the new councils, but he was defeated.

It was said afterwards in debate that some of the new town councils sold pictures by Reynolds that belonged to the old corporations.—James, House of Commons, March 6, 1845.

of the repeal of the Corn Laws and of the Ten Hours Bill. The Leeds Council after presenting a petition in favour of the first reform, rejected a proposal to petition in favour of the second by 22 votes to 7.[1] Yet the working classes in Leeds were notoriously anxious for the Ten Hours Bill, and a local petition in its support had been signed by 23 parsons, 3 Catholic priests, 2 Methodist ministers, 6 doctors, and 23 surgeons.[2] The objections to the property qualification were put strongly in the House of Commons in 1859, when it was stated that the town councils of Sheffield, Rochdale, and Oldham had complained that it was a serious obstacle to their efficiency.[3]

The second point is the character of the voters. The new Act established a uniform qualification. Anybody who paid rates and had resided in the town for three years was entitled to be put on the burgess' roll. "While we think," said Lord John Russell, "that it is but proper to have the permanent ratepayers of the town as the persons to elect the Council which is to have the government of the town, yet, at the same time, it seems to be as necessary to take some precaution that they are neither persons who are occasionally suffering under that pressure of distress which obliges them to receive parochial relief, nor persons unable regularly and for a length of time to pay their rates."[4] Place attacked this restriction in a paper, "Municipal Corporation Reform," of which a few numbers appeared in the summer of 1835, and he said that there was widespread opposition to it. It was significant that the opponents included Blackburne, who had been Chairman of the Commission of Inquiry, and two members with special knowledge, Ewart, who was familiar with the conditions of Liverpool, and Brotherton, who was familiar with those of Manchester. Brotherton pointed out that the Act would disfranchise a certain number of poor people and also a certain number of women who had voted as freemen. The qualification remained unchanged in form till 1869, when the qualifying period was reduced to one year and women were given the vote.

We can see from a study of the burgess lists that the working classes had very little voting strength. In 1835 Liverpool

---

[1] *Leeds Mercury*, May 16, 1846.   [2] *Leeds Intelligencer*, April 4, 1846.
[3] Speech of W. J. Fox, House of Commons, March 10, 1859.
[4] House of Commons, June 5, 1835.

(population nearly 200,000) had less than 6000 voters; Newcastle (population of 53,000) had 2500 voters; Preston (33,000) had about 2400; Stockport (41,000) had about 2300. The Yorkshire towns did a little better, for Leeds (123,000) had 6790 voters.[1] It is probable that the first lists were the most exclusive, for in 1839 Leeds had nearly 9000 voters,[2] but it was generally recognised that the Act created a middle-class electorate. In Norwich and Nottingham there were fewer voters under the new system than under the old: in Norwich 2401 instead of 3640; in Nottingham 2217 instead of 2880. " There never was such a coup as this municipal reform has turned out to be," wrote Creevey in 1836. " It marshals all the middle classes in all the towns of England in the ranks of Reform: aye, and gives them monstrous power, too." [3]

After 1850 the municipal franchise was extended by accident in certain towns. In that year an Act was passed to simplify the collection of rates in tenements, and a clause was inserted which gave the vote under certain conditions to occupiers of those tenements. In 1859 a Select Committee of the House of Lords took evidence on the effect of this clause.[4] It appeared that in Bolton the number of electors had increased from 2539 to 7107; in Bradford from 5058 to 14,094; in Newcastle from 2393 to 9850; in Preston from 1892 to 5738: in Warrington from 628 to 2721; in Wigan from 1227 to 3137. In other towns the increase was not in this proportion. The Lords Committee were in no doubt that the effects had been bad, and they pointed out that in this very year an Act had been passed by R. A. Cross for checking bribery. There was evidence, however, to show that the extension of the franchise in these towns had stimulated a new attention to sanitary and housing reform. Two witnesses said definitely that this had happened in Newcastle, and it is significant that the extension was followed in Bradford by an attempt to put down the building of back-to-back houses.[5]

The third point to notice is that the town councils were not allowed to absorb the various Improvement Commissions. The Act merely provided that such bodies should be at liberty to

[1] Somers Vine, *op. cit.* p. 30.   [2] *Leeds Mercury*, August 24, 1839.
[3] *Creevey Papers*, vol. ii. p. 308.
[4] See Report of Lords Committee on Rating of Tenements Act, 1859.
[5] Cudworth, *Historical Notes on the Bradford Corporation*, p. 145.

transfer their powers for paving, lighting, cleansing, and other purposes to the town councils if they pleased. Lord Morpeth said in 1847 that the Government took this course because they feared the new town councils would be too political.[1] The powers of these bodies were transferred in Manchester in 1842 and 1843, but Birmingham, which was incorporated in 1839, kept its Commissioners till 1851, and in some towns these bodies survived still later. Lord Morpeth, in 1848, when introducing his Health of Towns Bill gave some remarkable facts revealing the consequences of this decision. He said that there were only 29 towns in England where the powers of draining, cleansing, and paving were vested exclusively in the town council. There were 66 towns where those powers were exercised jointly by town councils and Commissioners. There were 30 towns where the town councils had no powers of draining, cleansing, and paving, and where these powers were exercised independently by Commissioners. Lastly, there were 62 towns where there was no authority whatever exercising such powers. Thus, out of 187 incorporated towns 62 were left without means of draining or cleansing, and only 29 had power to act through their elected government.[2] This was the state of municipal government in England thirteen years after the passing of the Municipal Corporations Reform Act.

The fourth point to notice is that the towns had very little more dignity or power after the revolution than before. The Act did not create a new town government inspired by generous ideas, exercising wide powers and seizing new opportunities for noble action. For the Act was really directed against a particular abuse, the enjoyment by a small body of property and patronage meant for the service of the community. The Bill was attacked on the ground that it interfered with property; it was defended on the ground that it protected property. The chief complaint brought against the old corporation was that of extravagance. The new government of the town was devised and exercised by men who thought this the chief evil in public life. We get a good idea of the spirit of the times in the argument of J. C. Knight, one of the lawyers who spoke against the Bill at the Bar of the House of Lords, drawing a picture of

---

[1] House of Commons, March 30, 1847.
[2] House of Commons, May 5, 1848.

the dangers to which the ratepayers would be exposed. " He would now briefly notice the 91st clause which related to the establishment of a borough fund, into which the profits of all hereditaments, the produce of all fines, etc., were to be thrown. This fund was to be devoted to various purposes, for the public benefit of the inhabitants and for the improvement of the borough. And it was provided that, where the ordinary resources of the fund were not sufficient to meet the charges upon it, that then the town council should cause a borough rate to be levied. Now, it was not unlikely that theatres, dancing-rooms, drinking-rooms, tea gardens, and other places of resort, might be very agreeable to the town council and their ladies, who might consider them necessary and proper for the ' improvement ' of any particular borough ; and, in case the borough fund was not sufficient for carrying these plans into effect, they had nothing to do but to lay on a rate, against the policy or necessity of which, as he read the clause, there was no appeal. That rate, be it observed, would be laid on by those who, in all human probability, and according to all impartial calculation, would either pay very little or nothing at all towards it. Were this bill to pass, and that he resided in a district subject to its operation, he should, if there were no place in England where he could escape from its enactments, fly from his native land, dearly as he was attached to it."[1] To this speaker, not throwing out some extravagance but seeking to convince his audience, the idea that his town might spend some of his money on entertainment, one of the first objects of city life to the ancient world, was so outrageous that he could only describe his feeling about it by saying that he would shake off the dust of his city from his feet rather than submit to the danger of such injustice. It was with this spirit in the ascendant that the towns started on their task of civilising the chaos of the Industrial Revolution.

[1] Speech of Jas. Lewis Knight, K.C., against the Iniquitous Corporation Bill, July 31 and August 1, 1835, published by C. F. Cock, 21 Fleet Street.

CHAPTER VI

THE NEW POOR LAW

THE organisation of town government was one of the two great English reforms of the Whigs ; the other was the reorganisation of the Poor Law. Disraeli said of this reform in 1841, that it was impossible " to conceive a revolution which exercised a greater influence upon the people at large. . . . If they had not, in passing the Poor Law, outraged the constitution or violated the law, they had done that which he conceived was of greater importance : they had outraged the manners of the people." [1] How far was Disraeli's description of the new Poor Law correct ?

If the historian of our age turns to the publications of the International Labour Office for light on our social life, he will find that certain arrangements are common to most European countries, designed to prevent or alleviate poverty, sickness, and misfortune. If he takes one of the more advanced nations, like Great Britain or Germany, he will find Trade Boards, Unemployment Insurance, Health Insurance, Old Age Pensions, Widows Pensions, special treatment for underfed children, special provision for insanity and other diseases, special arrangements for medical services. In some countries he will find all of these institutions, in all he will find some. If he turns to English life between 1800 and 1850 he will find, so far as the State is concerned, one single institution in use for the treatment of all these problems : the Poor Law. This was true before the revolution of 1834 : it was true after that revolution. What, then, was done by that revolution ; how did it outrage the manners of the English people ? To answer that question we must put the revolution against its historical background.

The escaped convict in Mr. Galsworthy's play reminds the parson, when he is found taking refuge in the vestry, that the

---

[1] House of Commons, February 8, 1841.

Church was once the sanctuary for fugitives. In England in the Middle Ages, as on the Continent of Europe, the Church took care, so far as care was taken, of the destitute and the sick.[1] The parish was the unit for these purposes. The cost was borne partly by alms, partly by parish property (parishes had property in different forms, sometimes in the form of an inn), partly by the proceeds of convivial entertainment known as Church Ales, and later by Church Rates. In the sixteenth century, as a result of a movement for reform, not peculiar to England, nor originating in England, for the chief name in its history is that of Vives, the State began to accept responsibility for the problem that had hitherto been thrown upon the Church. A number of Acts of Parliament, beginning with a modest Act in 1536 and culminating with the famous Act of 1601, made provision for the relief of the destitute. The justices were directed to see that every parish had a stock of wool, hemp, and other things, in order to provide employment; recalcitrants were to be committed to a house of correction, householders were to be compelled to contribute. This legislation was followed by half a century of remarkable activity, the Privy Council putting strong pressure upon the local authorities to carry out constructive schemes.

This short spell of centralised effort was followed by a long spell of local autonomy. Parliament stiffened the restrictions of Settlement Laws and Vagrancy Acts, but the administration of the Poor Law was left to local effort guided by Acts of Parliament. The Acts that concern our study are those of 1722, 1782, and 1796.

At the beginning of the eighteenth century the man or woman needing help could apply to an overseer who was an unpaid officer, or to a magistrate. He might be given help at home, or he might be relieved in the workhouse. In 1722 Parliament, anxious to make administration stricter, encouraged the building of workhouses, authorising parishes to build workhouses without a special Act of Parliament and enacting that any one who refused to enter a workhouse forfeited any claim to relief. This Act made the law more stringent. In 1782 a reformer named Gilbert carried an Act which in some respects made administra-

---

[1] Lord John Manners (House of Commons, February 23, 1843) would have liked to revert to this system.

tion more indulgent. Parishes adopting his Act, known as Gilbert's Act, could make special arrangements. In these parishes, grouped in incorporations, the workhouse was to be reserved for children and the aged and infirm ; the able-bodied were to be given employment outside the workhouse, or, failing employment, were to be given relief.

This was the state of the law when the French war broke out. There were a number of parishes in which the able-bodied were either employed or relieved in their homes by the parish, the workhouse being the refuge for special classes, and others where a person refusing help inside the workhouse lost his right to relief. The French war produced a crisis in which this system broke down. For in 1795 high prices created a position so desperate that it was universally recognised that something must be done for the agricultural labourer whose wages no longer maintained him. Arthur Young came forward with a proposal for the regulation of wages, and he was supported by Whitbread and Fox. Whitbread introduced two Bills for this purpose in 1795 and 1800, but Pitt threw his great influence against them and this plan was rejected. The method of relief adopted, that of making up wages out of the rates, has become famous in history as the Speenhamland system, for it was at Speenhamland that the country gentlemen of Berkshire met and drew up a scale of wages fluctuating with the price of bread, based on the size of a man's family, that was generally observed in other parts of England. The same year Parliament, acting in this spirit, passed a Bill introduced by Sir William Young, relaxing the restrictions of the Act of 1722 and sanctioning and encouraging outdoor relief.[1]

To understand the full effect of the Speenhamland plan of making up wages out of the rates, we must remember that it was soon mixed up with the Gilbert plan for public employment. One method for dealing with applicants for relief was to hire them out to the farmers in turn, the parish paying two-thirds of their wages, the farmer the other third. In some cases these labourers were put up for public auction every Saturday night.[2] The Poor Law soon became a vicious circle from which the poor man could not escape. Where things were at their worst

---

[1] 36 George III. c. 23.
[2] Speech of R. A. Slaney, House of Commons, March 19, 1841.

a man who had any savings could not get help from the rates : a man who did not get help from the rates could not get a farmer to employ him.

When the Royal Commission in 1833 examined the problem of Poor Relief, they discovered a number of abuses, but the abuse that stood out in their minds as the main cause of degradation and extravagance was the Speenhamland plan. The Commissioners, therefore, recommended the extinction of this system and a return to the stricter ideas of 1722. So drastic a change could not be carried out at once, if at all, by local authorities accustomed to the old habits and amenable to local influences.[1] It was therefore proposed to set up a central authority with exceptional powers and to reorganise local administration by combining parishes into unions, with Boards of Guardians elected for the whole district. The nation, that is, was to return to the method of the seventeenth century, when pressure was put upon the local authorities from the centre.

Lord Grey's Government introduced a Bill in 1834 to give effect to this report. The Bill contained 110 sections, but it did not attack in detail the evils exposed by the Commission. Instead it created a central department consisting of three paid Commissioners with a paid Secretary, with power to make regulations and orders. The administration of the relief of the poor was to be put under the control of this Commission. The alarm excited by the abuses and burdens of the Speenhamland system was such that the Bill passed its second reading by 319 votes to 20. There was great opposition in the press from the first, ranging from the *Times* to the *Political Register*, and certain of its proposals were fiercely attacked in Parliament, but the Bill became law in August of that year. Some Ministers were afraid that so drastic a measure might lead to an outbreak of violence, and Melbourne disliked giving a new authority power to issue mandatory orders without the sanction of the Secretary of State. But Nassau Senior, the famous economist, the ablest member of the Poor Law Inquiry Commission, who had great influence with members of the Cabinet, persuaded

---

[1] See Althorp's speech, April 17, 1834: " However excellent their motives," they would be apt to be " biased ... by local prejudices and local feelings." Senior put it, in arguing with the Cabinet for giving the Commissioners drastic powers, that the reform must be carried out by " those who had no stacks to burn."—Mackay, *History of the Poor Law*, iii. p. 121.

them that no methods less rigorous would meet the public need. So Ministers held on their course.[1] But it is significant that whereas the second reading passed by 319 votes to 20, the third reading passed by 187 to 50.

To men like Althorp and Lord John Russell, the Ministers chiefly concerned with this revolution, the problem seemed simple. The old Poor Law had become the degrading force that it was in the early nineteenth century, because a vicious method of public employment was combined with a vicious method of relieving the poverty due to low wages. The Poor Rate had grown into a vast burden because men and women were encouraged to find in subsidies from the rates the livelihood they ought to earn, and because the employer was encouraged to find in those subsidies a way of saving his pocket. Where this system prevailed " the farmer gained an advantage which he ought not to gain—namely, that of receiving assistance for the payment of those whom he employed." [2] The solution was to extinguish the practice of making up wages by devising a system of discipline that left no loophole for such methods. This could only be done by forbidding outdoor relief to the able-bodied and by making the condition of the pauper so undesirable that no one would become a pauper if he could help it. It was with this fixed idea in their minds that the Whig Ministers embarked on this revolution.

When we consider how jealous the English people have always been of centralised authority, the setting up of this Commission, a body not even responsible to Parliament, with power to override local sentiment and to overrule local authorities, seems an astonishing achievement. It was only made possible by panic : panic for private property threatened by the swelling rates, panic for the English character threatened by the Allowance System. But strong as was this panic, the Government did not dare to make the Poor Law Commission a permanent body. It was set up for five years.[3] It lasted in the end for thirteen years, being converted in 1847 into the Poor Law Board, a department of the usual kind.

The first Commissioners were T. Frankland Lewis, a Welsh

---

[1] Lansdowne declared that they must do their duty undeterred by such fears.—Mackay, *op. cit.* iii. p. 122.

[2] Althorp, House of Commons, April 17, 1834.

[3] Lord Salisbury suggested ten years in the House of Lords.

country gentleman who had served as subordinate minister under Canning, Goderich, and Wellington, J. G. Shaw-Lefevre, at the time an under secretary at the Colonial Office, who was one of the founders of the Athenæum Club, and George Nicholls, a retired sea captain, a bank manager, who had served as overseer in the parish of Southwell. In 1839 Lewis was succeeded by his famous son, Sir George Cornewall Lewis, and in 1841 Shaw-Lefevre was succeeded by Sir Edmund Head. But the Secretary of the Commission is better known to history than any of the men to whom he gave his disobedient service.[1] Edwin Chadwick had expected to be a Commissioner, and his natural intolerance of the opinions of others was encouraged by his conviction that a subordinate office hardly gave his talents room to turn round. The most successful work he did in the next ten years was not in administration, where his want of sympathy and his stiff bureaucratic temper made him a dangerous guide, but in the investigation and analysis of complicated abuses in which he excelled. A bad beacon, he was an admirable searchlight. If you wanted to prepare a peaceful revolution by blue book you could not choose a better agent; if you wanted to carry out a peaceful revolution by administrative action you could not choose a worse. The history of the Poor Law between 1834 and 1847 is the history of an experiment in centralised administration, and of what that experiment produced in the hard and energetic hands of Chadwick, checked from time to time, by wiser colleagues.

It was at first intended to prohibit all outdoor relief to the able-bodied from July 1, 1835, by a stroke of the pen. This clause was withdrawn in the course of the debates in Parliament, and the duty of deciding when this step should be taken in several Unions was assigned to the Commissioners.[2] If Chad-

[1] For Chadwick's unconventional behaviour, see Webb, Sidney and Beatrice, *English Poor Law History: The Last Hundred Years*, vol. i. pp. 167 ff., and evidence of Frankland Lewis and Chadwick before Select Committee on Andover Union, 1846, part ii. pp. 1085 ff.

[2] See the Second Annual Report of the Poor Law Commissioners, 1836, i. p. 6 : " In the Poor Law Amendment Bill as first submitted to the consideration of Parliament, a clause was inserted which directed that all relief to able-bodied paupers out of a Workhouse should cease on the 1st July 1835. In the progress of the Bill through Parliament this clause was withdrawn, and the Commissioners were charged with the important duty of fixing the time when, in each Union, that provision (which formed the first recommendation of the Commissioners of Poor Law Inquiry and is, in fact, the main object of the Poor Law Amendment Act) should take effect." See also Lord John Russell's speech, House of Commons, July 20, 1839.

wick had had his way the Commissioners would have acted promptly and firmly, but he was beaten and the new discipline was introduced by stages and never in its full rigour. The Commissioners began at once in the south of England. Several members of Grey's Cabinet had been afraid that if the Act were put into force in the agricultural districts it would lead to another outbreak of Swing riots. But this did not happen. The passing of the Act was followed by three very good harvests, and the rapid development of railway construction at the time eased the immediate difficulties of the transition. Wages rose a little, and though there were riots of a kind in East Kent, Chesham, and Bedfordshire, they were quickly suppressed. In the South, consequently, the Commissioners made rapid progress.[1]

When the Commissioners turned to the North they found a different state of things. The effect of the Speenhamland system in the South had been to demoralise completely the conditions of employment, to spread pauperism far and wide, and to turn the agricultural labourer in many parishes into a kind of public serf.[2] When it was abolished considerable suffering was caused, but most labourers found employment either on the farms or on the railways. The Speenhamland system was in force to some extent in the North, for outdoor relief was given in the industrial districts to some of the hand-loom weavers, a class by this time permanently underpaid, dying a lingering death.[3] The Assistant Commissioner, Gilbert Henderson, who reported on Lancashire, argued that there were important differences between the case of the hand-loom weaver and that of the agricultural labourer. The hand-loom weaver was a piece-worker, and the overseer could calculate what he ought to earn. The Allowance System in the opinion of the Assistant Commissioner had the effect, not of making the

---

[1] " Within nine months of incessant activity, the Commissioners and their dozen or more Assistant Commissioners had set up 111 Boards of Guardians, for as many newly created Unions, in which no fewer than 2311 parishes had been included, with a total population of 1,385,124, being about one-tenth of the whole kingdom ; and raising Poor Rates to the amount of £1,221,543, being (as these were districts more pauperised than the common average) about one-sixth of the total raised by Poor Rates."—Webb, *op. cit.* vol. i. p. 114.

[2] " Any law, however well meant as a law, which has become a bounty on unthrift, idleness, bastardy, and beer drinking, must be put an end to."—Carlyle, *Chartism*, p. 3.

[3] See the answers from Bolton, Oldham, Preston, Wigan, and Warrington, printed as an Appendix to the First Report of the Commissioners on the Poor Law, 1834.

hand-loom weaver relax his efforts, but of stimulating him beyond his strength. At Oldham the hand-loom weavers were reluctant to apply for relief, and were only driven to it when they had three or four children under ten.[1]

The Poor Law Commissioners themselves, reviewing their policy in 1847, drew a distinction between North and South. " They have considered the main object of the Legislature in passing the Poor Law Amendment Act to have been the extinction of the Allowance System, or the system of making up the wages of labourers out of the poor's rate. With this view their regulations respecting the limitation of outdoor relief have been almost exclusively confined to the able-bodied in health ; and these regulations have been issued particularly to the rural Unions, inasmuch as it was in the agricultural counties and not in the large towns of manufacturing districts, that the Allowance System was most prevalent and led to the most dangerous consequences." [2] It is significant that even staunch friends to the principle of the new Poor Law were not prepared to extinguish the practice of giving outdoor relief to hand-loom weavers. " In the Union with which he was connected," said Sir James Graham in the House of Commons, " there was a large body of hand-loom weavers, and he did not hesitate to say, during the last winter it would have been utterly impossible to have conducted the affairs of that Union without relief, though sparingly administered, and with great caution, to the able-bodied labourer." [3]

There was another class of able-bodied workmen receiving relief from time to time in large numbers from the rates. The industrial districts were liable to mass unemployment, a form of unemployment which was unknown in the southern counties. Edward Baines, the member for Leeds, like Graham a strong supporter in general of the new Poor Law, called attention to this difficulty. " Circumstances occasionally occurred there which

---

[1] So the Assistant Commissioner reported in 1833. (Extracts from the Information received by His Majesty's Commissioners, as to the Administration and Operation of the Poor Laws, 1833.) On the other hand, a very different description of the effect of relieving hand-loom weavers while in employment was given later by an Assistant Inspector named Mott, who said that he found in the Bolton and Macclesfield Unions all the evils that had arisen in agricultural parishes. This Report, written in 1841, was not published until 1846. See the Reports received by the Poor Law Commissioners in 1841 on the state of the Bolton and Macclesfield Unions, 1846.

[2] Webb, *op. cit.* vol. i. p. 147.   [3] House of Commons, July 20, 1839.

threw 400 or 500 persons in a single parish out of employment. In such cases could they enforce the rule ; or were they prepared to build enough workhouses to carry it out ? " [1] In these cases the granting of outdoor relief had clearly not entailed the consequences of personal degradation which had followed in the South, when parishes faced with their growing difficulties had so managed the Allowance System as to put a moral stigma upon the great body of agricultural labourers. The southern labourer had lost his status before the revolution in the Poor Law. But the poor man in the North, who had received poor relief in his home as a hand-loom weaver or as an unemployed workman, had not been under that stigma. He now found himself threatened with the punishment of the workhouse. Even men who had deep sympathy with the lot of the agricultural labourer believed that the new Poor Law, drastic as it was, was an improvement on the terrible conditions created in the villages by the abuses of the old. No person with such sympathies in the North could think with patience of punishing great masses of unemployed workmen, victims of the new industrial system, with the rigours that were meant for incorrigible idlers. [2] It is easy, then, to understand that the threat of the Bastille provoked in the North a storm of indignation which prevented the Commissioners from repeating the success they had achieved in the South. The *West Riding Herald* could boast, in July 1837, that " the new Poor Law has been suspended in the West Riding through the sturdy resistance of the people."

The new Poor Law had many enemies besides the poor : clergymen angry over the new Marriage Registration Act which had been hitched on to the Poor Law ; country gentlemen who disliked taking orders from Whitehall ; tradesmen who lost sources of profit, and good party men, who saw an excellent opportunity for heaping odium on a Government they hated. There were others, again, who acted from larger motives, country gentlemen, parsons, doctors, professional men, and manu-

[1] House of Commons, July 20, 1839.

[2] See Fielden's speech, February 24, 1837 : " This House refused to act upon my suggestions to regulate the rate of wages they should receive ; and now I put it to the House whether, if one of these hard-working men through sickness or accident becomes incapable of labour, it is just to treat that man as a criminal in the mode of giving him relief ? Is it just to make this man go into an Union workhouse and put on a prison dress, and submit to separation from his wife and children before you will aid him in his sufferings ? "

facturers, who thought the new law harsh and unjust and took an active part in agitating against it on these grounds.[1]

This resistance took various forms. Public meetings were held in the chief towns of the West Riding and South Lancashire, and organisations for obstructing the Poor Law were set up. The Government were so much impressed by these demonstrations that when the Assistant Commissioner visited Bradford in March 1837 to address the Guardians with a view to the formation of a Union, he went to extraordinary lengths in the attempt to disarm hostility. "There was a very prevalent opinion in the country that the Board of Guardians had not the power to administer outdoor relief. Now he wished it to be distinctly understood (and he spoke from authority) that the Boards of Guardians had control of their own funds and were invested with full power to afford either indoor or outdoor relief to any extent, entirely according to their own discretion, and in no instance were they dictated to by the Commissioners." The Assistant Commissioner, who was named Power, was pressed on this point by one of the Bradford members, E. C. Lister, who had voted against the third reading of the Bill, and he repeated his statement with emphasis.[2] These assurances, which read rather strangely in view of Section 52 of the Act, modified the objections to the proposal to form a Union, but did not remove the discontent with the Act itself. Opposition was still violent in the West Riding and in Lancashire. At Huddersfield, Rochdale, Todmorden, and other places the Guardians defied the Commissioners.[3] But resistance took also the form of popular rioting. There were riots at Bradford in November 1837,[4] at Huddersfield in May 1838, at Dewsbury in August, and at Todmorden in November of that year. At Bradford it was found necessary to bring soldiers from Leeds and Lancashire, and the West Riding accounts of 1838 show that £1000 was

---

[1] In 1846 a Poor Man's Guardian Society was founded "for securing the humaner dispensation of the law for the Relief of the Poor," and Dickens became a vice-president.—*Morning Post*, April 9, 1846. Dickens' dislike of the Poor Law was so strong that he thought seriously at one time of standing for Parliament for Reading.—Forster's *Life*, i. p. 225. Readers of R. S. Hawker's Poems will remember his descriptions of the workhouse.

[2] *Bradford Observer*, March 23, 1837.

[3] As late as 1845 the Commissioners reported that the Rochdale, Ashton, and Oldham Unions were acting as Registration Authorities but not as Poor Law Authorities. —Eleventh Annual Report, 1845, p. 19.

[4] See cartoon in *Cleave's Penny Gazette*, xii. 36.

spent on exceptional measures for keeping order at Dewsbury.[1]

The results of this opposition are evident in the reports and
decisions of the Poor Law Commission. In 1839 the Commissioners deplored the extent to which relief was given out of
doors. " Four-fifths of the money now expended on relief is
still outdoor relief. . . ." [2] But during the next few years the
number of paupers receiving outdoor relief increased from
rather under 1,000,000 in 1839 to over 1,200,000 in 1842.[3] The
Commissioners instead of narrowing had found themselves
impelled to increase " the discretionary powers of relief " of
which they had complained. In 1841 they published a list of
the Unions to which they had issued their order prohibiting outdoor relief. Not a single Union in Lancashire or the West
Riding appears on that list.[4] In that year, recognising that they
could not enforce their plan in the North, the Commissioners
issued an Outdoor Labour Test Order allowing relief to able-
bodied men in return for a task of work, and in 1843 nearly 40,000
able-bodied men were employed in Poor Law labour yards, very
many of them factory workers, victims of the depression of
trade.[5] The Commissioners had been as unlucky in the North
as they had been lucky in the South. The introduction of the
new Poor Law in the southern counties had been followed by
two years of abnormal prosperity : its introduction in the
northern counties by two years of abnormal distress. The

[1] *Leeds Intelligencer*, January 1839.   [2] Report, 1839, p. 9.
[3] See Sir J. Graham's speeches, House of Commons, July 20, 1842, and February
23, 1843.
[4] Report, 1841, p. 37.
[5] Tenth Annual Report of Poor Law Commissioners, pp. 467-470 ; Webb, *op. cit.*
vol. i. p. 365.

One of the Commissioners, Sir George Nicholls, commenting on this state of things
in his *History of the English Poor Law*, deplored the laxity that had allowed forty or fifty
thousand able-bodied males to receive relief, most of them out of doors. " In a
community such as now exists in this country, so largely occupied in commercial
industry, and liable to be affected by the changes continually taking place in trades
and manufactures, there must be alternations of prosperity and adversity, of activity
and stagnation, of the demand for labour exceeding the supply, and of the supply
exceeding the demand ; and such changes will necessarily have the effect of occasionally
throwing able-bodied persons out of employment. But this is a contingency against
which men may provide by the exercise of care and forethought. They can, however,
hardly be expected to do so, if on the occurrence of every reverse they are permitted
to fall back upon the poor rates for unconditional relief ; and the condition of the relief
being given in the workhouse is therefore as necessary for the protection of the ratepayers, as the relief itself is necessary for those who without it might be subjected to
the extremity of want."—*History of the English Poor Law*, New Edition, 1890, vol. ii.
p. 427.

Liverpool Courier, commenting on the figures given by Graham, remarked : " The present practice is a modification of the system forced upon its administrators by necessity or public opinion. . . . No country can safely continue to trample upon the rights of the labouring or destitute population. And, situated as the country now is, with the mass of poverty daily increasing through the accumulation of wealth into fewer hands and the rapid growth of machinery, the danger of alienating the lower classes from the ranks above them by harsh and oppressive usage is peculiarly great." [1]

The Whig Government which had set up the Poor Law Commission held office, except for a brief interruption, during the first seven years of its contentious life. Lord John Russell defended it in the House of Commons with the steady conviction of a man whose mind never travelled outside one simple idea on this question. He had presided over a Committee on labourers' wages in 1824. The evidence submitted to that Committee of the evils that had followed the Allowance System had made such an impression on him that he never could give any attention to any other aspect of the problem. The attacks from which he defended the Commission were led in the House of Commons by John Walter, editor of the *Times*, Thomas Wakley, editor of the *Lancet*, and John Fielden, the great factory reformer. In 1837 Disraeli entered Parliament, and from that time his biting tongue was at their service. These men did invaluable work, bringing abuses to light and checking some of the cruelties of the new system. Thus in the House the Opposition was that of free-lances, but it represented a great body of opinion in the country where Conservative sentiment was much more hostile both to the Act and to the Commission than

---

[1] *Liverpool Courier*, March 1, 1843.

In 1852 the Poor Law Board, which had taken the place of the Poor Law Commission after 1847, issued an Outdoor Relief Regulation Order which expressly permitted relief to the able-bodied under conditions which gave the Guardians a large discretion, and to the aged and infirm practically without restriction (Appendix to the Fifth Annual Report of the Poor Law Board). The Board explained in a circular letter that this Order had been substituted for an Order of August of the same year, in answer to representations, in order to meet the special difficulties arising from commercial and industrial depression. This Order was put into force throughout the industrial districts of Lancashire and the West Riding (see the list in Schedule A to the General Order, *P.P.*, 1852, liii.). In this letter the Poor Law Board explained that even persons in part-time employment might receive outdoor relief. So far as the battle over the new Poor Law was a battle between local autonomy and central authority, Chadwick had been beaten in the North.

the Conservative party in the House of Commons. The Conservative papers in Leeds, Halifax, Wakefield, Liverpool, Bolton, and other northern towns, used language on this question as vehement as anything said or written by the Chartists. During the General Election of 1837 which followed the death of William IV. this hostility found fierce expression. One of the Conservative candidates at Bradford described the new Poor Law as "that Bill which separated those whom God had joined together, gave a premium to murder, made poverty a crime, starved the poor man and tried to prove whether he could not live upon bread and water." [1] Beckett, the Conservative candidate at Leeds, said he had done his utmost to prevent the introduction of the Act into the West Riding, and Stuart Wortley, one of the Conservative candidates for the West Riding, stood as an opponent of the Poor Law. Reminded that Peel and Wellington had supported the Bill of 1834, these candidates replied that they were not bound by anything that their leaders had said, and Stuart Wortley argued that the Commissioners were worse than the Act. Even so orthodox a Liberal candidate as Lord Morpeth spoke in his election address to the West Riding of the necessity of compromise, and one of the Liberal candidates for Bradford declared : " What is good in the measure I will keep, what is bad I will exterminate." [2]

Politicians are often more violent in their views when their party is in opposition. In 1841 the Conservatives took office. Peel, the new Prime Minister, treated the angry sentiment of his party with characteristic independence. The hated Commission was prolonged first for six months, and then for five years. Fielden took the opportunity to ask for a Committee of Inquiry on the specific question of the influence of the new Poor Law on wages. The Government resisted the proposal, and Fielden was only supported by eight members, a distinguished little group, for it included both Cobden and Disraeli.[3] A Conservative member, Escott, raised a fundamental issue, for he moved to insert in the Bill, which was to prolong the life of the Commission, the following clause : " That it shall be lawful for all Boards of Guardians of the poor in England and Wales to grant

---

[1] *Bradford Observer*, June 29, 1837.
[2] *Bradford Observer*, July 6, July 13, July 20, 1837.
[3] House of Commons, July 19, 1842.

such relief as in their judgment shall be necessary to poor persons at their own homes, any order, rule, or regulation of the Poor Law Commissioners notwithstanding." [1] Escott admitted that this would open the door again to the Allowance System, and he was defeated by 90 to 55. Graham, in reply, argued that the figures which he gave, revealing the large increase in the volume of outdoor relief, showed that ample discretion was given to the local authorities in practice. But in 1844 the Government amended the law in some important respects, removing one great cause of discontent by dissociating from the Poor Law all legal questions relating to bastardy. At the same time, the administration of the law was relaxed, Chadwick having happily been diverted to more suitable tasks. In 1845, however, a storm broke which did more damage to the Poor Law Commission than any of the previous agitations.

One of the forms of task work imposed in certain workhouses was the crushing of bones, and the master of the Andover Workhouse was accused of so starving the paupers that they fought among themselves for the gristle and marrow to be found in the half-putrid bones given to them for this purpose. The indignation led to a demand for inquiry, so vehement and general that the Government had to yield, and the revelations that followed made a profound impression on the public mind.[2] For an inquiry that began with the Andover scandals ended as an inquisition into the life and methods of the Poor Law Commission. When asked for a Committee on the Andover Workhouse, Graham, who made a bad start, regretting the time Parliament was spending on " a workhouse squabble," felt himself obliged to give way to the insistence of the House of Commons. It was then proposed to extend the inquiry to the

[1] House of Commons, July 20, 1842.

[2] " We have read of nothing in the accounts of sieges or shipwrecks, nor even in the imaginative descriptions of the worst horrors which these calamities entail, that can be compared with the dreadful truth that has just been brought to light at Andover." —*Times*, August 14, 1845.

The *Leeds Intelligencer* wrote about this series of revelations at the end of the Inquiry : " As for the gross and cruel abuses which were for ten years perpetrated under their contemptible rule, unquestioned and unnoticed, in the Andover Union we have this at least to thank them for, that they have preserved to us an illustration of what the new Poor Law was as it came fashioned to us by the gaunt and bony fingers of political economy. Thanks to public indignation, a society so constituted as to engender poverty with the same certainty that it engenders wealth, was not permitted to treat poverty as an unpardonable crime."—August 29, 1846.

conduct of the Poor Law Commissioners. The Government resisted, but the motion was carried by 92 votes to 69.[1] The Committee was set up, and it was soon deep in the domestic quarrels of the Poor Law Commission. Frankland Lewis, no longer a Commissioner, spoke of his perpetual troubles with the secretary, " as unscrupulous and as dangerous an officer as ever I saw within the walls of an office." [2] Chadwick made it clear that in this uncongenial partnership there was about as much confidence on one side of the table as on the other. As Commissioners and Secretary had friends on the Committee, and as there were members who were glad enough to bring the Commission into discredit by pressing for disclosures, these recriminations let a great deal of unkind daylight into the past. They settled the fate of a body which, obnoxious already for its public transactions, was now mistrusted for transactions that had hitherto been private. Decisions that were unpopular did not gain in respect when it was known by what methods and in what kind of atmosphere they had been reached. The Committee, after condemning the administration of the law in the Andover Union, passed on Disraeli's initiative, by 8 votes to 4, a sweeping condemnation. " On a review of the proceedings of the Commissioners with respect to the Andover Inquiries and towards Mr. Parker and Mr. Day, the Committee are of opinion that their conduct has been irregular and arbitrary, not in accordance with the statute under which they exercise their functions, and such as to shake public confidence in the administration of the law."

Whatever might have been made, under different conditions, of an experiment in centralised administration by a body without a parliamentary head, it was clear that this particular experiment could be continued no longer. The Whigs came back to power in 1847, and Sir George Grey, the new Home Secretary, carried an Act setting up a new Poor Law Board in place of the Poor Law Commission. The new Board consisted nominally of the Lord President of the Council, the Lord Privy Seal, the Home Secretary, and the Chancellor of the Exchequer, together with the President, who was to be eligible to sit in Parliament, and two paid Secretaries, of whom one was also to be eligible to

[1] March 5, 1846.
[2] Report of Select Committee on Andover Union, 1846, part ii. 22620.

sit in Parliament.[1] The Act also contained provisions making the administration of the Poor Law more humane.

These changes did not, of course, reconcile the working classes to the new Poor Law. The Commission had gone, but the law remained. The law was administered by Guardians with a property qualification, elected by a system of voting which virtually excluded the wage-earning classes, that lasted until 1894. The 25,000 Guardians were mostly farmers and retail tradesmen, and the complaint of want of sympathy and consideration continued for half a century.[2] It might seem that the poor had gained very little by the change. Yet the Poor Law never again became the object of an agitation so violent and widespread.

To understand the episode of English history that began when Chadwick became Secretary of the Commission, and ended when the new Poor Law Board undertook the administration of the less rigid law, we must remember that between 1834 and 1847 every workman saw himself exposed to the danger of imprisonment in the Bastille, with the break-up of his family and home at the dictation of the Poor Law Commissioners. That is how the struggle appeared to the working-class mind. The Poor Law Commissioners stood for an alien power, inaccessible to pity or justice. In this struggle rumour flew from place to place, and local incidents were known from one end of the country to the other. In the eighteenth century brutalities in a particular workhouse were not heard of outside the district; in the nineteenth century any workman in Bradford or Gateshead could tell you that a man had died in the Eton Workhouse, who had not been allowed to see his wife alone, and that the Preston Guardians were debating whether or not a bell should be tolled at paupers' funerals. The press was a new propagandist force. The Conservative papers filled their columns with cases of hardship, and speakers like Parson Bull were reckless in bringing charges against the Commissioners and their subordinates on hearsay evidence.[3] Much was happening that deserved to be

---

[1] The first President was Charles Buller, whose early death was a calamity. The *Times* said of his tenure of office : " Compared with the long triumvirate of his predecessors his own brief reign was one of peace and goodwill."—November 30, 1848.

[2] See Webb, *Statutory Authorities*, p. 475, and *Poor Law*, vol. i. pp. 120 and 232. Duncombe tried to abolish plural and proxy voting, but he was defeated by 112 votes to 35.—House of Commons, July 29, 1839.

[3] Bull was called to account by the Commissioners for some of his statements, and

exposed and blamed, but in such an agitation it happens inevitably that the truth, bad as it is, becomes worse in the telling. The tone and language of the Commissioners embittered the struggle, and Peel protested strongly in the House of Commons against the indifference they displayed to the feelings of the poorer classes. The working-class world was reminded every day, in the press, on the platform, and in official documents, that the only choice for the poor man, when misfortune befell him, was the choice between starvation and disgrace. To understand how deep and vivid was this impression, we must turn to the workhouse.

The mixed workhouse of the eighteenth century has been described by Crabbe in a famous picture :

> " There Children dwell who know no parents' care :
> Parents, who know no Children's love, dwell there ;
> Heart broken Matrons on their joyless bed,
> Forsaken Wives and Mothers never wed ;
> Dejected Widows with unheeded tears,
> And crippled Age with more than childhood's fears ;
> The Lame, the Blind, and, far the happiest they !
> The moping Idiot and the Madman gay." [1]

The Commissioners who inquired into the Poor Laws in 1833 wished to put an end to the mixed workhouse. Nassau Senior and Bishop Blomfield were specially anxious to isolate the children; others to isolate the aged. Chadwick, who pressed this policy, argued that in this way the old could enjoy their comforts, the children receive education, and the able-bodied be subjected to necessary discipline. Unfortunately, Chadwick's good advice made less impression than his bad. The Poor Law Commissioners kept the mixed workhouse, and in improving it, turned it more definitely and grimly into a prison. Disraeli said in 1841 that no other term than that of imprisonment could

he cut a poor figure under examination. Lord Stanhope, who had quoted them in the Lords, had to retract. See Chadwick's letter to the *Bradford Observer*, February 23, 1837.

[1] Supporters of the new Poor Law, in answering attacks, called attention to scandals in some of the workhouses where that new law was not in force. See *Manchester Guardian*, November 11, 1840, on Bolton Workhouse; December 16, 1841, on Middleton and Stalybridge; and August 14, 1844, on the case at Wigan, where the governor refused to send for surgeon or clergyman for a dying man. All this was good enough for its dialectical purpose, but it did not make the Poor Law any more agreeable to the class which hated the workhouse, whether old or new.

be given to the confinement which the poor underwent in the Union workhouse.[1]

The Union workhouse was, of course, much larger than the old Parish workhouse. The larger the workhouse, the more detailed and exact the regulations that are necessary to keep order and arrangement. In this case these regulations proceeded from a central authority setting up, or seeking to set up, a system of discipline to be imposed upon Union workhouses all over the country. The Commissioners began by laying down the most rigorous rules. From 1836 to 1842 silence was prescribed at all meals,[2] a rule of which Wakley remarked that the silent system was generally regarded as the most severe form of punishment in prison life, and paupers could not see their friends except in the presence of Master, Matron, or porter. Playing at cards was forbidden. Such discipline could make no allowance for the circumstances of a particular workhouse, a particular class, or a particular pauper. It is easy to imagine what this iron discipline looked like to the poor of the West Riding, when they learned that the Dewsbury Guardians had wished to allow an old man to smoke a pipe but were warned that they would first have to get the leave of the Poor Law Commissioners.[3]

A lawyer, writing in 1852, said that he had visited many prisons and lunatic asylums, not only in England, but in France and Germany. " A single English workhouse," he went on to say, " contains more that justly calls for condemnation in the principle on which it is established than is found in the very worst prisons or public lunatic asylums that I have seen. The workhouse as now organised is a reproach and disgrace peculiar to England : nothing corresponding to it is to be found throughout the whole Continent of Europe." [4] The explanation is simple. There were collected in the workhouse young and old, sick and mad, vagrants passing a night, and crippled old men and women who could never hope to leave it, the victims of misfortune and the victims of vice. " It passed the wit of man," as Mr. and Mrs. Webb well put it, " to contrive a General Mixed Workhouse that should appear so uncomfortable as to deter from entrance every person who could possibly earn a bare living

---

[1] February 8.   [2] Webb, *English Poor Law Policy*, p. 73.
[3] *Halifax Guardian*, November 9, 1838.
[4] *Pauperism and Poor Laws*, 1852, p. 364, by Robert Pashley, Q.C., quoted by Webb, *English Poor Law History. The Last Hundred Years*, vol. i. p. 138.

wage; and yet be, in fact, so endurable, and withal, so improving, to those who could not possibly maintain themselves by work, as to induce them both to enter and voluntarily to remain for as long as was socially expedient." [1] It would have been difficult in any case to make the workhouse a terror to the idle and vicious, and a comfort to the sick and unfortunate. But in the minds of the Commissioners the workhouse was meant to be a deterrent institution for all sorts and conditions of the poor. " With regard to the aged and infirm," they wrote in 1840, " there is a strong disposition on the part of a portion of the public so to modify the arrangements of these establishments as to place them on the footing of almshouses. The consequences which would flow from this change have only to be pointed out to show its inexpediency and its danger. If the condition of the inmates of a workhouse were to be so regulated as to invite the aged and infirm of the labouring classes to take refuge in it, it would immediately be useless as a test between indigence and indolence or fraud." [2] This idea, that vice and idleness were to be discouraged by punishing the sick and the unfortunate, was carried so far that the Commissioners would not help to educate pauper children living on outdoor relief. Chadwick wanted to have a training establishment for all the children who came under the control of the Guardians, but the Commissioners were so afraid of taking the sting out of pauperism that they would not even allow the Guardians to pay the school fee of twopence a week for the children maintained on outdoor relief.[3]

The Commissioners kept the mixed workhouse, but they classified the inmates, forbidding any communication between the different classes. In this way husbands and wives, parents and children, were kept rigorously apart. Before 1834 the practice of workhouses varied. In some of the Lancashire workhouses, such as those at Liverpool, Oldham, and Wigan, married couples were not separated. At Manchester, on the other hand, they were always separated. " A case occurred where an old man of eighty, a tinker, who, though in great distress, turned back from the house when he found that he must be separated from his wife, an old woman of seventy.

---

[1] Webb, *op. cit.* p. 157.   [2] Webb, *op. cit.* p. 158.
[3] Webb, *op. cit* p. 104.

He was afterwards, however, compelled by want to take refuge in the house, and died there after remaining some time, according to the rule, deprived of his wife's society."[1] The Commissioners made a strict rule for all cases, and this rule was denounced again and again in the House of Commons by Walter and other critics of the Poor Law.[2] The Commissioners defended their decision in a characteristic passage in their First Report. " Under these circumstances, we cannot admit that the charge of undue severity attaches to the continued and more complete enforcement of the rule for the separation of the sexes during the temporary residence in the workhouse, as a condition of being relieved from the danger of perishing for want."[3] This feature of workhouse life inspired many passionate speeches. An address from Newcastle women spoke of the Poor Law as separating those whom God had joined together.[4] The Commissioners had to make concessions, and in 1847 Parliament passed an Act forbidding the separation of married people over sixty.

Peel and Graham both complained of the want of sympathy and feeling which the Commissioners exhibited in their public documents. One illustration shows vividly how little Chadwick, so admirable in his exposure of abuses, was able to understand human nature when he was called on to administer a policy. If one thing stands out in the records of the minds and feelings of the poor in history, it is the passionate concern for the treatment of the body after death. The inscriptions that tell us of proletarian life in the Roman Empire show that the mean and the miserable alike in the days before and the days after the introduction of Christianity clung to the hope that their friends would pay some tribute to their memory. The burial club is an institution so old and so common in the life of Europe that one might suppose that the fear of being thrown on one side as a nameless carcase after death has troubled and

---

[1] Henderson's Report for Lancashire, Extracts on Poor Laws, 1833, p. 358.

[2] There was a riot over the separation of parents and children in the parish of Steyning in Sussex, and dragoons had to be brought from Brighton to liberate a magistrate who had been locked up by the rioters.—*Annual Register*, 1835, *Chronicle*, p. 137. Gladstone, as Conservative candidate at Newark, " in great part concurred " with the general sentiment there against these arrangements.—Morley, *Life of Gladstone*, i. p. 140. [3] Report, 1835, p. 129.

[4] Quoted by Dolléans, *Le Chartisme*, vol. i. p. 240. When the question was discussed by the Halifax Guardians the local Conservative paper wrote : " Let them lay their hands upon their Bibles and do it if they can. Let them do it if they dare."—*Halifax Guardian*, July 16, 1838.

haunted the mind of man more persistently than the fear of sickness or starvation.

Chadwick trod on this universal sentiment as if all life had gone from it. The last touch of degradation was added to the lot of the pauper when, in response to a circular which he issued in March 1836, the Guardians in certain Unions decided that the bell should not be tolled at pauper funerals. Walter read a letter to the House of Commons from the Mayor of Morpeth stating that two men had been driven to suicide by the barbarities of the Poor Law. The Mayor went on to say that the Board of Guardians for the same Union (a Union embracing sixty or seventy townships) had only a few days before resolved that the common decencies of burial should not be observed as heretofore towards deceased paupers.[1] The Rector of Bishops Waltham, in criticising the new Poor Law before the Select Committee in 1837, remarked : " The mode of burying the poor, separation from their friends in death, the decent rites of interment not being provided, even the funeral bell not being tolled—all these things are an outrage upon the feelings of the poor." [2] Chadwick in this was overruled by the Commissioners. In a letter to the Guardians of March 1, 1836, he had included amongst the charges commonly found in overseers' accounts, but not authorised by any statute, charges for tolling bells at paupers' funerals. This letter went to every Union in the country, and it was clear from evidence taken by the Select Committee of 1837 that some Unions acted upon it. Lewis, however, intervened, and a corrected circular was sent out a month later in which the word " excessive " was inserted before the charges for tolling. Chadwick prevaricated when pressed on this point by Walter, and it was only under persistent cross-examination that the facts came to light, for the Annual Report of the Commissioners had printed as the circular letter of 1st March the letter in which the word " excessive " had been inserted.[3]

[1] February 24, 1837.

[2] See Committee on Poor Law Amendment Act, 1837, 27405.

It was stated at a meeting of the Bradford Guardians in 1848 that pauper coffins were made so cheaply that they came to pieces, and the corpse had in one case fallen out.—*Bradford Observer*, May 25, 1848.

[3] Minutes of Evidence before Select Committee on the Poor Law Amendment Act, Twelfth Report, 1837, 12599, 12600, 17165, 17167, 17189. See also Baxter's *Book of the Bastilles*, p. 592.

When the dirty linen of the Commission was being washed in public, before the Committee on the Andover scandals in 1846, both Frankland Lewis and Chadwick gave their version of the origin of this circular. Lewis said that the circular was brought to the Board by Chadwick in his absence ; that the circular might quite well have been kept back till his return to the office, and that next day, when he saw it, he said to Nicholls : " I would rather have cut off my right hand than have issued that, if I had had an alternative." The Commissioners, to meet his objection, agreed that future circulars should contain the word " excessive." Chadwick denied that he had taken deliberate advantage of Lewis' absence, or that he had any special responsibility for the inclusion of this charge in the general list. The facts were that the legal adviser had been asked to draw up such a list, and had put the charge for tolling among them. Chadwick had merely copied the list into his circular. He had since urged the Commission to get a Bill passed legalising this and other charges. When asked whether there was any minute recording this expression of his views, he said he could not find one, but that he had put the suggestion in the Fourth Report. In that Report, however, tolling the bell is not specially named.[1]

Chadwick's defence is illuminating. His tidying mind prompted him to put the Guardians' expenditure on a strict and legal footing. If he had had enough imagination to realise what impression would be created by warning the Guardians that they were not authorised by law to pay for the rites of Christian burial, he would never have sent out such a circular. The Guardians had no power to alter the law ; a statement of this kind from the Commissioners was equivalent to a warning not to break it. At a moment when a strong hand was being laid on the indulgence and the abuses that had demoralised the Poor Law, the Commissioners went out of their way to justify the worst that had been said of their indifference to the feelings of the poor. And Chadwick was so insensible to the emotions that move mankind that he never realised what a storm he was provoking.

Peel had much more understanding of the poor, and he opposed another project, that of building workhouse cemeteries,

[1] See his evidence before Select Committee on Andover Union, 1846.

which had excited popular indignation.[1] The rector of Pet-
worth quoted the observation of a pauper, that no consecration
by the Bishop would change the workhouse dunghill into a
burial-ground.[2] An Act passed by Peel's Government, authorising Guardians to bear the expense of burying paupers dying
out of the workhouse, directed that the wishes of the dead or
their friends in regard to their place of burial should be respected.

The doctrine that poverty was the consequence and the mark
of bad character, rather than of misfortune, was not new in the
England of the thirties or forties. It goes back to the harsher
teaching of Puritanism ; many politicians and magistrates in the
eighteenth century took a merciless view of their duty to the
poor. Workhouses were brutal places long before they were
given the name of Bastilles. The Speenhamland system had led
in some villages to practices as degrading and humiliating to the
poor as any of the scandals on which Oastler and Stephens called
down the wrath of God and man on Hartshead Moor. But the
system of 1834, bringing many detailed improvements in the
administration of the Poor Laws, gave to this doctrine a universal
rigour. The workman was regarded as a person who was to be
protected against the temptations of idleness by the stern choice
of starvation or loss of liberty as the alternative to persistent
effort. This principle was pushed to its extreme limit during
the first few years of the Poor Law Commission. " By the
workhouse system," Chadwick explained, " is meant having all
relief through the workhouse, making this workhouse an un-
inviting place of wholesome restraint, preventing any of its
inmates from going out or receiving visitors, without a written
order to that effect from one of the Overseers ; disallowing beer
and tobacco, and finding them work according to their ability ;
thus making the parish fund the last resource of a pauper, and
rendering the person who administers the relief the hardest
taskmaster, and the worst paymaster, that the idle and dissolute
can apply to." [3] It was believed that if the workhouse were
made less like a prison in any respect, or for any class, for the
unfortunate, or for the vicious, England would slip back again

---

[1] House of Commons, February 8, 1841.
[2] Select Committee on Poor Law Amendment Act, 1837, question 101.
[3] Webb, *English Poor Law History. The Last Hundred Years*, vol. i. p. 67. " If
paupers are made miserable, paupers will needs decline in multitude. It is a secret
known to all rat-catchers."—Carlyle, *Chartism*, p. 12.

into the abuses that had scared all educated men before 1834.
" What is a pauper ? " asked Cobbett, and he answered, " A
very poor man." That is what the pauper seemed to the poor.
He was a man on whom misfortune had fallen, whether it had
come as sickness or unemployment, as the paralysis of old age,
or the pinching want of the hand-loom weaver. The logic of
1834 rested on a different conception. The pauper was as much
culprit as victim. At any rate, he was so often a culprit that it
was dangerous ever to treat him as a victim. Even if he
happened to be a victim, to treat him as a victim would mean
that soon you would have to treat some one else as a culprit.
The common phrase of the time warned the tender-hearted
against opening any loophole to the evils of the past.[1]

Another grim idea lurks in the pages of the Commissioners'
Reports. Just as a slave in the ancient world was a man who
had been saved by his captor from death by violence, so a
pauper was a man who had been saved by the overseer from
death by starvation. In both cases it was easier to think of the
unfortunate as persons with obligations to others rather than as
persons with claims upon others. However harsh their treatment, was it not better than the fate that would otherwise have
overtaken them ? Thus the workhouse assumed in all its
aspects, whether as refuge or as deterrent, a penal and degrading
look. Yet of the men and women who listened to Stephens
asserting that God had given to every man the right to live,
nine out of ten, whether they were industrious or idle, skilled
or ignorant, knew that no effort of their own could make them
secure from the danger that hung like a cloud over the
working-class world.

[1] The *Times* had a good description of this type of mind in a reference to Brougham :
" In the treatment of starvation we do not think Lord Brougham the highest of
authorities. He appears to us unduly possessed with the fear that if you save a starving
man to-day, you may possibly find to-morrow that you must begin again."—July 22,
1847.

CHAPTER VII

THE STATE OF THE TOWNS

ABOUT the year 1840 those responsible for the government of England became painfully aware that during the preceding fifty years, in the course of an amazing growth of population, the proportions between town and country dwellers had completely changed; that whereas in 1790 the country labourers were about double the town workmen, the town workmen were now nearly double the country labourers;[1] that in spite of the general advance in the arts and amenities of life this new town population had what was graphically described as "a low and grovelling mode of living."[2]

The cholera epidemic of 1832 called public attention to the subject of the towns, and late in the thirties and early in the forties there were a series of inquiries which throw a vivid light on the conditions of town life. An attempt will be made in this chapter to reconstruct from the sometimes redundant and sometimes scanty material some picture of what daily life was like for the inhabitants of these towns. First, we must remember in thinking of the new urban population that the recent developments in industry had gathered together masses of men and women, not only to work in the industry for which the particular town or district was noted, but also to produce goods or supply services for those workers. Tailors, shoemakers, butchers, bakers, druggists, greengrocers, bricklayers, plasterers, masons, chimney-sweeps, and many others, all flocked to the centres of population. Leeds was reckoned the centre of the woollen trade, but it was estimated by a Statistical Committee of the Town Council in 1839 that out of a population of 82,120, only 12,684, including 594 mechanics, were actually employed

---

[1] 1840 Health of Towns Committee, p. iv.
[2] Of Coventry silk-workers. 1845 Health of Towns Commission, Second Report Appendix, part ii. p. 263.

in manufactures, the remainder of the population being made up as follows: 12,639 in "select trades," 17,916 in "miscellaneous ditto," 38,881 domestic servants, children, and "others not specified" (the domestic servants numbered 4509, and there were 27,299 children under thirteen years of age).[1] In the cotton town of Ashton-under-Lyne, on the other hand, out of a population of 22,700, 10,520 were said to be actually employed in the mills,[2] and in Bolton, in 1837, out of a population of 43,396 23,257 were said to be employed in work connected with the textile trade (11,961 in cotton factories, 2000 in print works, 500 in bleach works, 968 as counterpane weavers, 4300 as hand-loom weavers, and 528 in flax mills).[3]

Whatever the character of the population, shelter of some sort had to be supplied. Where an existing town like Leeds or Manchester formed the nucleus of the settlement, there was further crowding in the already overcrowded and insanitary quarters of the poor, but growing suburbs soon encircled the old centre. In some of the cotton and in many of the iron districts, villages or towns were now planted for the first time in sparsely populated regions. Under such circumstances the employers were often compelled to provide houses themselves.

Where the new population swarmed into a town, employers could leave this task to the speculative builder. A typical example of the result is given in a description of the growth of Liverpool. "The soil is subdivided into a multitude of holdings, and a man runs a new street, generally as narrow as he possibly can, through a field, not only to save the greater expense of soughing and paving, which, in the first instance, falls upon himself, but also that he may have a greater quantity of land to dispose of. The next owner continues that street, if it suits him, but he is not obliged to do so, and the consequence is, the growth of narrow thoroughfares, the erection of mean edifices, the utter neglect of proper sewerage, the inattention to ventilation, and that train of evils which is so much to be deplored, is the inevitable consequence."[4] The suburbs of

---

[1] *Journal of the Statistical Society of London*, vol. ii. pp. 409 and 412.
[2] 1844 Health of Towns Commission, First Report, Appendix, p. 81.
[3] See Summary of Statistics of Bolton, by Jas. Black, M.D., published in *Transactions of Provincial Medical and Surgical Association* in 1837.
[4] 1844 Health of Towns Commission, First Report, Appendix, p. 186.

Bradford grew up in the same way : " an individual who may have a couple of thousand pounds, does not exactly know what to do with it, having no occasion for it in trade ; he wishes to lay it out so as to pay him the best percentage in money ; he will purchase a plot of ground, an acre or half an acre ; then what he thinks about is, to place as many houses on this acre of ground as he possibly can, without reference to drainage or anything, except that which will pay him a good percentage for his money ; that is the way in which the principal part of the suburbs of Bradford has sprung up." [1]

The kind of building that paid the good percentage was described as follows : " An immense number of the small houses occupied by the poorer classes in the suburbs of Manchester are of the most superficial character ; they are built by the members of building clubs, and other individuals, and new cottages are erected with a rapidity that astonishes persons who are unacquainted with their flimsy structure. They have certainly avoided the objectionable mode of forming underground dwellings, but have run into the opposite extreme, having neither cellar nor foundation. The walls are only half brick thick, or what the bricklayers call ' brick noggin,' and the whole of the materials are slight and unfit for the purpose. . . . They are built back to back ; without ventilation or drainage ; and, like a honeycomb, every particle of space is occupied. Double rows of these houses form courts, with, perhaps, a pump at one end and a privy at the other, common to the occupants of about twenty houses." [2]

The houses that sprang up in the districts where there was no existing town were of much the same quality. Mr. Edmund Ashworth, himself an enlightened and kindly employer, gave a

[1] 1840 Health of Towns Committee, p. 89.

[2] 1842 Sanitary Condition of Labouring Population, General Report, p. 284. Compare Slaney of the Midlands : " The increased demand for workmen in these districts called for additional dwellings, which have been erected, or *run up*, as the phrase is, in many instances with extraordinary celerity, and with *no regulations* to ensure those conveniences which are necessary for the health and comfort of the inmates. The great majority of houses for the working classes thus built are the property of small capitalists, tradesmen, and others living on the spot, who only desire to make the largest interest on their money. Some are erected by building clubs, who are generally led by the same motive. Thus, rows of small houses are built by contract from time to time, the main object in almost all cases being to pack as many dwellings as practicable on any given quantity of land, and to build them at as little expense a, possible, consistent with their being let. . . ."—1845 Health of Towns Commissions Second Report, Appendix, p. 14.

vivid picture of them. "On the early introduction of the cotton manufacture, the parties who entered into it were often men of limited capital, and anxious to invest the whole of it in mills and machinery, and therefore too much absorbed with the doubtful success of their own affairs to look after the necessities of their workpeople. Families were attracted from all parts for the benefit of employment, and obliged as a temporary resort to crowd together into such dwellings as the neighbourhood afforded : often two families into one house ; others into cellars or very small dwellings ; eventually, as the works became established, either the proprietor or some neighbour would probably see it advantageous to build a few cottages ; these were often of the worst description : in such case the prevailing consideration was not how to promote the health and comfort of the occupants, but how many cottages would be built upon the smallest space of ground and at the least possible cost. We find many built back to back—a most objectionable form, as precluding the possibility of any outlet behind. People brought together as these were for a living had no alternative but to occupy such dwellings.[1] Whatever the weekly income, the wife could never make such a house comfortable ; she had only one room in which to do all her work ; it may be readily supposed the husband would not always find the comfort he wished in such a home. The public-house would then be his only resort. But here the evil does not end; the children brought up in such dwellings knew no better accommodation than such afforded, nor had they any opportunities of seeing better domestic management." [2]

The Ashworths themselves, it may be mentioned, started an interesting experiment in housing. After an outbreak of malignant fever among their workpeople, due to filth, they began a system of what would now be called " health visiting." This convinced them that habits and conditions were closely connected, and they proceeded to build bigger and better cottages for their workers. The taste for these cottages soon grew among the workpeople, who acquired in consequence

[1] Cf. : "The poor cannot afford to repair, decorate, and excavate. What they have given them, that they must keep ; what they can't mend, that they must endure. That is their condition in many things, but in nothing so much as in their tenements." —*Times*, May 7, 1847.
[2] 1842 Sanitary Condition of Labouring Population, Local Reports, p. 337.

"better habits and a more respectable feeling in society." [1] The best-sized house for general use they found to be one with a living-room 15 feet by 9 feet, a back kitchen of the same size, and three bedrooms over them.

When we think of the new houses crowding up, we must bear in mind that there were no building restrictions or town-planning schemes to hamper the impulse for economy in material and space. Each man could do what was profitable in his own eyes, and could exercise his ingenuity in packing on each acre the greatest number of human beings at the smallest cost. Such building Acts as existed applied only to parts of London and to a few other towns, and were concerned with regulations about the thickness of party walls between houses, designed to prevent the spread of fires.[2] In a few of the growing towns, where the land happened to belong to a single landowner of enlightened views, certain town-planning restrictions were enforced. But these places were an exception. Most notable among them was the cotton town of Ashton-under-Lyne, where the Earl of Stamford, who owned the town, made certain conditions about "good, firm, and substantial" building when he granted leases.[3] Though the old parts of the town had narrow streets and crowded back-to-back houses, the new parts, some seven-eighths of the whole, were said to show great improvement. "Lord Stamford," we read in the 1844 Report, "takes especial care to have all new buildings erected in airy, well-formed streets, and in all cases where leases expire of premises in the old town, his Lordship invariably binds the new tenants to widen the streets when necessary to relieve the overcrowding." [4]

At Huddersfield again, Sir John Ramsden, who owned the town, enforced wide streets and "good straught houses"; [5] and in the Glossop district of Derbyshire, owned by the Duke of Norfolk, which was passing from rural to manufacturing conditions, "the land is laid out in regular form, under the personal superintendence of the agent or surveyor of the owner of the soil, with a provision for the requisite streets, avenues, passages, drains, sewers, and other conveniences." [6]

---

[1] 1840 Health of Towns Committee, p. 110.
[2] See 1842 Sanitary Condition of Labouring Population, General Report, p. 280.
[3] 1844 Health of Towns Commission, First Report, Appendix, p. 81.
[4] *Ibid.* p. 74.   [5] *Ibid.* p. 177.
[6] 1842 Sanitary Condition of Labouring Population, Local Reports, p. 250.

A disastrous effect of abortive town-planning was seen at Chorlton on Medlock, one of the growing suburban townships of the borough of Manchester, where the streets as originally planned were to be wide and airy, with a front street and a back street to each row of houses, but as the first row did not stretch from front to back, another row was wedged in back to back with it, so that the original back street now became a front street to the second row.[1] This use of space originally designed for giving light and air was carried to an extreme in the St. Giles district in London, where an originally large square was gradually filled up from circumference to centre with buildings, like the nests of boxes with which children play.[2]

Not only were there no building restrictions, but there was actually a certain bonus given to bad building, by the fact that the worst class of houses often escaped payment of local rates.[3] The Window Tax, too, in spite of the fact that since 1825 houses with less than eight windows were exempted from its incidence, still served to discourage light and air.[4] As every window over

[1] 1844 Health of Towns Commission, First Report, Appendix, p. 60.

[2] 1840 Health of Towns Committee, p. 171 : It was said of Snows Rents in West-minster that the court was too wide, for it was possible for the surrounding houses, which had no back yards, to deposit all their refuse in it, whereas " had the court been narrower, this accumulation could not have taken place, for the houses would have been inaccessible, and some other provision for the refuse must have been made."—1844 Health of Towns Commission, First Report, p. 419.

[3] ". . . in almost every place the lowest class of houses, partly through the in-efficiency of the law and partly through the difficulty of enforcing it, pay scarcely any of the local rates, including the poor rate."—1845 Health of Towns Commission, Second Report, Appendix, p. 15.

[4] The Window Tax was first imposed by William III. in 1696, eight years after the repeal of the vexatious Hearth Tax. It was imposed as a temporary measure in order " to raise the £1,200,000 for supplying the Deficiency of the Clipped Money " ; it was " 2s. yearly upon each House ; four shillings upon every House having ten Windows, and eight shillings upon such Houses as have twenty Windows, over and above the said two shillings." This simple form was from time to time elaborated and recast when the tax was continued or reimposed ; thus Pelham in 1747, in addition to a standing charge of 2s. a house, imposed a duty of 6d. on every window from 10 to 14 in number, of 9d. on windows from 15 to 19, and 1s. on every window from 20 in number and upwards. In 1766, in addition to a charge of 3s. a house, 7 windows paid at the rate of 2d. each, 8 windows paid 6d. each, 9 paid 8d. each, and so on, rising by increments of 2d.   Pitt, when he came into office in 1784, after defeating the Coalition, largely increased the Window Tax, to make up for the reduction in the Tea Duties. All houses now paid a fixed rate of 6s., and in addition, houses with 7 windows paid 6s., with 8 windows 8s., with 9 windows 10s. 6d., and so on. In 1792 Pitt reduced the payment of 6s. per house to 3s. for all houses with less than 7 windows, but the French war made further reductions impossible, and instead the tax rose, till it reached its maximum in 1808, when houses with 6 windows and under paid from 6s. 6d. to 8s., according to their value, houses with 7 windows paid £1, houses with 8 windows paid £1, 13s., houses with 9 windows paid £2, 2s., houses with 10 windows paid £2, 16s., and so on.   Certain exemptions for trade premises and farm-houses were made in

the eight which were not taxed cost on an average 8s. 3d. a year, even though the opening might be only a foot square, architects and builders of any houses bigger than small cottages were naturally encouraged to devise structures with as few openings as possible, and the result was recognised as disastrous even in a generation for which fresh air had many terrors. In most new houses privies, closets, passages, cellars, and roofs were left without ventilation. " The legislature," declared a witness in 1844, " now says to the builder, Plan your houses with as few openings as possible, let every house be ill-ventilated by shutting out the light and air, and as a reward for your ingenuity you shall be subject to a less amount of taxation than your neighbours." [1]   Apologists for the Window Tax pointed out that, whereas there were 2,846,179 inhabited houses in Great Britain, only 377,471, or something between one-seventh and one-eighth, paid window tax; and they argued that the poor were therefore exempt.[2]   Opponents retorted that though the country poor might be unaffected, in towns it had a disastrous effect. " In London the poor do not live in cottages, but several families occupy lodgings in the same house, and that, perhaps, a house built with the maximum of untaxed windows allowed by the law." [3]

The worst consequences were seen in the northern towns such as Newcastle and Barnard Castle, where a large proportion of the poorer people lived in tenement houses which had known better days. In Barnard Castle four-fifths of the weavers and half of the rest of the working classes lived in large houses, one house sometimes containing fifty or more persons. The effect of the heavy charges on the tenement houses in Newcastle was described by a collector of assessed taxes who had been originally appointed in 1805. " No circumstance has contributed more to injure the habitations of the poor, and to diminish their healthiness, than the tax upon windows, the manner of its

1817; in 1823 the duties were halved, and in 1825 houses with less than 8 windows were exempted.   The Reform Government of 1832, which had denounced both the Window Tax and the Inhabited House Duty when in opposition, found itself in difficulties when expected to give effect to its denunciations.   After an episode which caused the resignation of Hobhouse, it ended by abolishing the Inhabited House Duty.   When the repeal of the Window Tax was finally carried after considerable agitation in 1851, the Inhabited House Duty was reimposed.
[1] 1844 Health of Towns Commission, First Report, p. 436.
[2] *Edinburgh Review*, July 1833, p. 437.
[3] 1844 Health of Towns Commission, First Report, p. 437.

assessment, and the high duty upon window glass. . . . This heavy taxation naturally induced proprietors of such property to close up every window not absolutely necessary for light. Many of the staircases were so darkened that it became necessary to grope the way up them, at noon-day, as at night. The effect of this process upon ventilation was deplorable, and continues to operate to this day, for although the tax upon windows is considerably reduced, yet it falls heavily upon such houses." [1]

Though the new districts and the new houses were squalid and unsightly, it is a nice question whether they were any worse than the older districts and older houses round which they grew. The new cottages round Manchester, as we have seen, were said to have neither cellars nor foundations. Round Leeds, on the other hand, the new cottages, though of flimsier structure than the old, were said to have larger rooms and cellars to keep them dry.[2] Opinions differed as to whether it was better to live in a jerry-built house with larger rooms or in a house that was smaller but substantially built. In Bradford, pronounced by James Smith of Deanston, the well-known authority on sanitation, to be " The most filthy town I visited," it was stated that there was no improvement in the " more recent arrangements for the abodes of the working classes." [3] But it is safe to say that the worst overcrowding was to be found in the old quarters of existing towns. Manchester, Liverpool, London were hard to beat ; Leeds could show districts where overcrowding could hardly be carried further ; but Nottingham was the worst example. For reasons described later, Nottingham could not grow easily, and it contained in a narrow space 11,000 inhabited houses laid out in narrow streets, many of them " built in confined courts and alleys, the entrance to which is usually through a tunnel from 30 to 36 inches wide, about 8 feet high, and from 25 to 30 feet long." Of the 11,000 houses upwards of 7000 were built " back to back and side to side." [4]

1845 alth of Towns Commission, Second Report, Appendix, part ii. p. 134. In 1834 an Act was passed (4 and 5 William IV. cap. 54) allowing occupiers, " if duly assessed " to the Window Tax in 1835, to open out as many windows as they liked without further payment, but it was complained that legal quibbles over the term " duly assessed " robbed this concession of its value.—1844 Health of Towns Commission, First Report, p. 436.

[2] 1840 Health of Towns Committee, p. 118.

[3] 1845 Health of Towns Commission, Second Report, Appendix, part ii. p. 315.

[4] 1844 Health of Towns Commission, First Report, Appendix, p. 132.

Overcrowding, however, was not the worst element in what one observer called " the perhaps unavoidably unpropitious position of the lower orders in densely populated manufacturing districts." [1] To describe the greatest discomfort, it is necessary to deal, however briefly, with the unpleasant but important subject of refuse. The problem of living in a closely packed community is, as every one knows, enormously complicated by the question of how to dispose of refuse, especially that most repulsive refuse which consists of the waste products of the human body. Now, in considering how this particular refuse was disposed of in the early nineteenth century, we must bear in mind that, as travellers to China soon realise, it has a considerable value as manure; [2] if left in heaps to rot and ripen, it acts as a strong fertiliser for the soil. In England in the early nineteenth century, farmers were glad to pay for it; it was, in fact, " a property highly prized." [3] In country districts it was the regular custom to hoard it. Contentment, no doubt, sat spinning at her cottage door, with a rich dung heap beside her, which would either serve to make her potato patch more productive or would bring in a few shillings from a neighbouring farmer. So long as there were not too many other cottages with similar heaps close by, and provided that the heap did not drain into the well, no one was much the worse, but when similar heaps were scattered about in the crowded quarters of Birmingham, or Leeds, or Liverpool, the consequences were dangerous as well as disgusting.

Sometimes there was not even provision for a midden. The cellar-dwellers of Manchester and Liverpool, some eighteen thousand in each town, had nowhere to put any refuse of any kind. It had to go either into the streets or into the already overcrowded receptacles of neighbouring courts.[4] Dr. Duncan, the well-known Liverpool sanitary reformer, writing in 1840, estimated, after a statistical investigation, that not only the cellar-dweller but a very large majority of the working-class

---

[1] 1842 Sanitary Condition of Labouring Population, Local Reports, p. 333.
[2]   ". . . in remotest orient lands
     whose cockcrow is our curfew, where Chineses swarm
     teasing their narrow plots with hand and hoe, carrying
     their own dung on their heads obsequiously as ants."
                              Bridges, Testament of Beauty, iii. 346.
[3] Sanitary Condition of Labouring Population, Local Reports, p. 2.
[4] 1845 Health of Towns Commission, Second Report, Appendix, part ii. p. 16.

inhabitants of that town, were in the same predicament.[1] There were whole streets of houses in Leeds where conditions were no better.[2] It was this state of things that provoked Chadwick's famous outburst: "Such is the absence of civic economy in some of our towns that their condition in respect to cleanliness is almost as bad as that of an encamped horde, or an undisciplined soldiery."[3] After describing the sanitary precautions embodied in certain Army Standing Orders, he continued: "The towns whose populations never change their encampment, have no such care, and whilst the houses, streets, courts, lanes, and streams, are polluted and rendered pestilential, the civic officers have generally contented themselves with the most barbarous expedients, or sit still amidst the pollution, with the resignation of Turkish fatalists, under the supposed destiny of the prevalent ignorance, sloth, and filth."

Even where provision for sanitation was made it was often grossly inadequate,[4] and the arrangements for clearing away the refuse were usually utterly defective.[5] It may be pleaded on behalf of the civic officers that the ownership of this filth, as we have seen, was a vexed question, and complicated the problem. Of the northern towns, Newcastle, Sunderland, Shields, etc., an observer wrote: "no circumstance appeared to me more fruitful of nuisance and disease than the attempt to accumulate the refuse of such privies and dust-bins as there were, for the purpose of selling it to the neighbouring farmers. . . . The landlords and farmers were led to encourage undue accumulations, and the local authorities were too often prevented from exercising their power in such cases as came under their jurisdiction, from the feeling that they were depriving the poor of a valuable source of income. . . ."[6] In the Midlands, again, the complaint was made that "In none of the towns visited is there

---

[1] 1842 Sanitary Condition of Labouring Population, Local Reports, p. 286.
[2] Ibid., Local Reports, p. 356. [3] Ibid., General Report, p. 43.
[4] For example, the Manchester district, where there were 645 houses with 7095 inhabitants and 33 "necessaries."—1845 Health of Towns Commission, Second Report, Appendix, part ii. p. 15.
[5] For example, the small back street of Chorlton on Medlock, where there were thirty-eight middens cleared at irregular intervals, so that on an average there were "nearly 20 tons of decomposing filth in the very confined space . . . of less than 500 square yards."—1844 Health of Towns Commission, First Report, Appendix, p. 68.
[6] 1845 Health of Towns Commission, Second Report, Appendix, part ii. p. 130. Cf. evidence of Kempson, a Birmingham surveyor before the Committee on the Building Regulations Bill, 1842.

any system of contracts with scavengers or nightmen to clear away at proper stated periods all refuse, filth, and night-soil from the courts and small streets inhabited by the poorer classes." Each inhabitant made his own separate bargain, with disastrous results.[1] Sometimes the midden was claimed as the landlord's perquisite. In the Lancashire towns the local Acts were said to have a clause " reserving the right of manure to the inhabitants of houses who are desirous to keep it." [2]

As the towns grew the demand for this manure fell off. The cost of cartage to more distant fields swallowed up all profit, and it became necessary to pay to have middens or cesspools cleared out. London reached this point early. By 1842 it could be said, " There is no filth in the metropolis that now, as a general rule, will pay the expense of collection and removal by cart, except the ashes from the houses and the soap lees from the soap-boilers ; and some of the night-soil from the east end of the town, where there happen to be in the immediate vicinity some market-gardens, where it can be used at once, without distant or expensive cartage. The charge for removing night-soil from the poorest tenements may be about £1 per tenement. One house with another, the expense may be said to be in London about 10s. per year, as the cesspools may be emptied once in two years." [3] This problem of what to do with London refuse became acute as the town spread and the regular dumping grounds were covered. When the new London University, Hyde Park Gardens, and Belgrave Square were built, useful places of deposit were lost.[4] " They drive us out," complained a contractor in 1844, ". . . they say they do not like our men, and they do not like our carts ; we are not very pleasant sort of people." [5]

<hr/>

[1] 1845 Health of Towns Commission, Second Report, Appendix, p. 3. In Nottingham, for example, " The refuse of the courts and alleys is saved up in the necessary-pits till the accumulation is very considerable, the inhabitants then sell it to ' muck-majors ' (as the dealers in excrementitious manures are here denominated) for a few shillings per load, and divide the amount so obtained amongst themselves. The refuse is carted away by the purchaser during the night, and not later than seven o'clock of the morning in summer, and nine in winter. This regulation is imposed by a bye-law of the corporation. The carts frequently let fall a portion of their semi-fluid contents in the public streets, notwithstanding a regulation exists to the contrary. . . ."—1844 Health of Towns Commission, First Report, Appendix, p. 132.

[2] 1845 Health of Towns Commission, Second Report, Appendix, part ii. p. 44.

[3] 1842 Sanitary Condition of Labouring Population, General Report, p. 379.

[4] *Ibid.* p. 381.

[5] 1844 Health of Towns Commission, First Report, p. 274. A nasty practice grew

Meanwhile the spread of water sanitation was changing the nature of the problem. The use of water to flush away refuse led to an increase in the number of cesspools. Filth and corruption were at any rate out of sight, deep in the earth, and though the solid matter had to be cleared out at intervals, the liquid took care of itself by soaking away. London became a honeycomb of cesspools. The architect in charge of the cutting of the Blackwall Railway described the results : " The soil in the immediate connexion with the houses and surrounding the foundations was so saturated from the cesspools as to be, in my opinion, in a worse condition than in dung-heaps." [1] London spring water acquired a curious colour and taste, but, fortunately perhaps, coal gas was often considered responsible for this. What was called, in 1834, " the increase of luxury and love of cleanliness which marks the present day," [2] in other words, the increasing use of baths, made the problem more difficult, for cesspools filled up too rapidly. A solution presented itself : Why not connect house drainage with the existing sewers and let everything be washed away together ?

The term sewer is now so much bound up in our ears with house drainage that it is important to remember that the sixteenth, seventeenth, and eighteenth century sewers were not constructed for anything of the kind. They were built to carry off the water from marshes and low-lying places, in other words, for surface land drainage, and were under the management of some hundred different authorities, called " Commissions of Sewers." Henry VIII., in 1532, " like a virtuous and most gracious Prince, nothing earthly so highly weighing as the advancing of the common profit, wealth, and commodity of this realm," [3] had first established them. The story of the inefficiency, and in many cases corruption, of the various London Commissions during the time that the town was spreading in the early nineteenth century, has been told by Mr. and Mrs. Webb.[4] It was into these sewers, constructed for surface water, and managed by inefficient bodies, that house drainage,

up of drying the manure, packing it in the empty sugar hogsheads and sending it out to the West Indies to enrich the soil there. See *ibid.*, and also Sanitary Condition of Labouring Population, General Report, p. 379.

[1] 1844 Health of Towns Commission, First Report, p. 414.
[2] 1834 Report of Select Committee on Sewers, p. 108.
[3] 1845 Health of Towns Commission, Second Report, Appendix, part ii. p. 40.
[4] See *English Local Government : Statutory Authorities*, chap. i.

provided a sewer was near enough, was now discharged. The results of the new system were tersely described in 1840 : " . . . the Thames is now made a great cesspool instead of each person having one of his own." [1]

The change, of course, did not take place all at once, and the two systems long went on side by side. In Liverpool the Commissioners of Sewers forbade the connection of house drainage with their pipes, though a good deal of filth got down from the streets, but in most towns people began to use the sewers for the disposal of house refuse. The results in manufacturing towns, where a river ran through the town and was used for water power, were particularly disastrous. As the flow was stopped by dams or weirs, a series of huge open cesspools was created. Leeds, Bradford, Halifax, Sheffield, Coventry, Derby, Birmingham,[2] Manchester, all suffered alike. For those who lived near its banks the famous Bridgwater Canal was associated, not with the triumph of engineering skill, but with " disgusting odours " of which the victims complained to the trustees.[3] Sanitary reformers urged, that since steam power had largely superseded water power elsewhere, the use of steam instead of water in establishments near rivers should be made compulsory, so that the water should be able to carry away its cargo unchecked. Even where no dams obstructed the flow, a slow stream produced much the same effect : " The sewers of Bolton empty themselves into the small rivers which wind sluggishly through the town, and yield to the air, in their passage, the most offensive emanations." [4] The Serpentine itself, intended by the original designer of Kensington Gardens and Hyde Park as an ornamental water, became " an open sewer " which drained Kilburn, Paddington, and Bayswater. " It is, indeed," said John Martin the artist, " a scandal upon the greatest metropolis in the world, that the only place near it in

---

[1] 1840 Health of Towns Committee, p. 209.

[2] Of the Rea Brook at Birmingham it was said : " The *cloaca maxima* of Birmingham differs from that of ancient Rome ; that whereas in the latter art was employed to effect what nature had left undone, here art has been employed to obstruct the useful course of nature."—1842 Sanitary Condition of Labouring Population, General Report, p. 387.

[3] 1845 Health of Towns Commission, Second Report, Appendix, part ii. p. 2. " A constant decomposition of the filth at the bottom of the canal is going on, and large quantities of carburetted hydrogen bubble up, causing an appearance like strong ebullition."—1844 Health of Towns Commission, First Report, Appendix, p. 68.

[4] 1845 Health of Towns Commission, Second Report, Appendix, part ii. p. 9.

which the public can bathe is an open drain to a populous district, the filthy bed of which, when disturbed by even a single bather, causes the most unwholesome and disgusting effluvia imaginable." [1]

Apart from the contamination of rivers and streams, the new use of sewers for house drainage produced a volume of sewer gas. Most sewer pipes were not even round; they were flat-bottomed, and laid with little fall, so that great deposits were formed at intervals. When the way was completely blocked these deposits were cleared out, but before that happened they had generated quantities of sewer gas which escaped either into the houses connected with the sewers or through gratings into the streets. The smell from these gratings was the cause of much complaint. " I find it every day in walking," said one witness, " as I daresay we all do, a very great inconvenience, to say the least of it." [2] Proposals to provide shafts for ventilation in place of the street gulleys were frowned on by the sewer authorities, who feared that they would only lead to the bottling up of the gas, and so increase the danger to their workpeople. "Explosions," said George Saunders, the Chairman of the Westminster Commission, " are continually taking place and our people are frequently sent to the hospital. Our surveyor can show a specimen of an entire new skin to his hand, and he had an entirely new skin to his face, and laid up in a very dangerous state." [3]

The escape of sewer gas into the streets affected rich and poor alike, but in other respects the poor were less exposed to its dangers than the well-to-do whose houses were connected with the sewers under the new system. The " gentleman of distinction " who nearly abandoned his house, " in consequence of the unpleasant smells which were continually arising," but " arose in the greatest strength whenever he had parties," was a case in point. His drains were imperfectly trapped, and " whenever he had a party there was a stronger fire in the kitchen, and stronger fires in other parts of the house, and the windows and external doors being shut, and a greater draught created, larger quantities of the foul air from the sewers rose up." This illustration was used as a much-needed warning to the enthusiasts

---

[1] 1834 Report of Select Committee on Sewers, p. 167.
[2] *Ibid.* p. 64.   [3] *Ibid.* p. 11.

who hoped to solve the problem of refuse by connecting " the house of the poor man " with the sewers. " When the door was shut, and he sat down to enjoy his fireside, he would have a stench." [1] As things were, the stench came from outside, and was perhaps less dangerous.

Street cleansing, like street paving, was originally considered to be an obligation on the householder.[2] Both became gradually a municipal duty. In the case of street cleaning there are three stages : (1) the householder does (or neglects to do) the work himself ; (2) the householder piles up the dirt and the scavenger removes it ;[3] (3) the scavenger both sweeps and removes the dirt, with the exception that the householder is still expected to sweep the footway in front of his house. In accepting accounts of the cleansing of particular towns considerable caution is needed. Dr. Southwood Smith described the experience of " a distinguished foreigner " who was sceptical of the statements in the Reports on Fever in the metropolis, because " from the cleanliness, neatness, and apparent healthfulness of the main streets and thoroughfares in London, he could not bring himself to believe that there could be large districts containing hundreds of thousands of the people allowed year after year to remain in such a neglected and poisonous condition." A visit to these places convinced him that the picture had been under-coloured.[4] Dr. Lyon Playfair, who wrote a report on Lancashire towns for the 1844 Health of Towns Commission, inserted an illuminating table on the subject.[5] Taking the ten towns, Liverpool, Manchester, Salford, Chorlton on Medlock, Rochdale, Preston, Ashton, Bolton, Bury, and Wigan, he set out in each case the authorities, the number of scavengers, the stated periods at which the streets were cleaned, and various other facts. If we look only at the information about the stated

[1] 1842 Sanitary Condition of Labouring Population, General Report, pp. 319 and 320.
[2] Webb, *Statutory Authorities*, pp. 316 f.
[3] Thus, *e.g.* under the 1748 Statute 21 Geo. II. cap. 24, dealing with building a church in Liverpool, and with " enlightening and cleansing " the streets, all inhabitants were ordered to cause the streets and lanes before their houses to be swept twice a week at least, and to bring out refuse to the scavengers, who will carry it away, together with the street sweepings, twice a week at least. It is noteworthy that the scavengers are to go to " every Court, Alley, and Place into which the said Carts and Carriages cannot pass," and to " abide and stay there a convenient Time," so that the inhabitants can bring out their refuse.
[4] 1844 Health of Towns Commission, First Report, p. 69.
[5] 1845 Health of Towns Commission, Second Report, Appendix, part ii. p. 13.

periods at which the streets were cleaned, we find that Liverpool, Manchester, Salford, Rochdale, and Preston were cleaned once a week, Chorlton on Medlock thirty-eight times a year, whilst Ashton, Bolton, Bury, and Wigan had no regular intervals. Once a week sounds fairly satisfactory, but the question in a further column " Are Courts and Alleys cleaned ? " is answered " No " for each one of the ten towns. A further question as to whether " undedicated streets " are cleaned, is also answered in the negative by all the towns except Liverpool and Manchester, where the answer is "seldom." Of Manchester, we read, " The only streets recognized by the authorities are those dedicated to the public. Unpaved and unsewered streets are not so dedicated, and, therefore, although from their bad condition calculated to retain filth of every description, they do not receive the benefits arising from the visits of the public scavenger." [1]

These answers show that we must beware of thinking that the whole of a town was cleaned because a local Act gave powers of cleansing and scavenging to some authority or other. In the first place, the Act probably covered only certain streets, for the Lancashire towns were not peculiar in this respect. In Leeds, for example, in 1842, out of a total of 586 streets, 68 streets were said to be " the only ones which are under any regulation, whether as to paving, draining, sewering, or cleansing." [2] In Bradford, again, with its population of nearly 100,000 in 1840, street cleansing was " attended to " only in the actual township, for the local Act did not touch the suburbs, " by far the largest portion of the town." [3] In Shrewsbury and Norwich only the old parts, within the walls, were cleansed ; [4] all over England, in town after town, courts and alleys were looked on as " private property."

In the second place, local Acts were not always carried out. Manchester illustrates this point. To say that under the local Act of 1791, which appointed Police Commissioners for Manchester, the streets were swept twice a week, sounds well on paper, but a study of the local records shows it to be misleading.[5]

[1] *Ibid.* p. 12.
[2] 1842 Sanitary Condition of Labouring Population, Local Reports, p. 398.
[3] 1840 Health of Towns Committee, pp. 88 and 89.
[4] 1845 Health of Towns Commission, Second Report, Appendix, p. 11, and Appendix, part ii. p. 284.
[5] See Webb, *Manor and Borough*, part i. p. 109. In 1799, for example, complaint was made that the streets remained " uncleansed and without lights."

Dr. Playfair showed, by comparing the number of scavengers and the number of streets in Manchester and Liverpool, that the public streets could only be cleaned in Manchester once a fortnight, in Liverpool once every three weeks.[1]   The actual regulations in force till Whitworth's sweeping machine was introduced in 1844, were that first-class streets should be swept once a week, second-class streets once a fortnight, third-class streets once a month, courts, alleys, etc., not at all.[2]   It is not surprising that when a statistical investigation was made in the township of Manchester by District Boards of Health, during the cholera alarm of 1832, it was found that in 352 out of 687 streets visited there were "heaps of refuse, stagnant pools, ordure, etc."[3]

What happened, it may well be asked, in the courts and alleys which the scavengers did not visit?   Apart from that cleansing "which Providence showers from the clouds,"[4] their state seems to have depended on the initiative and resource of the inhabitants.   In Liverpool they sometimes remained a whole year uncleaned.[5]   At the end of that time the pile of muck and ashes might be worth a contractor's while to remove.   In Birmingham people often tipped out their refuse from the courts by night into the streets.[6]   Newcastle was not the only town where it was possible to talk of "that mass of filth that constitutes the street."[7]

Such were the surroundings in which the new town population lived.   What was life like for the housewife?   An old judgment declared that "three great commodities" were essential to a man's house : "air for his health, light for his profit, prospect for his pleasure."[8]   Prospect and light were scarce enough in the crowded quarters, and air was none too common in the houses of the poor with that "close, unpleasant smell" of which their betters complained.   In many cases the excuse "were the closed windows opened, it would frequently

[1] 1845 Health of Towns Commission, Second Report, Appendix, part ii. p. 12.
[2] 1842 Sanitary Condition of Labouring Population, General Report, p. 53 ; and 1844 Health of Towns Commission, First Report, Appendix, p. 206.
[3] Sir James Kay-Shuttleworth, *Four Periods of Public Education*, p. 13.
[4] 1844 Health of Towns Commission, First Report, Appendix, p. 188.
[5] 1840 Health of Towns Committee, p. 144.
[6] 1842 Sanitary Condition of Labouring Population, Local Reports, p. 195.
[7] 1845 Health of Towns Commission, Second Report, Appendix, part ii. p. 129.
[8] 1842 Sanitary Condition of Labouring Population, General Report, p. 291

be only to admit a worse compound, the air from neglected privies, and the miasma from the wet and undrained court or street," [1] might be valid, but it must be admitted that however pure the air outside, there was then, even more than now, a strong prejudice among rich and poor alike against admitting it to their houses.   Fresh air was well enough in its place—out-of-doors.   The description of the agricultural labourer at home applied to all classes : " He appears to be insensible to anything but changes of temperature, and there is scarcely any stench which is not endured to avoid slight cold." [2]   It was sometimes assumed that the objection to fresh air was increased by the habit of working in heated factories, but it is hard to believe that any factory was worse than the tailor's shop of which the master cheerfully said, " Oh, there is no necessity to take particular means to warm it, the animal heat brings it up high enough," [3] or the stocking-weaver's shed where a weaver explained that it was impossible to open the windows during the fourteen or sixteen hours' work, for it "would not be prudent, as our confinement makes us susceptible of cold." [4]

It must be remembered that the open window was counted a danger by current medical opinion, and the Scottish doctor who used to " begin his prescription by breaking a pane or two of the window with his walking-stick, which he made good again at the end of the illness," [5] was before his time.   Children might faint from the foul air in school, but the teachers were commended for keeping the steaming windows tightly closed.[6] Fresh air, indeed, was advised, but in very moderate quantities.

---

[1] 1842 Sanitary Condition of Labouring Population, General Report, p. 129. Bad air in small rooms is, of course, more offensive than bad air in large rooms, and in the older towns, where personal contact between different classes was still customary, attempts were made to teach the benefits of fresh air.   Thus we read of the dwindling manufacturing town of Frome : " The ventilation of the habitations is left to the feelings of the inhabitants.   Sometimes the visiting charitable ladies—and they are many— when the windows have no openings, order the glazier to alter them."—1845 Health of Towns Commission, Second Report, Appendix, p. 125.

[2] 1842 Sanitary Condition of Labouring Population, General Report, p. 232.

[3] 1844 Health of Towns Commission, First Report, p. 203.   In justice to the master, it should be mentioned that the men had stopped up his ventilators.

[4] Ibid. p. 50.   This man complained that his fellow-workers would not open the windows even when work was over.   " When I have mentioned the injurious effect that this vitiated air had upon my constitution, that I felt it exhausting my strength, it was looked on as a sort of nonsense and a new-fangled notion that was not worth attending to."—P. 51.

[5] Ibid. p. 203.

[6] See 1845 Health of Towns Commission, Second Report, Appendix, part ii. p. 27.

"Windows," wrote one medical authority, ". . . are not recommended as affording the best means of insuring ordinary ventilation, though they may be resorted to with advantage when the weather is not severe, or under peculiar circumstances, and should therefore always be available when large supplies of air are required." [1]   What is needed, he explains, is "a much less extended opening."   The Sanitary Reports of the time are full of ingenious devices for " mechanical ventilation," which will introduce a sufficiently small amount of air.

Air, then, the poor neither had nor wished to have ; but there was another " commodity," water, which they certainly desired, but did not obtain.   The dearth of it made life a hard struggle for housewives who tried to keep up some standard of cleanliness.   It was generally assumed that country people were cleaner than townsfolk, but in the country a little washing went a long way, and it was possible to produce a cleanly appearance with a very small amount of water.   In the towns, on the other hand, there was dirt in the streets, and worse still, dirt in the air ; torrents of black smoke took all heart out of the housewife. Water was seldom close at hand, and the labour of fetching it in quantities sufficient to keep person and house clean became a weary task.   " The whole family of the labouring man in the manufacturing towns," wrote Chadwick, " rise early, before daylight in winter time, to go to their work ; they toil hard, and they return to their homes late at night.   It is a serious inconvenience, as well as discomfort to them to have to fetch water at a distance out-of-doors from the pump or the river on every occasion that it may be wanted, whether it may be in cold, in rain, or in snow.   The minor comforts of cleanliness are, of course, forgone, to avoid the immediate and greater discomforts of having to fetch the water." [2]   It is no wonder that the suggestion was made that " it is only when the infant enters upon breathing existence, and when the man has ceased to breathe— at the moment of birth and at the hour of death—that he is really well washed." [3]

Often it was necessary to pay water-carriers, or to buy water from carts.   Mr. Thomas Ashton of Hyde, the benevolent

[1] *Ibid.* p. 139.
[2] 1842 Sanitary Condition of the Labouring Population, General Report, p. 70.
[3] 1845 Health of Towns Commission, Second Report, Appendix, part ii. p. 303.

cotton employer, put water into the colony of 320 houses where his workpeople lived, and found that whereas they paid 3d. a week for his good supply, they had formerly paid at least 1d. a day, and some as much as 1s. a week, to water-carriers for a small quantity.[1] In Leeds, some families paid as much as 2s. a week for water from carts.[2] The charge per gallon varied considerably in different places; at Chorlton-on-Medlock and at Bradford, 1d. was charged by the carts for three gallons; in Preston, where there was competition with the waterworks, the charge was ½d. for three gallons; in Nottingham, before the regular supply was introduced, the charge varied from ¼d. to ½d. a bucket according to distance; in Carlisle, water was sold at 1d. for eight gallons. In the squalid pages of the inquiries of the time, the tale of the spring at Frome which supplied a hundred families stands out. It was the property of " a man in humble life, named Flower, who, though possessed of little else than it, freely gives its waters to all who ask, denying no one. He even supplies his poor neighbours with cups and bowls, with which to dip the water out of the spring." [3]

In towns where there was an organised water supply in pipes, the water might be better and purer, but it was seldom laid on to working-class houses, and the business of fetching it was more difficult than in the case of wells or rivers. The supply was usually intermittent, and it was distributed to poor quarters by means of stand-pipes, one to some fifteen or more houses, out of which water poured for half an hour or an hour twice or thrice or oftener in the week. In Liverpool, for example, where the water was " pure and good," we read that " In the poorer neighbourhoods there is usually a cock in each court, and the inhabitants carry it and store it in jugs or wooden vessels from day to day ; but, compared with the dense population, the supply is totally inadequate, as the turn-cocks of the company cannot allow it to run a sufficient length of time ; and many of the habitations of the poor (whether from this circumstance or from inherent habits of filth, I do not venture to say) have never had their boarded floors properly scoured since the

---

[1] 1844 Health of Towns Commission, First Report, pp. 331 f.
[2] Report of Statistical Committee of Town Council, 1839, published in *Journal of Statistical Society of London*, vol. ii.
[3] 1845 Health of Towns Commission, Second Report, Appendix, p. 124.

houses were erected.   Many of the poor beg water—many steal
it. . . ."[1]   "How do people get their water, when they are out
of work?" a London witness was asked.   "They generally have
some of their children at home," he answered, " to empty it into
a tub, or something of that kind.   To the better sort of tenants
we give a water-tub ; but in cases where they have no water-
tubs or water-tanks, some of the family must be at home to take
it in." [2]   The fetching of water did not lead to good relations
among neighbours ; " I have seen as many as from 20 to 50
persons with pails waiting round one or two stand-pipes.   Then
there is quarrelling for the turn ; the strongest pushing forward,
and the pails, after they are filled, being upset." [3]   There were
lively scenes in Snows Rents in Westminster, where the one
stand-pipe that supplied sixteen houses was turned on for about
five minutes on Sunday, the principal cleaning day.[4]   There
were four grades of water storers : the lowest had only a tea-
kettle or a saucepan or jugs to store it in ; the next grade bought
a butter tub, costing 1s., and holding 8 gallons ; the third grade
rose to the purchase of a pork tub for 2s. 6d., this held 42 gallons;
the highest grade, " those who wish to be quite comfortable,"
invested from 16s. to 20s. in a wine-pipe, which held some 125
gallons.[5]   The wine-pipes were used in a few houses of a better
description, where water was laid on in the yards.   Sometimes
the landlord provided the water-butt.

Two towns enjoy an honourable distinction in respect of
their water supply.   In Preston and Nottingham the houses
might be overcrowded and insanitary, and the death-rate might
be high, but life, while it lasted, must have been made much
more tolerable than in most places by abundance of water.   In
both towns the water was always on, and in Nottingham two-
thirds of the houses were supplied.   The manager of the
Preston Water Works strongly advocated a constant supply

[1] 1844 Health of Towns Commission, First Report, Appendix, p. 189.   Things
were no better four years later if we can judge from a bitter paragraph in a Liverpool
comic paper : " A handsome reward will be given to any person or persons who may
discover in any part of the town of Liverpool pumps, wells, cisterns, or other reservoirs
of water, yielding sufficient supply to accomplish the necessary ablutions in any court,
street, or lane, solely occupied by the cottages of the poor.   The advertiser is not so
unreasonable as to expect that the Irish immigrants arriving can be washed here at
any price."—*The Liverpool Lion*, January 1, 1848.
[2] 1844 Health of Towns Commission, First Report, p. 222.
[3] 1844 Health of Towns Commission, First Report, p. 397.
[4] *Ibid.* p. 419.   [5] *Ibid.* pp. 256 and 260.

with taps as more economical than the intermittent supply of running water customary elsewhere.[1]

How much water was needed in a town to keep a house and family reasonably clean ?   A civil engineer, who had considered the matter carefully, declared that in London the actual consumption of " the family of an English workman of the cleanest kind," consisting of five persons, was under 20 gallons a day, or 4 gallons a head.[2]   Of the 20 gallons, 10 were used for cooking and personal washing.[3]   The other 10 were used for washing the rooms, washing the linen, and watering the flowers.[4]   The experience of Nottingham and Preston, however, showed that when water came to the door it was consumed in double that quantity.   In Nottingham the average consumption of the labourer's family was estimated at 40 gallons a day ; in Preston, at 45 gallons.[5]

It is interesting to speculate how far cleanliness is a natural and agreeable state for which sacrifices are willingly made, or how far dirt is natural and cleanliness an acquired virtue.   The Rev. Whitwell Elwin, Chaplain to the Bath Union, a man, doubtless, of considerable experience, was a strong champion of the latter view.   After explaining that even in " gentlemen's houses " shifts were resorted to in order to avoid the cost of an extra pail of water, he continued : " With the poor, far less obstacles are an absolute barrier, because no privation is felt by them so little as that of cleanliness.   The propensity to dirt is so strong, the steps so few and easy, that nothing but the utmost facilities for water can act as a counterpoise ; and such is the love of uncleanliness, when once contracted, that no habit, not even

---

[1] *Ibid.* Appendix, p. 159.
[2] *Ibid.* pp. 259 f.   20 gallons per head is considered a moderate allowance nowadays.
[3] They were divided thus :

Washing potatoes and vegetables, about . . .	2 galls.
Breakfast, tea, and washing up, about . . .	2 galls.
Boiling vegetables and meat, about . . .	2 galls.
For persons " when very clean," about . . .	4 galls.
	10 galls.

[4] These 70 gallons a week were distributed as follows :

Washing rooms	10 galls.
Washing linen	50 galls.
Watering flowers, etc.	10 galls.
	70 galls.

[5] *Ibid.* p. 303, and Appendix, p. 159.

drunkenness, is so difficult to eradicate."[1] But on the other side there rise up to confute him those clothes-lines of Leeds, where, on the weekly washing day, half the streets in the township were " so full of lines and linen as to be impassable for horses and carriages, and almost for foot passengers " ;[2] a danger to traffic, no doubt, but the symbol of a gallant struggle against almost overwhelming odds.[3]

It was difficult, as we have seen, to wash at home, and there were few towns where it was possible to wash elsewhere. The price of such baths as existed was usually prohibitive. Liverpool was an exception, after 1842, for in that year the Corporation started baths and wash-houses where 2d. was charged for a warm bath, 1d. for a cold bath, and 1d. for the use of a tub and hot water for washing clothes.[4] The chief credit for this reform is due to an Irish immigrant, Mrs. Kitty Wilkinson, a poor woman of noble character who offered the use of her kitchen to her neighbours in the cholera epidemic for washing their clothes. William Rathbone, who knew of her successful enterprise, persuaded the Corporation to establish public baths and to put her in charge of them. Her remarkable career has been commemorated in a window in Liverpool Cathedral. At Leeds in 1842 there was said to be a large swimming-bath owned by a private company, open to the working classes every Saturday for 2d.,[5] and in Westminster an enterprising proprietor conducted with success an establishment with two swimming-baths side by side : one at 1s. for the middling class, the other at 3d. for mechanics. The water for the middling-class bath was being continually replenished, and then passed through a filtering bed into the bath for the

---

[1] 1842 Sanitary Condition of Labouring Population, General Report, p. 70.

[2] 1840 Health of Towns Committee, p. 98 ; and 1842 Sanitary Condition of Labouring Population, Local Reports, pp. 352 and 402.

[3] The introduction of cotton clothing had, of course, increased the work on washing day. The old custom of wearing woollen clothes till they dropped off was unhygienic, but labour-saving.

[4] See *Memoir of Kitty Wilkinson*, by H. R. Rathbone, 1927, and Ramsay Muir, *History of Liverpool*, p. 311. For particulars of these baths, see 1844 Health of Towns Commission, First Report, Appendix, p. 195. A grim instruction for the conduct of these wash-houses runs : " Many of the clothes are full of vermin, which boiling does not destroy ; the clothes of the clean should therefore be boiled together, and those of the dirty together, in the second boiler when it is not wanted for infectious clothes. The woman must be very cautious, however, how she gives such reason, or she will give great offence."—*Ibid.* p. 198.

[5] 1842 Sanitary Condition of Labouring Population, Local Reports, p. 402.

" humbler classes." [1]   But these baths were exceptions, and as a rule the only bathing possible was in the rivers and canals, too often polluted by sewage or industrial refuse.[2]

The medical men whose evidence forms so large a part of the 1844 Health of Towns Report, took a more kindly view of shortcomings in cleanliness than some of the observers who lived under the shadow of the Poor Law Commission.   They realised that the work of fetching and storing even twenty gallons of water is considerable, and that to empty out dirty water when there are no proper sinks takes time and energy ; they could sympathise with the plea " We are so knocked up with the day's work that the water must wait until to-morrow when we shall be able to remove it." [3]   Even in Bristol, where " the dwellings of the lower classes " were said by Dr. Lyon Playfair to be " generally abominably filthy, full of vermin, and in a condition such as I have not seen in any of the large towns of Lancashire," he ascribed it " wholly to the want of means, and not to any inherent habits in the people themselves, from whom we, in very many instances, received loud complaints on this subject." [4]   Bristol was particularly badly off for water ; except in the case of the wealthy inhabitants its large population depended on scanty supplies from public or private wells ; of one private well it was reported that the owner " is obliged to pump twice a week with a steam-engine for the poor, in self-defence, for they rush in and take the water by pails." [5]

The town housewife had other difficulties besides want of water.   In summer, we read of the Derby courts and yards, " the passages are covered with creeping insects," [6] and the swarms of flies, bred in the universal refuse heaps, can be easily imagined.   The discovery that flies cause disease was not made till modern times, and nobody then connected them with the unquestionable fact that town dwellers were forced to live from

---

[1] 1840 Health of Towns Committee, p. 183.

[2] The Coroner for Middlesex complained in 1833 that children bathing in the Lea were chased by the police from their accustomed places where they knew the depth, and in consequence went into deep water and were drowned.—1833 Committee on Public Walks, p. 22.

[3] 1844 Health of Towns Commission, First Report, p. 340.

[4] 1845 Health of Towns Commission, Second Report, Appendix, part ii. p. 37, and Appendix, p. 72.

[5] 1844 Health of Towns Commission, First Report, p. 262.

[6] 1845 Health of Towns Commission, Second Report, Appendix, part ii. p. 274.

hand to mouth because no food would keep. The much-praised prudent housewife, with her little store of provisions, was only to be found amongst the ill-paid agricultural labourers ; if she moved into a town, though earnings might be doubled, prudence was useless ; meat turned at once, butter became rancid, bread became " dry and disagreeable." [1]

Man's life in crowded towns was bad, but woman's was infinitely worse ; it was the housewife who suffered most from the misery of defective sanitary arrangements, and from the constant struggle with dirt. That so many kept up some standards of decency and comfort is a marvel. Of the efforts made in the Yorkshire manufacturing towns, James Smith of Deanston gave a moving picture. " In the perambulation of the lower districts inhabited by the poorer classes, it was often very affecting to see how resolutely they strove for decency and cleanliness amidst the adverse circumstances ; to see the floors of their houses and the steps washed clean, made white with the hearth-stone, when the first persons coming into the house must spoil their labours with the mud from the street, kept filthy by neglect of proper scavenging ; to see their clothes washed and hung out to dry, but befouled by soot from the neighbouring furnaces ; and to see their children, attempted to be kept clean, but made dirty from the like causes ; and sometimes to see those children, notwithstanding all their care, pale, sickly, and droop-ing, evidently from the pestilential miasma of a natural stream converted into a sewer, and dammed up for the sake of mill power, in the hands of persons of great influence in the return of members to the town council, who are deaf to all statements of evidence of the evil, or of the possibility of amendment." [2] Many failed, and their case is put with sympathy and insight by R. A. Slaney : " Amidst these scenes of wretchedness, the lot of the female sex is much the hardest. The man, if, as is usually the case, in employment, is taken away from the annoyances around his dwelling during the day, and is generally disposed to sleep soundly after his labours during the night ; but the woman is obliged to remain constantly in the close court or neglected narrow alley where she lives, surrounded by all the

[1] 1842 Sanitary Condition of Labouring Population, General Report, p. 130.
[2] 1845 Health of Towns Commission, Second Report, Appendix, part ii. p. 319. James Smith of Deanston, the well-known agricultural engineer, afterwards became an inspector under the Public Health Act of 1848.

evils adverted to; dirty children, domestic brawls, and drunken disputes meet her on every side and every hour. Under such circumstances, the appropriate employments of a tidy housewife in brushing, washing, or cleansing, seem vain and useless efforts, and she soon abandons them." [1] Whether they struggled, or whether they abandoned the struggle, soured tempers and peevish complaints were the result of continual frustration. The melancholy of the town populations and their lack of animal spirits were conspicuous. It is almost a relief to read the description of the ill-cared-for house at Ashton-under-Lyne, where the mother went out to work ; squalid children might sprawl " on the flags, near the fire in danger of being burnt," the chairs, tables, stools, and culinary vessels might be " in dirt and disorder," but at any rate there was the gay sight of " two or three young nurses and their friends playing at shuttle-cock, and other games." [2]

A cynic might say that it was the Irish, with their low standards of cleanliness and comfort, who best adapted themselves to the conditions of town life. They found dirt, and they multiplied it lavishly, but they preserved a contented spirit however degraded their surroundings,[3] and their very recklessness helped them to keep clear of the trade in opiates, or the dealings with burial clubs, which formed a constant temptation to overwrought and harassed mothers.[4]

One fact must always be borne in mind in any attempt to picture the lives of the new industrial populations : they were in the main country folk by feelings and tradition, with their roots in fields and not in streets or courts. " A great deal of their pallid and care-worn appearance," said an acute observer of the inhabitants of Manchester, " is not so much to be attributed to the factory system, as it is to be attributed to the sweeping together of large masses of people, with little intelligence, under circumstances so unfavourable." These people, he

[1] 1845 Health of Towns Commission, Second Report, Appendix, p. 16.
[2] 1844 Health of Towns Commission, First Report, Appendix, p. 80.
[3] 1840 Health of Towns Committee, p. 150. Cf. John Roberton, *Observations on the Mortality and Physical Management of Children*, 1827, p. 32.
[4] " They said : ' God took care of young children who died,' " explained a doctor, commenting on the callousness of certain mothers; " they said, ' that their deaths did not much matter ; that life was full of hardships and misery ; and that the child was provided for when it died.' "—1844 Health of Towns Commission, First Report, p. 203. For opiates and burial clubs, see specially 1845 Health of Towns Commission, First Report, Appendix, part ii. pp. 61 ff. and 71.

explained, " were not brought up in or prepared for the new circumstances in which they have been placed." [1]   One illustration will serve to show what this change meant : In the Appendix to the First Report of the Health of Towns Commission [2] there are some plans and a vivid picture of a new suburb that was growing up on the outskirts of Preston.   With an eye to the future the builder has economised space, and set down in the fields two rows of eleven houses, each with a minute back-yard.   The yards of the one row back on to the yards of the other row, separated only by a long and narrow fosse or ditch, four feet deep, which acts as an open cesspool for these twenty-two houses, and for four more houses which are built up at one end of the two rows.   " The surface of refuse and decomposing matter," says the Report, exceeds " 3000 square feet."   Any visitor to this settlement would be aware of what Slaney once called " the absence of the decencies of life and the constant presence of disgusting and dirty objects."   And yet the inhabitants of these squalid houses had something of which the town populations were deprived.   " One woman expressed her great satisfaction at having removed from Albert Street to her present abode : it was ' so pleasant to hear the birds singing in a morning, and to see the flowers growing in the spring.' "

[1] 1840 Health of Towns Committee, pp. 72 and 73.   [2] P. 34.

CHAPTER VIII

THE LOSS OF PLAYGROUNDS: I

Wolves with the hearts of devils !
They steal our footpaths too !
The poor man's walk they take away,
The solace of his only day,
Where, now unseen, the flowers are blowing,
And, all unheard, the stream is flowing !
What worse could devils do ?

 EBENEZER ELLIOTT.

THE WEAVER

That beauty's in the handiwork of God,
The flowers I toil to imitate declare,
Tho' what their brightness on the earth's green sod
Be, I know not—I never saw them there.

The Poor Man's Guardian, August 1833.

In England it is not only children for whom play seems to be a necessity of life. A modern wit has drawn the English character in an epigram which gives to the passion for amusement its due place in English history. " One Englishman a fool: two Englishmen a football match ; three Englishmen the British Empire." This taste for games is not, of course, a recent development. Chamberlayne, writing on the English people in 1660, remarked that " the common people will endure long and hard labour, insomuch that after twelve hours' hard work, they will go in the evening to football, stockball, cricket, prison base, wrestling, cudgel playing, or some such like vehement exercise for their recreation." At all times there have been critics who have accused the English people of thinking their play more important than their work.

As industry turned country into town in the early nineteenth century, this national habit was checked and repressed in a drastic manner, for old playgrounds disappeared and new playgrounds were not provided. This change did not pass unnoticed, for a few far-sighted men in Parliament pressed for an inquiry, and secured the appointment of a Select Committee in 1833 to consider the deficiency of " Public Walks and Places of Exercise." The facts were presented to Parliament by this Committee. " As respects those employed in the three great Manufactures of the Kingdom, Cotton, Woollen, and Hardware, creating annually an immense Property, no provision has been made to afford them the means of healthy exercise or cheerful amusement with their families on their Holidays or days of rest." Nor did the Committee find other large towns in any better case. Of all but a very few they wrote : " With a rapidly increasing Population, lodged for the most part in narrow courts, and confined streets, the means of occasional exercise and recreation in the fresh air are every day lessened, as inclosures take place and buildings spread themselves on every side." This neglect, suggested the Committee, might be due to preoccupation with the late war. A century later it is easy to see that this is too simple an explanation, and that there were strong forces at work which public opinion, even when unpreoccupied, was powerless to control.

We propose in this chapter to examine the position of towns in whose neighbourhood there were commons or common fields.

In a community where there is plenty of waste land, and games are rude and uncomplicated, those who wish to play can easily find a playground. The people who live near what is called a common have no doubt that they can use it for recreation, whether stock is turned out on it or not by the Lord of the Manor and commoners. No questions of legal ownership trouble their minds. The difficulties begin when land rises in value, for legal rights then become important and the inhabitants become aware, from painful experience, of what has been called " the difference between popular conceptions and traditions and legal rights and conclusions." [1] Fortunately, it is not necessary to discuss at length the legal complexities, but it is necessary to understand how serious was the difference between the expectations encouraged by custom and history, and the rights recognised by the law, as the law stood, whilst the manufacturing towns were growing, and as it still stands, with certain recent modifications.

According to the legal view which ignored ancient tradition and relied upon the imposition of the feudal system as the

[1] Eversley, *Commons, Forests, and Footpaths*, p. 8.

starting-point of common rights, all rights of common came from the grant or permission of the Lord of the Manor who owned the soil of the common or waste. It might have been argued that since the lord owned the soil in virtue of a grant which carried with it the performance of certain duties,[1] the whole position should have been revised when those duties lapsed. But it was not revised, and in the eyes of the law the framework of feudalism still stood intact. Common rights came into being, said the law, because at some time or other the lord had granted his tenants the right to graze cattle or sheep or to cut wood or turf on the waste of the lord's manor. It was then from the lord's grant or permission or sufferance that all common rights were derived.[2]

Now, in a famous case in 1603 (Gatewards case) it was laid down that these rights could not be held by the inhabitants of a village or district merely as inhabitants. The term, said the judges, was too vague; common rights could only be held by owners of property. Thus if you owned a cottage by a common and were in the habit of turning out stock to graze on it, your right of common would probably be recognised as a legal possession in case of enclosure : you would have to be consulted, however perfunctorily, before enclosure could take place, and on enclosure some compensation, whether adequate or not, would be awarded you. If, on the other hand, you rented the cottage, however long you might have been in the habit of using the common for your animals, you had in law only been using your landlord's right, and when enclosure turned your cattle off, the compensation went, not to you, but to your landlord. But if you had only been using the common for walks or for games, there was no question of any right or of any compensation.[3] You might have had access to the common all your life; your forefathers for generations might have walked and played there; it would make no difference. Nobody

---

[1] Compare Fawcett, *Fraser's Magazine*, February 1870 : " When grants of land were originally made to private persons there was always associated with its possession the performance of some duty. The monarch made grants of land to barons on the condition that they should render to him a certain amount of armed assistance."

[2] See Scrutton, T. E., *Commons and Common Fields*, 1887, p. 41.

[3] It is true that by a judgment given in Charles II.'s time, the judges had decided that the inhabitants of a village in Oxfordshire had the right to play games on a village green, if they were accustomed to do so, even though the ground on which they played was private property; but this judgment seems to have lain in abeyance for many generations, and was not used in order to save spaces for recreation at the time of the enclosures.

had any legal right to be consulted about the common or what happened to it except the Lord of the Manor, the tithe owner, and the owners of property to which common rights were attached. In the words of one who fought a long and valiant battle in the second half of the nineteenth century and later, on behalf of public interests in common land : " According to the strict technical law, invented by the feudal lawyers—and superseding a much wider and more popular law, under which undoubtedly the commons were the common property of the village or community—the commons were the property of the Lords of Manors, and the tenants of their manors, and the public had no right to them, no matter how long or how much they had used them for recreation, no matter how necessary they might be for the health of the district." In the case of commons near towns, the public, Lord Eversley pointed out, had taken the place of cattle. " People took the place of cattle, they wore down the grass in lieu of browsing on it, the turf was more useful for games than for burning. The law, however, had not been pliant enough to recognize this practical transfer of user and custom, or to legitimize the public user which had thus ousted the private user." [1] The legal position was clearly put by a member of the 1844 Committee : " Notwithstanding that all the world are in the habit of walking about on commons, and turning themselves on, in fact they have not acquired any legal right by that, but, practically, they would lose something if they were deprived of it." [2]

It would seem reasonable to expect that old paths and rights of way across land that came under enclosure would remain intact even if the public were no longer free to use the common. But this was not the case. In Enclosure Acts the Commissioners were usually empowered, or rather ordered, to take the map of the area to be enclosed, wipe out existing ways (turnpike roads sometimes excepted), and refashion the whole highway system. When they had done their work, any paths that did not appear in the map attached to their award ceased automatically to be rights of way.[3] Commissioners were also sometimes empowered to stop up ways over old enclosures. The General Inclosure Act,

---

[1] House of Commons, February 18, 1876.
[2] 1844 Select Committee on Inclosure, p. 14.
[3] This provision has left an evil legacy to the present day.

passed in 1801, an Act designed to cheapen the expensive process of Parliamentary Enclosure by providing model clauses to be incorporated by reference in each private Enclosure Bill, expressly authorised Commissioners to " divert, turn, and stop up " ways. At the same time, it was enacted that if the Commissioners were empowered by any private Enclosure Bill " to stop up any old or accustomed Road passing or leading through any Part of the old Inclosures, in such Parish, Township, or Place," they had to obtain the concurrence of two Justices of the Peace " not interested in the Repair of such Roads." Enclosure thus might deprive you not only of your accustomed walks on the common, but also of footpaths in other parts of the parish as well.

An illustration will show that this legal interpretation of the rights of property put into the hands of the landowners in many places an almost unlimited power of depriving a community of its customary places for walks and games. We will take the case of Basford. In this small framework knitting town, a few miles north of Nottingham, with 1200 acres of forests, commons, and waste lands at its doors, the inhabitants before 1793 probably never thought about their playgrounds or wondered how they had been provided. They took them as a matter of course. After 1793 there were no playgrounds to think about, for an Inclosure Act swept the whole area into private hands.[1] The inhabitants of Basford did not easily adapt themselves to the changed conditions. Fifty years later it was stated that the want of open land for recreation was "a fruitful source of bickering and recrimination between the young men of the parish and the owners and occupiers of lands, trespasses on the part of the young men, for the purposes of cricket-playing and other games, being very common. There are now no common lands belonging to the parish. Formerly there were very extensive grounds of this class, but in 1793 these rights were resumed and the grounds enclosed, but without leaving a single acre for the use of the public." [2]

At Basford the disaster was catastrophic; in other cases, Sheffield for example, the process was spread over several years. Enclosure of one common was made easier by the fact that a

[1] 32 Geo. III. cap. 67, Private.
[2] 1845 Health of Towns Commission, Second Report, Appendix, part ii. p. 258.

second remained open ; enclosure of the second made easier by the precedent of the first. Enclosure Acts, it may be noted, were usually justified on the ground that the land was in its present state "incapable of improvement," whereas, if enclosed and handed over to private ownership, it would yield bounteous harvests. Round towns the big proprietors, and sometimes the small ones too, easily persuaded themselves that crops of villas (or slums, as the case might be) were as desirable to grow as crops of corn.[1] Incidentally they were even more profitable to the grower.

How little the need for recreation had been recognised in the growing districts, is illustrated in the case of enclosures at Bolton, Oldham, and Gateshead. A great deal of waste was enclosed in East Lancashire before this time, in the sixteenth and seventeenth centuries, by agreement or moral compulsion. Didsbury Moor, Withington Moor, Kersal Moor, and Chorlton Moor, and other waste land near Manchester, had been enclosed by the eighteenth century. But there were Acts for enclosing waste at Bolton and Oldham at the time when these towns were growing very rapidly. The Bolton Act, dated 1792,[2] contains rare, if not unique, provisions for applying the proceeds of enclosure to public purposes. Unfortunately recreation was not amongst those purposes. Although Great and Little Bolton were described in the Act as "large, populous, and trading Towns, and daily increasing," they were still large villages surrounded by open country. The Act directed that the 270 acres of Bolton Moor should be enclosed, and, after allotment of one acre for stone, and one-fifteenth for the Lords of the Manor, should be divided up into lots of not more than 4 acres and sold for 5000 years for the best annual rent offered, subject to the immediate payment of £10 an acre. The money was to be spent by trustees, who were given large powers by the Act, on widening, paving, lighting, watching, cleansing, and otherwise improving the streets of Great Bolton, and on supplying water for the free use of the inhabitants.[3] Any surplus was

[1] Compare the witness before the 1844 Committee on Inclosure (p. 373), who urges the enclosure of Heswall Common in the Wirral peninsula. "It is rocky ; a good portion of it would be scarcely fit for cultivation." Q. "What would you do with that?"—A. "It is valuable for the sites of villas."
[2] 32 Geo. III. cap. 71, Public.
[3] This purpose was not fulfilled, for a later Act of 1824 (5 Geo. IV. cap. 130, Local) established a company for supplying Great and Little Bolton with water.

to go towards the Poor Rates. Seventy-one trustees were appointed to administer the Act, forty-one for Great Bolton, with a residential qualification of £1000, and thirty for Little Bolton, with a qualification of £500. Two other Enclosure Acts of the usual type swallowed up other moor land in the Bolton district ; Chew Moor (68 acres) was enclosed in 1807,[1] Tonge Moor (acreage not stated) in 1812.[2] In neither case was any allotment made for recreation. The result was described in 1833. " The population of Bolton being nearly 45,000, there are no public walks, or open spaces in the nature of walks, or public gardens reserved at all in its vicinity ? "—" No." But, though no part of the moor was reserved for the purpose, games were still allowed on sufferance on ground that was technically enclosed.[3]

The case of Oldham is specially interesting. An area of 300 Lancashire acres (that is, about 480 ordinary acres), consisting of Green Acres Moor, North Moor, Hollingwood, and other commons and wastes, was inclosed in 1802 without any allotment for recreation.[4] Public interests, however, were not ignored, for 16 acres were allotted for a workhouse. It happened that Oldham was already well provided in this respect, and the land so reserved was left idle. In 1826 another Act was passed.[5] The population of Oldham had nearly doubled in the interval, and the case therefore for reserving this land for recreation was very much more pressing. The promoters of the Bill recognised the fact of this increase, but they asked for, and obtained, an Act, not to make provision for recreation, but to enable the churchwardens and overseers to let this site for building land in aid of the rates, since Oldham " hath become very populous and is rapidly increasing in population." [6]

At Gateshead 600 acres of Gateshead Fell were divided by an Act passed in 1809,[7] without any allotment being made for any public purpose, except one acre for a church and churchyard.

[1] 47 Geo. III. cap. 26, Session II., Local.   [2] 52 Geo. III. cap. 102, Local.
[3] 1833 Committee on Public Walks, p. 55.
[4] 42 Geo. III. cap. 59, Private. A curious feature of this Act is that the Lord of the Manor receives in his share all encroachments made within sixty years (those made by persons entitled to an allotment excepted), " whereon any Buildings have been erected or now forming, or being a Garden, Orchard, Yard, or Fold whether the same shall have been so inclosed with or without " the consent of the Lord of the Manor.
[5] 7 Geo. IV. cap. 67, Local.
[6] Population of Oldham : 1801, 21,677 ; 1821, 38,201 ; 1831, 50,513.
[7] 49 Geo. III. cap. 135, Local.

On the enclosure of a further 200 acres of commonable land in 1814,[1] the Windmill Hills, an area of about 10 acres, were left open and vested in the borough holders and freemen. It was disputed later whether this land belonged to its holders as their private property, on which they could build houses, or was, as the Corporation argued, merely vested in them for the benefit of the public. Gateshead, meanwhile, was reported as being in great need of public walks.[2] The question was not finally settled till 1861, when the borough holders handed over the ground to the Corporation, under a deed, with stipulations that it should be made an agreeable place of resort to the public.[3]

Blackburn affords a case where the need for recreation was recognised in the early seventeenth century, but forgotten later. In 1618 the 1266 acres[4] of common and waste lands were enclosed and divided up amongst the owners of land in Blackburn, but some 18 acres[4] were to be set out and used "for the mustering and training of people in that part, and for the recreation of the Inhabitants of the said Town, and for the good and profit of the said Town and Poor thereof, as a gift for ever. . . ." The rights of recreation had apparently been lost by 1833. "Is there any place," William Feilden, M.P. for Blackburn, was then asked, "to which the children of the humbler classes may resort for any game or exercise, any of those games they have been used to on holidays?" "None whatever," was the answer. Here, too, as in the case of Bolton, a certain amount of trespass on fields was permitted.[5] It is stated that "the remnant of the public recreation ground on the Towns Moor (set apart on the enclosure of Waste Lands in 1618)" was sold to a Railway Company in 1845 for £4701, and the proceeds used towards the purchase of Corporation Park in 1855.[6]

---

[1] 54 Geo. III. cap. 184, Local.

[2] "Few places stand more in need of public walks, or at least of vacant ground for the recreation and exercise of the inhabitants generally, and of the children in particular, than Gateshead."—Health of Towns Commission, Second Report, 1845, Appendix, part ii. p. 177.

[3] For this information we are indebted to the kindness of the Town Clerk of Gateshead.

In 1880 the Corporation bought Saltwell Park, an area of some 60 acres, for a recreation ground.

[4] The customary acres ($7\frac{1}{2}$ yards to a perch) are here turned into statute acres.

[5] 1833 Committee on Public Walks, p. 55.

[6] For particulars about Blackburn, see *History of Blackburn*, by W. A. Abram (1877), pp. 256, 259, and 378.

In some towns Lammas rights, that is, common rights of pasture for a limited period, not over commons or waste lands, but over cultivated fields or over meadows, after the harvest,[1] afforded the inhabitants valuable opportunities for games.[2] Nottingham is the most striking example. This town was hemmed in and its growth checked by large common fields, some 800 acres in extent, over which the freemen of the borough, about 3000 in number, possessed Lammas rights.[3] The freemen steadily opposed enclosure ; the Corporation supported them, and the result was an ingenious " heaping and clubbing of buildings upon one another " in the actual town. This condition of things was severely denounced by the Municipal Corporations Commission, and by the Health of Towns Commission, but it might be argued on the other side that, though nobody but the freemen had a legal right of common on the Lammas lands, in practice the public used them for recreation, and a bad slum in Nottingham with open fields close by, which could be used for games in summer, might be preferable to a less bad slum in Manchester, surrounded by other slums. We have a pleasing picture of these Lammas fields in summer in 1844.[4] " Does not that afford from the end of June to a certain period in the winter, a great space for recreation and amusement and so forth ? "—" No doubt ; at this season of the year you see it covered with parties playing at cricket and other games . . . I observed the meadows, as I came across last night, actually covered with cricket parties ; I should think not less than a hundred parties at various games . . ." The free-

[1] Under the old common field system of cultivation, after the harvest on Lammas day, August 12, " the hayward removed the fences, and the livestock of the community wandered over the fields before the common herdsman, shepherd, or swineherd."—Ernle, *English Farming, Past and Present*, p. 25.

[2] Compare Walsall, where the freeholders had rights of pasture over 20 acres of Lammas lands belonging to the Earl of Bradford ; " when the grass is mown it is used as a play place by children, and as a general walk by the inhabitants."—1833 Committee on Public Walks, p. 37.

Compare also Godalming, where extensive enclosures had been made in 1803 without any allotment for recreation. A witness before the 1844 Committee on Inclosure (p. 75) was asked : " How is Godalming itself off in point of greens, such as would afford the means of playing at cricket ? "—" We have no places of that description for the public except on certain meadows, after the grass is taken off ; we have a good deal of Lammas land. . . ." " That Lammas land does afford for a certain period of the year, a considerable means of recreation to the inhabitants ? "—" It does."

[3] " There is no doubt that at an early, and indeed till a comparatively recent period, the right was enjoyed by all the inhabitant householders paying scot and bearing lot."—Health of Towns Commission, Second Report, 1845, Appendix, part ii. p. 254.

[4] 1844 Committee on Inclosure, pp. 248 and 298.

men of Nottingham, however little they may have been moved by public spirit, did in fact perform a public service in delaying enclosure till public opinion had been educated.   When later the enclosure took place, a considerable area was set apart for recreation, and certain town-planning provisions introduced, which, however inadequate, made the new districts less insanitary than the old.[1]

But in other towns the public received less generous treatment from the freemen.   There were extensive Lammas fields at Coventry, but apparently they were not available for popular recreation.   The Health of Towns Committee reported in 1840 that enclosure of other open spaces (not apparently by Act of Parliament) has had great effect upon the habits of the weavers.[2] They had been accustomed to spend much of their very considerable leisure time in " football and quoits, and bandy and bowls, and cricket, which has been a game used from very early times."   " There was a large open space of several hundred acres, on which the poorer inhabitants used to desport themselves, in those games and amusements which gave them health, on times of holidays, which land has been enclosed, and from which amusements they are now debarred ? "   " Yes; it formed part of the old Royal Manor ; it is now called the Park, and is enclosed, and forms part of the property of the Marquis of Hertford."   The Mayor of Coventry, himself a weaver in his youth, was quoted as describing " the habits of the weavers of former times as those of greater activity though of more rudeness ; that they were more robust, though more rude ; that they had then abundant opportunity for exercise, but that now the lands are enclosed, and that they have only the roads to walk upon, or the pot-house to go into."   The freemen still had their Lammas rights, for the common fields were not enclosed until after this date, but it is clear from this description that the public were not allowed to use them.

The records of parliamentary enclosure are unsatisfactory, but in the case of non-parliamentary enclosure, there are no records at all.   Statistics of the total acreage enclosed by Acts of Parliament are largely guesswork ; nobody ventures even to guess the amount enclosed without resort to Parliament.   If a lord of the manor could win over the commoners to consent or

---

[1] See p. 296.   [2] See 1840 Health of Towns Committee, pp. 69 and 70.

to silence, either by buying up their common rights or in some other fashion, there was no legal obstacle to the enclosure of a common.[1] " Formerly," said a witness before the 1844 Committee on Inclosure, " twenty or thirty years ago, during the war, small commons were always so inclosed that I was concerned in."   But even supposing the commoners objected, if they were not people of substance, it was easy enough to ignore their objections.   The process can be watched in later times when a vigilant searchlight was turned on to it.   " He knew now an instance," said Fawcett in 1876, " of a common of which a few years ago not a single acre was inclosed ; but every autumn lately when he had visited it, there were 50 or 100 acres inclosed, and the commoners could not take any steps to resist it because a suit would cost from £1500 to £2000.   This was not justice.   It was a scandal which the House had power to prevent.   Thousands of acres of land were being inclosed in this illegal and arbitrary manner.   How had any illegal inclosure been prevented but by the public spirit of some influential person in the neighbourhood who was willing to go to the expense of a law-suit ? "[2]   Another speaker had quoted the notorious instances of Berkhampstead and Plumstead where public spirit and a long purse had recently saved valuable open spaces from arbitrary encroachments, in the first case by Lord Brownlow's Trustees, in the second by Queen's College, Oxford.   There is no reason to think that in earlier times lords of the manor were less acquisitive.   We hear less about it because the educated opinion of the day was all in favour of inclosing, and not anxious to protest against technical illegalities.

The circumstances that made it easy to enclose land made it easy also to close footpaths.   We have seen that arbitrary power was given to Enclosure Commissioners.   In cases where there was no enclosure any landowner could shut up a footpath, provided he could obtain the sanction of two Justices of the Peace, to be confirmed at the next Quarter Sessions.[3]   This sanction

---

[1] Nor was there till 1926.   [2] House of Commons, February 18, 1876.
[3] The absence of open spaces increased the probability that footpaths would be closed by landlords anxious to protect themselves from trespass.   " In the neighbourhood of many large towns it is shown in evidence that much damage is done by trespass on the fields adjoining footpaths, owing to the people having no other spot to which they can resort, and the damage is continually increasing as the population are more confined. . . ."—1833 Committee on Public Walks, p. 9 n.

was for the most part easily obtained. "The arbitrary power lately assumed by Magistrates in closing footpaths," said Mr. Harvey, M.P., in 1833, "had engendered much discontent among the poorer classes, who were thereby shut out from all means of wholesome recreation."[1] Here again, unless there happened to be in the neighbourhood a man of public spirit, able and willing to spend money in opposing him, a landowner could safely take liberties with the law. In Manchester, a Footpaths Preservation Society, composed of well-known citizens, was called into being in 1826 by a particularly notorious instance, where a magistrate himself flouted public opinion and public rights. This particular case was won, but "at a cost of £750 to the spirited vindicators of a public privilege."[2] By 1845, unfortunately, this society seems to have lapsed.

Apart from deliberate inclosures, as towns grew, opportunities for recreation were restricted by the advance of building on land in private hands. Thus, in Birmingham, though there were no parks, or public open spaces, or common lands, yet in the early nineteenth century a considerable portion of the population had gardens of their own. ". . . It is the custom at Birmingham," said a witness in 1833, "for the working men to have gardens at about a guinea a year rent, of which there are a great number round the town, and all the better parts of the workmen spend their leisure hours there; a considerable portion of land in the immediate vicinity of Birmingham is let at £12 an acre for these small gardens." "Are they enabled," he was asked, "to go there with their children?" "Their children and families," was the answer, "they have little summer-houses, where they spend their evenings and Sundays."[3] Nine years later it was reported that the gardens in which the mechanics "took great delight" were "now for the most part built over, and the mechanics of the town are gradually losing this source of useful and healthy recreation."[4] The Spitalfields weavers suffered the same loss. A description given in 1833 of the London of the past shows that it had been a less sombre town. "Do you remember," a witness was asked, "a time when the humbler and middle classes used either by usage

[1] House of Commons, February 21, 1833.   [2] Prentice's *Manchester*, p. 293.
[3] 1833 Committee on Public Walks, p. 36.
[4] 1842 Report on Sanitary Condition of Labouring Population, p. 275

or by sufferance to enjoy themselves in the fields in its vicinity?"
"I remember," he answered, "the fields at the back of the
British Museum being covered every night in summer by at
least from 100 to 200 people at cricket and other sports . . .
wherever there was an open space to which people could have
access they would play, but now they are driven from all." [1]

It was not only in the towns that games were discouraged.
Chadwick, giving evidence about drunkenness in 1834, mentioned
that "in rural districts, as well as in the vicinities of some of the
towns" he had heard "very strong representations of the mischiefs
of the stoppage of footpaths and ancient walks, as contributing,
with the extensive and indiscriminate inclosure of commons
which were playgrounds, to drive the labouring classes to the
public house." [2]   Sometimes a landowner with a larger outlook
intervened to save playgrounds, like Mr. Monck, of Coley
House, Reading, who realised that neither grown-up villagers
nor their children could live by work alone.   "Since the enclosures have been made," he said, "I think some place should
be provided for the exercise and recreation of the working
classes, and especially for their children."   He set aside a four-
acre field as a playground.   "They have now their cricket
matches, their quoit playing, and their revels there.   Sheep and
cows feed on it; so it is no great loss to me.   I let it for four
pounds a year to a man, on condition that he cuts the hedges
and keeps it neat." [3]   Where there were no Mr. Moncks, and
they were not common, the country people might be even worse
off than the inhabitants of a growing town.   In the latter, fields
awaiting the builder often afforded temporary playgrounds; since
they were useless for agriculture there were no crops to injure,
and the question of trespass was not looked into too closely;
bricks and mortar would anyhow soon oust the intruders.   "In
the rural districts," on the other hand, "the children and young

---

[1] A less agreeable aspect of the use of open spaces in London is given by William
Lovett, who described how when he first came to town in 1821 he used to see "the
working classes of London flocking out into the fields on a Sunday morning or during
a holiday in their dirt and deshabille, deciding their contests and challenges by pugilistic
combats.   It was no uncommon thing at that time on taking a Sunday morning's walk
to see about twenty of such fights."—1849 Committee on Public Libraries, p. 178.
Cf. also Place on the duck-hunting, badger-baiting, and the setting of dogs at cats
in the water in the fields and ponds to the east of Tottenham Court Road.—1835
Committee on Education, p. 70.
[2] 1834 Committee on Drunkenness, p. 36.
[3] 1842 Report on Sanitary Condition of Labouring Population, p. 278.

persons of the villages have frequently no other places for recreation than the dusty road before their houses or the narrow and dirty lanes, and accidents frequently take place from the playing of children on the public highways.   If they go into the fields they are trespassers, and injure the farmers." [1]

Nowhere was the neglect of any provision for exercise and open-air amusements more striking than in Manchester.   The commons and wastes of the district had been, for the most part, early enclosed, and were now swamped by the tide of buildings. Newton Heath, a common or waste of 140 acres which survived through the eighteenth century, was enclosed in 1802. [2]   No provision was made on its enclosure for any recreation, but a liberal allotment was made in aid of the Poor Rates.   " At present," wrote Dr. J. P. Kay in 1833, " the entire labouring population of Manchester is without any season of recreation, and is ignorant of all amusements, excepting that very small portion which frequents the theatre.   Healthful exercise in the open air is seldom or never taken by the artisans of this town, and their health certainly suffers considerable depression from this deprivation.   One reason of this state of the people is, that all scenes of interest are remote from the town, and that the walks which can be enjoyed by the poor are chiefly the turnpike roads, alternately dusty or muddy.   Were parks provided, recreation would be taken with avidity, and one of the first results would be a better use of the Sunday, and a substitution of innocent amusement at all other times, for the debasing pleasures now in vogue.   I need not inform you how sad is our labouring population here." [3]   Ten years later the position was unchanged.   " With a teeming population," wrote Mr. Mott, " literally overflowing her boundaries, she has no public walks or resorts, either for the youthful or the adult portion of the community to snatch an hour's enjoyment."   On one occasion, and one only, such institutional gardens as existed were opened to this melancholy population : " On the holiday given at Manchester in celebration of Her Majesty's marriage, extensive arrangements were made for holding a chartist meeting, and for getting up what was called a demonstration of the working classes, which greatly alarmed the municipal

[1] 1842 Report on Sanitary Condition of Labouring Population, p. 277.
[2] 42 Geo. III. cap. 107, Private.   [3] 1833 Committee on Public Walks, p. 66.

magistrates. Sir Charles Shaw, the Chief Commissioner of Police, induced the mayor to get the Botanical Gardens, Zoological Gardens, and Museum of that town, and other institutions thrown open to the working classes at the hour they were urgently invited to attend the chartist meeting. The mayor undertook to be personally answerable for any damage that occurred from throwing open the gardens and institutions to the classes who had never before entered them. The effect was that not more than 200 or 300 people attended the political meeting, which entirely failed, and scarcely 5s. worth of damage was done in the gardens or in the public institutions by the workpeople, who were highly pleased. A further effect produced was, that the charges before the police of drunkenness and riot were on that day less than the average of cases on ordinary days." [1]

[1] 1842 Report on Sanitary Condition of Labouring Population, pp. 275 and 276.
A writer in 1842, speaking of the Botanical Gardens in Manchester, makes this remark : " Once in the year, indeed (a circumstance which is lauded by your nonthinkers as a mighty stretch of benevolence), the Sunday School children, amounting to several thousands, are permitted to walk through these beautiful grounds; and let it be remembered that on such occasions, not a shrub or flower has been injured—a fine commentary upon the charges generally brought against the people in excuse for our neglect of them. During the remaining part of the year ' the brazen gates are closed,' except to annual subscribers, admitted by ballot."—" Characteristics of Manchester," *North of England Magazine*, vol. i. p. 164.

CHAPTER IX

THE LOSS OF PLAYGROUNDS: II

LITTLE notice was taken, till 1833, of the social consequences of enclosure near the towns. In that year, as we have seen in our last chapter, an active and public-spirited member, R. A. Slaney, brought the subject before Parliament, and a Select Committee was appointed to consider " Public Walks and Places of Exercise." Slaney pointed out the advantage of the presence in the Reformed Parliament of members representing the large towns. The Committee in their Report recommended a liberal provision of public walks, proposing that in all future Acts for Turnpike Roads or Canals to towns above a certain population, a clause should be inserted reserving land on either side of the road or the canal to some 100 yards in breadth, for a certain distance, for " a broad and ample Walk, with two Rows of Trees, and room for Seats." They attempted to disarm opposition to this scheme by pointing out the enhanced value of building plots behind these strips. They laid stress on the social advantages of such promenades, which would stimulate the care for " cleanliness, neatness, and personal appearance." For open spaces in general they trusted largely to private liberality, suggesting that when this failed, there should be public grants or help from the rates.

The recommendations of the Committee had little immediate effect,[1] but they had considerable influence on the mind of Parliament. This was illustrated in the debates on a Bill of Lord Ellenborough's in 1834, to facilitate the enclosure of

[1] The purchase of Primrose Hill from Eton College in 1842 for £20,236, supplied by the Land Revenues of the Crown (see Returns relative to Metropolitan Parks, 1854) was the first result. The Committee had urged the Government to acquire this " healthy open spot which the humbler classes have been in habit of visiting with their families in fine weather time out of mind " and so save it from being used for building purposes.

common fields. Lord Ellenborough announced (February 11) that he was against the enclosing of wastes; few of them were profitable to cultivate at the present price of corn. " Besides this, he thought a right to common was a public advantage. The poor man saved a small sum and bought a small piece of land, the great benefit of which to him was, that there was connected with it a right of common." His aim was only to prevent the inconveniences of the common field system of agriculture. The Bill passed the Lords, and went down to the Commons, where it was bitterly attacked (July 31 and August 4), partly on the misconception that commons would be enclosed under it, partly on the good ground that it would interfere with recreation. Supporters of the Bill, including T. G. Estcourt who had charge of it, declared that recreation was not affected by it, since it was concerned only with agricultural improvement, but John Cam Hobhouse, now member for Nottingham, spoke against the Bill on behalf of his constituents who, if it passed, would lose the cricket and other sports now allowed on the Lammas lands. In spite of the willingness of the promoters to introduce an amendment exempting land round big towns,[1] the Bill was defeated by 34 votes to 14. In the course of the debate many speakers condemned enclosure as interfering with " healthful recreation and innocent enjoyment," and mention was made of successful opposition to attempts to enclose Hampstead Heath.[2]

The strength of the new anti-enclosure movement was shown again, though in a less vigorous fashion, in 1836, when the Bill for enclosing common fields was again considered. Though the Act was passed,[3] a clause was inserted exempting common fields within a certain radius of big towns from enclosure under the Bill. The importance of Lammas lands for recreation was thus recognised. It was specifically stated in the Act that nothing in it was to authorise the " Inclosure of any Waste whatsoever," and the radius round towns in which common

---

[1] Potter and Cutlar Fergusson pointed out that the rapid rise of northern towns made such an amendment of little use.

[2] Potter (July 31) rejoiced that the House of Commons had that session thrown out three Enclosure Bills on the grounds of injury to the poor. These were Bucklebury in Berks, Aston and Coate in Oxon, and Kingsclere in Hants. There was an interesting debate on the Bucklebury Bill due to John Walter's exposure of its injustice.

[3] 6 and 7 William IV. cap. 115.

fields were not to be enclosed under the Act was as follows :

Towns of	5,000 inhabitants	.	.	1 mile.
,,	15,000 ,,	.	.	$1\frac{1}{2}$ miles.
,,	30,000 ,,	.	.	2 ,,
,,	70,000 ,,	.	.	$2\frac{1}{2}$,,
,,	100,000 ,,	.	.	3 ,,
London	. .	.	.	. 10 ,, [1]

Perhaps the most interesting example of the awakened interest in public rights was Peel's attempt to amend the Municipal Corporations Bill in Committee in 1835. We have seen that there were attached to many towns common lands over which the privileged class of freemen had legal rights, which the public in some cases could use for recreation. When the Whigs brought in their measure for reforming the government of towns, Peel obtained the insertion of a clause which, had it survived, might have made considerable difference to the disposal of these lands.[2]

Peel's view was " that most of the property of corporations was intended for the benefit of the community at large, and it would be desirable that the community should recover it as soon as possible." By long prescription it had been appropriated to the use of certain descriptions of inhabitants only, and it was now desirable that it should be put "into the hands of the commonalty as speedily as possible consistent with justice to the rights of individuals." [3]   The Whigs accepted Peel's views ;

[1] The Act simplified and cheapened the procedure for enclosing common fields and common meadows. Two-thirds in number and value could appoint a Commissioner or Commissioners, without application to Parliament. Seven-eighths could manage the business without a Commissioner at all.

The same year (1836) the Over Enclosure Bill was defeated after a lively debate (May 18, 1836).

[2] See debate in House of Commons, June 24, 1835.

[3] ". . . Mr. Maitland, in his interesting work *Township and Borough* (Cambridge, University Press, 1898), suggests that the rights of pasture of freemen in a corporate borough are a survival of the rights which existed throughout the village communities of England. A township of size and importance was able to assert itself as a community, and by degrees to obtain recognition in that capacity. A small rural township, on the other hand, for the sake of obtaining some cohesion, and under the pressure of troublous times, gradually crystallised round the Lord of the Manor as its nucleus, and thus the property in the waste lands, which in the one case became vested in the Corporation, in the other was ascribed to the lord, the actual use of the land remaining, throughout the Middle Ages, the same in both cases."—*Open Spaces, Footpaths, and Rights of Way*, Sir Robert Hunter, Second Edition, p. 87.

but there was some discussion as to the rights of individuals. Should "inchoate rights" be considered, or only existing rights? Some Tories offered violent opposition, but ultimately two clauses were inserted in the Bill to the effect that in future the common lands and public stock of the town, and the rents and profits thereof, were to belong to the borough and not to certain individuals, though the present privileged holders and living persons, who would in the natural course of events obtain the privilege (sons, daughters, apprentices), were to retain their privileges till death, after which they would accrue for the benefit of the Borough Fund. The Council of the Borough were also given power to buy up the rights of common and other privileges at a price determined by a Jury of Quarter Sessions. These clauses were sent up to the House of Lords unanimously. There they were turned out of the Bill. The House of Commons and the House of Lords looked at the question from opposite points of view. Whereas a custom had prevailed of taking the common lands and rents and profits " for the particular Benefit " of certain persons, " and of not applying the same to public purposes," it was desirable, in the view of the House of Commons, that the common lands, etc., should revert to the public. Whereas the custom had prevailed of using the common lands, etc., for the particular benefit of certain persons, and not for public purposes, it was unjust, in the view of the House of Lords, to deprive the beneficiaries of their privileges.[1] The House of Commons was unhappily so much occupied with fighting the Lords on other points, that it accepted defeat on this.

The next move for the defence of public rights was made by Hume. On March 9, 1837, he proposed a resolution in the House of Commons " that in all Inclosure Bills provision be made for leaving an open space sufficient for the purposes of exercise and recreation of the neighbouring population." Peel, then leader of the Opposition, though doubtful about the actual form of the resolution, gave warm support to Hume's object. He pointed out, with truth, that the subject had been urged on the attention of the Legislature, but that the Legislature had

---

[1] Compare Raumer's comments on this incident, *England in 1835*, vol. iii. p. 310 : " In the first place the Upper House has in the whole discussion kept in view and advocated private rights; the Lower House, public rights."

refused to attend.   He laid down a sound doctrine that though the people might have no legal right to portions of waste lands or commons " they had a moral right," and he urged that even where no enclosure took place it would be a " wise and prudent expenditure of public money " to give a grant of £5000 or £10,000 to aid local authorities.

Hume's motion was passed.   It was supplemented two years later by Harvey, who moved (April 9, 1839) a resolution, afterwards made into a standing order, that in all Enclosure Bills " provision be made for leaving an open space in the most appropriate situation sufficient for purposes of exercise and recreation of the neighbouring population," and that provision be made " for efficient fencing of the allotment."   Harvey made a long speech about the iniquities of Enclosure Bills, and the small allowance made for recreation allotments, instancing 3 acres out of 1300, or 10 to 20 out of 10,000.   He suggested that there should be " a poor man's Commissioner " to see that a suitable reservation was made, and urged the House to protect the poor in view of the " spirit of the times and the symptoms moving around them."

The intentions of the House of Commons were good, but the actual allotments made under these standing orders were meagre.[1]   An illustration is afforded by the case of Bradford. Near Bradford there was an open space of from 20 to 30 acres called Fairweather Green.   According to a witness before the 1840 Health of Towns Committee,[2] this space was used for games by " the population for five and six miles round, it is the only place for the purpose in the whole neighbourhood."   But whilst this Committee was sitting, a private Bill was passing through Parliament, prepared by Mr. Lister, one of the largest proprietors concerned, to enclose this green and some other parcels of waste land, amounting in all to 170 acres.[3]   Mr.

---

[1] A parliamentary return for 1841, giving the Bills passed since 1837 and the number of acres allotted for recreation, supplies some information, but it is defective.   Out of 63 Acts mentioned, particulars are given in only 34 cases.   These cover an acreage of 41,420, out of which some 222 acres are set apart for recreation, that is 1 acre out of every 186.   If one peculiar case (Haverford West), where 88 acres out of 600 are reserved, be excluded, the proportion works out at 1 acre to every 304.   Compare the proportion from 1845 to 1875 of 1 to every 352.   See Eversley, op. cit. p. 16.

[2] Pp. 91 and 92.

[3] 3 and 4 Vict. cap. 3, Private.   The witness explained the absence of public opposition to the enclosure as follows : " This ground has been latterly used by the Chartists, and it has got into bad odour, but I do not think that a good reason for inclosing the

Joseph Ellison, the witness referred to, protested against the reservation in the Act of 3 acres only " as a Place of Exercise and Recreation for the neighbouring Population," a population that he estimated at 120,000. On Fairweather Green, he pointed out, it was the custom to play at cricket, and " a game we call spell and nur; they will drive a ball, 10, 11, 12, 13 and 14 score; they cannot play at those games in three acres." [1]

When considering the small size of the recreation allotments, we must remember that a tiny playground, combined with a fairly broad walk, was all that most members of Parliament thought necessary for the working classes. Roebuck was almost the only man who saw the need for bigger spaces. " On the commons, the sports of the village took place. (Laughter.) They might laugh if they liked ; he considered this to be a point of much importance. He liked that the poor should have the right of going on the commons with their wives and families ; he liked to go himself among the furze bushes, and he did not wish to take away what he enjoyed himself from them. . . ." When reminded by another speaker that already in all Enclosure Bills " a portion of land for the exercise of the poor " was set aside, Roebuck retorted, " Yes, a small space ; I am for a large common." [2]

There was another use of land that was of great value to inhabitants of towns. To indoor workers gardening can be an amusement. The allotment system, it was truly said, " partly supplies that deficiency of innocent amusement and rational recreation which weighs so particularly upon the lower

ground. I am happy to say that Chartism is very rapidly dying away, but if the lower orders have not places where they can engage in sports, it is the very thing to drive them to Chartism ; there cannot be a better thing to keep their minds engaged in matters of that kind."—P. 92.

[1] Compare also the recreation allotment at Llangerniew in Denbigh, 1840 (3 and 4 Vict. cap. 11, Private). Out of the 1500 acres enclosed the Commissioner was instructed to set out not more than 4 or less than 2 acres for a place for exercise and recreation for the neighbouring population. We have his own description of how he interpreted this. " I set out two acres ; I consulted with all the neighbours where I should put out those acres of recreation-ground, and they suggested that I should add it to the turbary in the bog which we drained to produce the turbary ; the two acres are added there, and they joke me and say it is a place for bog-trotting." " Do you think the turbary would make a very good cricket ground ? "—" Yes, now it would ; it is very soft." " Perhaps it is a little too soft ? "—" No, it is dry since drained." " You have two acres added to the turbary ? "—" Yes ; it adjoins the turbary, and is a turbary." The same witness was asked : " There is plenty of space for people to run about in after this inclosure is made, is not there ? " He answered : " Yes, along the roads."—1844 Committee on Inclosure, p. 162.

[2] House of Commons, June 21, 1843.

classes of this country." [1]   Naturally the chief demand was
from districts where the workers still regulated their own hours.
A witness before the Select Committee on Allotments described
the enthusiasm for allotments among the framework knitters of
Hinckley.   The operatives worked from 13 to 16 hours a day,
but did no work after 12 on Saturdays, or on Mondays.   He
explained that they could work their allotments on Saturdays,
instead of going to the public-house.   Otherwise Saturday
afternoon was a dreary time.   " It is very uncomfortable for
a poor man to stay at home if his wife is cleanly and wishes to
clean up for Sunday ; it is very uncomfortable to sit in the
midst of the damp." [2]   A letter to the Committee from a man
who had set out 2000 allotments on the Duke of Newcastle's
land in Notts, for labourers, colliers, and mechanics, also described the advantages. [3]   Allotments were desirable, he said,
under every enclosure, specially near towns, for when a man left
work in the summer, " What can he do ?   How can he pass his
time ?   The extent of his habitation being, perhaps, a room
12 feet by 14 feet in a close court, and with three, four, or five
children, he cannot remain there until bedtime ; if he goes out,
he has no resort but the beer-shop."   Round Nottingham
itself, in spite of all the open land, the appetite for allotments was
widespread ; there were quantities of little gardens near, some
said 1000, some said 5000, rented at 1d. a yard, and used " for
growing flowers, and the growing of fruits for prizes to a very
considerable extent, and the cultivation of vegetables for the
family." [4]

In the Midlands there was a flourishing society known as the
Northern and Midland Counties Artisans' Labourers' Friend
Society, with branches in Leicestershire, Derbyshire, Northampton, Notts, and Warwickshire. [5]   Its object was to promote
allotments by acquiring and letting land.   There were 63
branches, letting out about 800 acres, in quarter of an acre plots ;
the society acted as middleman, inducing the landowner to let

[1] Select Committee on Allotments, 1843, p. iv.
[2] *Ibid.* p. 82.   [3] *Ibid.* p. 137.
[4] Select Committee on Inclosure, 1844, pp. 227 and 297.   Compare also William
Miles, M.P., before 1843 Committee on Allotments, p. 115, on the large number of
gardens round Nottingham, held generally by stocking weavers.   ". . . they seem,
instead of frequenting the pot-house, to work early and late in the gardens, and it is
a source of amusement to them."
[5] Select Committee on Allotments, 1843, pp. 90 and 101.

the land, and paying him a lump sum.   The Secretary mentioned that the Earl of Chesterfield had given up twenty more acres for allotments near Nottingham, because there had been less poaching on his game preserves since they had come into being; also "the cultivation of allotments withdrew their attention from politics."[1]

In Yorkshire there seems to have been a considerable demand. A land agent, who was about to lay out some land in allotments for Lord Dartmouth near Huddersfield, described "the desire to possess land in manufacturing districts" as "extraordinary."[2] At Leeds there were thirteen acres let in allotments by Mr. Marshall, the flax mill owner, to some 140 holders, of every factory trade.   They were almost all new to the work, but the success had been such that many operatives were now anxious for land.   Mr. Gott, the woollen manufacturer, also let a few allotments.[3]

But though allotments were successful when tried, the supply did not equal the demand.   The 140 holders in Leeds represented about one in a thousand of the population.   Even in the framework knitting areas the 3200 holders under the Labourers' Friend Society, and the 2000 under the Duke of Newcastle, added together, do not cover a large proportion.   William Cowper mentioned a society in Leicestershire of 1000 members in different parishes, all wanting allotments but unable to get hold of a single acre.[4]   The districts where the supply equalled the demand were, in fact, a very small part of the country.[5]

It might seem at first sight that enclosure would afford a good opportunity for making allotments, for when land was enclosed other considerations were thrust aside in the interests of increased cultivation.   But spade cultivation counted for little on these occasions.   The objection was put bluntly by one of the members of the 1844 Committee on Inclosure (p. 11) : the more

---

[1] Select Committee on Allotments, 1843, p. 93.

[2] *Ibid.* p. 42.

[3] In the Manchester district, on the other hand, one witness (pp. 62 and 64), the relieving officer of the Chorlton Union, said that allotments would be useless.   "I do not see that it (*i.e.* garden ground) would be any advantage to the operatives, inasmuch as they go to the mill at half-past five in the morning, ˚nd do not leave till half-past seven at night."   Again : ". . . taking Manchester as the data, a man would become sufficiently weary with his fourteen hours a day, and I think he could never apply himself to anything else."—*Ibid.* p. 126.

[4] House of Commons.   Debate on Field Gardens Bill, July 10, 1844.

[5] See *ibid.* March 4 ,1845.

you took for allotments, the less there was to be divided up amongst the various proprietors. In case of enclosures near towns, land was of course more valuable, so this objection operated there even more strongly. This was well illustrated by the evidence of an experienced land agent in the Liverpool and Birkenhead district, who was urging enclosures in the Wirral peninsula.[1] " Do you think, in case of inclosure, there would be a general willingness to give allotments of land to the cottagers ? "—" I am persuaded that would be the first object of the principal landowners." " To those who have no rights of common ? "—" Yes." " Are allotments now given to the labourers in the adjoining townships which are inclosed ? "— " I do not think they are." " In the event of the inclosure of these commons, do you think there would be any objection on the part of the proprietors, and persons having rights of common, to give up a portion for allotments to the poor, whether in their own or in the adjoining townships ? "—" I think there would be considerable objection on account of the lands growing into such great value. It would be giving what they would not like to give." " From their being of such great value, as being near Liverpool and Birkenhead ? "—" Yes."

The Committee on Allotments (1843) thus described the position. " Garden allotments are to be met with in all agricultural counties, but have not become universal in any one of them ; they have existed in the manufacturing districts for a short period and to a limited extent." What was the cause ? " The desire of obtaining the tenancy of land appears to be universal among the mechanics and artisans of manufacturing towns and villages, as well as among the inhabitants of rural districts ; but in both cases the difficulty of procuring land has opposed a continual obstacle to the gratification of this desire." Some landowners, as we have seen, were willing to let their land in this way, but the business of collecting the rents and dealing with a large number of tenants made the system unpopular with land agents.

Attempts were made in Parliament, both before and after the Report of the Committee on Allotments, to increase the supply.[2]

---

[1] Select Committee on Inclosure, 1844, p. 376.

[2] *E.g.* in 1833 Mr. Pryme moved that in all Inclosure Bills the Commissioners should set aside 1 acre to every 25 inhabitants for allotments, and early in 1843 Mr. Stanton and Mr. Ferrand both made proposals on the subject.

Lord Ashley and William Cowper[1] both introduced Bills for overcoming the difficulties on lines suggested by the Committee. Ashley, who pointed out the trouble and expense to landlords of letting small portions of ground, with the consequent scarcity of field gardens in crowded districts, proposed the establishment of a Board in London with powers to purchase and hire and let allotments, and to set up loan funds. He mentioned the existence near many large towns of plenty of waste and common land that might be used for allotments.[2]   Cowper, whose proposal had a rather longer life, suggested the establishment in every parish, where a majority so desired, of a Field Gardens Board, with power to lease and to let.[3]   His Bill, in a mutilated form, passed the Commons and reached the Lords, who rejected it, and the only result of the Allotments agitation, so far as parliamentary action was concerned, was a meagre clause in the General Enclosure Act of 1845.

We have seen that during the thirties there was considerable concern in Parliament for the loss of public rights by enclosure. Yet in 1845 Parliament passed a General Enclosure Act[4] making it easier to convert land that was still available for the public enjoyment into private property. Legally, as we have said, the public had no claim to use or to wander over this land ; practically they were not and could not be kept out. To obtain the full benefit of what the law said belonged to them and to them alone, to shut up the land and shut others out, the lord of the soil and the owners of common rights had to gain in each case the consent of Parliament. In the Act of 1845 a general consent was given. What had become of the concern of the thirties ? Why was Parliament so ready to give this consent, and to allow the closing-up of vast tracts that had lain open from time immemorial ? Population was increasing rapidly, means of transport were increasing rapidly, and people were moving about outside towns. It would have seemed reasonable to expect that Parliament would be not less but more concerned in the forties than in the thirties.

The answer is to be found in the peculiar circumstances of

---

[1] Afterwards Lord Mount Temple. Well known later as an active member of the Commons Preservation Society.
[2] House of Commons, July 24 and 26, 1843.
[3] House of Commons, July 10 and 17, 1844 ; March 4, April 9, May 7, July 2, 1845.
[4] 8 and 9 Vict. cap. 118.

agriculture, combined with a disastrous confidence in statistics. The pressure for making enclosure easier and cheaper, which had produced the 1801 Act, became vigorous again in the early forties. The agricultural depression, in the course of which the Board of Agriculture had been dissolved, in 1822, began to lift. Eighteen thirty-seven has been given as the year which marks the beginning of the period of high farming.[1] With the researches of the great German chemist Liebig, agricultural chemistry opened up new vistas of improvement; artificial manures, guano, rape dust, bones, etc., were introduced, new systems of drainage were discussed and employed, new agricultural machinery came into use. The *Journal of the Royal Agricultural Society* (founded 1838) which began publication in 1840, reflects this new confidence in the application of science to agriculture.

As we have pointed out, the 1836 Act to facilitate the enclosure of common fields without recourse to Parliament had expressly excluded commons and waste lands from its scope, and Lord Ellenborough, who originally introduced the measure, deprecated any interference with them. [2] But by the forties the attitude towards commons was changed, for the new science of agriculture seemed to promise that these waste places would blossom under private ownership. The question of the expense of enclosure became vital. The best common field districts had mostly been already enclosed; the common fields that remained were not so productive, the commons and wastes obviously required a good deal to be spent on them before they could become profitable. Meanwhile the price of corn had gone down. Thus whereas in 1801 the high price of corn gave an impetus to enclosure, in the forties the low price of corn had a similar effect.[3]

In 1843 the movement for enclosure received a fresh and

---

[1] See Lord Ernle on the revival, *English Farming, Past and Present*, chap. xvii.

[2] A good deal of waste land was illegally enclosed under the 1836 Act (6 and 7 William iv. cap. 115): see 1844 Committee on Inclosure, p. 18. The enclosure was legalised by the 1845 Act.

[3] See Memorandum to 1844 Committee on Inclosure, p. 259 : " Now, so long as the produce of land (wheat, for instance) fetched £4, £5, or £6 per quarter, this expense in many cases was submitted to rather than forego the advantage of enjoying lands in severalty and improving their cultivation. But, since the price of wheat has sunk to 50s. or 55s. a quarter, the expense attending inclosures by Three Commissioners could no longer be endured, and, comparatively, no Inclosure Bills have been applied for."

disastrous impulse from the statisticians. A parliamentary return asked for by Lord Worsley was published (June 9 and 14, 1843) giving an estimate of the common or waste land in the parishes in which tithes had been commuted under the Tithes Commutation Act of 1836. The total quantity of land in these parishes amounted to 8,616,115 acres; the estimated quantity of common or waste land in those parishes to 1,860,234 acres. As the total area of England and Wales is some 37 million acres, a simple and irresistible rule-of-three sum gave a total area of some eight million acres of uncultivated common or waste land; this seemed to mean that more than a fifth of the whole soil of England and Wales was lying ready for the application of artificial manures. Add to this eight millions a rough estimate of two million acres, still under the common field system of cultivation, and you had a round total of ten million acres awaiting improvement.

The prevailing optimism was well expressed by Lord Palmerston. "In England and Wales there were about 37,000,000 acres, and it was calculated that of these 37,000,000 acres 10,000,000 would come under the operation of the present bill, and it was in evidence before the committee that setting aside the temporary employment which would be given in their enclosure, and in drainage, tilling, and in erecting those buildings which would be consequent on enclosure, the permanent additional employment given to the labouring classes might be stated at one labourer and his family for every 50 acres; so that if this calculation were applied to the 10,000,000 acres, there would be given by their enclosure additional employment to 200,000 agricultural families." [1]

A later and more sceptical generation has pointed out, first, that the estimate of the commons or wastes in the commuted parishes was hastily and incorrectly made; second, that the area of the commuted parishes was too small to admit of any trustworthy generalisation.[2] A parliamentary return of 1873 made a more modest estimate of 2,632,772 acres of commons or common fields, which with the 618,000 enclosed since the former estimate, would have made the total some three and a

---

[1] House of Commons, July 4, 1845. See *Times* Report, July 5.
[2] See Sir Robert Hunter, "The Movements for the Inclosure and Preservation of Open Lands," *Journal of Royal Statistical Society*, June 1897.

quarter instead of some ten millions. Even this reduced total, it may be noted, has been subjected to devastating criticism as regards the common fields.[1] At the time of the first estimate the statisticians were unchallenged. To those living in the hungry forties, the ten million acres opened up a vast prospect. The anti-Corn Law campaign made the whole question acute. Repealers, however anxious for importation, could hardly oppose a measure to increase home-grown supplies; anti-repealers saw here an answer to the agitation. Instead of allowing foreign wheat to enter free, turn those 60,000 acres in Surrey, and those wide Yorkshire and Welsh moors, and that great stretch of hills that runs from Derby up into Scotland, into prairies of waving corn, tended by prosperous, industrious, and virtuous labourers. Nothing seemed impossible with the growth of scientific agriculture.

In the year in which this return was printed, Lord Worsley, who, it should be noted, was himself unconnected with any enclosure and acted solely in the public interest, introduced a Bill for the enclosure of commons, if two-thirds of those interested asked for it, by means of a permanent public department of Commissioners, without any application to Parliament, and without any specific provision for recreation allotments or for field gardens. The only safeguards provided in the Bill against wholesale and anti-social enclosure were (1) a provision that when the draft award was drawn up, one-fourth of those interested could petition Parliament to suspend proceedings, and (2) an injunction to the Commissioners to have " regard as well to the health, comfort, and convenience of the inhabitants of any neighbouring cities, towns, villages, or populous places, as to the advantage of the Proprietors and persons interested." The Bill was introduced late in the session and dropped. It reappeared early in 1844. A few warning voices were heard, mostly from those already identified with opposition to enclosure. Sibthorp (February 29) asked, Why widen streets in towns, when you were at the same time shutting out the poorer classes from their pastimes ? Hume (March 3) attacked the Bill with his usual vehemence : " Open spaces were required for the health of the population. At present the poor were driven into dusty roads whenever they wanted a mouthful of fresh air."

[1] See Slater, *English Peasantry and Enclosure of Common Fields*, pp. 36 ff.

But the most striking speech was made by Peel, who announced that he would vote for the second reading, but that he looked with great jealousy on the enclosure of commons near towns.

Peel spoke, as in 1837, of " moral " as opposed to " legal rights." " He thought it would be very unwise to apply the rigid principles of political economy, and to say that by enclosing these spaces a greater quantity of vegetable produce could be procured. He thought you had a perfect right to set considerations of health, of innocent recreation, of moral improvement, against the mere considerations of pecuniary gain ; and if you were to prove that by the enclosure of the land for a certain period of time, there would be a demand for labour, and ultimately and apparently an increase of produce, these facts would not be considered by him as conclusive ; he would consider the other question, whether or no you were interfering with the healthful amusements and recreations of the people. He could conceive many cases in which, unless you gave the poor the means of protecting their interests, you ran the risk of doing great injury, and of having all these spaces, not merely near towns, but near villages, totally lost to the public." He pleaded the case of those who might indeed have no legal right to wander over an unenclosed open space, yet whilst it remained unenclosed had, as a matter of fact, the privilege of access. He pictured a case where such land belonged to a corporation ; the corporation cajoled those who had common rights on it to agree to enclosure ; enclosure took place ; " the corporation is benefited ; but he should like to know what were the poor to do ? He was speaking of men who had no right but that of the privilege of access. As to the actual right, the House must be cautious how they dealt lightly with these rights. It might be a question of feeling. Honourable members had their feelings, and the poorer classes of the community had feelings on this subject. The right of common connected them with the soil ; the right of turning a goose on a common made a man feel interested in the tenure of the land. It might be more beneficial to a tenant that he should accept £2 or £3 ; but recollect that you were not dealing with the rights of the individual, but with those of his successors. Therefore the more you could multiply this feeling on the part of the poor, the more you strengthened the foundations of landed property.   Recollect that what was done was irrevocable.   These towns might increase ; and that was an additional reason why they should not permit too hasty an interference with those uninclosed lands." [1]

Impressed by these arguments, Worsley agreed to modify his Bill, and instead of proceeding with it that year (1844), he moved for a Select Committee on the subject of Inclosure, a project blessed by Peel (June 27).   " He had originally entertained very strong objections to the Bill ; but in justice to the noble Lord he must say that the strongest disposition had been evinced by him to remove the objectionable features of the measure, and to prevent its undue interference with the rights and enjoyments of the people."

" The Select Committee to inquire into the expediency of facilitating the Inclosure and Improvement of Commons, and Lands held in common, the Exchange of Lands, and the Division of intermixed Lands ; and into the best means of providing for the same," was appointed on June 27, and its report was printed on August 5.   It consisted of fifteen members, including Lord Granville Somerset, Chancellor of the Duchy, William Cowper, and Brotherton.   Hume said next year (July 4, 1845) that " he would be glad to hear what trouble had been taken by the Committee to get the evidence of the poor man and the labourer on the matter ?   What evidence had they from the poor who used the commons ? "   The answer is, None. Lord Granville Somerset, it is true, put many questions to the witnesses from the poor man's point of view, but he did not produce any witnesses to bring forward that point of view themselves.   The thirty-two " competent and experienced " witnesses who gave evidence consisted of the two Tithe Commissioners, whose evidence fills many pages of the Report, twelve land agents or surveyors, six lawyers concerned with the management of property, a parliamentary lawyer, a parliamentary agent, a civil engineer, and nine men of the well-to-do land-owning or occupying class.   One of these, who is described as a yeoman, owned some 600 acres and rented another 600.

Several of the witnesses laid great stress on the demoralisation of the commoners ; " uninclosed commons are invariably

<hr />

[1] House of Commons, March 3, 1844.

nurseries for petty crime," said one ; [1] they rarely go to a place of worship or send their children to school, said another ; [2] but where an enclosure had taken place all this was altered, and " the parties are a respectable class, looking up to the wealthier classes for labour."   "It is generally alleged that in the vicinity of commons there is a great laxity of morality, and that I believe to be perfectly true, and to be the fact," said one of the Tithe Commissioners ; [3] " I have no opinion," said the other, " of the advantages of people living on the edge of a common ; they are generally the most immoral and worst portion of the rural population." [4]   Part of the unpopularity of the commoners was explained by a description of some near Matlock : " it [the moor of 300 acres] makes them idle ; they can get a bare existence by putting a few geese or something of that sort upon it, and they will not work." [5]   Some of them were doubtless uncomfortable neighbours, *e.g.* the stubborn fellows who, when turned out for non-payment of rent, put up hurdles on the common " and made habitations for their family." [6]   " I think," said the witness who described this, " it is a confirmed habit, their living in that wild state ; they prefer it ; it is more suitable to their notions."

Other witnesses, whilst urging the advantages of reducing mountain-sides to severalty ownership, drew a very unattractive picture of the habits of the owners of stock on big moors, specially in Wales, of the constant fights and quarrels about sheep and cattle, of the cruelty involved in the habitual " dogging."   The Duke of Beaufort's agent, Mr. T. Davies, who claimed to have let more farms in Wales than any other man, declared that these tales were exaggerated.

No evidence was heard as to the demoralisation of landowners into whose private ownership commons had passed.

Walter, who so often took a larger view, once put an aspect of the use of commons which was overlooked in the evidence before the Committee.   Speaking in the House of Commons on the Kingsclere Inclosure Bill,[7] he said, " the result of his inquiry was, that there was no way of compensating the poor generally for any loss of this common by any addition to the allotment of individuals. . . . The loss to be inflicted was real, substantial,

[1] P. 364.   [2] Pp. 305, 306.   [3] P. 45.   [4] P. 8.
[5] P. 149.   [6] P. 304.   [7] June 5, 1834.

and durable ; and it was attempted to repair it by means artificial —he had almost said frivolous ; for the right of common was a perpetual right—a right of which the poor could not dis-seize themselves—of which an improvident father could not rob a meritorious son. All that these people wanted was to be left alone in the enjoyment of that which nature had brought to their doors."

Most of the witnesses declared themselves in favour of leaving town greens and village greens untouched. Even the two Tithe Commissioners, with all their enthusiasm for enclosure, would have left any land open that was " subservient for the health, recreation, or amusement of the population." One of them thought it inadvisable as a rule to touch small commons of from 100 to 200 acres, specially if they were near a village ; [1] the other remarked that though a common of from 100 to 200 acres was too big for a village green, yet " if it did not exceed one hundred acres, and was near a village, and that a populous village, I conceive it might not be expedient to meddle with it." [2]

The Committee, as was natural on the evidence they had heard, reported strongly in favour of making enclosure easier. " The evidence of competent and experienced Witnesses " had convinced them that a large portion of the Waste Land of the Kingdom was " capable of profitable cultivation, or of other improvement." The unenclosed lands were, in several localities, " a source of serious injury and inconvenience to the surrounding neighbourhood, by their effect upon the character of the population." The present time was particularly favourable, thanks to tithe commutation, to drainage and to artificial manure. The Committee recommended the establishment of some central body to consider applications and to carry out enclosures. Lord Granville Somerset, who alone seems to have recognised the superficial character of the inquiry they had made, fought in a minority of one against the Report, proposing that they should announce that the evidence was not sufficiently complete to justify any opinion on the subject. Most of his amendments were defeated, but he succeeded in carrying one to the effect that parliamentary sanction should be necessary in the case of all enclosures carried out by the Board,

[1] P. 12.   [2] P. 51.

instead of " such revision and control being required as might be thought necessary and expedient." The Committee reported in August (August 5, 1844), too late for parliamentary action that year. Next year Lord Worsley dropped his Bill in favour of a Government measure introduced by Lord Lincoln. The Government Bill adopted a good many of Lord Worsley's clauses, but introduced additional safeguards for public rights. Lord Lincoln, in his introductory speech on May 1, 1845, disarmed opposition by his assertions that although in the private Inclosure Bills of the past, in nineteen cases out of twenty the rights of the poor had been neglected, ample securities against injustice to the individual and to public interests would now be provided. " I certainly do intend," he announced, " to impose such additional restrictions as may be necessary for thoroughly protecting the rights of the poor, and for securing to the working classes in great towns, open spaces for recreation and amusement."

Outside the House the *Times* attacked with vigour what it called " this agricultural interest endowment scheme," but in Parliament itself the Bill met with remarkably little opposition. On the motion in the Commons (July 4) that it should go to a Committee, Sharman Crawford, a consistent opponent of enclosure, moved its postponement on the ground that " the rights of future generations " were being sold. Sibthorp also spoke against it. Hume opposed it as " taking away the little public property which still remained available for the health and enjoyment of the community, in order to divide it amongst the landed proprietors." But these were the only critics. Palmerston from the Whig benches gave it a fatherly blessing, suggesting that it might be called a Bill for the interests of agricultural labourers, since nothing was worse for them than the existence of commons, and nothing could be better for the labouring classes than " constant employment, where moral conduct was regarded, and where there was a strict attention to the rights of others." [1] Lord Lincoln defended his Bill against such criticisms as had been raised, and the opponents of the

[1] In commenting on Palmerston's argument that enclosure would provide additional employment, the *Times* remarked : " To snatch from the poor their commons and give them the job of fencing in the waste, is like picking a pocket of a handkerchief and employing the owner to mark it with the initials of the thief."—*Times*, July 7, 1845.

Bill only mustered 11 votes as against 121. In its final stage in the Commons a division was again challenged by Sharman Crawford, but as the only two opponents were the Tellers for the Noes, Sharman Crawford himself and Colonel Sibthorp, the Bill passed its third reading by 48 votes to none (July 17). The House of Lords introduced certain small amendments, and the Bill became law on August 8.

The 1845 Act (8 and 9 Vict. cap. 118) revolutionised, quickened, and cheapened the whole procedure of enclosure. Instead of each enclosure requiring its own separate machinery, a permanent department was now set up with three Commissioners at its head, the First Commissioner of Woods and Forests, together with two other Commissioners, one of them paid, nominated by the Secretary of State. These three Commissioners were empowered to carry out the Act. The expenses of enclosure were no longer provided entirely by the enclosers, for the department was supported out of public funds.[1]

To set the machinery for enclosure in motion, applicants representing " at least one-third in value of the Interests in the Lands " in question had to apply to the Commissioners on a special form provided for the purpose, and if the Commissioners thought the application reasonable they referred it to an Assistant Commissioner, who made inquiries on the spot, heard objections, and reported on the matter. The Commissioners, if they still thought enclosure desirable, next issued a provisional order, giving an outline of the scheme, and proceeded to obtain the necessary consents. The owners of two-thirds in value of the interests in the land proposed to be enclosed had to consent before any further steps could be taken. Meanwhile in their Annual Report, sent in each year in January, to be laid before Parliament, the Commissioners gave tables and certain particulars of all the applications for enclosure they had received, and of the amounts to be set aside for allotments for recreation and the labouring poor, if any. The cases where the consents had been obtained were all embodied together in what was

---

[1] On this the *Times* remarked (June 26, 1845) : " Let those who *obtain enclosures* pay for them, this is the least they should do when they shut out their neighbours from the free soil ; when they fence in what could and would have been reclaimed long ago, if it had been worth cultivating." One Commissioner received £1500 a year, and the Assistant Commissioners were to receive not more than three guineas a day when on duty, plus reasonable travelling allowances. Under the old system the Commissioners had received three guineas a day.

called the Annual Enclosure Act, which authorised enclosure of certain specified areas mentioned in a schedule to the Bill. The only particulars given in the Act were the name of the area, the county, and the date of the Provisional Order.

Such, briefly, was the procedure. What safeguards were there against arbitrary and unjust enclosure? What provision for public interests? How far had Lord Lincoln fulfilled the promise to secure to the working classes in great towns open spaces for recreation and amusement?

(1) In the first place, the independent public department provided by the Act, with its machinery for local inquiry and its officials who had no personal interest in the matter, seemed to ensure fair treatment for personal and for public claims.[1]

(2) In the second place, parliamentary supervision and sanction were still required in the case of the enclosure of any common or waste land over which there were rights of common all the year round, and also of any land within a certain distance of towns (15 miles of London, 4 miles of a town of 100,000 inhabitants, $3\frac{1}{2}$ of a town of 70,000 inhabitants, 3 of a town of 30,000, and 2 of a town of 10,000 inhabitants). Thus the enclosure of common fields with Lammas rights near towns, such as those at Nottingham and Coventry, would still require the sanction of Parliament. By an amending Act of 1852,[2] all enclosures dealt with by the Commission required the authority of Parliament.

Thus, theoretically, such provision as already existed for the ventilation of grievances and cases of injustice remained. This was an improvement on Lord Worsley's Bills, which provided that Parliament could only intervene if expressly petitioned to do so. This provision proved useful in the sixties and seventies.

(3) In the third place, the Act itself provided certain rules for the guidance of the department, embodying the public interests. As in Lord Worsley's Bills, the Commissioners when inquiring into expedience were ordered to have " regard as well to the health, comfort, and convenience of the inhabitants of any neighbouring cities, towns, villages, or populous places, as to

[1] Compare William Cowper, House of Commons, March 13, 1844.
[2] 15 and 16 Vict. cap. 79.

the advantage of the Proprietors and persons interested. . . ."
In addition to this rather vague general injunction it was
decreed " that no Town Green or Village Green shall be subject
to be inclosed under this Act " unless it was allotted as a recreation allotment.   Further, where commons or wastes were enclosed the Commissioners could require as a condition of
enclosure the appropriation of an allotment " for the Purposes
of Exercise and Recreation for the Inhabitants of the Neighbourhood."   This clause was a legal embodiment of Hume's
resolution (see p. 124), and also laid down directions as to the
amount.   The maximum amounts were fixed as follows: for
populations under 2000, 4 acres; for populations between
2000 and 5000, 5 acres; for populations between 5000 and
10,000, 8 acres; for populations of 10,000 and over, 10
acres.   A similar provision was enacted with regard to an
allotment for gardens for the " labouring poor," but here no
definite directions as to size were given; the area was to be
such " as the Commissioners shall think necessary, with reference to the Circumstances of each particular Case."   If the
Commissioners failed to require these allotments for recreation and for gardens, they had to give their reasons in their
Report.

These provisions proved miserably inadequate, but it is clear
that although a few opponents of enclosure deprecated the
simplification and cheapening of the method, most people,
including many critics of enclosure in the past, thought that
whilst national difficulties demanded acceleration of the process,
ample measures had been taken for safeguarding public interests.
They compared the Act with Lord Worsley's Bills, and found
a great improvement; there would be allotments for recreation
and for gardens; village greens and town greens were not
to be enclosed; a public department could be trusted to look
after public interests.   They hoped for the best, were glad to
hand over responsibility, and forbore to scrutinise the provisions
too closely, to consider the meagre size of the allotments permitted, to press for a legal definition of a village green, or to ask
how far these greens were protected from enclosure not under
this Act.

The *Times* saw further than the preoccupied and apathetic
members of the House of Commons, and attacked (July 7) " the

Pecksniffian provisions for the exercise and recreation of those whom the measure is designed to deprive of what they are entitled to." It pointed out that even were the allotments for recreation adequate at the present time, no provision was made for future growth of population. It realised the worthless character of the clause exempting village or town greens. "There is a sentimental section which professes to exempt the 'village green' from the operation of the act, but the character of this piece of twaddle may be conceived from the fact that on Lord Lincoln being asked to say what is meant by a 'village green' he declined describing it. The exemption, however, is of no real value, for the clause provides that instead of requiring that other land be allotted for the purposes of exercise and recreation out of the commons to be enclosed, the 'village green' is to be allotted for the purposes alluded to. This arrangement entirely dissipates the little air of romance with which the framers of the bill had endeavoured to invest the 'village green,' which is only exempted that the landlord may have the whole of the common enclosed, without taking out of it even a small slice for the poor's recreation and exercise."

The next twenty years afford a melancholy picture of the disregard of public interests by a department well-intentioned, but deficient in imagination and foresight, and untouched by any criticism. Year after year the Inclosure Commissioners presented their Report, and followed up the Report with an Annual Bill which was passed as a matter of routine without discussion.[1] A false sense of security had engendered apathy in place of those spasmodic and occasionally effectual protests evoked by the more flagrant earlier abuses. Parliament trusted to the Commissioners, the Commissioners trusted to Parliament to protect public interests.[2] In 1862, for the first time after the passing of the 1845 Act, Parliament intervened

---

[1] It is significant that when Charlotte Brontë wrote *Shirley*, the first idea of a public-spirited man was to obtain an Act for enclosing the neighbouring common. *Shirley* was written in 1848. Trollope wrote *The Prime Minister* in 1876. There an M.P. who wants to make himself useful in Parliament cherishes precisely the same project.

[2] Compare the evidence of one of the Inclosure Commissioners before the 1865 Committee on Open Spaces in the Metropolis, p. 6. He explains that the Commissioners, when applied to, proceed with the work of enclosure "if we find that there are advantages in an agricultural point of view, because I take it we do not consider that it is for us to determine whether upon public points of view it is right that they should be inclosed, because they come before Parliament afterwards. . . ."

and made an alteration in the Annual Inclosure Bill, in the case of Chigwell, but it was not till 1865 that public interest was effectively roused.   With the formation of the Commons Preservation Society and the action of Eversley, Fawcett, and many others, a new era begins.   But the story of that long struggle does not come into this book.

CHAPTER X

DRINK

OPEN air and exercise might be denied to the town workers, but another form of recreation was supplied in increasing abundance: the ginshop and the beerhouse welcomed them on every side. "You would scarcely now be able to put your foot down without meeting with a public-house," said a magistrate of the northern towns in 1834.[1] A brief sketch of eighteenth-century legislation about liquor is necessary in order to understand how this had come about.

After the Revolution of 1688, in the course of commercial warfare with France, the distilling of English spirits was encouraged, and it was made possible for any one who paid certain duties to distil and to retail spirits made from English corn. The result of this encouragement of home industries is well known. The poor, who had hitherto drunk beer, in amazing quantities if the statistics are to be trusted,[2] turned now to spirits. Ginshops, with straw-strewn cellars for the drunk and disabled, sprang up everywhere; "drunk for 1d., dead drunk for 2d., straw for nothing," was a common sign. Hogarth's brush has preserved for later generations a record of the revolting orgies of the time; some think there has been another and a disastrous legacy. "Small as is the place," says Lecky, "which this fact occupies in English history, it was probably, if we consider all the consequences that have flowed from it, the most momentous in that of the eighteenth century— incomparably more so than any event in the purely political or military annals of the country. The fatal passion for drink was at once, and irrevocably, planted in the nation."[3]

---

[1] 1834 Committee on Drunkenness, p. 311.
[2] "It was computed in 1688 that no less than 12,400,000 barrels were brewed in England in a single year, though the entire population little exceeded 5,000,000."— Lecky quoting Gregory King, *History of England in the Eighteenth Century*, vol. ii. p. 100 (1898 edition).
[3] *History of England in the Eighteenth Century*, vol. ii. p. 101 (1898 edition).

Attempts were made to check the evil, taking the form at first of practical prohibition.[1] In 1729 a licence was fixed at £20; this partially successful Act was repealed in 1733 on a complaint from the farmers, but after a brief interval a new attempt was made, and in 1736 the cost of the licence was fixed at £50, and a tax of 20s. per gallon, to be paid by retailers, was put on spirits. The measure of attention paid to this attempted prohibition can be judged by the fact that in seven years only three licences were taken out. The Act, said a speaker in the Lords in 1743, " gave such a turn to the spirit of the people, that no man could with safety venture to become an informer." [2] Less ambitious legislation from 1743 to 1751, fixing lower prices for licences and putting the control of licensing into the magistrates' hands, was more successful, and the figures for the consumption of spirits, which had stood at more than a gallon per head of the population in 1740 and 1750, fell to ·36 in 1760.[3] As, however, all the figures relate to the spirits that paid duty, they must be used with discretion, for any increase in duties or in the price of licences automatically increased illicit distilling and smuggling. England, after 1750, became no doubt less drunken, but she was probably not as sober as the figures would suggest.

In 1785 the duties on spirits were reduced, with the result that the amount of duty-paying spirit rose considerably, from ·31 per head in 1780 to ·48 in 1790.[3] At the same time began that interesting campaign of regulation and suppression by the magistrates, of which a full account is given in the *History of Liquor Licensing in England*. Mr. and Mrs. Webb have suggested that the limitation of opportunities for disorderly drinking between 1787 and 1825 contributed largely to the advance in respectability of the working man during that period. Huskisson in 1822 declared that " no person who had lived so long as he had but must perceive that a greater degree of sobriety prevailed amongst the lower classes now than was formerly the case." [4] The movement, it is true, had little effect in London, but in the provinces Sunday closing became usual,

---

[1] For an excellent description of the whole episode, see *London Life in the Eighteenth Century*, by M. Dorothy George, pp. 28 ff.
[2] Lord Cholmondeley, *Cobbett's Parliamentary History*, vol. xii. p. 1215.
[3] *Population Problems of the Age of Malthus*, by G. Talbot Griffith (1926), p. 201.
[4] House of Commons, July 18, 1822.

and in many counties houses were made to close at 9 P.M. in winter and at 10 P.M. in summer.

The control of the magistrates after 1825 was weakened by various causes. The magistrates had made themselves unpopular, sometimes for good, sometimes for bad reasons, and there was also a growing movement against any form of monopoly. The effect of this last movement on some of the Justices themselves was described by a Durham magistrate later. Formerly, he said, the licensing system acted as a considerable restraint, then the " general principles of free trade " gained the day, and the magistrates relaxed their vigilance, thinking that they would in this way destroy the brewers' monopoly and improve the quality of the beer. Spirits and beer, in fact, were treated like groceries.[1] Those magistrates whose minds were not influenced by these new ideas, and who were still zealous to exercise their authority, found a considerable check imposed on their activities in 1828 by the codifying Act, commonly called Estcourt's Act,[2] which repealed a multitude of existing licensing statutes, and simplified the law, at the same time leaving the magistrates' position in considerable uncertainty. The spirit in which Estcourt, a Tory member, introduced his measure illustrates the unpopularity which surrounded magisterial control. " It was his original intention," he announced, " to have proposed the doing away with the licensing system altogether " ; but when his attention was called to the evils which would follow he thought better of it and brought forward this Bill instead.[3]

In Estcourt's Act the magistrates retained their old power of licensing at Brewster Sessions, though an appeal was now allowed to Quarter Sessions. They were given specific powers of interfering and closing a licensed house in cases of riot or tumult, and many magistrates interpreted this to mean that they had no power of direct interference otherwise. But the most important point raised by the Act was the question of hours. Hitherto the regulation of hours had always been supposed to come within the magistrates' province. By the last Licensing Act of 1822,[4] the licence-holder undertook not to allow drinking during the hours of Divine Service on Sundays, and not to keep

---

[1] 1834 Committee on Drunkenness, p. 311.
[3] House of Commons, May 21, 1828.
[2] 9 Geo. IV. cap. 61.
[4] 3 Geo. IV. cap. 77.

his premises open " during late Hours of the Night or early in the Morning." It was the custom of the Justices to specify what " late hours " meant, and to fix 10 or 11 P.M. as the closing hour on week-days, as a condition of the grant of a licence. But in Estcourt's Act all reference to week-day hours was omitted. The licence-holder undertook to shut his house during the usual hours of the morning and afternoon service on Sundays, Christmas Day, or Good Friday, but there was no mention anywhere of week-day closing. Had the magistrates still the power to fix the closing hours at night? Different magistrates gave different answers; some held that the power had been definitely taken away from them:[1] others argued that though no hours were mentioned in the Act, yet a house which kept open all night might be considered a disorderly house and thus come under their jurisdiction.[2] This was said to have been Estcourt's own view.[3] But this indirect control over hours, even where it was believed to exist, proved unsatisfactory, and as time went on fewer attempts to fix any hours were made. When the Commissioner of Metropolitan Police was asked in 1849 " Do not the Magistrates fix certain hours for public-houses to be closed?" he answered, "No; the public-houses may be open all night;[4] there is no law to prevent it in the Metropolitan Police District."[5] We have, in fact, as a result of Estcourt's Act a growing dislike on the part of the magistrates to interfere with the question of hours.[6]

[1] Cf. evidence of Chief Constable of Hants before the House of Lords Committee on the Sale of Beer, Minutes of Evidence, 1849, p. 62, on the subject of Estcourt's Act and its predecessors. Q. " Used the Magistrates under that Act (the 1822 Act) practically to regulate the hours of public-houses? "—A. " Yes." Q. " Has that now entirely ceased?"—A. "It has; now they may keep open all night long." Q. " Would it be considered evidence of irregularity if they kept their houses open all night? " —A. " No ; it would be committing no offence against the terms of the licence."

[2] The licence-holder promised, amongst other things, that he would not " wilfully or knowingly permit Drunkenness or other disorderly Conduct," and an offence against the tenor of his licence was punishable by a maximum fine of £5 for the first offence, £10 for the second, and £50 or a possible cancelling of the licence for a third offence.

[3] See evidence of Worship Street Police Court Magistrate before 1834 Committee on Drunkenness, p. 20. Compare also Melbourne's speech in the House of Lords, September 6, 1831, for conflicting views of magistrates.

[4] Except, of course, Saturday nights after 1839. See p. 163.

[5] House of Lords Committee on Sale of Beer, Minutes of Evidence, 1849, p. 7. Cf. Birmingham, where public-houses were said to be allowed to remain open all hours except on Saturday night, ibid., Minutes of Evidence, 1850, p. 63 ; and Liverpool, where they were often open all through Saturday night till the Police Act of 1842.

[6] The Manchester magistrates, as late as 1834, seem to have thought that they had the right of fixing the closing hour at 11 P.M. See evidence of late Boroughreeve before the Select Committee on Drunkenness in 1834, p. 56.

The decline of magisterial control synchronised with an important reduction in the duties on English-made spirits. These duties, which had been already reduced in 1823, underwent in 1825 a further reduction from 11s. 8¼d. a gallon to 7s. a gallon, and the publican's licence for the sale of spirits was also reduced from five to two guineas. The sale of whisky was at the same time legalised in England for the first time. Much whisky had been drunk before, but it was whisky smuggled over the Scottish border. Hume had boasted in Parliament that he had some of this smuggled whisky in his house, " if such foolish laws were made, they ought to be broken." [1]   The policy of reduced duties, which was part of what Professor Smart called the second Free Trade Budget, was explained by its author, Robinson, as an attempt to put down smuggling, which had reached enormous proportions in the border district, since Scotland's spirit duty had been reduced to two shillings. Figures for English spirits manufactured and charged to duty rose from 3,684,049 gallons in 1825 to 7,407,204 in 1826,[2] but it is impossible to believe that consumption was more than doubled in twelve months. An alarming increase there undoubtedly was. Hume, when advocating a reduction of duties,[3] had laid down the proposition that " it was the disposition of man, when he could only obtain an indulgence occasionally, to get as much of it as he could ; but, if circumstances enabled him to obtain the gratification regularly, the temptation to commit an excess was removed." Unfortunately this doctrine proved as false when applied to indulgence in spirits now as it had a century before. " Making all proper allowance," said Brougham seven years after, " for the conversion of the contraband trade to a duty-paying trade, the result of his inquiry, and of his personal observation, was that the increased consumption of ardent spirits must have been frightful since the diminution of the duty." [4]   Blomfield, Bishop of London, described in 1832 " a most frightful increase " of intemperance. " I never saw, when I first came to London, a female coming out of a ginshop ; but I have since repeatedly seen females with infants in their arms, to whom they appeared to have been giving some part of their liquor. I almost think I have seen more women than men

----

[1] Smart, *Economic Annals*, 1821-30, p. 220.   [2] Talbot Griffith, *op. cit.* p. 201.
[3] House of Commons, April 22, 1825.   [4] House of Lords, August 29, 1831.

coming out of these shops." [1]   This increase in spirit-drinking was one of the causes contributing to that amazing piece of legislation, the famous Beer Bill of 1830.

To understand the circumstances that made the Beer Bill possible we must consider the public opinion of the time.   The public had been shocked by gross evidence of magisterial corruption in certain districts of London revealed in the Committee on the Metropolitan Police in 1817; the publicans, no amateurs in the arts of propaganda, resented what they considered interference by licensing magistrates; the general feeling of the day was hostile to all monopolies, and with the growth of the tied-house system more public-houses were coming under the control of the big breweries.   Beer, as opposed to spirits, held a high place in public estimation.   Teetotalism was practically unknown.   Social reformers were anxious, not that the working classes should cease to take alcoholic drinks, but that they should turn from spirits to beer.   " Ale, taken to excess," said Slaney, " might make a man dull and drowsy; but it would not ruin his health by destroying his liver." [2]   Plenty of beer, easily obtained, would cure the poor of their craving for spirits, and the beer itself would be better, for, with free competition, adulteration would cease.   Beer, again, was the good old national drink, and its consumption had gone down to an alarming extent; whereas in 1722 a barrel per head a year had been drunk, in 1830 only half a barrel was consumed.[3]   This reduced consumption hit the agricultural interest, whose fortunes were at a low ebb; if more beer were drunk, more barley and hops would be wanted.   The big brewers indeed could not and did not plead poverty or a failing revenue, but they pointed out that the taxation paid on beer was enormous.   A quarter of barley cost 35s.; when converted into malt it paid 20s. 8d. duty; when the malt was converted into beer and sold it paid a further 35s., so that the total tax on 35s. worth of malt was 55s. 8d., or 160 per cent.   Port wine paid 56 per cent.; claret 27 per cent.; and champagne only 26 per cent.[4]

The result of these various influences and of the political circumstances of the moment was that in 1830 the Tories, under

[1] Select Committee on Observance of the Sabbath, 1832, p. 248.
[2] House of Commons, May 21, 1830.   [3] See Talbot Griffith, *op. cit.* p. 202.
[4] T. Fowell Buxton in Committee on Sale of Beer, 1830, p. 19.

Wellington, by their Beer Bill, introduced free trade in beer, as one of their last acts before the tide of reform swept them away for ten years. The Government was in difficulties. Wellington had alienated his Canningite followers by his intransigent attitude to the mildest proposals for reform ; the high Tories, on the other hand, had been outraged the year before by the passing of Catholic Emancipation. Misery and discontent outside strengthened the hands of the Government's opponents within Parliament. There was a certain surplus in the revenue, and nothing seemed more obvious and suitable than to use it to relieve that distress with which opponents made such play. Beer was regarded as a necessity of life for those who could not afford to drink anything better, and it was decided to take off the whole tax on beer itself, though the tax on malt remained. To ensure to the poor man the full benefit of the reduction in price, the sale of beer was to be opened to any one who chose to pay an excise licence. Thus it was hoped that adulteration, tied houses, and gin-drinking would all vanish, whilst agriculturists would be helped by the increased demand for barley and hops. The Chancellor of the Exchequer, Goulburn, even persuaded himself that the cause of law and order would be promoted, since the present system of a few licensed houses caused crowds to collect, and crowds meant disturbances.[1]

It seems curious now that the decision to throw the trade open and to put an end to the system of licensing by the magistrates should have been taken so lightly.[2] A Select Committee appointed by the Government in 1830 to examine the laws and regulations affecting the sale of beer had indeed reported strongly in favour of free sale. No magistrates were examined before this Committee, and no evidence was taken as to probable effects on public order. Many witnesses had emphasised the hardships free sale would inflict on the present holders of licences.[3] But these vested interests were swept aside by

---

[1] House of Commons, March 4, 1830.

[2] "The political history of this period is bewildering to the student, and rich in paradoxical happenings, because, while the old parties are breaking up, "the spirit of the age," and the constant pressure of the unenfranchised from without, overwhelm from day to day the policies of the nominal holders of power."—G. M. Trevelyan, British History in the Nineteenth Century, p. 216.

[3] The big brewers, indeed, whilst suffering as owners of tied houses, would benefit as brewers; it was the independent publicans who stood to lose, and to lose heavily.

Wellington's Government with a martial decision characteristic of the Duke's attitude to opposition, whether from his enemies or his friends.[1]   He denied, indeed, that there were any vested interests, since the licences lasted for a year only, and the magistrates had the power to refuse to renew them.   The Chancellor of the Exchequer declared that " the brewers and publicans were the parties on one side, the labouring population of England on the other."   The brewers did not oppose the Bill as it passed through Parliament, but the publicans sent petition after petition. There were 8 petitions for and 483 against the Bill.   The petitions had no effect.   A few Cassandras foretold scenes of drunkenness and debauchery, amongst them Michael Thomas Sadler, who described the measure as " offering a bonus to tipplers."   Opposition in Parliament was concentrated on amending the Bill so that the new Excise licences should give the power to sell, but should not allow consumption on the premises.[2]   These off-licences, it was argued, would do less harm to the present publicans, and would encourage the labourer to consume his beer " in the bosom of his family."   Though the second reading of the Bill had been carried by 245 to 29 votes, two amendments in Committee to this effect were only defeated by majorities of 38 and 30 (180 to 142, and 138 to 108).

In its original form the Bill had contained no restrictions on hours of sale.   Later, the closing hour was fixed at 10 P.M., a clause severely denounced by Hume.   Here was a Bill, he said, to promote the free sale of beer, and yet every clause was a restriction.   There was no division on the third reading in the Commons, and in the Lords, though there were strong speeches criticising the Bill and the Government's action by Lord Malmesbury and the Duke of Richmond, opposition was weaker than in the Commons, and an amendment to introduce off-licences only was defeated by 60 votes to 15.   Lord Malmesbury, it is interesting to note, championed the magistrates,

[1] Cf. *The Chartist*, March 16, 1839 : " How the deuce the Beer Act ever passed we cannot very well comprehend.   No one, certainly, but the Duke of Wellington could have done it.   He did it at a time when it was quite necessary to do something in order to gain a little popularity throughout the country. . . . The Duke, however, is an imperious commander ; he ordered, and they obeyed."

[2] It may be noted that an Act of 1823 (4 Geo. IV. cap. 51) had made it lawful to sell a weak form of beer called " intermediate beer " for consumption off the premises without a magistrate's licence, but this intermediate beer was little drunk.

declaring that the Bill was an unjustified attack upon them. The Duke of Wellington, who conducted the measure through the Lords, made light of the supposed dangers to peace and injury to property, and laid stress on the " beneficial conse- quences to the lower orders." [1]

The Beer Act became law in October, 1830.[2] After that date, any householder except a sheriff's officer could obtain an Excise licence to sell beer, provided that he paid two guineas and produced one surety for £20 or two for £10 each.   These sureties also had to be householders.   The control of the magistrates over these Excise-licensed houses was reduced to the power to close them in cases of riots or tumults.   Penalties were enacted for permitting drunken or disorderly conduct on the premises, such penalties varying from a minimum of 40s. for the first offence to a maximum of £50, with a possible dis- qualification for two years, for the third offence.   Adulteration of beer was also to be punished by fines varying from £10 to £50, with a possible disqualification for the second offence. Closing hours were fixed by the Act from 10 P.M. to 4 A.M. every day, and on Sundays, Good Friday, Christmas Day, and other days appointed for fasts or thanksgivings, the houses were also shut from 10 A.M. to 1 P.M. and from 3 P.M. to 5 P.M.   There was to be a fine of 40s. for each sale outside the proper hours.   Public-houses where spirits were sold were un- touched by the Act, and remained as before under the control of the magistrates.

The effects of the revolution were rapid and startling. Crowds of little beershops sprang up in every town and all over the country.   In 1829 there were 50,660 publicans licensed to sell beer ; in 1830 the publicans numbered 51,482, but there were 24,342 beerhouses as well.   In 1831, whilst the number of publicans remained stationary (51,488), the beerhouses had risen to 30,978, and they continued to rise steadily at a more rapid rate than the public-houses, till in 1836 the relative numbers were : public-houses, 55,192 ; beerhouses, 44,134.[3] Small trades-

---

[1] The chief debates in the House of Commons were on April 8, May 3, 4, and 21, June 3 and 21, July 1 ; in the House of Lords, July 6 and 8.
[2] 11 Geo. IV. and 1 William IV. cap. 64.
[3] 1870 Report of Commissioners of Inland Revenue, vol. ii. p. 44.   In the iron district round Pontypool in 1831 there were 37 public-houses; in 1840 there were 38 public-houses and 132 beerhouses.   " According to their own confession," 1962

men, mechanics, even journeymen and labourers added to their earnings by keeping a beerhouse.[1] Thus in Sheffield, where 280 beerhouses flourished in addition to 386 alehouses, the former were largely kept by working men, grinders, cutlers, and the like, whose wives managed the premises in their absence. Hand-loom weavers found a new opening, widows a new way of earning a livelihood; enterprising parish officers were said to save the rates by setting up paupers as beerhouse keepers.

In Staffordshire, the new beerhouse became often a tommy shop. Miners were engaged by "butties" or small contractors, and these butties kept beerhouses where the men for whom they found employment were compelled to spend a good part of their wages. Iron-workers were also victims of this system.[2]

In villages, the autocratic rule of the landed proprietors which had kept the labourer sober against his will was rudely shaken. Beershops rose up where public-houses had been forbidden, and farmers and gentry wrung their hands over the orgies of the labourers. In towns, where it had been easy to get beer before, it was now made easier still. "Everybody is drunk," wrote Sydney Smith, a fortnight after the Beer Bill had come into force. "Those who are not singing are sprawling. The sovereign people are in a beastly state." The best illustration of the immediate effects is given in some statistics produced by the Chief Constable of Leeds in 1833. For the three years before October 1830 the number of persons brought before the Leeds magistrates for drunkenness was 639; for the two years and seven months after October 10, 1830, the number was 2023, or more than three times as many.[3]

It seems at first sight strange that the Reform Government which entered upon an inheritance of riots and disorder, charged with the mission of carrying a great constitutional change, made no attempt to stem this tide of beer. It was no more dependent than Wellington's Government had been on the votes of those

persons, that is 16·6 per cent. of the population above twelve years old, were drunkards. See statistics of a recently disturbed district (parish of Trevethin).—*Journal of Statistical Society*, vol. iii. (1840), pp. 371 and 400.

[1] 1833 Committee on Sale of Beer, p. 253.

[2] Evidence of J. H. Hatton (Chief Constable), Lords Committee on Sale of Beer, 1850, p. 524.

[3] 1833 Committee on Sale of Beer, p. 246.

who soaked themselves in the beer, for neither before nor after the Reform Bill had these people the suffrage.   But action was not easy.   Lord Althorp, Chancellor of the Exchequer, perhaps the best type of the honest Whig aristocrat, admitted candidly in 1834 " that the question was one which ought to have been taken up by Ministers ; but it was so surrounded with difficulties, that they could not easily make up their minds respecting it."   These difficulties were obvious.   The traditional method of controlling the sale of drink was by means of the magistrates.   But the magistrates had made themselves exceedingly unpopular ; the Tories had diminished their power, and a Whig Government that tried to restore it would have had great trouble with its followers.   For the magistrates were generally Tory in politics.   It is significant that leave to bring in a Bill for putting the beerhouses under the magistrates was refused to a private member in the reformed House of Commons by 109 to 12 votes.[1]   It would not have been easy to find an alternative plan of control, for the police system was only just being created, and it was generally regarded with dislike and suspicion.   Moreover, every interference with personal liberty was resisted fiercely by the Radicals.   Hume denounced all encroachment on the freedom and comforts of the poor ; Cobbett, the most temperate of men in his habits, except that of speech, derided the efforts of statesmen to improve moral conditions by law.   " There must be something left to the pulpit— there must be something left to the parents—there must be something left to the moral teacher." [2]   And Hume and Cobbett struck a sympathetic chord in the heart of Whig supporters.

Critics of the beershops did not make matters easier by their exaggerations.   A good deal of the outcry against the beerhouses was organised by their rivals, the publicans, and was felt to be unfair.   Beerhouses in lonely spots, on the edges of commons, might and did act as receivers of stolen goods, but the average beerhouse was not a haunt of thieves and profligates. Many of them were unpretentious cottages where bread and cheese could be bought as well as beer.   It became, however, a regular custom for prisoners, in conversation with magistrates or chaplains, to attribute their downfall to the beerhouses.   The

[1] May 31, 1832.   [2] House of Commons, May 27, 1834.

confession was too common to be convincing.[1]   The connection between beerhouses and crime was clearly brought out by
Lord Melbourne.   If crimes were planned in them it was
because they were "places of meeting, not because liquor
was sold there."   "Where were thieves to meet?" he asked.
"They must meet somewhere to concert their plans; and the
most convenient houses were houses of this description."[2]
The ordinary beerhouses in villages were not meeting-places for
thieves, but they did serve as meeting-places for the labourers.
They tempted the poor man to waste his pittance of a wage on
drink, but they also acted as his club.[3]   The labourers had had
nowhere to meet together freely before, and they seized their
chance eagerly.   At the public-houses they had always been in
the presence of their betters; as an experienced magistrate's
clerk expressed it, "the public-house is frequented by people of
a better description, and I conceive, therefore, that there is a
degree of moral restraint over the lower class frequenting a
public-house which does not exist as a beerhouse."[4]

A House of Lords Committee later pointed to this as one
of the disadvantages of beerhouses.   ". . . It is no small evil
to have a class of houses thus established, frequented exclusively
by the labouring population, who thus lose the benefit of some
control from contact with persons of superior station, such as
was exercised when both the employers and the employed
frequented the same Public-house."[5]   The farmers went to the
alehouse and the labourers to the beerhouse.   The many
denouncers of country beerhouses were emphatic on this aspect.

---

[1] See House of Lords Committee on Sale of Beer.   Minutes of Evidence, 1850,
pp. 86 ff.   *The Chartist*, March 31, 1839, commented on this practice: "Does he
frequent beershops, was the question which was always asked after a poor wretch
had been convicted; and as all poor men do frequent beershops, the answer was
pretty generally in the affirmative, and put on another month or two to his sentence. . . .
Then again, when a poor wretch is convicted of some capital crime, the parson comes
in and treats him with as much distinction as though he had been born to the distinction
of having a private chaplain.   The good man is vastly affectionate, pictures all the
characteristics of the next world as graphically as if he had been there, and, after getting
from him a confession, exhorts him to employ his last moments in an earnest philippic
against the beershops.   It is extraordinary that all murders are committed upon beer—
gin is quite a tranquillising humanity-teaching liquid."
[2] House of Lords, June 17, 1839.
[3] Godolphin Osborne argued that the right remedy was to be found in rival attractions, and urged the establishment of village clubs, open for reading on Sunday.   See
his essay in *Meliora*, edited by Lord Ingestre.
[4] 1833 Committee on Sale of Beer, p. 96.
[5] Committee on Sale of Beer, 1850, p. v

To talk was counted a greater crime than to tipple. " The general character of an Englishman," said the energetic Hampshire parson magistrate, the Rev. Robert Wright, " is something like the loadstone and the needle ; the beerhouse is an attractive thing to him ; it is not altogether the beer, but the fellowship they meet with, and the conversation they get into, and the petty publications which are continually carried round to those houses and which they get to read ; I think as long as they can get to those houses, mischief will ensue." [1]   Complaints against country beerhouses were loudest, but the country gentlemen who were the chief sufferers were not conspicuous for their support of the Government, and it seemed unnecessary to handle a thorny question in order to oblige them.

In towns the question was more complicated.   A crowd of beerhouses sprang up,[2] and, as we have seen, drunkenness increased, but the worst excesses came from spirit drinking.[3] Spirits were not supplied by beerhouses, and the houses that did supply them were still under the control of the magistrates.   The truth was that after the first bout of drunkenness the disastrous effect of the beershops in towns was largely indirect.   Pressure of competition drove the public-houses to lower their standards and to rely on the attractions of spirits. " The old public-houses," said the Worship Street Police magistrate in 1834, " where a man could have his steak dressed, and sit down and take his ale, are extinct ; they are obliged to convert them into splendid houses, and sell gin at the bar." [4] Many of them started special spirit vaults, or dram shops, with a separate door, where small quantities were sold.   In Manchester it was calculated that the 430 public-houses had 322 gin-shops attached to them.[5]   " In Manchester a person can do . . .

---

[1] 1833 Committee on Sale of Beer, p. 9.   Cf. : " And their wish to frequent these beerhouses arises from the love of society ? "—" Yes."—*Ibid.* p. 137.

[2] *E.g.* Leeds, 280 alehouses and 251 beerhouses ; Stockport, 89 alehouses and 99 beerhouses ; Sheffield, 386 alehouses and 280 beerhouses.

[3] An increase of indigestion among the working classes was attributed by two medical men before the 1834 Committee on Drunkenness to the growth of spirit drinking.   One of them, Dr. Gordon of the London Hospital, seemed, curiously enough, to think that the malady was unknown before.   " Yes.   Indigestion is quite a new disease amongst the lower classes."   " Do you attribute the introduction of it to the use of spirits ? "—" Yes, I attribute it, as a physician, to the facility which the poor people possess of procuring, without loss of time, without inconvenience, and without shame, day and night, Sunday and working-day, any quantity of spirits."—P. 197.

[4] 1834 Committee on Drunkenness, p. 15.

[5] Kay-Shuttleworth, *Four Periods of Public Education* (1862), p. 34.

as low as a pennyworth of rum and a halfpennyworth of gin." [1]
London set the example of fine gin palaces; the provinces
followed suit. There was no conviviality in these places, not
even seats to sit on. Through their glittering gimcrack
splendour a procession passed all day of men, women, and
children. In the evening hours this procession quickened its
step. Statistics had come into fashion, and social observers
stood and counted the numbers. Fourteen of the chief ginshops
in London were visited, so it was calculated, by 269,438 persons
one week.[2] A big Manchester ginshop was entered during
Saturday evening by an average of 412 persons an hour.[3]

As the beerhouses were bound by law to close at 10 P.M., a
rule which their rivals took care to see enforced in towns, their
customers often went on to the public-houses, which closed much
later, at 11 or even 12, and the partisans of the beerhouses argued
that many of the evils attributed to them were really due to this
exodus into the public-houses. The idyllic picture of the working of the Beer Act in Devonport, where the people were said
to visit the beerhouses and to go thence to the Mechanics'
Institution,[4] was certainly not true of other towns, but on the
other hand there was much evidence to show that many, at any
rate, of the beerhouses in towns were well conducted, and served
a useful purpose, cooking food as well as supplying in a pure
and cheap form what so ardent a social reformer as Slaney
called "the second necessary of life." It became almost an
axiom, even with critics of beershops, that in towns their evils
were trifling; the beerhouses were, as Buckingham described
them, the gnat, the spirit-houses were the camel. And all the
while the sale of spirits continued to be licensed by the magistrates, who still had a certain power of controlling the licence-

---

[1] 1833 Committee on Sale of Beer, p. 152.
[2] 1834 Committee on Drunkenness, p. 2.
[3] Kay-Shuttleworth, *op. cit.* p. 35. Cf.: "You close the Picture Gallery and
Museum on holidays and feast days, but you leave wide open the Gin and the Beer
shop, hating convivial meetings, you make the people unsocial drunkards. This
ginshop that you love, because it increases your revenue, look at it, go into it, and
behold its horrible appearance. A flaring gas-light is over the door, *which door never
shuts.* Push it aside, go in, look around—splendid windows, brass rods and ornaments,
a fine showy counter, immense tubs of spirits, and gay damsels ready to serve it.
But no chairs. No one sits in a ginshop. The customer comes in, '*pays for his glass
of poison,*' drinks it off at one gulp, and goes away to make room for a succeeding
customer."—Roebuck, J. A., "Pamphlets for the People," 1835. (Quoted by Dr.
F. R. Lees, *An Argument for Prohibition,* 1857, p. 118.)
[4] Sir E. Codrington, House of Commons, May 16, 1834.

holders by refusing to renew the licences.   It may well be asked why they were so supine, and why they made no attempt to control the gin palaces.   The answer seems to be that they had lost all heart.   Brougham described them in 1839 : " they now had their conduct so narrowly scrutinized, that no persons led more the life of a toad under a harrow than they did." [1]

The last and the most important obstacle to any reform was that the Beer Bill had created a host of new vested interests. Every proposal for suppression, limitation, or regulation met with clamorous opposition from the many champions of the poor men who had invested their little all in beerhouses on the strength of a Government Act.   Every year the number of the poor men grew, and their power became more formidable.   It is a melancholy thought that Wellington, who alone had the power and the will to brush aside vested interests, and to pursue his path unconcerned by the cries of their champions, should have used that power only to increase their numbers.

It must not be supposed that the Government and Parliament sat entirely still whilst petitions to amend the Beer Act poured in from every side, from clergy, magistrates, and " respectable inhabitants."   In the ten years that followed the Beer Act there were perpetual debates, a fair number of abortive proposals, two Committees of Enquiry, and two mild Acts.

An attempt was made by Melbourne in 1831 to bring the beerhouses under some kind of discipline.   The agricultural rising of the previous winter was believed by many to have been fomented in the new beerhouses, and Melbourne carried a Bill through the Lords authorising constables or police officers to enter beerhouses without a warrant, but the Bill was thrown out by the Commons.   In 1833 a Select Committee on the Sale of Beer was appointed by the Commons.   Many witnesses were heard before them.   Some denounced, some praised the new beerhouses.   The Committee recommended higher charges for licences, certificates of character before renewal, stiffer penalties, Sunday morning closing, regulation of hours for evening closing (within limits) by the magistrates, and, finally, a revision of the whole licensing system.

The Whig Government, though unprepared to act, declared themselves willing to support any measure that did not interfere

[1] House of Lords, June 3, 1839.

with open competition, and they gave a qualified support to a Bill brought in next year, 1834, by a high Tory county member, Sir Edward Knatchbull, who had fought hard to modify the 1830 Beer Bill. This Bill embodied some of the Committee's recommendations. In its original form certificates of character were to be made compulsory for all beershop licences where beer was consumed on the premises, but during its passage through the House Knatchbull made a rather ignominious surrender to the claims of property, by offering to exempt towns with more than 5000 inhabitants from the operation of the Bill. After this the Government adopted the Bill and carried it. An amendment that in the exempted towns no licence should be granted for consumption on the premises to houses of under £10 in value was carried by a private member, Mr. George Wood, on the third reading of the Bill. The Act, 4 and 5 William IV. cap 85, in its final form, in addition to requiring a certificate of character in the country and a £10 qualification in towns, gave the constables and police officers the right of entry at all times,[1] and placed the regulation of hours, within certain limits,[2] in the hands of the Justices.

This Act did not fulfil the hopes of its promoters. It was indeed described as "a complete nullity" when the question of the regulation of beerhouses came up again for serious consideration. But in certain districts the magistrates seem to have taken their new duties seriously, and in St. Pancras they closed the beerhouses at 9 o'clock.[3] In the same year, 1834, a small interference with the vested interests of spirits was ventured upon by Lord Althorp, Chancellor of the Exchequer. He noted the alarming increase in the consumption of ardent spirits, but did not propose to deal with it by any increase of the ordinary spirit duties. "Upon such a subject," he remarked, "taxation could not very well be productive of morality."[4] But he introduced an increase of 50 per cent. in the price of retail spirit licences, in cases where they were under ten guineas a year. By this he hoped apparently either to

---

[1] An amendment inserted by the Lords.

[2] The houses were not to be open before 5 A.M. or after 11 P.M. on week-days, or before 1 o'clock on Sundays.

[3] House of Lords Committee on Sale of Beer, Minutes of Evidence, 1849, p. 39, and Minutes of Evidence, 1850, p. 24.

[4] *Annual Register*, 1834, p. 291.

improve morality, or to benefit the revenue to the extent of £160,000. The experiment was too short-lived to produce any lasting result, for his successor, Spring Rice, under strong pressure, repealed the additional duties in 1836.

A flood of light was thrown on the general problem in 1834 by the appointment of a Select Committee of the House of Commons on Drunkenness. The affair was stage-managed by that erratic reformer, James Silk Buckingham. About 235 petitions had poured into Parliament, demanding an inquiry into the causes of Drunkenness, and the Committee appointed consisted of 36 members, including Peel and Althorp and many others of exceedingly moderate views. Very few of the members seem to have troubled to attend the meetings, at which a great mass of interesting evidence was given, and the Report seems almost undiluted Buckingham. Some opposition to printing it was raised by members of the Committee and by others, including O'Connell, who declared that " if they allowed this Report to be printed, they would encourage every drivelling Legislator. Oh, yes ! they would have some snail-paced Legislator moving for a Committee to inquire into the best means of preventing flies from destroying butter or honey."[1]

In spite of these objections, the House decided to print the Report together with the evidence. A remarkable document, long-winded and florid, it begins by describing the consequences of drunkenness to individual character under six headings, to national welfare under eleven headings. The immediate remedies proposed are given under nineteen heads and include a new classification of houses for the sale of intoxicating liquors, a limitation of licences by population, the handing over of all licensing to the magistrates, earlier closing, abolition of spirit rations to the Army and Navy, the provision of open spaces and of a National System of Education, which should amongst other things teach the poisonous nature of spirits. But the most startling and subversive part of the Report was that which came under the heading " Ultimate or Prospective Remedies." These included nothing less than total prohibition. This, it is true, was not given as the Committee's own recommendation, but as having been strongly urged by several witnesses, " when public opinion shall be sufficiently awakened to the great

[1] House of Commons, August 5, 1834.

national importance of the subject." In its concluding paragraphs, however, the Report urged that the Government should be requested to make a declaration that early next session they would introduce " some general and comprehensive law, for the progressive diminution and ultimate suppression of all the existing facilities and means of Intemperance, as the root and parent of almost every other vice." It is not surprising that Lord John Russell rose at once to explain that he, for one, would be no party to such a measure. So far, indeed, were the Government from meditating any drastic temperance measures, that, as we have seen, next year they repealed Althorp's increase in the price of licences.

Buckingham, whose valiant attempts to introduce social amenities we have described elsewhere, brought in a Bill in 1835 embodying some of the recommendations of his Committee, but in face of overwhelming opposition dropped it, and concentrated his efforts on the provision of open spaces, libraries, museums, etc. The principle of open competition had by this time become firmly established, and the liquor interests were strong enough to resist any further encroachments. Brougham, indeed, whose views on beerhouses had become violently hostile, proposed in the House of Lords, in 1839,[1] a measure that meant a practical repeal of the 1830 Beer Act, advocating his proposals with his usual flow of elaborate eloquence, and denouncing beerhouses as haunts of " profligacy and crapulous vice." On the evils of public-houses and ginshops he was silent. His proposal died in Committee stage.

A more modest measure was brought forward in 1839, and carried in 1840 by Mr., afterwards Sir John Pakington, a Tory member. In 1831 the agricultural riots, and now the Chartist disturbances, in especial the Newport rising, produced a certain panic about beerhouses. Chartist meetings, it was said, were held in them ; in Dukes Town, the chief seat of Chartism in Monmouth, out of the 151 houses, 5 were public-houses and 28 were beershops.[2] Pakington's measure[3] seems now a curiously mild Act to have evoked so strenuous a defence of beerhouses and of the property invested in them from the Chancellor of the Exchequer, F. Baring. No proposal was made for limitation by

<hr/>

[1] June 3.   [2] Pakington, House of Commons, February 19, 1840.
[3] 3 and 4 Vict. cap. 61.

population or for confiscation, and most of the provisions of the 1830 and 1834 Acts still stood.[1]   In its final form the new Act merely imposed a certain qualification of value for all beerhouses according to their situation,[2] but exempted existing holders of licences from this regulation.   The clauses of the original Beer Act, and of the 1834 amending Act on the subject of hours, were repealed and statutory hours laid down, approximating to those during which public-houses were usually open.   Thus, in the cities of London and Westminster and in certain other London boroughs, beerhouses might be open from 5 A.M. till 12 P.M. ; in places with a population of over 2500, from 5 A.M. till 11 P.M. ; and in other places from 5 A.M. till 10 P.M.   On Sundays everywhere they were to be closed till one o'clock, and at other hours when licensed victuallers were shut.

These provisions about hours brought beerhouses more or less into line with public-houses as regarded week-days,[3] though in towns like Manchester and Liverpool there was a tendency for the closing hour of the latter to approach midnight.   Eleven might be the nominal hour, but there was " no severity " exercised in enforcing it.   On Sundays, however, there was still a considerable distinction.[4]   By the terms of their licence all publicans were obliged to close their houses during the hours of Divine Service.   For the rest of Sunday they might keep open.   Thus as the churches filled, the public-houses emptied.   The result was that church and chapel goers found the streets thronged with staggering or sprawling figures.   The disgusting scenes in London on Sunday mornings had formerly been notorious ; Manchester and Liverpool were now no better. A stipendiary magistrate, later, thus described the state of Liverpool before 1842 : " In the populous Parts of the Town many of the Public Houses were open all the [Saturday] Night ; others only closed from Two to Four o'clock ; and the Consequence was, that they were filled with People drinking, and . . .

---

[1] An amendment, proposed by Lord Sandon, that licences in future should be only for " off " consumption was defeated by 91 votes to 47.   It is interesting to notice that the minority included Gladstone, the only occasion, so far as is recorded in Hansard, when he voted on any of the above-mentioned measures.

[2] £15 a year for places with a population over 10,000 ; £11 a year for places with a population over 2500 ; £8 a year elsewhere.

[3] The recognised hour for closing in London seems to have been midnight.   A London magistrate said in 1834 that seventeen years earlier London public-houses had been forced to close at 10 P.M.—1834 Committee on Drunkenness, p. 292.

[4] Except as regards London.   See p. 163.

People were not turned out of them until the Proprietors of the Houses dreaded the Operation of the Law which prohibits the Sale of Beer during the Hours of Divine Service. . . ." [1] The use of carriages to take people to church, deprecated by the stricter Sabbatarians, was defended on the grounds that the streets were impassable on foot. It is significant that no attempt was made to check this public nuisance by strengthening the hands of the magistrates or by altering the terms of the licence. It was made a matter of police regulation, and handled piecemeal. In 1839, by a special Police Act, all places in London for the sale of intoxicating liquor were ordered to be closed from midnight on Saturday till one o'clock on Sunday. Liverpool followed in 1842, Manchester, Newcastle, and Sheffield a few years later, and in 1848 Sunday-morning closing was made compulsory for the whole of England. [2]

We have described parliamentary action. Let us now consider how that action affected the ordinary man and woman in the new industrial towns. In any community, however happy the conditions of life, unlimited and unregulated facilities for obtaining alcohol would be dangerous. In these towns the conditions of life were far from happy. " I quite believe," said Dr. Southwood Smith, " from what I have observed of them, that the inducement to take the most pernicious amount of stimulants often arises from a sensation of lassitude and languor, the direct result of the debilitating causes that are incessantly acting upon them, and that renders them so incapable of physical and mental exertion. Every one who has observed his own sensations during the few days which precede an acute attack of fever, can well appreciate that feeling of *malaise*, more intolerable than pain ; and it is no wonder that they fly to anything which affords a prospect of temporary relief from it." [3] When ginshops and beerhouses were multiplied this deadly escape from wretchedness was hard to resist. In the words of another wise and humane physician, Joseph Toynbee: "When I see the working man and his wife living in a dark, damp kitchen, or in a close attic, supplied with a deficient quantity of impure water, the odour throughout the house being most

---

[1] House of Lords Committee on Sale of Beer on Lord's Day Regulation Bill, 1847-48, p. 15.
[2] 11 and 12 Vict. cap. 49.
[3] 1844 Health of Towns Commission, First Report, p. 73.

offensive—paying for this accommodation an exorbitant rent, I must confess that the wonder to me is, not that so many of the labouring classes crowd to the ginshops, but that so many are to be found struggling to make their wretched abodes a home for their family." [1]

Though reformers like Buckingham were able to achieve little in Parliament, there grew up among the working classes in the north of England a considerable movement against the evils of drink. Henry Forbes, a Bradford merchant, started the first Temperance Society in England at Bradford in February 1830. Similar societies were formed in other towns, Leeds, Bolton, and Birmingham, and others in the same year. A London society called the British and Foreign Temperance Society was also started the same year under distinguished patronage. These early societies did not forbid the use of wine or beer ; their hostility was directed solely against spirits and against excess in other alcohol. No doubt they did much good work, though their record has been rather put in the shade by the more sensational developments later. In 1832 a new movement for total abstinence from all intoxicants was started by a band of some thirty-three men [2] at Preston, a town afterwards called " the Jerusalem of teetotallers." The best known of the band was Joseph Livesey, a cheese factor who had started life as a weaver, a remarkable man, who after a short time at a Dame School, had picked up his education by reading as he worked at his loom. All but two or three of the thirty-three were working men. They were inspired with boundless zeal for the cause. " They felt," wrote Livesey afterwards, " that they had discovered a remedy for the greatest curse that the world had to endure. It was like the discovery of the gold diggings, crowds rushed in to gain the prize ; and for the first few years the meetings were crowded, and we had an array of reformed drunkards, not a few of them speakers, such as we have never seen since." [3]

It was one of the reformed drunkards, Richard Turner by name, who coined the word which caught the popular fancy, " tee-tee-totalism." As was to be expected, a fierce opposition rose up, and one at least of the band lost his work

---

[1] *Ibid.* p. 340. [2] Seven men signed the original pledge.
[3] *Reminiscences of Early Teetotalism*, by J. Livesey, 1867, p. 4.

in consequence. This was Henry Anderton, a saddler, who wrote a great quantity of popular verse for the cause.[1] His trade was largely dependent on the coaches, and the coaches were owned by the publicans. It must often have needed as much courage to be a teetotaller at this time as it had needed once to be a Methodist, for drinking customs prevailed in almost every occupation, and, if the writer of a book on the subject in 1839 is to be trusted, in some trades those who refused to conform were roughly handled.[2] Meetings in Preston were held at the Cockpit, built for cock-fighting by the Earl of Derby, but deserted by that nobleman when his son was defeated by Henry Hunt at the 1830 Election. But meetings were not confined to Preston ; " there was scarcely a night in the week on which a party was not holding a meeting in some of the adjoining villages," and in 1833 a week's missionary tour to other Lancashire towns was undertaken by seven of the enthusiasts. The movement spread rapidly, not only in Lancashire but all over the country. Even London was visited by Livesey. As the movement grew, larger and more formal societies were started—the British Association for the Promotion of Temperance, founded 1835, was the first general society—and a mass of rather dreary periodical literature was issued.

Two points may be noticed about the early career of the movement : a good deal of energy was spent in attacking what the zealots considered the pernicious doctrine of partial abstinence. " As Christianity was fettered for a long time with Judaism," explained Livesey later, so was the new movement fettered with its predecessor. But it did not take long to win over most of the existing societies to the new rule of total abstinence. Secondly, there was a certain hostility between the early teetotallers and some of the representatives of the churches.[3] To certain Christian ministers total abstinence seemed a crude and fanatical doctrine, contrary to Christ's teaching, and advocated moreover by men some of whom were of heterodox opinions.[4] Opposition to the movement on these

---

[1] See *Poems of Henry Anderton*, with Memoir by E. Grubb.
[2] See Dunlop, *The Philosophy of Artificial and Compulsory Drinking Usage*, by John Dunlop, President of the General Temperance Union of Scotland, 1839.
[3] See P. T. Winskill, *The Temperance Movement*, 1892, vol. ii. chaps. xx. and xxii.
[4] John Finch of Liverpool, one of the most prominent early teetotallers, was an adherent of Owen.

grounds was not confined to any one sect,[1] but it was most prominent among the Wesleyan Methodists. This was felt the more bitterly because the early meetings were largely held in Methodist chapels; the Primitive Methodists and the Independent Methodists were mainly friendly. Methodists, including ministers, were amongst the keenest and most unsparing advocates of total abstinence, and Wesley himself had preached the doctrine. "Nevertheless, for a long series of years the majority of the leading officials and ministers of the Wesleyan Methodist or parent Methodist Society were bitterly opposed to teetotalism, as were also a considerable number of the ministers and official members of some of the other branches of the Methodist family, although many of them professed to be friends of what they pleased to denominate as temperance—the moderate use of alcoholic liquors. . . . This opposition culminated and took an official form in 1841, when the Conference which met in Manchester that year passed the three following resolutions:

1st. That no unfermented wines be used in the administration of the sacrament throughout the Connexion.

2nd. That no Wesleyan chapel be lent for the meetings of the Temperance Society.[2]

3rd. That no preacher shall go into another circuit to advocate teetotalism without the consent of the superintendent of the circuit to which he may be invited."[3]

The teetotallers, on their side, did not weary in drawing attention to the fact that part of the basement of the Wesleyan Centenary Hall in London was let to a wine and spirit dealer. The teetotallers inside the denomination formed their own Temperance Association, and many ignored the resolutions. It was many years before the breach was healed.

Some idea of the temperance activities of the forties can be gained by glancing at an account of Hull in the *National Temperance Magazine* for April 1846. There were three distinct temperance societies in the town with which religious leaders and medical men were associated. Four evenings a week there were meetings held in connection with one or other of these societies, and they all joined together to

---

[1] See Rev. T. Spencer's pamphlets.   [2] This meant the Teetotal Society.
[3] Winskill, *op. cit.*, vol. ii. p. 54.

support a missionary. Livesey, writing in 1867, suggested that when the help of other classes was enlisted some virtue had gone out of the movement. In early days " The conflict was fierce ; and the resistance, manifested in hostile opposition, served only to fire our zeal. We seemed as if we would turn the world upside down. We scarcely feel in this mood now. Our working men—sawyers, mechanics, and men of all trades—were constant speakers at the meetings ; they went everywhere, and no others were listened to with equal attention. Instead of these fearless heroes, reverend gentlemen and professional lecturers, to a great extent have taken their place. . . ." [1] Such reflections are not uncommon when a crusader looks back upon his life. In the forties, at any rate, the age of the fearless heroes had not passed ; the help of persons of good worldly position had not interfered with the formation of numerous small temperance societies of working men. Their growth in Leeds was described by Mr. Thomas Beggs, formerly Secretary of the National Temperance Society. " Then there have sprung up a great number of temperance societies ; almost every little neighbourhood having its separate temperance society with its committee, whose business it is to distribute tracts and hold weekly meetings in order to give lectures on the subject of temperance ; and the last time I was in Leeds there were 28 of these societies, holding weekly meetings. As many as I could crowd into three or four evenings' stay in Leeds I visited, and the average attendance seemed to be from 300 to 400 working men, and women, and sometimes boys." [2] Mr. Bishop, Minister of the Liverpool Domestic Mission Society, said that there was scarcely a large town in England without one or more Temperance Societies, " but such societies are mainly supported and worked in this country by the operative classes themselves. Here and there they have the support of a clergyman or gentleman connected with the wealthier classes, but, for the most part, their meetings are conducted, their rooms are taken and the rent paid by the pence of the operatives." [3]

[1] Livesey, *op. cit.* pp. 37 and 38.
[2] Select Committee on Public Houses, 1852-53, p. 325. [3] *Ibid.* p. 320.

CHAPTER XI

EDUCATION

IN 1834 the passion for social improvement and for accurate information induced a body of gentlemen in Manchester, who had formed a Statistical Society, to start an inquiry into the state of education in that town. The inquiry spread to neighbouring towns, to Salford, Liverpool, Bury, Bolton, Ashton, Dukinfield, Stalybridge, and even to York. Later, Birmingham and Bristol were also investigated in the same way. The results were digested and published in different reports, mostly between 1834 and 1837, and, from the remarks of the investigators, even more than from the numerous statistical tables, it is possible to form some estimate of the opportunities for schooling in the towns of that time. There was no compulsory attendance except for children working in factories (see p. 181), and there the schooling existed chiefly on paper.

Let us suppose that the parents of a small intelligent boy in Manchester, of what we should now call school age,[1] were anxious that he should learn his letters and whatever else he could pick up. In 84 out of the 86 Sunday-schools in Manchester, he would be taught to read after a fashion, and in 10 of those schools he might learn writing too, but the process would be long and tedious, and we will suppose that his parents wished for instruction on week days. He would first be sent to one of the many Dame Schools scattered about the town (there were 230 of them in Manchester), where reading, and, for girls, sewing, were taught. If he were lucky he would live close to one of the old-fashioned type, where a tidy old lady would teach habits of neatness, even though her literary stan-

---

[1] Robert Owen had set the example of infant education in his well-known establishment at New Lanark. There were a few infant schools in the English towns, started by Samuel Wilderspin (1792?–1866), a man of great public spirit, whose ideas were, in many respects, more enlightened than those of his contemporaries. In Manchester there were about 650 children taught at these schools.

dards were not high. If he were very fortunate he would find himself at the school " kept by a blind man who hears his scholars their lessons and explains them with great simplicity." The blind teacher was liable to be interrupted by being called to turn his wife's mangle, but probably the lessons were none the worse for that. If he were less fortunate he would find that the Dame School was a dirty, close room, where children were sent not so much to learn as " to be taken care of and to be out of the way at home." " If I can keep a bit of quietness," said one of the Dames, " it is as much as I can do and as much as I am paid for,"—where books to read and fresh air to breathe were equally scarce, where discipline depended on the rod, where the only saving grace was a certain slackness so that in hot weather, for instance, the children could stretch out their limbs (provided there were room) on forms or floor, and sleep away the weary afternoon. As a Bury mistress remarked with truth, by way of apology, " they were better so than awake." For the privilege of sending a child to one of these Dame Schools parents paid as a rule 4d. a week, some more, some less. The average income of the Manchester Dames was calculated to be £17, 16s. or 6s. 10d. a week, in Bury it was put at £19 a year. It was supplemented by earnings from other sources such as shopkeeping, sewing, or washing. Teaching might be combined with keeping a cake shop, for which the pupils provided a clientele, or with selling milk, in which case the scholars could amuse themselves with dabbling in the cans. Occasionally the poor rates provided the necessary supplement, but this was rare.

In his next stage the boy would go to what the Statistical Society called a " Common Day School," [1] that is a school kept by a master or mistress who made his or her living by it. This was the type of school at which the majority of boys and girls in Manchester obtained their education, such as it was. The charge was higher than at the Dame Schools, from 6d. to 9d. a week, and the average master made 16s. or 17s. a week, the capable master a good deal more. Too often the teacher's qualification for his job was that noted in the case of the old men who kept Dame Schools : " unfitness for every other."

[1] Kay-Shuttleworth, *Four Periods of Public Education*, 1862, p. 104, calls them " Adventure Schools," as they were kept by " private adventure teachers."

These masters and mistresses, however, had a better opinion of themselves than that held by their investigators. " Some intelligent masters," it was said, " . . . conceive there is something in the occupation which begets self-sufficiency." Whatever the truth of this, these Common Day School masters were " strongly impressed with the superiority of their own plans to those of any other school, and very little inclined to listen to any suggestions respecting improvements in the system of education that had been made in other places." These schools professed to teach reading, writing, and arithmetic. Penmanship was considered essential, and specimens of fine writing exhibited to attract parents. In some of the better ones a little grammar and geography were thrown in for an extra penny or so a week. Occasionally they soared higher. In one school the master dilated on the various sciences he could teach : Hydraulics, Hydrostatics, Geography, Geology, Etymology, Entomology. The visitor remarked : " This is *multum in parvo* indeed." To which the master immediately replied : " Yes, I teach that : you may put that down too."

The premises of these schools were not much better than those of the Dame Schools. Perhaps the worst example was a school in Liverpool, where a garret, measuring 10 feet by 9 feet, contained one master, one cock, two hens, three black terriers, and forty children. Bad air, dirty rooms, incompetent teachers, disorderly ways (" tiresome task this teaching," remarked one master, " there is no managing them "), absence of books or other apparatus, were characteristics of these schools. A floating population of boys and girls resorted to them ; in most boys' schools there were some girls, and in most girls' schools some boys, and the children learnt or failed to learn the elements of the three R's, to the constant accompaniment of the birch. On the other hand, the masters and mistresses were occasionally persons of ability, and even when ability was absent there was also an absence of the monotony and routine which improved methods often brought with them. School life must have had attractions and surprises under the master who was met by the investigator " issuing from his school at the head of all his scholars, to see a fight in the neighbourhood ; and instead of stopping to reply to any educational queries, only uttered a breathless invitation to come along and see the sport." These schools were severely blamed for their neglect of any systematic religious and moral instruction, but a good many children surfeited with this teaching in National or Lancasterian schools might have done better in the care of the master who, when asked his method of religious teaching, answered " I hear them their catechism once a week," and to the question how he taught morals, replied, " I tell them to be good lads, you know, and mind what I say to them, and so on." Perhaps they might have done no worse under the gentleman who, when asked if he taught morals, observed : " That question does not belong to my school, it belongs to the girls' schools." One of these masters, held up to ridicule in the Manchester Report, seems to have been before his time. He stated that " he had adopted a system which he thought would at once supply the great desiderata in education. ' It is simply,' he said, ' in watching the dispositions of the children and putting them especially to that particular thing which they take to.' In illustration of this system, he called up a boy of about ten years of age, who had *taken to* Hebrew, and was just beginning to learn it ; the master acknowledging that he himself was learning too, in order to teach his pupil. On being asked whether he did not now and then find a few who did not take to anything, he acknowledged that it was so, and this, he said, was the only weak point in his system, as he feared that he should not be able to make much of those children."

It might have happened that the boy whose experiences we are attempting to imagine, instead of going to one of the ramshackle, self-supporting schools, went instead to a school dependent on public subscription and conducted on the lines of one of the two societies for educating the poor, whose methods and rivalries fill so much of the educational literature of the time. In the Manchester Lancasterian School, connected with the British and Foreign School Society, he would have found over a thousand close-packed children, sitting on benches, all being taught together in one room, with only two masters and one mistress in charge. At first the noise would have been deafening, the crowd bewildering, but soon he would have noticed that there was order and system in the apparent chaos, that the multitude obeyed certain words and commands such as " sling hats," " clean slates," and acted as one child, that each nine or ten boys were in charge of another boy called a monitor, who taught them the lesson that he had lately learned himself, either summoning them to stand round him in one of the semi-circles marked in the passage at the end of the forms and teaching them to read from a board with the lesson printed large upon it, or else standing at the end of the form on which they were sitting and dictating to them words of the number of syllables suitable to their particular class. Dictation for the whole school was a triumph of organisation. On the platform at one end sat the master, and at a signal from him, or from the " monitor-general," a sort of sergeant-major amongst children, the monitor of the highest class would lead off with his four-syllabled word, followed in turn by each monitor in the hierarchy down to the bottom. When the process had been repeated for six words, each monitor examined the slates of his charges and signalled to the master by means of a " telegraph " or signboard fixed at the end of the form ; as soon as corrections were made, and all the telegraphs turned the right way, the master gave the signal again and another six words were dictated.[1]

If the boy were specially bright he might find himself, even at the early age of seven, chosen by the master to be trained as a monitor. The master would teach him a lesson and he would repeat it like a little gramophone to his small group. His authority over his group or " draft " would not extend to chastisement, but he was expected to become a rather stern disciplinarian. If he perceived " a pupil untidy, talking, or idle," it was " his duty to put a disgrace or accusation-mark about his neck, having first warned him." He was to take away the disgrace-mark as soon as the pupil showed that he was corrected of his fault, or as soon as he perceived " that another pupil had committed a similar offence." " Incorrigible pupils " he would send up to the master's platform. Even these boys were not whipped, for in marked contrast to the Common Day Schools, the Lancasterian and National Schools trusted to a system of rewards and of confinement for their discipline.[2] Dirty boys were " sentenced to have their faces and hands washed before

[1] See British and Foreign School Society Manuals of 1816, 1831, 1843.
[2] The Manchester Statistical Society's Report on Education in York in 1836-37, p. 10 footnote, states that originally it was the custom in Lancasterian Schools for a boy to " wring the ears of all whom he superseded " as he went up the class after a successful answer.

the whole school and to be confined for half an hour " ; talkers, players, and idlers were also given half an hour's confinement, but by an ingenious arrangement of barter each half-hour's confinement could be paid for by a " merit ticket." But those culprits whose supply of tickets failed were " taken to the bottom of the school by the monitor of bad boys," and there made to do dictation of an appropriate kind for the allotted period. Good boys and monitors could exchange their merit tickets, each of which was worth half a farthing, for books or clothing at the end of the month.

School began and ended with the reading by the master of a chapter of the Bible ; the Bible was the only reading-book, and on the Bible all lessons were based. In some schools there were libraries from which the more promising pupils might borrow books to read out of school hours, but these books generally had " a bearing towards the works of God or the word of God." [1] By 1831, in order to counteract the deadly effects of mechanical instruction which were very obvious, attempts were made to teach the children the meaning of the words or sentences that they read or spelt or wrote, by a system of interrogation that had been hitherto confined to the highest class. [2] Thus if the reading lesson had consisted of the first verse of Genesis, the following interrogation would take place :

" *Monitor.* Who created the heavens and the earth ?

Pupil. God.

Monitor. When did God create the heavens and the earth ?

Pupil. In the beginning.

Monitor. What did God do in the beginning ?

Pupil. He created the heavens and the earth," etc., etc. [3]

If the boy remained long enough at school he would learn reading, writing, and the first four rules of arithmetic ; if he stayed longer he would be instructed in " geography both ancient and modern." This, as we shall see, contained also

---

[1] 1834 Select Committee on Education, p. 97.

[2] Francis Place in 1813 had tried to introduce into Lancasterian Schools a series of elementary reading lessons on such subjects as implements, *e.g.* the pickaxe and spade. The " fanatics," as he called them, turned them down. When he tried to start a Lancasterian School in which such lessons would be given, " These men said they would much rather destroy the undertaking than permit any but Bible lessons, and they did so."—1835 Committee on Education, pp. 76 and 77. By 1831 the spelling lessons were used as general information lessons, and the words spelt were ranged under various heads, *e.g.* saddler, bricklayer, farmer.—1834 Committee on Education, p. 93.

[3] *Manual* of 1816, p. 20.

scraps of historical information.   We will take a sample lesson, which was the ideal for the most forward children.   Tyre was the subject.   The monitor had loaded his own mind with various particulars about Tyre, acquired either from the master or from books studied in the school library.   He would then, supposing there was a map, put it up, point out the position of Tyre, and proceed to relate his various items of information. After this he would question them on what he had told them, as follows :

" *Monitor.* Where is it ?
Pupil. On an Island.
Monitor. Describe the situation of the Island ?
Pupil. It is at the eastern extremity of the Levant, opposite the northern part of the Holy Land, from which it is separated by a narrow strait.
Monitor. What occasioned its erection on an Island ?
Pupil. Its being attacked by Nebuchadnezzar.
Monitor. In what tribe was it included ?
Pupil. Asshur.
Monitor. For what was it remarkable ?
Pupil. Commercial prosperity.
Monitor. In what class of powers should we place it ?
Pupil. Naval.
Monitor. Was the second Tyre ever taken ?
Pupil. Yes.
Monitor. By whom ?
Pupil. Alexander the Great.
Monitor. Cite a passage of Scripture relating to that event ?
Pupil. Isaiah xxiii.
Monitor. What is Tyre now ?
Pupil. A place resorted to by fishermen to dry their nets.
Monitor. The prophecy respecting this ?
Pupil. Ezekiel xxvi. 14."

And so on, till Ezekiel, Isaiah, Alexander and Nebuchadnezzar were exhausted.[1]

In the thirties, and still more in the forties, an attempt was made to relax the strict reference of all knowledge in the Lancasterian Schools to the Scriptures, and though no language was

[1] *Manual* of 1831, p. 45.

taught, ample explanations were given of the roots of words. This was probably not unconnected with the fact noticed by Kay-Shuttleworth : " Those who have had close intercourse with the labouring classes well know with what difficulty they comprehend words not of a Saxon origin, and how frequently addresses to them are unintelligible from the continual use of terms of a Latin or Greek derivation. . . ." [1] A short illustration will show how it was attempted to make these words intelligible. In the highest divisions of the school, reading-books containing varied subjects, including " general history, physics, and natural history," had been introduced. A lesson on natural history would be given thus. The boys would read : " Ruminating animals. Cud-chewing or ruminating animals form the *eighth* order. These, with the exception of the camel, have no cutting teeth in the upper jaw, but their place is supplied with a hard pad. In the lower jaw there are eight cutters ; the tearers, in general, are absent, so that there is a vacant space between the cutters and grinders. The latter are very broad, and are kept rough and fit for grinding the vegetable food on which these animals live, by the enamel being disposed in crescent-shaped ridges." And so on for a long time. Interrogation on this lesson would then take place :

" *Monitor*. What have you been reading about ?
Boy. Ruminating animals.
Monitor. Another name for ruminating ?
Boy. Cud-chewing.
Monitor. What is the root of the word ?
Boy. ' Rumen,' the cud.
Monitor. What does the termination *ate* mean ?
Boy. To do or act on in some way.
Monitor. Ruminate, then, is to —— ?
Boy. To act on the cud,"

and so on. And later :

" *Monitor*. You read in the lesson *the enamel is disposed in crescent-shaped ridges*. What is the enamel ?
Boy. The hard, shining part of the tooth.
Monitor. What part of our tooth is it ?
Boy. The covering of that part that is out of the jaw-bone.

---

[1] Kay-Shuttleworth, *Four Periods of Public Education*, 1862, p. 339.

Monitor. What do you mean by disposed?
Boy. Placed.
Monitor. The root?
Boy. 'Pono,' I place.
Monitor. What is crescent-shaped?
Boy. Shaped like the moon before it is a half-moon.
Monitor. Draw a crescent. (*Boys draw it on the blackboard.*)
Monitor. What is the root of the word?
Boy. 'Cresco,' I grow," etc., etc., etc.

It is not remarkable to read in a footnote, "At this point it would be necessary for the monitor to put many of these questions over again, to ascertain that there has been perfect comprehension of the subject." [1]

Possibly during his school years the boy's parents would move house, and it would be more convenient to send him to a school under the auspices of the National Society for Promoting the Education of the Poor in the Principles of the Established Church. He would probably have noticed little difference. The forms would be arranged differently, but he would still be taught by monitors or teach others as a monitor. The repertory of religious instruction would be enlarged; he would hear a good deal about something called doctrines; in place of continual "catechetical interrogation" on the text of the Bible, he would now learn to repeat the creeds and the catechism, whilst words like "justification" and "sanctification" would loom large on his horizon. If he stayed long enough at school, he might know less about the connection of Tyre with Nebuchadnezzar and Alexander than if he had stopped at the Lancasterian School, but on the other hand he might hope to rival the class of children, aged ten to fourteen, described by Bishop Blomfield, who passed an excellent examination in the first nine chapters of Romans, explaining any passage on which they were questioned, and referring readily to parallel passages, and this in addition to showing knowledge of "almost all the principal facts connected with the history of the New Testament, the application of the leading prophecies, and the common geography of the Holy Land." [2]

On leaving school the boy we have tried to describe might not be altogether clear in his head about the doctrine of redemp-

[1] *Manual* of 1843, pp. 19 ff.   [2] 1834 Education Committee, p. 190.

tion and sanctification, or the pomps and vanities of the world, but he would have been still more puzzled to explain the declaration of the National Society whose school he had been attending, that they would not "timorously, unwisely and supinely . . . give up into the Hands of our Enemies that sacred and victorious weapon, which we have so long and successfully wielded in the Defence and Preservation of the Religion, the Virtue, the Welfare and Happiness of our Country." [1] To understand it he would have had to know something of the history of education during the preceding thirty years. That history would have made him aware that all the while, over the unsuspecting heads of the little boys and girls in the " Society " schools who were busy spelling out " The way of God is a good way," or " Bad men are foes to God," or adding up the children produced by Jacob's various wives,[2] a battle was raging among the Olympians for the possession of their young souls. A brief sketch of that battle is essential if we are to understand the state of education when public help was first given to it.

At the end of the eighteenth and beginning of the nineteenth centuries, in the age of mechanical inventions, two remarkable men, Dr. Andrew Bell, a Church of England clergyman, and Joseph Lancaster, a Quaker, invented separately new and similar systems of teaching. Both discovered that education could be greatly cheapened by the employment of child labour ; schoolmasters, except as heads, were superfluous ; scholars could be used to teach each other. For the credit of this discovery there was fierce controversy between the partisans of the two men. Lancaster began his teaching career in London : Bell started his system as a chaplain in Madras, and hence it was often called the " Madras system." Never have educationalists or their friends made higher claims. Lancaster, who announced that he had " invented, under the blessing of Divine Providence, a new and mechanical system of Education," showed that one master " might conduct a school of 1000 children with perfect ease." [3] Bell, who had a lively fancy, though he did not mention the figure of a thousand, was no less sanguine. " On

---

[1] Quoted, S. E. Maltby, *Manchester and the Movement for National Elementary Education*, p. 41.
[2] See F. Adams, *History of the Elementary School Contest*, p. 102.
[3] By 1831 the B.F.S.S. *Manual* had altered this to " several hundred."

this principle a superior can conduct any institution, how numerous soever, through the instrumentality of its own members. In a school it gives to the master the hundred eyes of Argus, the hundred hands of Briareus, and the wings of Mercury. In other words, by multiplying his ministers at pleasure it gives to him indefinite powers, and enables him to instruct as many pupils as any school will contain. While it bears a manifest analogy to the mechanical powers, it infinitely surpasses them in simplicity, economy, force, and effect. With great propriety it has been called the STEAM ENGINE of the MORAL WORLD. The intellectual machinery costs nothing, grows in force and efficiency, by the use that is made of it, and with the work which it has to perform : viresque acquirit eundo. In a word, it is the *lever of Archimedes* transferred from matter to mind." [1] Nor were his adherents less enthusiastic in their language. "If we do not reproach the philosophers of old time with the ignorance of what a Newton saw and investigated, we must not find fault with those good men for not having forestalled the merits and anticipated the discoveries of a Bell," said the Dean of Chichester of those who had tried to educate the young in the past. The new arrangement of the school-room seemed indeed to make it possible to educate a large number of children at a small expense. "Suppose," wrote Bell, "that in two empires consisting each of 2,000,000 children to be educated, the one on the old plan, in schools of 50 pupils each, the other on the new, of 500, at the stipend of £50 to each master. The amount of school fees, in the one case, would be £1 a scholar, or £2,000,000; in the other, 2s. a scholar, or £200,000 —the difference being £1,800,000. But, allowing the Madras master double this stipend, the difference would then be £1,600,000." [2]

Enthusiasts for education grouped themselves behind the two men according to their colour, and societies were founded to promote their respective principles. The Lancasterian Society (1808), afterwards called the British and Foreign School Society (1814), was unsectarian, and drew its main support from Whigs and Nonconformists. In its schools the Bible was taught without comment. The Society which followed Dr. Bell was

[1] Bell's *Manual of Public and Private Education* (1827), p. 15.
[2] Bell's *Mutual Tuition or Manual of Instruction* (1823), p. 121.

called "The National Society for Promoting the Education of the Poor in the Principles of the Established Church," and taught Church doctrines in addition to the Scriptures. The National Society, in addition to its enthusiasts, harnessed to its purposes a good many who had before been lukewarm, if not hostile, to scattering schooling wholesale. William Cotton, the philanthropist, giving evidence on behalf of the National Society, summed the matter up very justly, when he said that whilst the main supporters and real workers (of the National Society) were quite unaffected by any question of rivalry, yet "the success of Joseph Lancaster created a considerable sensation among those who were not very friendly to the education of the poor, but who would rather see the people educated by the National Church than by Joseph Lancaster, I readily admit."[1] However this may be, and whatever the motives of its subscribers, the National Society was the wealthier of the two.

Let us now consider the position of education for the working classes when the Reformed Parliament began to sit in 1833. Whitbread in 1807, and after him Brougham, had pressed in vain for some scheme of national education. A large number of the existing schools were still (specially in towns) affairs of private enterprise. The extent to which the working classes in the industrial towns were supporting schools out of their pockets has perhaps been overlooked. In Manchester, for 4070 children attending schools that were either free or partially assisted, there were 13,108 children attending entirely self-supporting schools.[2] In Bury, the proportions were 652 to 1799. In Salford, 1950 to 3709. In Birmingham, 4066 to 8248. In West Bromwich, 423 to 1131.[3] In York, where there were many endowments, the figures were reversed, for there were

---

[1] 1834 Committee on Education, p. 145. Compare Bishop Tomline on Bell's system in a charge to his clergy in 1822. " If the plan of Education recently adopted in this country, be generally maintained in its True Spirit and Extent, and the children, when transferred from these schools into the various walks of humble and active life, be afterwards regularly supplied with suitable books, to foster and confirm that principle of Religion which has been instilled into them, and that sense and habit of submission to which they have been accustomed, we may defy all the machinery of domestic foes to subvert our constitution or disturb our internal tranquillity, and all the exertions of foreign enemies to deprive us of our prosperity and glory as a nation."—Bell's *Manual* of 1823, p. 36.

[2] In these totals the " superior and private boarding-schools " are omitted. For these and following figures, see Reports published by Manchester Statistical Society.

[3] *Journal of Statistical Society of London*, 1839, vol. ii. p. 377.

2697 free and assisted scholars to 1294 in self-supporting schools. In Bristol and Liverpool, too, there was a small majority of free and assisted scholars. In Bristol, the figures were 7207 to 6494; in Liverpool, 13,000 to 12,000. If an inquiry by the Manchester Statistical Society into Rutland may be taken as typical, there was a majority in country districts of free and assisted scholars; in Rutland it was 1610 to 1218 self-supporting scholars.[1] The payments at the self-supporting schools in all the places investigated were much the same; 3d. to 4d. was usual at Dame Schools, 8d. to 9d. at the Common Day Schools. The Bristol Statistical Society made the interesting calculation that in that town, out of a population of some 120,000, working-class parents were paying no less than £15,202, 19s. 6d. for the education of their children, that is, more than half the total parliamentary grant.[2]

Important though these self-supporting schools were, public interest was centred on the work and the rivalries of the two Societies. That there was a lamentable deficiency in means of education was generally agreed; the full extent of that deficiency was a matter of guesswork. An ambitious attempt to clear the ground before action was made early in the new Parliament by Lord Kerry, who asked (May 24, 1833) for a return, which amounted to an educational census. Rickman, who had achieved brilliant results with the population returns, took it in hand, unpaid. The answers to the 15,000 circulars, enclosing elaborate schedules, sent out to overseers, were remarkably numerous and full.[3] From this portentous mass of information, published in three volumes, it was calculated that out of an estimated population for England and Wales of 14,400,000, 1,276,947 children, or 1 in 11 of the population, were attending day schools of some sort or other,[4] whilst 1,548,890, or 1 in 9

---

[1] *Ibid.* pp. 303 ff.

[2] *Journal of Statistical Society of London*, 1841, vol. iv. p. 253. The total is made up of £2390, 17s. 9d. to Dame Schools, £10,298, 11s. 8d. to Common Day Schools, and £2513, 10s. 1d. to the aided schools.
It was estimated that in Birmingham (population, 180,000) parents paid annually £9922 to the self-supporting schools.—1838 Committee on Education, p. 121.

[3] All places were stated to be covered, with the exception of thirty-eight, containing some 19,000 inhabitants.

[4] 1835 Abstract of Education Returns, vol. iii. p. 1330. In 1922, 1 in every 7 of the population were attending elementary schools in England and Wales, and there was school accommodation for 1 in 5. For a full discussion and estimate of the number of children attending school, see M. E. Sadler, "Elementary Education in England and Wales, 1833 to 1870," in Board of Education Special Reports, vol. ii. 1898.

of the population, were attending Sunday-schools. Unfortunately, although the returns were numerous and full, they were found on more careful investigation to be hopelessly incorrect. As an example, the Manchester Statistical Society found that in Manchester, where the total school-going population was about 18,500, allowing for certain mistakes which cancelled each other, the Kerry returns omitted 181 schools with 8646 scholars.[1] The truth was that the attempt was too ambitious. The experiences of the Manchester investigator throw light on the errors. At York, the masters of the Endowed and Charity Schools " answered all interrogations with the utmost caution and in the vaguest manner," each seeming to think that his own school could be omitted without affecting the accuracy of the total. At Salford, many of the mistresses, with a caution for which one cannot blame them, asked a " prudent neighbour " to come in before answering the questions. If *viva voce* questions were bad, elaborate schedules were worse. Apart from the universal dislike of filling up forms, detailed knowledge of the Scriptures had persuaded some that counting numbers was unlucky. " No, no," said one teacher, " you shan't catch me counting ; see what a pretty mess David made of it when he counted the children of Israel." [2]

Whilst the Kerry papers were being sent out the Government took two important steps. In the first place, they included in their Factory Act of 1833 provisions for the compulsory education of factory children. On paper every child was obliged to attend school for two hours a day, and if a suitable school was wanting, the Inspector was " authorized to establish or procure the establishment of such schools." As, however, no funds were provided, and as the relevant sections were carelessly drafted, these well-intentioned provisions were often a dead-letter, and, where carried out conscientiously by employers, were a tax on industry.[3] The second step taken by the Government was to make a grant in aid of education. Their plan avoided the pitfalls of religious controversy. They proposed, on August 17,

---

[1] In Bury, with 2474 scholars, 19 schools with 861 scholars were omitted ; in York, with 4707 scholars, 53 schools with 1650 scholars were omitted.
[2] 1838 Committee on Education, p. 103.
[3] See for account of the provisions of the Act, etc., the Special Report on the Establishment of Schools in Factory Districts, by R. J. Saunders, published amongst the Factory Inspectors Reports for 1843.

1833, a vote of £20,000 to be distributed between the two Societies, in aid of subscriptions for building schools. Before any grant was given, at least half the sum required must be raised by subscription.[1]   The proposal was carried by 50 votes to 26, the opposition including Cobbett, who objected to any public help (" Education," he said, " had been more and more spread, but what did it all tend to ?   Nothing but to increase the number of schoolmasters and schoolmistresses—that new race of idlers.   Crime, too, went on increasing "), and Radicals like Hume, Fielden, Potter, and Brotherton, who wanted a national system, and thought this a harmful substitute.   For five years this non-committal grant was distributed by the Lords of the Treasury.   The National Society, as the wealthier and larger, had the lion's share, £69,710 during the five years, whilst the British and Foreign School Society received £35,285.[2]

In the sixth year, 1839, the Government took a further step, a step from which we may date the beginning of public education in England.   The credit for this departure rests with Lord John Russell.   In the autumn of 1838, when the Government had lost its popularity, he decided to grasp the nettle of the religious difficulty, though that nettle had not lost its stinging properties.[3]   As far as the grant was concerned, relations had been harmonious between the two Societies, and its distribution, as the *Annual Register* put it, had " been attended with the happiest consequences to the poorer classes." But in questions outside the grant, relations between the Church and Nonconformists had been embittered by the grievance of Church rates, and Cobden's jest is well known that the Corn Law agitation was " light amusement " compared with his attempt to unite the different sects for education in Manchester in 1836.[4]

During the five years a good deal of information about the state of education had been published.   Apart from the reports of the Manchester Statistical Society there had been three Parliamentary Committees.   The first was appointed at the instance of Roebuck, in 1834, to inquire into " the present

---

[1] See Treasury Minute, quoted Kay-Shuttleworth, *op. cit.* p. 235 footnote.
[2] 1838 Committee on Education, p. x.
[3] It was perhaps unfortunate that he happened to be connected with the British and Foreign School Society, of which he had been a Vice-President since 1824.
[4] Quoted Maltby, *op. cit.* p. 48 footnote.

state of Education of the People in England and Wales, and into the application and effects of the Grant made in the last Session," and to consider the question of further grants. This Committee merely reported the evidence, which was given mainly by spokesmen of the two Societies. The Committee was re-appointed in 1835, and again reported the evidence without making any recommendations. In 1837 a new Committee was appointed, at the instance of Slaney, " to consider the best means of providing useful Education for the Children of the Poorer Classes in large Towns throughout England and Wales." Slaney was chairman, and Peel, Ashley, and Wyse[1] were among the members. This Committee made full use of the Manchester Reports, and took a considerable amount of varied evidence. It reported, in July 1838, six months after Brougham had made a forcible plea for a Board of Education in the House of Lords, and a month after Wyse in the Commons had only lost his motion for the establishment of a central Educational Authority by four votes. Owing to disagreements on the Committee its report was timid in tone. After laying down as an end the ideal that education should be provided for 1 in every 8 of the population in great towns, the only means that the Committee proposed was a continuance and increase of the grants to the two Societies, with a modification of the conditions about sub-scriptions in the case of poor districts.

From the evidence before the various committees two points had stood out clearly : the need of trained teachers, and the absence of effective provision for training them. The National Society took young men and women at the age of twenty-one onwards and gave them five months' training. Most of them had tried other professions or callings ; some had come from " very respectable situations in life in which they have not been successful." [2] The British and Foreign Society took them from nineteen years old to twenty-three or twenty-four. Their candidates were mostly ex-mechanics who had acquired a taste for teaching by helping in Sunday-schools. If they kept any of that taste after the three months' intensive training that was given them, they must have been remarkable persons. " Our object," said the Secretary, " is to keep them incessantly em-

---

[1] President of the Central Society for Education.
[2] 1834 Committee on Education, p. 9.

ployed from five in the morning until nine or ten at night. We have rather exceeded in the time devoted to study the limit we would choose, on account of the very short period we are able to keep them, and we have found in some instances that their health has suffered on account of their having been previously quite unaccustomed to mental occupations."[1] The future schoolmistresses seem to have stood the training even less successfully. "I think women have not generally the same vigour of mind."[2] It is only fair to say that neither of the Societies thought their few months' training sufficient, but the great demand for teachers, and the want of funds, caused the stream through their training schools to flow fast.

The provision of a Normal School for training teachers was a main feature of Lord John Russell's educational scheme. On February 12, 1839,[3] he briefly announced his new plan in Parliament, at the same time laying on the table his correspondence with Lord Lansdowne, Lord President of the Council, on the matter. He proposed to set up by Order in Council a body of five persons, consisting of the Lord President of the Council, the Lord Privy Seal, the Home Secretary, the Chancellor of the Exchequer, and the Master of the Mint, " for the consideration of all matters affecting the Education of the People." They were to have charge of any sums voted for education, and one of their first cares would be the establishment of a Normal School. In his letter to Lord Lansdowne, Lord John Russell, after describing the differences of opinion on the question of religious instruction, went on to use language of a curiously sanguine nature : " In the midst of these conflicting opinions, there is not practically that exclusiveness among the Church societies, nor that indifference to religion among those who exclude dogmatic instruction from the School, which their mutual accusations would lead bystanders to suppose. Much, therefore, may be effected by a temperate attention to the fair claims of the Established Church, and the religious freedom sanctioned by law."[4] He was soon to find his mistake. On April 10 the

---

[1] 1834 Committee on Education, pp. 16 and 17.
[2] *Ibid.* p. 25.
[3] Cf. *Memoir of Bishop Blomfield*, edited by his son, p. 194, extract from his diary, January 22, 1839 : " Went with the Archbishop to Ld. John Russell about education : asserted the claims of the Church to conduct the education of the people."
[4] Quoted Kay-Shuttleworth, *op. cit.* p. 240.

four Cabinet Ministers already mentioned were appointed by Order in Council as a Committee of the Privy Council to superintend the application of the parliamentary grants to education. The Master of the Mint had dropped out, and so had the more ambitious task of considering all matters affecting the education of the people. On April 17 were published extracts from the Minutes of the newly appointed Committee, which caused widespread excitement. These Minutes contained a detailed scheme of the proposed Governmental Normal School, and of the Model School to be set up in connection with it. They also contained a resolution " not to adhere invariably to the rule which confines grants to the National Society and the British and Foreign School Society " and not always to make the amount of the grant depend on the amount subscribed. A Secretary was to be appointed, and two Inspectors, who were to disseminate a knowledge of improvements among those engaged in education and to keep the Committee informed of progress. Dr. Kay, afterwards better known as Sir James Kay-Shuttleworth, was the first Secretary. He was a great public servant of independent mind and enlightened ideas, of whom it has been said : " To him more than to any one else we owe it that England is supplied with schools for the children of her people, and that this costly work has been accomplished without a breach between Church and State." [1]

A storm of criticism greeted these Minutes. The Church was outraged because in the Model School, attached to the Normal School, religious instruction was divided into " general " and " special," and the special instruction might be given, if desired, by Dissenting ministers. The candidate teachers in the Normal School could also have their special religious instruction provided from Nonconformist sources. This was taken to foreshadow a general " right of entry " into all schools. Nor were certain Nonconformists any better pleased. In the regulation that " either at the time fixed for reading the Scriptures, or at the hours of special instruction," Roman Catholics might read their own version of the Bible, the Wesleyan Methodists saw the triumph of the Scarlet Woman. This recognition by the State of " the corrupted Romish translations " they declared to be " a direct violation of the

---

[1] Sir Michael Sadler, in Introduction to *Life of Kay-Shuttleworth*, by Frank Smith.

first principles of our Protestant Constitution."[1]   In vigorous language the *Times* (June 3) described the horror of Nonconformists at seeing their children " herd with the leprous young brood of Papists, Socinians, Freethinkers, and fanatics, about to be forced upon them by the Whigs." The *Leeds Mercury*, though friendly to the Government, declared the scheme unworkable, putting the Nonconformist objections temperately but firmly. " Dissenting Ministers *might* come, by permission, to instruct the children ; but they would not, except in rare cases, be paid for it ; and most of the Dissenting Ministers have their hands already too full of work to be relied upon for a daily attendance on the schools."   The Church, on the other hand, had its equipment all ready.   As a consequence, " The Church Establishment would be immensely extended— an extension which, we hope, all Dissenters would feel it their duty to oppose." [2]

These religious clauses roused the more violent feeling, but the proposals to give grants outside the two Societies, and the appointment of Inspectors, were also unpalatable.   The five years' distribution between the two Societies had created vested interests.   It was now proposed to let others share in the benefits, and, worse still, to make inspection a condition of the grant.   The additional jam, in the shape of an increased grant, did not compensate for this powder.

The Government, discredited by the Bedchamber incident (May 3–May 13), and unwilling to face the storm, threw, to use Lord John Russell's expression, the Normal School to the wolves.   The wolves tore the corpse and demanded fresh victims.   The Report of the Committee of Council of June 3, in which it was announced that the scheme for the Normal School was dropped " until greater concurrence of opinion is found to prevail," whilst the £10,000 earmarked for the scheme would be divided equally between the two Societies, expressly retained the right of making grants in particular cases although the applications did not come from either Society, and also laid down the rule that grants in future should carry with them the right of inspection.   In a vigorous debate on the order for a Committee of Supply on June 14, adjourned till June 19 and 20,

[1] See Resolutions of Conference, *Leeds Mercury*, May 25, 1839.
[2] *Leeds Mercury*, May 25, 1839.

Lord Stanley, declaring that " education was the peculiar province of the clergy and was a spiritual matter to be entrusted to their superintendence," demanded the rescinding of the Order in Council. Statistics, always a special feature of debates on education, were hurled backwards and forwards with equal effect to prove opposite conclusions. Prisons and penitentiaries were ransacked to show that education cured or encouraged crime. In the end the Government only escaped defeat by five votes (280 to 275).[1] Four days later, when Lord John Russell moved the vote of £30,000 for education,[2] the majority was still narrower, 275 to 273.

In the Commons the Government had scraped through and had saved the grant by two votes ; in the Lords, faced with episcopal rhetoric, they could not avoid censure. The Archbishop of Canterbury (July 5) proposed a series of resolutions drawn up by Peel[3] deprecating the Government's action, and proposing to present an address to Her Majesty to ask that no plan for general education should be established without consulting the House of Lords. The new powers of the Committee of Council " ought not to be committed to any public authority without the consent of parliament." It was in vain that Lord Lansdowne pleaded that the change was a small one, and that the new Committee only discharged functions performed since 1833 by the Treasury. The sentence in the original letter to Lansdowne, about considering " all matters affecting the education of the people," and still more the deceased scheme for a Normal School, were treated as revelations of the Government's true intentions, and of their underlying hostility to the claims of the Church. By 229 votes to 118 the Lords passed the resolutions. They waited on Her Majesty with their remonstrances. As was to be expected, she did not show them much sympathy. Whilst regretting that they had taken this step, she assured them that she was sensible of her duties, and hoped that the money would be distributed with due respect to the rights of conscience and with a faithful attention to the security of the Established Church.

The Government had won a victory of a kind, but the Church

---

[1] June 24.
[2] Reformers were fond of pointing out that £70,000 was voted the same year for building Royal Stables.
[3] G. Kitson Clark, *Peel and the Conservative Party*, p. 436.

had other weapons at her command. The new Committee existed to distribute public money, of which the lion's share was to go to the Church, and the Church began to refuse to take it. To soften hostility the Committee issued regulations that the inspectors were not to interfere with religious instruction or with discipline, but were merely to collect facts and information.[1] It was explained that exceptions to the usual division between the two Societies would be very exceptional. Applicants not connected with either Society would have to explain their objections to such a connection and to give the fullest particulars of the religious instruction provided. Even then their chances of success seemed small.[2] Towards the end of December the Rev. John Allen and Mr. Seymour Tremenheere were appointed Inspectors. The Committee on January 4, 1840, gave them long instructions, of which the gist was that they were to be tactful and not meddle or intrude where they were not invited to go. Further, " in order to allay unfounded apprehensions " they were bidden to leave religious instruction alone, unless expressly asked to examine it. A parliamentary return on Education, of March 17, 1840, showed how serious the boycott was. Out of 393 applications for assistance from the £30,000 grant, the National Society had made 228, asking for £31,683. They had been offered £19,895, and had accepted only £5369, refusing £12,504. The balance was under consideration. They had also refused the £5000 allotted them for their Normal School. The indefatigable Secretary of the Education Committee poured out building plans and detailed specifications for the guidance of patrons of schools, but they were of little use if schools connected with the Establishment kept aloof. Matters, however, were settled in the summer of 1840, by a virtual capitulation of the Government. The Archbishops were given not only a veto on the appointment of inspectors of Church of England schools, but also the power of discharging them at any time. They were to be consulted about the general instructions to inspectors, and were themselves to draw up instructions about the inspection of religious

[1] The Committee of Council told the National Society in August 1839 that they had asked the Bishop of Chichester to recommend an inspector for National Schools. See *Life of Kay-Shuttleworth*, by Frank Smith, p. 95.

[2] See Minutes of December 3, 1839, published among Minutes of Committee of Council on Education, 1840, p. 7.

teaching. Copies of all reports on Church schools were to be sent to the Archbishop of the province and to the Bishop of the Diocese. Grants, with certain exceptions, were to be given in proportion to the number of children and to the amount of the contributions. When this was settled the new machinery was allowed to work.[1]

Thus, in 1839, the Government only escaped defeat by throwing several limbs of their proposals to the wolves of the Church; in 1843, when the next attempt was made, this time by a Tory Government, to introduce a considerable measure of education, the wolves of Dissent claimed and obtained the whole body. In the meanwhile the two inspectors had been very busy writing long reports of the various districts which they were asked to study. Several of these reports are accounts such as an explorer might give of the manners and customs of a new country, and contain much interesting information not closely connected with education. Mr. Tremenheere's report on the Monmouth Mining Districts and their " moral and social habits " attracted most attention, as the Newport rising was of recent date. After 1840, although the Church had been placated, relations between the British and Foreign School Society and the Education Committee were not running smoothly. From 1833 to 1839 the British Society had been technically on an equality with the Church, although, owing to her greater wealth and activity, the Church had obtained the larger share of the grants. But in 1840 the National Society had been put in a superior position, by the power given to the Archbishops. A long letter of complaint in January 1841 produced little satisfaction. The Whigs were succeeded by the Tories in September 1841, and the British Society now dealt with Lord Wharncliffe as President of the Council. They had become uneasy about the condition of inspection attached to the grants given to their new Normal School, for inspectors' comments were proving unpleasantly outspoken. Criticisms of the Glasgow Normal School had been published, and they feared that similar criticisms of their own establishment might dry up the stream of subscriptions and discourage the teachers. " Its reputation is its life," they pointed out. " In order to be useful,

---

[1] Extracts from Minutes of Committee of Council on Education, 1840, p. 2. See also *Life of Lord John Russell*, by Spencer Walpole, vol. i. p. 344.

it must possess the unlimited confidence both of those who sustain it and of those who are benefited by it." Matters were not improved when Mr. Tremenheere, to whom had been allotted the inspection of British and Foreign Schools, produced, in July 1842, a shattering report on 66 British and Foreign Schools in the Metropolitan district.[1] A very small number of these schools had received grants entailing inspection, the rest had asked for his visit of their own free will. The Society explained that they urged inspection on schools connected with them, never imagining that the report might be adverse.

It was hard for a Society which existed to enable the enlightened rich to bestow the blessings of knowledge on the grateful poor, to be told that out of 35 boys' schools in the London district all but a very few were in " various stages of mediocrity," that their cherished monitorial system, which was the pivot of their whole scheme of education, produced " mere mechanical reading," and that the monitors themselves (whose average age was ten and a half) did not show " more than a very slender capacity to maintain authority and attention while teaching, and still less to give anything of an intellectual character to the work they were entrusted with." Nor was this the worst. The inspector discovered a " great and lamentable " ignorance of the Scriptures, even amongst children who had been from two to six years at day and Sunday-schools. This is perhaps not surprising since " the reading in the lower divisions consists generally of Scripture extracts, placed before the children, not with reference to any connected train of historical instruction, but according to the number of syllables composing the words of the sentence." In reporting cases to illustrate this " absence of all memory for the facts which have formed the almost exclusive subject of their lessons or of all power to express any ideas they may have received," he seemed to hold up the schools to ridicule. The questions were clearly not put in the expected order. A few examples will show this : *Q.* Who were the Gentiles ?—*A.* People of God. *Q.* Who was Moses ?—*A.* Apostle of Christ. *Q.* Who was Peter ?— *A.* An angel. *Q.* Where was Christ crucified ?—*A.* Eng-

---

[1] For the whole episode, including Tremenheere's Report, see Return to House of Commons, April 1843, of Correspondence about the Borough Road Normal School. For Tremenheere's Report, see pp. 22 ff.

land. *Q.* Who was Jesus Christ the son of?—*A.* Son of David. *Q.* Who then was David?—*A.* Son of Jesus.[1]

The wrath of the Society at Mr. Tremenheere's criticisms was not averted by his suggestion that " a somewhat too continuous contemplation of merits may have helped to perpetuate imperfections."

Into the long-drawn controversy between the Education Committee and the British and Foreign School Society it is unnecessary to enter, though what seems a parliamentary echo of it may be noticed. In July, 1842, Wharncliffe, who had made a conciliatory statement about the claims of dissenters a few days previously,[2] was rebuked by the Bishop of London, who reminded the Lords that " the Church of the country was entitled to claim the instruction of the people, though it did not assert the right to teach the children of those who differed from it." [3] The importance of the controversy here is that it was helping to embitter relations just at the time when the Tory Government was producing its new education scheme. This scheme in its short life of three months in the spring of 1843 produced, outside Parliament, a storm of hatred and indignation so great that its astonished creators could only bow before it, and decide that the question of education was unsafe to handle.

To understand the conditions under which the scheme was put forward we must recall the atmosphere of 1843. The uneasiness caused by the Newport Rising of 1839 and by the Chartist agitation in general, had been increased by the riots of 1842. By 1843 it was generally acknowledged that an ignorant populace was a dangerous populace. From this point of view education was regarded as a means of enabling the working classes " to govern and repress the workings of their passions," [4] and the school was advocated as the alternative to the prison. This plea for education as an insurance against social danger was most frankly expressed in a letter from the Education Committee dated November 13, 1840. The Monmouth Mining Proprietors had been urged, and, with the excep-

---

[1] Borough Road Normal School Correspondence, pp. 51 and 52.
[2] He had " confessed that he should be ashamed if in a matter of education any difference should be made between Churchmen and Dissenters."—House of Lords, July 12.
[3] House of Lords, July 25, 1842.
[4] Ashley, see *Annual Register*, 1843, p. 53.

tion of Sir Thomas Phillips to whom the letter was addressed, urged in vain, to establish schools in their neglected districts. " My Lords," ran the letter, " conceive that the same motives which induce merchants and manufacturers to devote a portion of their annual profits to the insurance of the capital they employ in trade ought to be sufficient (even without any reference to moral considerations of much greater dignity and importance) to deter sagacious men, from leaving their wealth exposed to the dangers of popular tumults and secret violence, when a comparatively small annual expenditure, judiciously employed in introducing the elements of civilisation and religion, would render society harmonious and secure." [1]

It was in this atmosphere of alarm that the scheme of 1843 was born. Ashley, on February 28, in a resolution on the need for education, drew a horrifying picture of the moral condition of great towns. Sir James Graham, in reply, lamented that England had failed to profit by the warning of the French Revolution.[2] Such dangers might have been expected to make sectarian strife less acute. Unfortunately the National Society claimed peculiar success for Church Schools as an antidote to disorder. " Wherever means of Church-instruction were best provided, there the efforts of the disaffected were least successful. In whatever districts Church-principles predominated, no out-break took place, however grievous the privations of the people, except in cases where the rightly disposed inhabitants were over-powered by agitators from a distance." [3] This claim, it may be noticed, was afterwards translated by the *Times* (June 17,

---

[1] Minutes of Committee of Council on Education, 1841, p. 17. Cf. Report of the Commissioners into the State of Popular Education in England, 1861, vol. i. p. 33 : " The general principle upon which almost every one who, for the last half-century, has endeavoured to promote popular education has proceeded, has been that a large portion of the poorer classes of the population were in a condition injurious to their own interests, and dangerous and discreditable to the rest of the community ; that it was the duty and the interest of the nation at large to raise them to a higher level, and that religious education was the most powerful instrument for the promotion of this object. The parents, on the other hand, cannot be expected to entertain the same view of the moral and social condition of their own class, or to have its general elevation in view."

[2] " . . . while all the other governments of Europe, warned by the melancholy events which darkened the latter years of the last century with scenes which it would be too painful to dwell on—warned by those bad lessons, had directed their earnest, their unceasing attention to the moral training and religious education of their people, England alone, Protestant Christian England, had neglected this all-important duty of giving her people that training, that education, which so intimately concerned, not only their temporal, but their eternal welfare."—*Annual Register*, 1843, p. 57.

[3] Thirty-second Report of National Society (1843), p. 2.

1843), the Church's champion, into " Those connected with her schools held back as one man—those engaged in Dissenting establishments embarked in shoals in the disturbances of last year."

The rather intricate scheme of education proposed by the Government is most easily mastered if we take one of the budding social dangers, in this case a factory child, and examine what the Bill meant for him in the matter of schooling. The proposals were part of a Factory Bill, and dealt primarily with factory children, though it must be remembered that Sir James Graham, the author of the Bill, hoped that the schools established would provide education for all children in factory districts, whether employed or not. The child in question, whom we will suppose to be between the ages of 8 and 13, would work for $6\frac{1}{2}$ hours at the factory, either in the morning or in the afternoon. In the other half of the day he would go to school for three hours. Out of these three hours a large portion would be spent in religious instruction. At the beginning and at the end of school the master would read something from the Bible, and the children would repeat the Lord's Prayer. There would also be two distinct sets of religious lessons. In the first place, every day the master would read a portion of the Bible and would explain it after the manner of the British and Foreign School Society, that is, without any doctrinal interpretation. Secondly, on three or more days a week one hour would be spent in learning the catechism and the various doctrines of the Church of England, after the manner of the National Society. Thus by the ingenious scheme of those who framed the Bill, the child would have the benefit of both systems of religious teaching. On Saturday he would be free from school, but on Sunday he would not only be taken to church by the master with the other scholars, but would have three hours of doctrinal teaching as well.

The child's cup of religious instruction was indeed brimming over, but if his parents did not like the character of the contents and were willing to take a certain amount of trouble, they could announce that " on the ground of religious objection " they wished him to be exempted from the doctrinal teaching on week days, and from church and the Sunday-school on Sundays. If this were done, he, with the other Dissenting children, would be given some secular lesson whilst the rest of the children were learning catechism and doctrines. To pay for his schooling he would find that 1d. out of every shilling, up to 3d., was being deducted from his wages by his employer, who was bound to pay it over and to procure a certificate from the school every week to show that the boy had attended. He could not go to any school that he or his parents happened to fancy, for no school would be allowed to grant certificates except the new schools and schools connected with one of the two Societies.[1] The new schools were to be built partly out of Government funds, partly out of private subscriptions; they were to be supported by the scholars' payments and by the rates, and were to be managed by seven trustees: the clergyman, the two churchwardens, and four others nominated by the magistrates, two of them, if possible, being millowners. Any one trustee had the right of appealing to the Education Committee of the Privy Council against a master who broke regulations, and the Education Committee could dismiss the master.

Whatever the shortcomings of these proposals, it is clear that their promoters acted in good faith. They thought that by including religious teaching of both species, and by inserting the conscience clause, they had produced a compromise " consonant with the principles of the Established Church, and at the same time to the utmost extent consistent with the honest principle of toleration." [2]   Their eyes were fixed on the Church and on the concessions that she was making, for the Bill by no means satisfied extreme Churchmen, who felt that in these new schools, with their exemptions for Dissenters, and their magistrate-made trustees, the Church was being lowered to the rank of a State establishment. The reception of the Bill in Parliament did not undeceive them, for it was allowed to be read a second time without a division. Ewart and Hume, indeed, criticised the education proposals strongly, but Lord John Russell, Sir George Grey, and Cobden, were in favour of amendments at a later stage, Cobden remarking that in spite of shortcomings it was an advance to find that the Church cate-

---

[1] The power of granting certificates could be taken away by the Education Committee of the Privy Council if the inspector reported unfavourably on school or master.
[2] Sir James Graham, *Annual Register*, 1843, p. 195.

chism was not made obligatory.[1] Outside Parliament, however, the atmosphere was very different, and the proposals were denounced at once as violating the elementary principles of religious liberty.   The management of the new rate-aided schools was to be handed over entirely to the Church of England.   Other day schools would be at a disadvantage, and, worst of all, existing Sunday-schools would suffer.   To realise the importance of this grievance, we must remember that Sunday-schools were the strongholds of Dissenting bodies.[2] Nonconformists of every sect united in meetings and petitions. Under the able editorship of Edward Baines, the *Leeds Mercury* devoted itself to an eloquent campaign.   The unpopularity of the Puseyites was a useful weapon.   The scheme, said the *Mercury* (March 18), was an attempt " to teach the doctrine of baptismal regeneration, the efficacy of the sacraments in communicating divine grace, apostolical succession, and all the mummery of the Puseyites, over the whole of the manufacturing districts, at the expense of the parishes and of the public."   The parents of Sunday-school scholars were exhorted (April 8) to resist a measure which aimed at " removing your children on the Sabbath from the sweet influences of pious benevolence and zeal, to the soulless discipline and task-work of the paid master who whips them during the week . . . away from the hearing of simple Gospel truth, to be taught the superstitious forms and beggarly elements of Puseyite-Popery."

On April 10, whilst petitions in unprecedented numbers were

[1] Cf. Morley's *Life of Cobden*, vol. i. p. 300 : " Popular education had been the most important of all social objects in his mind from the first, and in spite of drawbacks, which he did not despair of seeing amended, he saw more good than harm, in the new proposals."

[2] In Manchester in 1834 there were 19,032 Dissenting Sunday-school scholars and 3812 Catholic scholars to 10,284 Church of England scholars.   In Salford the figures were—Dissenting 6250, Catholic 613, Church of England 2741 ; in Liverpool—Dissenting 8350, Catholic 700, Church of England 6318 ; in Birmingham—Dissenting 11,830, Church of England 4500; in Bristol—8477 to 2631.   (See 1838 Report of Committee on Education, p. ix.)   In Bury the figures were 3056 to 1013.   (See Report of Manchester Statistical Society on Bury.)   In Ashton they were 7025 to 3100, and in Oldham 5400 to 1400.   (See Factory Inspectors Reports for 1843, pp. 6 and 22.)   At the Coronation festivities at Halifax in 1837, 4032 Sunday-school children marched in procession, of whom 1242 were Church of England (*Halifax Express*, January 30, 1837.)   The Education Report of the 1851 census, commenting on the fact that the Church of England had over four-fifths of the day-schools, but less than half of the Sunday-schools, remarks : " In fact it is only in comparatively recent years that the Sunday-school has found much favour with the Church of England generally—many clergymen apparently possessing conscientious scruples as to the employment of lay agency for religious teaching."—P. lxxvii.

pouring into Parliament, Lord John Russell gave notice of certain resolutions that he intended to move, expressing the hope that they would be discussed in a moderate and temperate tone. Lord John had certainly done nothing to fan the flames ; he had not even consulted any Dissenting body about his resolutions. Before they could be discussed Sir James Graham, on May 1, announced certain important concessions giving effect to many of the resolutions.

In the first place, with regard to the trustees, Lord John Russell's resolution that the ratepayers should be represented on the Board was accepted, though his further suggestion that the chairman should be elected by the Board was ignored. The clerical trustee was to remain chairman over a Board composed of one churchwarden, one member elected by donors and subscribers, and four trustees elected by £10 ratepayers. To ensure the representation of the minority, no ratepayer was to vote for more than two trustees.[1] But this provision was double-edged, for, as Lord John Russell pointed out, in the places where Dissenting ratepayers were in the majority, the Church minority would be enabled to elect members, thus ensuring a permanent Church majority, on a Board which started with two *ex-officio* Church members. The trustees still appointed the master and the assistants, and the Bishop had to approve of the appointment of the former. As Lord John Russell's suggestion that the doctrinal teaching should be given by the clergyman or his nominee and not by the master was not accepted, appointments in the new schools were still confined to members of the Church of England.

In the second place, freedom of choice was enlarged. Any school selected by the parents was to be authorised to give a certificate to factory children, provided it was inspected, and provided the Scriptures were taught in it. This met the objection that such schools as the Wesleyan Day Schools would be crushed out, but did not alter the fact that the new schools alone would be helped by the rates.

In the third place, the proposals about the Sunday-schools and religious teaching were modified; the Sunday church-going and the Sunday-school were no longer to be obligatory for all

---

[1] Sir James Graham calculated that the minority would secure representation, unless the majority was one of more than two-thirds.

whose parents did not notify religious objections. Only children whose parents desired it were to be obliged to attend them. Other children would be free to go to any Sunday-school without any trouble about notification. With regard to the doctrinal teaching on week-days, children would now be exempted from it if their parents merely announced that they wished for exemption. No formal statement of religious objection was necessary. The doctrinal teaching was to be at the beginning or the end of school, in a separate room, on three days a week. To make matters even between the Dissenting minister and the clergyman, the former, or some person appointed by him, would be able to give religious instruction to the children from his flock for three whole school hours on one of the week-days " at some convenient place other than the school-house."

These were considerable concessions. In the House of Commons, Lord John Russell (May 1), again appealing for " calmness," received them as improvements,[1] and, after certain criticisms, hoped that they should proceed to a consideration of the Bill, " with the prospect of wiping away from this country the stain of not having an efficient education for the working classes." Some opposition was offered, mainly by the advocates of secular education, but there seemed no doubt that the education clauses, whether further amended or not, would pass through Parliament. But outside Parliament there was no lull in the storm and no slackening in the stream of petitions against the Bill.[2] The *Manchester Guardian* (May 8), which had not joined in the hue and cry, pleaded for dispassionate consideration and for the concessions from both sides demanded by any scheme of national education, but nobody listened.

[1] In a private letter to Kay-Shuttleworth, Lord John Russell laid stress on " the one point upon which he (Graham) has not yielded " as being very important, namely, the ensuring of a majority of Churchmen on the Board, and the restriction of masterships to Churchmen ; " here is a new civil office with a salary paid by the public, restricted to Churchmen by a method as sure as the Sacramental test."—*Life of Sir James Kay-Shuttleworth*, by Frank Smith, p. 151. It is worthy of notice that, with a curious want of logic, R. J. Saunders, the Factory Inspector, one of the chief forces behind the proposals, had argued that as the British Schools accepted not only Dissenters but Churchmen as masters, therefore " no just offence can be taken to the selection of such persons (Churchmen) . . . for the joint instruction of Churchmen and Dissenters."—Special Report of 1842 on Schools in Factory Districts, p. 8.

[2] There were 170 petitions with 312,669 signatures for the educational clauses of the Bill, and 25,535 petitions with 4,064,832 signatures against them.—Hume, House of Commons, July 25, 1843.

Had the concessions been embodied in the original proposals, it is probable that the opposition would never have acquired its overwhelming force. As it was, nothing could satisfy it but destruction.

To the moderate man the outstanding feature of the proposed new scheme was the abatement of the claims of the Church, and her recognition of the civil power.[1] The Dissenters, on the other hand, could see nothing but the Bishop enthroned over every school. It is, however, doubtful whether the civil power was any more congenial to them at the moment than the Episcopal Bench, for their experience of inspectors and Commissions had not given them much confidence in State control. Tremenheere's scathing report on 66 schools of the British and Foreign Society we have already mentioned, and the correspondence on the subject was published on April 28, 1843. Just at this very time the Factory Inspectors too were embittering the atmosphere. " I have been disappointed," wrote Leonard Horner, " to find so little disposition on the part of the more wealthy Dissenters in my district to come forward in the cause of the education of the working classes : all the activity which has come under my notice, in places where schools are most wanted, has been on the side of the Church. This apathy is much to be regretted ; not only on account of the deficiency of schools for the children of Dissenters, but because that wholesome rivalry is diminished which, ever since Joseph Lancaster opened his school in the Borough Road, has worked so beneficially in stimulating the Church to exertion in the cause of education." [2]

Still more unfortunate were the activities of another Factory Inspector, R. J. Saunders, known as a staunch High Churchman who had been concerned in preparing the educational proposals of the Bill. His report for the quarter ending December 31, 1842 (published 1843), described at considerable length the advantages of a definitely Church education over undenominational religious instruction in teaching " all social, moral, and

---

[1] " Churchmen," wrote Kay-Shuttleworth, explaining his position to Lord John Russell, " are thus prepared to confide the chief control of education to the civil power —to submit their schools to the management of a trust of mixed character, chiefly elected by popular suffrage—to afford complete protection to all classes of Dissenters and Romanists—and even to admit into the schools an inspector appointed by the civil power alone. . . ."—*Life*, by Frank Smith, p. 148.

[2] 1843 Factory Inspectors Reports, p. 23.

religious duties," and impressing on the pupils the "weakness and sinfulness of human nature." The account of how he managed to procure such teaching at National Schools for 940 of the factory children under his charge, in spite of the fact that the majority were probably Dissenters, cannot have been soothing reading for the angry protesters.[1] In addition to this, to add fuel to the flames, the second Report of the Children's Employment Commission (p. 202)[2] criticised Sunday-schools and their teaching severely. It spoke of "the teachers volunteering their meritorious efforts, which, however, are altogether unsystematic and feeble," and stated that "great numbers of those Children who had been in regular attendance on Sunday-schools for a period of from five to nine years, were found, on examination, to be incapable of reading an easy book, or of spelling the commonest words; and they were not only altogether ignorant of Christian principles, doctrines, and precepts, but they knew nothing whatever of any of the events of Scripture history, nor anything even of the names most commonly occurring in the Scriptures."

The concessions then fell on stony ground. The *Leeds Mercury* (May 6) summed up the insuperable objections: the ascendency of the Episcopal Church and the Episcopal clergy remained; Dissenters would be proscribed as masters; Dissenting scholars would feel themselves to be "a lower and certainly not a favoured class." Even the improved facilities for exemption failed to please, for the fact remained that the majority of parents, as R. J. Saunders had discovered, were wholly indifferent, and many of them would have no objection to instruction in "the principles of Mahomet, or the worship of blocks and stones," provided that the fees were low.[3] Hence no exemption clause could abolish the advantage of the Church. "Dissenters," said the *Leeds Mercury*, "will have to make an *effort* and to perform a *disagreeable duty*, and the children will be put in a position that cannot be pleasant. To Churchmen all will be smooth and easy, like gliding down a stream—every-

---

[1] The special Report on the Establishment of Schools in Factory Districts by R. J. Saunders, dated February 1842, in which the plan afterwards adopted by the Government was outlined, was not published till August 1843.

[2] Presented to the House of Commons, February 20, 1843. It may be noted that two of the four Commissioners were Leonard Horner and R. J. Saunders, so that the Dissenters might well have complained of a stage army of critics.

[3] Factory Inspectors Reports, 1843, p. 34.

thing is made to flow and tend towards the Church; whilst Dissenters will require to be ever on the alert and making exertion, like men who have to stem the current. Even the neglect and indifference so prevalent among the working class are thus made to answer the purposes of the Church."

A motion of Roebuck's on May 18 illustrated the different points of view. Roebuck urged that the State should abstain from "peculiar religious teaching." Mr. Hawes, on the other hand, as spokesman for the Dissenters, claimed, not the abolition of religious teaching, but complete equality in the matter between Dissent and the Church; whilst Sir James Graham contended that though Dissenters had a right to security, yet "while the Church of England remains established, the preference must be given in favour of that establishment." Roebuck's motion was rejected by 156 votes to 60.

Faced by continued hostility, the Government decided to submit. The contested clauses could, indeed, be carried through Parliament, but the trouble would only begin then. It was not a question of a Treasury grant, but of rates, and the Dissenters threatened to refuse to pay rates. There had been enough trouble over Church rates and the Poor Law to make any Government hesitate. Nor could support from the Church side be counted on. The Bill, said the *Times* (May 12), was now unworkable. By its provisions the master had to play a double part: he must give one lesson as an "expositor" of the Scriptures; for a second lesson he must become a "commentator." If he put a little too much of the latter character into the former part, a dissenting trustee could now complain to the Privy Council, and possibly have him dismissed. The lukewarmness of the Church was not counterbalanced by the championship of the *Northern Star*, in which Feargus O'Connor turned his powerful invective against "the hungry and aspiring hordes of Dissenters yelling and clamouring against Mother Church," whilst all the time "seeking to occupy her place" (May 6). Chartist advocacy and Chartist petitions did not strengthen a Government's cause. One last effort was made at a meeting between representatives of the United Wesleyan Committee on one side and Peel and Graham on the other, but it failed.

In a dignified speech on June 15, Graham announced that the

Government would not proceed with the clauses. He paid a tribute to the forbearance of the parliamentary opposition, but pointed out that since hostility outside Parliament was not mitigated by the recent concessions, the proposals, even if carried successfully through both Houses, would be inoperative, and would only embitter religious discord. In less dignified language the Government's strange ally, the *Northern Star*, described the defeat (June 17). " . . . the Government of this country have actually cowed before the bristling, bustling, bullying of Mr. Edward Baines and a few scores of hypocritical, ignorant, and malignant Dissenting parsons, acting as cat's-paws for the mammonocracy by which their several conventicles are upholden."

It is difficult not to trace a recognition of the growing power of nonconformity in the last Act of the quarrel between the British and Foreign Society and the Education Committee. In January 1843, Lord Wharncliffe had announced that though the Committee would endeavour to make an appointment that would inspire confidence, they could not " consent to the exercise of any control over such an appointment by the British and Foreign Society." [1] In November he wrote that " no Inspector for them (the British Schools) will be appointed without the full concurrence of your Committee." [2]

Dissent had won a great battle. The Church, it might be said, had claimed a monopoly of education from mediaeval times; the Dissenters had claimed an equal share from Sunday-school times. The victorious Edward Baines, after collecting and publishing statistics to show that the manufacturing districts and their schools had been maligned, now devoted his energies to organising the Voluntaryist campaign for founding schools that should be free from Government money and Government inspection. An immense impulse was indeed given by the fierce controversy of 1843 to both sides to found new schools. By the end of 1844 it was calculated by Kay-Shuttleworth that the National Society had raised £160,000, the Congregationalists £70,000,[3] and the Wesleyan Methodists another £70,000.[4]

[1] 1843 Borough Road Normal School Correspondence, p. 69.
[2] Kay-Shuttleworth, *op. cit.* p. 466 footnote.
[3] The *Leeds Mercury*, May 23, 1846, stated that the Congregational Union had subscribed £100,000 for education during the previous two and a half years.
[4] *Life of Kay-Shuttleworth*, by Frank Smith, p. 157.

Applications for building grants were doubled in the following year. Unfortunately enthusiasm did not extend to maintaining the schools in an efficient condition; sometimes it did not extend to maintaining them at all.

Kay-Shuttleworth, distressed no less than Peel and Graham at the collapse of the 1843 plan, turned his active and resourceful mind to other and less controversial methods of action. The Government agreed, in November 1843, to extend the grants to the building of houses for masters and mistresses, and to the provision of furniture and apparatus at the starting of a school. Additions were also made to the staff of inspectors. Other changes the Committee of Council either rejected or failed to carry out. Thus Peel and Wharncliffe agreed in principle to a scheme for maintenance grants for pupil teachers but went no further in the matter. They had burnt their fingers badly over education in 1843, and they were to burn them worse over Maynooth and the Corn Laws. It is therefore not surprising that they left education alone.

Outside official circles a bold suggestion for settling the religious quarrels about education was made in July 1846, from the Church side by the well-known Vicar of Leeds, Dr. Hook. In a vigorous pamphlet he exposed the failure of existing attempts at popular education.[1] " With one voice, the Church and Dissent demanded that they might be permitted to attempt [the] universal education of the people. . . ." They had been allowed to do so, and they had failed. Readers of Reports of Societies must not be misled; " societies are from their constitution braggarts." " Reports are drawn up as advertisements, failures are judiciously passed over, and by that very circumstance the good accomplished is given in an exaggerated and therefore an untrue form." Much, it was true, had been done, but " we have lighted a lanthorn which only makes us more sensible of the surrounding darkness." How, indeed, could we expect schools to be efficient when we underpay schoolmasters and " commit the education of the people of England to the wisdom, experience, and discretion of unpaid instructors in the shape of monitors, whose average age is ten years." Church schools were not spared. " Is it not a mere

---

[1] On the Means of Rendering more Efficient the Education of the People. A Letter to the Lord Bishop of St. Davids, by Walter Farquhar Hook, D.D., Vicar of Leeds.

mockery to tell persons that there is a religious education given in our National Schools, because the children are permitted to dog's-ear a Bible ? "

Hook's remedy was clear and simple. Let the State provide literary or secular schools, financing them partly by grants, partly from the rates, and let the Church of England and other denominations provide religious teaching, both at their own Sunday-schools and on Wednesday and Friday afternoons at the State secular school, where special rooms would be set aside for the purpose. To any " general " religious teaching by the State he was vehemently opposed : " Satan could devise no scheme for the extirpation of Christianity, more crafty or more sure than this. . . ." On the other hand, the Church was to have no special pecuniary aid, but must be treated on the same basis as other corporations. If the Church claimed exclusive rights, she must produce the money herself,[1] not ask for it from taxes collected from persons of all religions. Such were the main features of Hook's scheme.[2] Unfortunately they were too liberal either for the Church or for Dissent. Brougham's description given in 1843 was still correct. " The Church was anxious to educate the people, but the Church was still more anxious to get the better of the sects; the sects were anxious to have popular education, but the sects were still more anxious than this to overturn the Church." [3]

In July 1846 the Whigs again came into power, and the insistent Kay-Shuttleworth could now press his reforms on less embarrassed ears. Statistics about illiteracy were beginning to alarm politicians. Each year since 1839 the Registrar-General had given the number of married persons who signed with a mark. This percentage had remained practically unchanged. It had been 41·6 in 1839 (men, 33·7 ; women, 49·5),

---

[1] Hook suggested that the bishops might obtain powers to sell their estates. " It would be better for the Church to have a pauperised hierarchy than an uneducated people ; and never could the hierarchy be more respectable than when pauperised in such a cause."

[2] Hook's dislike of local authorities was illustrated in the scheme. "Let me conjure you," he wrote to Kay-Shuttleworth, "not to permit town councils to have anything to do with it. I have had twenty years' experience of corporations, reformed and unreformed, and I have always found them, no matter what party is in power, so influenced by little, local, party, jobbing, petty, paltry feelings, that they do injury to any and every cause they take in hand."—*Life of Kay-Shuttleworth,* p. 176 footnote.

[3] House of Lords, May 5, 1843.

it remained at from 40 to 41·4 during the next six years.   Yet schools had undoubtedly increased during the school years of the brides and bridegrooms.   No time was lost.   In August an outline of the new proposals was issued, followed in December by further details.   The proposals consisted of an elaborate scheme for the reorganisation of school teaching, and the improvement of the teachers' position.[1]   Monitors were to be replaced wherever possible by pupil teachers, apprenticed for five years.[2]   Grants were to be given to the pupil teachers and to the teachers who trained them.   When the apprenticeship was finished, the further training of the pupil teachers for three years at a normal school was to be encouraged by a system of scholarships and grants.   Teachers thus trained were to enjoy certain additions to their salaries provided by grants, and retiring pensions were to be given under certain conditions. The establishment of the pupil teacher system in a school, and the additions to salaries, were dependent on a favourable report from an inspector, and it was an inspector who conducted each year the examination of the pupil teachers.   Thus the Education Committee for the first time obtained a certain control over the schools it inspected and subsidised.   The qualifications of the pupil teachers for giving religious instruction were to be tested in Church Schools by the inspector, with the assistance of the parochial clergyman ; " in other schools " the managers were merely required to certify that they were satisfied with the candidates' religious knowledge.

These proposals were not an attempt to grasp English education and remould it into a national scheme.   No Government was likely to try its hand at that for some time.   They were a scheme for improving existing schools without altering the existing basis.   No new principle of distribution was introduced, for National or British Schools were equally qualified to claim and obtain the benefits.   But this was not the aspect under which Dissenting circles represented by the Voluntaryist movement saw the proposals.   The Church was the enemy. The Church, having more schools and less objection to subsidies, stood to gain by the grants ; therefore talk of equality was

---

[1] See Kay-Shuttleworth, *op. cit.* pp. 531 ff., for details.
[2] In rural districts a sort of second-grade system of " stipendiary monitors " with lower qualifications and lower grants was allowed.

absurd, and the proposals must be fought.   If, as the *Manchester Guardian* expressed it (April 10, 1847), education was to be regarded merely " as a machine for spreading particular religious opinions," opposition was inevitable.   Curiously enough, it was the State's determination to encourage and not to supersede voluntary effort which led to the movement against State interference in education.   For the policy of giving grants in aid, equitable though it sounded, had resulted in the richer body obtaining an overwhelming share.   Mr. Horace Mann explained the Nonconformist point of view very clearly in the 1851 Census Volume on Education.[1]   " The taxes taken from the nation generally (nearly half consisting of dissenters) are appropriated in a vast preponderance to the schools of the Established Church."   Dissenters, he pointed out, argued that " neither the possession by particular sects of conscientious scruples, nor their want of worldly wealth, afford . . . any valid reason why they should be taxed to aid such other sects as may be both unfettered and rich. . . ."   Behind the question of the aggrandisement of the Church there lay also the dislike of the individualist to the increase of State interference in any form.   The common argument that the grants would foster corruption by creating a host of Government functionaries might be ridiculous enough, but it was true that the schools which benefited would, as we have said, come under a measure of State control.   We must also remember that the Voluntaryists always assumed and asserted that education was going on very well as it was, so that there was no cause for any interference.[2]

Again, as in 1843, meetings and petitions were organised, and again Baines of the *Leeds Mercury* was the protagonist.   The result was a sorry spectacle, moving the young James Martineau, then a Unitarian minister at Liverpool, to a strong protest. " For his own part, he would rather choose to increase the power of the Church of England, which is under some check, from the

---

[1] P. lxxxv.

[2] Cf. Horace Mann on the Voluntaryists, *ibid.* p. lxxx. : " Whether convinced, by the nature of the legislation actually attempted, of the impossibility of any equitable treatment, by the State, of all religious bodies—or deriving, from the progress of opinion on the free trade question, an enlarged idea of the hurtfulness of Government assistance generally—or impressed, by many evidences, with a sense of the enormous power of individual enterprise and charity when left to their own resources—it is certain that a very considerable number of the earnest friends of education gradually came to the conclusion that the increase and improvement of our popular day-schools would be best promoted without any intervention by the State."

control of the State, and the good sense of the representative power of the country, than he would extend the power of the Dissenters who did not appear to him to understand at all the principles of religious liberty."[1]   Early in the campaign the Voluntaryists suffered a severe loss, for the Wesleyans were won over.   The story does not reflect much credit on the parties to the transaction.[2]   It was explained to the Wesleyans, between whom and the Government Lord Ashley acted as intermediary, that their schools would be eligible for grants, and that they would be consulted before any inspector was appointed to visit them.   This seemed satisfactory, but the Wesleyan representatives smelt a Popish rat.   The Minutes referred to " any school under inspection " as being eligible for grants ; what if Roman Catholic schools were eligible too ?   Now the Government had not yet gone closely into the question of eligibility.   They had vaguely intended " to remove the stringency of the preamble " to the Minutes of December 3, 1839, governing grants, which stated that " special circumstances " must be shown before any grant could be given outside the two Societies.[3]   They now found on looking it up that the Minute of December 3[4] limited grants to schools where there was a daily reading of the Scriptures.   To this, it was explained to the Wesleyans, their Lordships of the Education Committee intended to adhere, and it was further explained that their Lordships required the entire Bible in the authorised version to be used.[5]

This provision, as the Wesleyans saw, ruled out the Roman Catholics from the grants.   But the Government did not pledge themselves never to give grants to Roman Catholics ; on the contrary, they foreshadowed further Minutes which would " make a separate provision " for Roman Catholic Schools.   They pointed out, however, that there would be opportunity " for the consideration and discussion of such minutes," and stated that " no one who agrees to accept aid under the present Minutes will be therebye in any degree pledged to approve these future

---

[1] *Manchester Guardian*, April 7, 1847.

[2] For an account of the affair, see Lord John Russell's speech, House of Commons, April 20, 1847, and Minutes of Committee of Council for 1847.

[3] The only grant hitherto outside the Church of England or the British and Foreign Society was £222 to one Wesleyan school in 1843.   See returns relating to Parliamentary Grants for Education, March 10, 1851.

[4] See p. 188, footnote 2.

[5] An exception was made for the British and Foreign Schools, which used extracts.

Minutes, or precluded from offering to them such opposition as he may think expedient." It is only fair to the Government to explain that later in the same year, on December 18, they did by their Minutes admit Roman Catholic Schools to the grants. Meanwhile their assurances had converted the Wesleyans to approval of the Minutes. " What though the Government," exclaimed the *Watchman* (April 7), " may not (and, alas ! in the present state of public parties and public feeling, we have little hope that *any* Government *will*) preclude themselves from granting sooner or later, in some shape or another, aid for Romish schools, yet this single regulation, supposing it to be faithfully carried out, will erect in the land a barrier against error and a bulwark for the truth, of incalculable value to the rising generation. For the BIBLE is the best book ever written, against either Popery or Infidelity." Whatever the motives of the Government, it is hard to resist the conclusion of the *Leeds Mercury* (April 17). " No sane man can doubt that if the apparition of evangelical clergymen and Wesleyan Committees had not risen before the eyes of Ministers, the dusty Minute of 1839 would have slept undisturbed to this day, and its repeal by the new Minutes making national what had been partial, would have been considered *un fait accompli.*"

Inside Parliament the agitation was better represented than in 1843, since Bright's powerful voice was now raised against the Minutes. Macaulay devoted one of his rare speeches to an exposition of the duty of the State to educate the people.[1] Bright set himself to answer this.[2] The question at issue, he declared, was not the general question of Education, but the question of the Minutes : " their object, their tendency, and the effect they will produce upon the position of the Established Church and the Dissenting bodies in the United Kingdom." The Dissenters, he explained, had approved of the establishment of the Committee of Council in 1839, hoping that it would act as a check upon the pretensions of the Church. They had been disillusioned, for every step had tended to aggrandise the

---

[1] House of Commons, April 19, 1847. He only spoke five times in Parliament as a Minister during the sessions of 1846 and 1847. Macaulay, during the Maynooth agitation, had used the words " Exeter Hall sets up its bray," a phrase which had much annoyed the Nonconformists.—*Life of Macaulay*, by Trevelyan, 1923, vol. ii. pp. 453 and 465.

[2] April 20.

Church, and after 1843 they had come to the conclusion that it was dangerous for Government to interfere with education, because they could not interfere "without giving increased power to the clergy of an already dominant church." Apart from the question of the Church, State help for education was, he argued, unnecessary. Things were going on well. Had not the number of scholars in day-schools increased 210 per cent. since 1818? Peel and Graham both supported the Minutes, whilst regretting that Roman Catholics were refused the grants. The vote of supply was passed, April 2, 1847, by 372 votes to 47. Outside Parliament the Voluntaryist movement continued its campaign and achieved certain successes against Government candidates in the Election that summer. Macaulay lost his seat at Edinburgh, and his defeat was largely due to the energetic campaign of the Voluntaryists against the defender of State education and of the Minutes.

If we leave the warring sects and politicians and come down again to the small boys and girls for whose souls they fought, what changes do we find? The self-supporting Dame Schools and Common Day Schools were dwindling in number, and the Denominational Schools were increasing. Manchester afforded an extreme example of this change. Whereas in 1834-35 there were some 409 Dame and Common Day Schools with 11,512 scholars, in 1852 there were only 126 of these schools with 4334 scholars. The children at National, British, and Denominational Schools meanwhile had gone up from 3818 to 15,270.[1] Whereas at Ashton and Oldham in 1842, with a population of 105,000, there was no public day-school for working-class children, in 1846 there were twenty schools of the kind with 3459 scholars.[2] But the private schools died hard. In 1851 it was calculated that 35·1 per cent. of working-class scholars attended them; in 1858, 33·9 per cent.[3] Judging from descriptions given later to the 1861 Commission on Popular Education, the character of these schools remained much what it was in the thirties. One is tempted, however, to think that the school mentioned where the kitten "to which all the children

---

[1] 1852 Committee on Manchester and Salford Education, pp. 23, 40, and 60.
[2] See *Leeds Intelligencer*, Feb. 14, 1846.
[3] This calculation deals with ten representative districts, covering one-eighth of the population. See Report of Commissioners into the State of Popular Education in England, 1861, vol. i. p. 636.

were very attentive " was the chief text-book,[1] may have given a better education than some schools where the Bible took its place.

Most of our knowledge about schools in the forties comes from inspectors' reports, and these, of course, deal mainly with the grant-aided Church or Society Schools. Now it would be possible to pick out things said of these schools by the inspectors as harsh as anything said of the Common " Adventure " Schools by the Manchester Statistical Society, but we must not assume that they were worse than they had been ; probably they were a good deal better. The truth was that the inspectors were the first people who discovered that a fog enveloped the children's minds, and that it was possible to read intelligently and even to answer questions correctly without having the slightest notion of the meaning of the words uttered. Any deviation from routine produced chaos. Mr. Tremenheere's report on the British Schools we have mentioned. As inspectors were chary of criticisms on these schools for some time, most of the information is about Church Schools. The cross-questions and crooked answers of which Mr. Tremenheere gave examples were not confined to British Schools or to Bible knowledge. The National Schools with their catechism provided equally striking examples.

"*Q.* Who gave you the name which you received in baptism ? —*A.* God.

Q. What did your godfathers and godmothers promise and vow for you respecting the pomps and vanities of the world ?— *A.* All the sinful lusts of the flesh.

Q. I asked what they promised and vowed respecting the pomps of the world ?—*A.* That I should believe all the articles of the Christian faith.

Q. What do you mean by those articles ?—(Silence.) The articles of the faith means all the truths of the gospel ; will you tell me any one of the truths of the gospel which your godfathers vowed you should believe ?—Five were silent, the sixth answered, ' The Commandments.' " [2]

But though the children might seem to have lapsed into what

---

[1] *Ibid.* p. 92.
[2] Minutes of Committee of Council on Education, 1841, p. 81.

Mr. Moseley, the inspector with perhaps the most vivid pen, called " that vagrant state of mind, approaching to idiocy," [1] yet, if appropriately handled, they could perform feats at the public examinations held before admiring subscribers, causing the audience, in the same inspector's bitter words, to " go away with the impression that the children of the poor are receiving a better education than they did themselves." [2]   The feats of etymology or mental arithmetic were " wonderful only as long as the short methods used in producing them are unknown." [3] Etymology itself he described as a method of " directing their attention to the derivation of one language, with which they are comparatively unacquainted, from another, of which they are profoundly ignorant." [4]

The severest indictment of the elementary education of this time was made, not by the school inspectors, but by the Children's Employment Commission in their Second Report of 1843 (p. 202).   " In all the districts," they stated, " many Children who had been returned as able to read, when examined were found to know only the letters of the alphabet ; a very small proportion indeed being able to read well an easy book." Even of those " who could read fluently, very few, when questioned, were found to have any conception of the meaning of the words they uttered, or were able to give any intelligible account of what seemed to the examiners to be simple and easy terms and things ; so that, as far as regards the acquisition of any useful knowledge, or the accomplishment of any higher purpose to be answered by education, these Children, in great numbers of instances, were as little benefited, after years of so-called tuition, as if they had never been at any school."   Mr. Moseley in 1845 calculated that out of the 11,782 children covered by his inspection, some 75 per cent. would leave school unable " to read the Scriptures with tolerable ease or correctness." [5]   Mr. Watkins reported in 1846 that out of 15,466 children in the schools he visited, a little under half were in the elementary stages of learning to read, whilst about a quarter

---

[1] *Ibid.*, 1847, p. 97.   [2] *Ibid.*, 1845, p. 247.
[3] Cf. the Rev. F. Watkins (Minutes, 1847, p. 208) on the " solemn and self-deluding mockery " of these public examinations.   He gives a description of one, and of the preparation for it.   Cf. also Kay-Shuttleworth : " the annual field-day of a paraded exhibition, when the children are initiated in a public imposture, and the promoters of the school are the willing and conscious dupes of a pious fraud," *op. cit.* p. 479.
[4] Minutes, 1846, p. 151.   [5] Minutes, 1845, p. 242.

could read simple narratives, and a quarter could read with ease.[1]
When we remember the short time spent at school it seems
remarkable that the percentage of illiteracy was so low.

From one aspect it is fortunate that these schools housed
a fleeting population. Their ventilation was, by any modern
standards, appalling. The school in the famous Enon Chapel
near the Strand, where the children sat on rafters over piled-up
corpses, may have been an exception, though it was paralleled
by a large free school at Bishop Wearmouth,[2] but the best
standards of space and air were lamentably low. Seven square
feet per child, with six square feet as a minimum, was the allowance recommended by the National Society.[3] Windows were
looked on with suspicion as means of ventilation ; valves in the
floor to let air in, and valves in the ceiling to let it out, were
recommended. Out of 35 London British boys' schools inspected by Mr. Tremenheere, 17 were reported to have a
depressing want of light and ventilation, 9 of them being under
chapels.[4] Of all the inspectors, the Rev. F. Watkins, who had
charge of the northern district, possessed the keenest taste for
fresh air, and showed the greatest interest in the subject. He
reported in 1845 that out of 114 schools that had been aided by
grants from the Treasury, 39 had sufficient, 21 had imperfect,
and 54 had bad ventilation. Included in the 54 were 5 which
had none. " I have found it difficult," he wrote, " to stay in
schools, in which the children have been for some little time
previous to my arrival." The teachers felt no inconvenience.
" I have sometimes seen the steam covering the windows, and
perspiration streaming down the children's faces, without (apparently) a suspicion on the part of the teacher that the room
was insufferably and unhealthily hot and close." [5] An even
more painful picture was given by Lyon Playfair in the Health
of Towns Commission Report ; writing of the Lancashire
schools he says, " It is by no means an uncommon thing, on
entering public schools, to observe children carried out in a

---

[1] Minutes, 1847, p. 209.
[2] 1840 Health of Towns Committee, p. 188, and 1845 Health of Towns Commission,
Second Report, Appendix, part ii. p. 200.
[3] Minutes, 1840, part ii. p. 5. The British and Foreign Society plans for a school
for 500 children work out at 6·8 square feet per child.—Manual of 1831, p. 76.
[4] Borough Road Normal School Correspondence, 1843, p. 41.
[5] Minutes, 1846, p. 283. Cf. the Rev. W. H. Bellairs, who remarked that the brain
did not work in foul air, *ibid.* p. 338.

fainting state, and the visitor, who feels the contaminated state of the air on entering it from a purer atmosphere, cannot be astonished at the occurrence."[1] Whatever else the children carried away from school, they must often have taken away the seeds of consumption.

The Reports give, on the whole, a picture of a brave struggle against overwhelming odds, in which the combatants are handicapped by poverty. The unfortunate idea that, thanks to the system of monitors, education could be provided cheaply had become firmly fixed in the public mind.   Thus as more schools were built, whether as an insurance against social dangers, or as pawns in religious controversy, it was the miserable facilities of a cheap education that were extended.   Even so, the burden of maintaining the schools at all fell heavily on many of the clergy.   There are many tales of sacrifice and struggle, and some of success.   Hook described in his famous pamphlet the efforts of a clergyman to start a school, " the weariness and painfulness of begging from day to day," the inadequate results at the end.[2]   Poverty too often impaired every effort ; the buildings were miserable, the books were a " tattered assemblage of miserable pamphlets,"[3] or else were paid for out of the parson's pocket.   Often from lack of funds, not as in the case of the British Society from principle, no text-book but the Bible could be used.[4]   The teachers were underpaid, and though Macaulay's picturesque description of them as men, " whom no gentleman would trust with the key of his cellar, and no tradesman would send of a message,"[5] was a travesty, it was true that the poor pay attracted to the calling many persons who, like the Manchester Dame School keepers, had shown their " unfitness for every other."   Kay-Shuttleworth, who was in a position to know the facts, wrote, " it is

---

[1] 1845 Health of Towns Commission, Second Report, Appendix, part ii. p. 28. Lyon Playfair also gives some statistics about the schools in Preston.   From these we learn that in 62 schools with 4541 scholars, the area per child varied from 2·44 feet in Dame Schools to 3·87 in Church Schools.

[2] Cf. the " spiritless if not a lifeless existence " that some of the schools were said to drag out.—Minutes, 1846, p. 165.   Cf. also Mr. Bellairs, who said that clergymen often spent a tenth of their benefices on schools, *ibid*. p. 335.

[3] Minutes, 1846, p. 156.

[4] Mr. Moseley reported that in 69 out of 103 Church Schools visited, no other book was used.   The New Testament could be purchased for 6d., the fourth reader of the S.P.C.K. cost 1s. 6d.—Minutes, 1845, p. 250.

[5] House of Commons, April 19, 1847.

reported that a great number of the candidates and students of the Normal Schools show signs of scrofula, and that generally their physical temperament is sluggish and inert." [1] It was masters from material of this kind who would divide 44 children into 6 classes with 6 little monitors, in a slavish adherence to Dr. Bell's system,[2] instead of teaching them all themselves.

The best masters were naturally to be found in large schools in towns, where higher salaries were given. But here under existing conditions, owing to numbers, the use of monitors was necessary. Dr. Bell and Joseph Lancaster would have been pained at the harsh language used about these monitors by most of the inspectors. Mr. Cook, while admitting that monitors could be very useful, said of the young ones that " their influence in many, if not the generality of cases, is positively detrimental to the moral character, while it is assuredly of no great benefit to the intellectual improvement of our schools." [3] In 411 out of 441 schools, wrote Mr. Watkins, the only help for the masters comes from " generally unwilling and almost always ignorant monitors." [4] He laid stress on the parents' dislike of the system ; they sent their children to school to learn and not to teach ; " They say, ' What 's master for ? ' " He suggested that the unpopularity of National Schools sometimes noted by the inspectors, was due to this cause. Even the mechanical perfection achieved in big schools under the monitorial system had no charms for the initiated. " To the Inspector," wrote Mr. Moseley, " such a scene has lost its interest —he is familiar with it ; and all his respect for it has been sacrificed by the neglected state of the education of the individual children, which he finds to be consistent with it." [5]

This detailed examination of the state of the schools brings out the importance of the Minutes of 1846. The pupil teacher system has an ugly sound in the ears of a generation unacquainted with monitors. The reforms of 1846 recognised, however imperfect their plan and methods, that the great

---

[1] *Op. cit.* p. 480.   [2] Minutes, 1847, p. 95.
[3] Minutes, 1845, p. 67.   [4] Minutes, 1846, p. 298.
[5] *Ibid.* p. 156.   Mr. Allen, one of the original inspectors, wrote in 1845 : " Right training cannot be looked for from our ordinary monitors, and is seldom found in our large schools ; the money that in England has been spent in raising such has commonly, as I believe, been ill spent."—Minutes, 1846, p. 63. The National Society, in their Thirty-fifth Report, 1846, explained that the monitor system was by no means ideal, but was adopted " as being the least amidst a choice of imperfect methods."

discovery for which Bell and Lancaster disputed the credit, the discovery that children could be taught cheaply, had been a curse to education.   The Government now set themselves with slow and feeble steps to the task of training efficient teachers, and creating efficient schools.

It is curious to reflect that education, which made its way with such difficulty, was, in one sense, in a specially favourable position.   For, if we take the two opposing philosophies of the time, we see that they were in principle agreed on this question. The fundamental philosophy underlying the humanist protest against the gospel of the Industrial Revolution—the idea that man was a complex character, and society a complex body, not to be left to the steam-engine and the railways for the satisfaction of instincts and tastes that had created and demanded, in other ages, art, culture, and religion—this idea, which inspired, in different forms, the teaching of Wordsworth and Coleridge, Dickens and Carlyle, gave great importance to education as a national need.   But the same conclusion was reached by the school that simplified human nature, taking individual opportunity for its watchword, looking to the incentive of gain as the moving power.   For this school, as we have seen, did not consider that existing institutions gave full scope to the virtues of the economic system.   " Remove all obstacles," they would have said, " to the spirit of initiative and enterprise, if you would see what the Industrial Revolution can do towards giving you a rich people instead of a poor people : a happy instead of a discontented people.   Encourage thrift ; abolish abuses in State, Church, and law ; get rid of the Corn Laws which check the flow of exchange ; spread education.   Men may by force of genius make their way without education, but, if the principle of your social life is to be universal opportunity, universal education is essential."   Thus, if education was demanded by Carlyle, who said " That a man should die ignorant, who had the capacity for knowledge—this to me is tragedy," it was also demanded by those who would have said, " That a man should die poor, who had the capacity for wealth —this to me is tragedy."   Men who differed on almost every other question agreed on this.

Unhappily the effect of this agreement was destroyed by another influence, the religious discord of the time.   Religious controversy has not always been mischievous. The quarrels of the seventeenth century did good as well as harm. If they made the English people more combative and more intolerant, they made it also more democratic and more vigorous. Historians, describing the rise of the Independents and the Baptists, trace to the revolt against control the religious vitality, and the sharp and stern sense of personal obligation which gave spiritual power to democratic ideas and democratic institutions in England.[1] But of the religious quarrels of the forties, the feuds of Church and Chapel, of Catholic and Protestant, of High Church and Low Church, the mischief clearly outbalanced the advantages. "Such was the mild spirit of antiquity," said Gibbon in a famous passage, " that the nations were less attentive to the differences than to the resemblances of their religious worship." There was more religious strife in Manchester or Bradford in the forties than in the Roman Empire under the rule of Augustus.[2] For men sought to recommend their own religion by exposing the vices of others, and when a popular orator like Stowell stood on a Manchester platform, thundering against the Churchmen who differed from him, he was more like a dervish or a medicine man beating his tom-tom than a preacher expounding Christian ideas. Wesleyan and Catholic, Puseyite and Dissenter, Baptist and Churchman, Evangelical and Tractarian, denouncing one another, treated St. Paul's famous letter on charity and the needs of the English child with equal indifference.[3]

This spirit opposed a fatal obstacle to reform. " One day,"

[1] Gooch and Laski, *English Democratic Ideas in the Seventeenth Century*, and A. D. Lindsay, *The Essentials of Democracy.*

[2] " There never was an age, since the days of the Apostles, in which the Catholic spirit of religion was so dead, and put aside for love of sects and parties, as at present."— Coleridge, *Table Talk*, p. 157, December 1831.

[3] To an evangelical gentleman who accused him of infidelity, because he supported the Minutes of 1846, Peel replied : " This is not the place to make professions of faith ; and no words that can fall from that honourable gentleman shall induce me to say one harsh word with respect to him. But as to infidelity, I say at once, that I cannot believe—and I say it with all reverence—that that God, who is the author of peace and lover of concord—who gave us his commandment, that we should believe in the name of Jesus Christ and love one another—I cannot believe, I say, that that Almighty God will think that we are fulfilling that commandment when we hate one another, and allow thousands and tens of thousands of children, who ought, whatever be their form of faith, to believe in the name of Jesus Christ, to pass through this mortal life and be launched into eternity without having ever heard of the name of Jesus Christ ; for such is a true statement with respect to education in some parts of this country."— *Annual Register*, 1847, p. 154.

said Peel, "the Dissenters refuse their assent because they are afraid the Church will derive some advantage; on the next occasion the Church is opposed to any measure for fear of some recognition of the principle of Dissent. But in the meantime, while all these disputes go on, it is for us to ask ourselves what is to become of the 800 children who are born every day? What is to become of the 300,000 persons who are added every year to the population?"[1] We can understand the strength of the obstacle to which Peel referred when we see that a leading Churchman like Bishop Blomfield, and a leading Dissenter like Bright, both of them exceptional men with wide experience of affairs, preferred to leave the English nation to such arrangements as we have described, rather than take the risk, in one case of reducing, in the other of increasing, the influence of the Church.   Or let anybody turn from the pages of the *Watchman*, in which a devout Wesleyan editor combats the proposal to allow public help to be given to any Roman Catholic school to the picture drawn by Peel of the Roman Catholic children of Manchester, without natural protectors or wealthy friends, who were to grow up in ignorance.[1]   The struggle over this question was a struggle between men who took a large view, like Russell, Peel, Cobden, and Hook, and men who took a small view, like Blomfield, Bright, Baines, and the editor of the *Watchman*.   The men who took a small view were strong enough to keep the English people behind the leading nations of Europe.[2]   We know from the *Life of Cobden* that it was this obstacle that deterred the most persuasive advocate of the day from taking up the cause of national education and pressing it with the ardour that he devoted to the Repeal of the Corn Laws. Cobden's decision was one of the calamities of the age.

---

[1] House of Commons, April 22, 1847.

[2] After the Religious Census was published in 1854, the *Times* pointed the moral reminding these fierce sectarians that though they had kept back education they had not helped religion.   An intelligent person was invited to inquire into his own district. "He will see that the working people are not in his church; and if he goes to the next parish church and the nearest chapel of ease and the proprietary chapels about him and to the Dissenting chapels—to every place where God is worshipped in any manner whatever, he will still find the working classes are not there; the working classes who, when we first began to talk and write of these things, were boys and girls learning 'Crossman's Catechism' and thumbing Mrs. Trimmer's Scripture History, if indeed they were receiving any education at all . . . the classes who now have been dosed and drilled for two generations, have been dosed and drilled with the multiplication table, catechism, and penmanship in mystic and inseparable alliance, are now grown up ill-educated and almost wholly irreligious."—January 29, 1854.

CHAPTER XII

RELIGION

THE ESTABLISHED CHURCH

" The middle classes have augmented rather than diminished that devotional sentiment and strictness of attention to religious services by which, for several centuries, they have so eminently been distinguished.   With the upper classes, too, the subject of religion has obtained of late a marked degree of notice, and a regular church attendance is now ranked amongst the recognised proprieties of life.   It is to satisfy the wants of these two classes that the number of religious structures has of late years so increased.   But while the *labouring* myriads of our country have been multiplying with our multiplied material prosperity, it cannot, it is found, be stated that a corresponding increase has occurred in the attendance of this class in our religious edifices.   More especially in cities and large towns it is observable how absolutely insignificant a portion of the congregation is composed of artisans.   They fill, perhaps, in youth, our National, British, and Sunday Schools, and there receive the elements of a religious education ; but, no sooner do they mix in the active world of labour than, subjected to the constant action of opposing influences, they soon become as utter strangers to religious ordinances as the people of a heathen country."

Census of 1851, *Religious Worship in England and Wales*, abridged from the Official Report made by Horace Mann to George Graham, Registrar-General, p. clviii.

A HAMPSHIRE clergyman, when a witness before a Parliamentary Committee in 1833, told the story of his success in sending certain village labourers to the gallows.   These men set fire to ricks in the distress and disorder of the winter of 1830.   Suspicion fell upon them, and the parson, who was a J.P., locked them up.   He failed, however, to obtain satisfactory evidence, and he decided to give them their liberty, thinking that he was more likely to find such evidence when they were out of prison. They were released ; twelve months later the necessary proof was supplied and the men were hanged.   The parson told the story to support his case against the Beer Act, for he said the unhappy men had said to him before they died that they blamed the beerhouse for their dreadful end.   About the justice of taking their lives his remarks show no trace of compunction or misgiving.[1]

---

[1] 1833 Select Committee on the Sale of Beer, pp. 7 f.

This incident helps to explain why the Church as an institution was regarded with such bitter hatred by the working classes at that time.   There were individual parsons of wide sympathies and humane feeling, but this parson magistrate, who took credit for putting to death men who had set fire to a hayrick more than a year after their offence, was typical of a character too common and too prominent in the life of the age.   Cobbett had no sectarian dislike of the Church ; he called himself a Churchman, and the savage things he said of parsons were certainly not prompted by any tenderness to the Methodists.[1] His violent rage was inflamed by a feeling that was common throughout the whole working-class world, the feeling that there was something false to the spirit of Christianity in the conduct of men who read the New Testament in church on Sundays and turned so ruthless a face on week-days to miserable men whose lives a savage law had brought within their grasp. It is not surprising that parsons who served their religion by lives of self-sacrifice and devotion made less of a mark on the imagination of the times than the parsons of Peterloo, or those who threw weavers into prison on the evidence of spies, or those like this Hampshire justice who demanded the blood of ignorant men, their neighbours in daily life, made desperate by hunger.[2]

Anybody who studies the newspapers and periodicals that were read by the workmen at this time must be impressed by the space and energy given to the attacks on the Church.   Attacks are directed sometimes against its religious teaching, but the chief cause of the Church's unpopularity was this reputation for inhumanity : the feeling that the Church gave its sanction to all the injustices and abuses that degraded the poor and outraged their self-respect.   An example is provided in the agitation against flogging in the army.   This was a barbarity that stirred the working-class sentiment deeply, for it was the symbol of the humiliation of their class, and the clergy took no part in helping to remove it.

" How many instances have we had within the last twelve

---

[1] " Hostile to freedom as the established clergy has been, its hostility has been nothing in point of violence compared to that of these ruffian sectaries."—*Political Register*, January 3, 1824.

[2] It is significant that the Bishop of London (Blomfield) told the Committee on Sabbath Observance (1832) that he had always avoided acting as a magistrate in his own parish unless obliged.—P. 348.

months of soldiers being carried off from the halberds in a state of entrancement, after their backs had been mangled into a jelly and their manhood for ever degraded before the disgusted circle of their comrades, and what priest or swaddler was ever known to denounce the atrocity from the pulpit, or to invoke the Legislature against this bloody and soul-degrading practice ? Oh, no, the vile wretches would cant about beershops and tea-gardens and Sabbath-breaking, or anything else that afforded innocent pleasures to the poor, but not a word would they say on behalf of the poor tortured soldier for fear of giving offence to the ' order ' from which the officers are taken." [1]

It is not surprising that the Church was apt to be regarded by the Radicals as an organ of class government. Of the bishops eleven in 1815 were of noble birth : ten had been tutors or schoolmasters to a prince or a duke or a statesman. Of the 11,700 benefices in England and Wales about half were in the gift of the landowning class.[2] Bulwer Lytton thought the Church suffered more than it gained from this close association with the aristocracy, but Wordsworth in the Preface to the *Excursion*, written in 1814, took the opposite view and said that he was glad to have an opportunity of describing " a country clergyman of more than ordinary talents, born and bred in the upper ranks of society, so as to partake of their refinements, and at the same time brought by his pastoral office and his love of rural life into intimate connection with the peasantry of his native district." [3] No doubt there were many parsons like the pastor in the fifth book :

> " a genuine Priest,
> The shepherd of his flock ; or, as a king
> Is styled, when most affectionately praised,
> The father of his people."

But the spiritual condition of the new industrial districts could not have been described as it was by speakers friendly to the

[1] *The Poor Man's Guardian*, September 7, 1833. " Swaddler " was a name given to itinerant preachers in Ireland, and it was applied to Methodist preachers in England.
[2] Halévy, *England in 1815*, pp. 344 and 345. In 1854 the patronage was thus distributed. The Crown had 1144 livings ; the Bishops, 1853 ; cathedral chapters, 938 ; universities, 770 ; ministers of mother churches, 931 ; and private patrons, 6092. —*Times*, January 9, 1854.
[3] *Poetical Works of Wordsworth*, edited Knight, vol. v. p. 3. Cf. *ibid.* : " It has ever appeared to me highly favourable to the beneficial influence of the Church of England upon all gradations and classes of society, that the patronage of its benefices is in numerous instances attached to the estates of noble families of ancient gentry."

Church in the reports and debates of the time, if such men had been very common.

For the Church, like every other part of the system of aristocratic government, had been corrupted by the abuses that come thick and fast when the sense of property is stronger in any body of men than the sense of duty.   We can see from a debate in the House of Lords in 1810 what a hold the sense of property had on the ecclesiastical system and the ecclesiastical mind. For eleven years, from 1809 to 1820, a yearly grant was made by Parliament to help the poorest livings.   In June 1810, when the grant was under discussion, Lord Holland suggested that the richer benefices rather than the nation should be taxed for this purpose.   Lord Harrowby replied to Lord Holland : " The first objection to a general tax upon the higher clergy, in which the parochial clergy were included, was this : About three-fifths of the livings in this country were in lay patronage, and the advowsons were a part of the estates of the proprietors bought and sold like other estates for a valuable consideration, upon the faith that they were only subject to taxation in common with other estates." [1]   Harrowby went on to his second objection, which was that if the higher incomes of the Church were reduced, an incitement to diligence would be removed. Now Harrowby was a leading reformer.   The Church was regarded, like the pocket boroughs, as a great system of patronage and property.   This system defeated in the Church, as in Parliament, the purposes that the institution over which it had spread its enveloping hand was meant to serve.

For the manner in which the duties laid upon the Church were carried out was determined by this view of its benefices as so much property at the disposition of the richer classes. Parsons could hold several livings together, putting curates, who were paid in some instances like the poorest labourers, in the less desirable and less healthy parishes.   In 1810 there were 6000 livings in which the incumbent was non-resident.[2]   Hay, the Vicar of Rochdale, one of the richest livings in England, was non-resident most of the time.   Even as late as 1838 there were over 4000 non-resident parsons.[3]   Chapters were as greedy

---

[1] Parliamentary Debates, House of Lords, June 18, 1810.   The advowson of Liverpool Rectory was sold for £8150 to Mr. John Stuart of Liverpool in 1839.— *Leeds Intelligencer*, May 4, 1839.

[2] Halévy, *op. cit.* p. 349.   [3] See Return in 1840, p. 57.

and as ruthless as individuals. A Dean and Chapter would take £1000 or £2000 from a parish and pay somebody like Parson Andrewes to do the work £50 a year, or even less.[1] The Church thus combined in its ranks men with princely incomes for which some of them rendered no service at all, and curates who were as badly off as the village labourer who was driven to live on the Speenhamland dole.[2] With a Church so governed and inspired there was, of course, no relation between spiritual needs and the ministrations of the Church. It was characteristic that neither Manchester, Birmingham, Liverpool, nor Leeds had a bishop; there was not a single bishop in Lancashire or the West Riding until 1836.[3] Churches were, like members of Parliament, most numerous where least needed.[4]

It is not surprising that a Church of which all this could be said took a prominent place among the scandals that were denounced in the agitations that produced and followed the reform of Parliament.[5] It is highly significant that ten or twenty years later the agitation had dropped to a much quieter note. It is true that there was still a demand for the separation of Church and State (the Chartists included this in their last programme), that there were grievances like Church rates that caused bad blood, that cases of mean and petty oppression over the marriages and burials of Nonconformists from time to time excited passionate feeling. But the Church presented a much smaller surface for attack because the great sensational abuses had been remedied, partly by the influence of reformers within

---

[1] Halévy, *op. cit.* p. 348.

[2] Readers of *Tom Jones* will recollect that the father of the wife of Black George, the gamekeeper, and the grandfather of Mrs. Honour, Sophia Western's maid, were both clergymen, and that Fielding put a footnote in chapter xiv. : " This is the second person of low condition whom we have recorded in this History to have sprung from the clergy. It is to be hoped that such instances will, in future ages, when some provision is made for the families of the inferior clergy, appear stranger than they can be thought at present." *Tom Jones* was published in 1747.

[3] Ripon was made a see in 1836, Manchester in 1847.

[4] A common saying in the populous part of South Staffordshire was, " as scarce as parish churches."—Midland Mining Commission, p. 586.

[5] " The law-established THING is one of the main causes of the misery of the people." —*Pioneer*, January 29, 1831. " The nuisance must be abated, the monstrous hypocrisy and injustice be put down."—*Pioneer*, September 10, 1831. The incomes of some of the bishops were the object of a great deal of satire and invective. Landor laid stress on this in his " Letters of a Conservative," 1836 : " A prelate must no longer be estimated at thirty admirals ; a greater number than ever were in commission at once during the most prosperous of our wars."

the Church, partly by legislation initiated by Peel [1] and carried on by Russell. An organ for internal reform was set up in the Ecclesiastical Commission; [2] scandals disappeared : attempts were made to supply the neglected districts by new bishoprics at Manchester and Ripon ; the glaring inequality between the incomes of different sees was removed ; members of Chapters were forbidden to hold more than one benefice or to belong to more than one Chapter, and it was made illegal to hold two benefices if they were more than a mile apart, or if the additional stipend exceeded £1000. Lord Holland's suggestion in 1810 for redistributing income within the Church was carried out in part in 1840 when a number of canonries was suppressed, and the income so saved was assigned to raise the poorer stipends. [3] The sense of obligation was now strong enough to challenge the sense of property, and to give the Church a new character. The effect of the reforms of the thirties was to convert what had been a great system of patronage and private property into a responsible semi-public corporation. It is impossible not to admire the success with which this conversion was effected. Dicey put it that so far as the great scandals of pluralism, non-residence, and neglect of duty were concerned, the establishment of 1850 was not the establishment of 1800 or of 1832, but the establishment of 1905. [4]

If the bishops had been a little wiser a grievance that did serious injury to the Church for the next thirty years would have been removed in 1836. Althorp had wished to abolish Church rates and to apply £250,000 a year from the Land Tax

---

[1] Peel's view was well explained in a letter he wrote to the Rev. John Peel, January 17, 1835. " In my opinion the time is come when clerical sinecures must share the fate of civil sinecures. They must be extirpated gradually and justly and injuring no existing interest, but to an end they must come. . . . Lord Nelson may storm and Bailey may stand aghast, but to this we must come, and the sooner we come to it— under the conduct of real friends and well-wishers to the Church—the better will it be for the Church and every interest of the Church temporal and spiritual."—Additional MSS., 40410.

[2] First set up by Peel in 1834 ; incorporated 1836.

[3] The fear of touching private patronage was still an obstacle to any attempt to remove the inequalities in the value of livings; see the speech of Sir Robert Inglis, May 4, 1838 : " With respect to the Hon. Member's recommendation of raising small livings by taking away from the larger he must remark that such a principle was founded neither on justice nor on law. A patron of a living had as much right to his income as any gentleman to his private property." Inglis was M.P. for Oxford University, having turned Peel out on Catholic Emancipation. He admitted in the same speech that the sale of advowsons was perhaps indefensible.

[4] *Relation between Law and Public Opinion in the Nineteenth Century*, p. 342.

to the repair of parish churches. The Nonconformists objected. In 1836 the Government returned to the question. It was now believed that if the bishops' estates were well managed enough money would be saved to make Church rates unnecessary. The Government devised a scheme for this purpose, but the Church objected, the bishops on the Ecclesiastical Commission going so far as to decline to act while this scheme was under discussion, on the ground that it violated a pledge given to the Commission when Melbourne's Government was formed in 1835. For the bishops on the Commission had extorted pretty stiff terms from Melbourne at that time, and among other things a promise not to depart from the principle of Althorp's proposed measure, which had recognised the repair of the churches as an obligation on the State. The bishops got their way, but if they had been less exacting or less successful they would have saved the Church a great deal of odium in the next twenty years.[1]

Russell, Peel, Melbourne, and the other statesmen of the time did for the Church what they did for the Poor Law and the government of the towns. They put an end to great and manifest scandals; they introduced a new principle of coherence and authority; they made the Church much more efficient for its tasks. The only serious opposition came from within. For a school in whose outlook an imposing sense of duty was adorned by a picturesque sense for the spiritual and historical character of religion, dreaded all interference by the State with the liberty of the Church, and thus, by a curious irony, it was not the vices of the eighteenth century but the attempt to reform them that provoked Newman's beautiful protests. In other respects the conditions were propitious for reforms which abated abuses but at the same time gave the bishops more power. For though the Act of 1836 constituted a Commission with a majority of laymen, later legislation added all the bishops. Such changes could not have been made if the Nonconformists had been in the same uncompromising temper as the Radicals,

---

[1] For the full story of this incident, see Walpole's *Life of Lord John Russell*, vol. i. p. 290.

For the bad blood caused by Church rates, see the case of Bradford, where Scoresby, a public-spirited vicar, lost a great deal of his influence in consequence. There as at Rochdale there was a perpetual struggle over these rates. At Doncaster, a Unitarian minister was sent to prison for refusing to pay the rate, and his case (see, *e.g.*, *Leeds Mercury*, September 11, 1847) caused widespread indignation. At some places the Church gave the rates up spontaneously with excellent results.

but the largest body of Nonconformists, though jealous of any measure that gave the Church control over education, were not hostile to the establishment itself or unconcerned for its improvement; they were not in the mood to say that the only reform of the Church that they would countenance was its separation from the State.[1]

With these reforms there disappeared the resounding scandals that had filled so many sparkling pages in the Radical pamphlets of the time. Cobbett's *Legacy to Parsons* was now a book for the library shelf rather than the political platform; a stern hand had been laid on the corruption which had displayed so splendid a target for his incomparable invective. This was a great achievement, but it would be false to say of it that it had solved the urgent problem that faced the Church: all that could be said is that it had removed obstacles that made any attempt at a solution desperate. It was one thing to put an end to sinecures and abuses and to give a serious and responsible character to the office of its parsons, hitherto regarded and held with such levity; it was another to satisfy the imagination of the great population on whose daily life of bleak and monotonous toil those civilising influences to which mankind has looked for comfort, ever since the first city found shelter behind its circling walls, shed a light so pale and doubtful. How far could the Church succeed in helping men and women to turn away from the hard face of a struggle, in which wealth brought fame, and poverty contempt, to this mysterious atmosphere, where the soul of Dives was no more esteemed than the soul of Lazarus? The importance of religion, like the importance of culture, or the importance of beauty, in the social setting examined in these pages, depended on its power to create a world of its own, with standards, duties, and satisfactions other than those set and sought in the race for wealth.

The difficulties of the Church were not new; they are almost as old as Christianity. Dr. Gore has described in his vivid sketch the changes that came over Christianity with the " transition from a Church sometimes grudgingly tolerated, and sometimes fiercely persecuted, to a Church seated in the high

---

[1] On the burning question of Church rates leading Wesleyan ministers supported the Church. See meeting reported in *West Riding Herald*, February 24, 1837.

places of government and power." [1]   The Church never afterwards found it easy to become what it had tried to be in early life, " a spiritual aristocracy which could draw and convert the world by the spectacle of a life so different from its own." [2] In the sixteenth century when wealth had become strong enough to challenge feudal prestige, Columbus, speaking bitterly of the adventurers whose avarice had spilt so much unbaptized blood in the distant land he had discovered, left behind him a phrase which reminds us how much the Church he loved had learnt from the world whose prizes they pursued; how deeply the imagination of the one had been coloured by the habits of the other.   For he spoke of gold as enabling a man to rescue the souls of his friends from purgatory. [3]

Historians have shown how in the movement of revolt, that was in part inspired by horror of this doctrine, the same difficulties recur.   They have drawn a picture of the phases through which the conscience of Christian Europe passed in its effort to discover and define the place of religion in the elaborate economy created by the rise of capitalist commerce. [4]   Of that picture we can say that, alike in the eighteenth and the fifteenth centuries, a man looking to religion for an escape from the pattern of the world might find that he was looking into its mirror.

Nor were the special characteristics that made the English Church look so much the church of the rich, the internal arrangements and the system of pew rents, peculiar either to England or to the nineteenth century.   The great in the world have often received special honour at church.   St. James had to rebuke the early Church for such distinctions.   St. Ambrose had to rebuke the Emperor Theodosius for taking his seat within the sanctuary rails, and the Emperor and his successors sat afterwards outside them.   In the reign of Queen Mary nobles and patrons were removed from choirs and chancels, where they had been accustomed to worship.   A learned authority, discussing the origin and history of pew rents in 1872, said that the pew rent system was common in Holland, Scandinavia, North Germany, and the extreme north of France, as well as in England, and that it was only in Spain and Italy

---

[1] *Christ and Society*, p. 89.   [2] *Ibid.* p. 105.
[3] Raleigh, *English Voyages of the Sixteenth Century*, p. 28.
[4] Compare R. H. Tawney, *Religion and the Rise of Capitalism*, p. 89.

that the appropriation of chairs or pews was quite unknown. The first record of a pew rent appears in the archives of St. Margaret's, Westminster, in 1504.[1] Pepys tells us in his Diary how he was locked out of his own pew in 1661.[2]

Pew rents were not new, then, in early nineteenth-century England, but the Acts of Parliament of the time show that they had become a serious obstacle to the progress of the Church at this time. When Parliament turned its mind to the need for more churches, Acts were passed (the first in 1818) for encouraging church building. In the earliest of these Acts it was stipulated that a fifth of the seats in the churches built with the help of public money should be free, and marked with the word " free " ; in the second, that in all churches rebuilt with the help of public money, half of the additional accommodation should be free. In the course of the next twenty years about a million and a half of public money was spent under these and later Acts. Charlotte Brontë explains that the opening sentence of *Shirley*, " Of late years an abundant shower of curates has fallen upon the North of England," refers not to the time of her story, 1812, but to the time of its composition, 1849. A study of the returns presented to Parliament shows that a large proportion of the new churches were built in the West Riding. But it was easier to build churches than to break down a bad tradition. Bishop Blomfield described the difficulties when giving evidence before the Committee on the Observance of the Sabbath, in 1832 : " It is the object of the Commissioners for building new churches, as far as they can, to intermingle the seats of the rich and the poor, so as to afford the latter nearly the same facilities for hearing which the former enjoy. We have found considerable difficulty in realising our own wishes in that respect, on account of the objections which were made by the richer classes to too great an intermixture of the poor among them, objections which it was absolutely necessary to attend to because the whole income of the Minister depends on the pew rents accruing exclusively from the richer classes." [3]

---

[1] See Heales, A. C., *History and Law of Church Seats or Pews*, 1872, vol. i. pp. 63, 79, 152, 185.

[2] " 1661. Dec. 25. In the morning to church where at the door of our pew I was fain to stay because the sexton had not opened the door. A good sermon by Mr. Mills."

[3] See also Blomfield's letter to a clergyman in 1851, *Memoir of Bishop Blomfield*, p. 325.

In 1832 Mr. Price obtained an Act (2 Geo. iv. cap. 79) for enlarging a church at

The system of pew rents was attacked by the High Church review, the *British Critic*, and Kohl remarks in his *Travels in England* that the abolition of pews was the chief of the reforms at which the Puseyites were aiming.[1] These reformers, who were strongly supported by the *Times*, condemned pew rents and the general arrangement of many of the town churches on the ground that they made a distinction between rich and poor, and also on the ground that they destroyed the character of the Church as something more than a place where men and women assembled to hear sermons. Those who cared about the spiritual significance of their religion, and those who cared about the historical traditions of their architecture, united in protest on this subject. The Camden Society, founded in the early forties, published several pamphlets. "For many town churches have been so spoilt by misshapen additions made to enable them to hold more people, besides having sometimes had little of the true plan of a church at first, that now unless you were told it you would often scarcely know that you were in a church."[2] "... Some churches indeed or rather

Birkenhead, providing a parsonage and an endowment of £30 out of the pew rents. He was to have the patronage and sell or let pews and receive all rents or monies from such letting or sale "as a remuneration for the great expense which he had sustained in the building of the Church and which he may sustain in making any additions thereto." A few years later the Price trustees endeavoured to lock up unlet pews, whereupon the parson made an arrangement by which the trustees received 400 guineas per annum.—Sulley, *History of Ancient and Modern Birkenhead*, 1907, p. 93.

[1] P. 322. Compare: "Observe, again, in the churches of the metropolis and large manufacturing towns, the scanty space allotted for what are called, in the language of modern days, '*free sittings*,' while the larger part of the building is occupied with galleries for the genteelly-dressed and profitable 'pews'; and well may you ask for the palpable evidences of that blessed Gospel which has 'lifted up the poor out of the dust, and the beggar out of the mire, that it may set them with princes.'"—*British Critic*, vol. 29, p. 56.

At a meeting to promote church building at Halifax, one parson said that some rich people in that town rented pews in two or three churches at the same time.—*Halifax Guardian*, December 15, 1838.

[2] "A few words to Churchwardens on Churches and Church Ornaments suited to Town and Manufacturing Parishes," 1842. A good illustration of the strange arrangement of many of the churches of that time, with a chancel blocked by pews, is the picture of the Bradford Parish Church given in the book, *Old Bradford* (Scruton). See on the subject of the ill-treatment of the chancel, *The Gothic Revival*, by Kenneth Clarke. In another publication of the Camden Society the writer remarked: "We are not now called on to prove that Gothic is the only Christian architecture. We believe that after a well-fought battle the point has been conceded."

Pugin, of course, took the same view, and Coleridge had contrasted the Greek church, which was beautiful and charmed the eye, with the Gothic cathedral, which was sublime, filling him, when he entered, with devotion and with awe; but Newman dissented, saying that however much his reason might go with Gothic, his heart had ever gone with Grecian. "I love Trinity Chapel at Oxford more than any other building. There

sermon houses, for they are not fit for prayer, remind one rather of auction or assembly rooms ; the inside being full of comfortable boxes, and the outside having a fine portico for the company whose carriages roll up with pride and bustle and strife." It is easy to imagine how such a church was regarded as a place of fashionable entertainment where people in local society assembled on Sunday morning for a pleasant ceremony : the idea given by an advertisement quoted in an article on church architecture at this time. "Plan and elevation for a Gothic church upon a large scale, to seat upwards of 1500 persons. . . . The handsome vestibule entrance with an enriched groined ceiling, and the noble staircase on each side, which lead to the gallery, give to the design a grand and noble effect, suitable to the character of a wealthy and extensive parish. Here are also a number of free seats." [1]

It was not only among High Churchmen and persons with a sense for architecture and history that the subject excited attention. It affected the popular imagination. When Oastler stood as Conservative candidate for Huddersfield in 1837, he put the question in his programme, saying that he would make every seat in the parish church free to the first comer. The Chartists took it up, and attendance at Church was one of their favourite methods of asserting their principles. Large numbers used to assemble before the hours of service, march to church, and occupy the seats. This was done in all the chief towns in 1839 : in Manchester, Bradford, Newcastle, Bristol, Norwich, Bolton, Blackburn, Stockport, and other places. Disraeli said in *Sybil* that this plan very much affected "the imagination of the multitude." Sometimes the Chartists gave notice to the parson, and even suggested a text. Dr. Whittaker of Blackburn, having been invited to preach on the text, "Go to now, ye rich, weep and howl for your miseries that are coming upon you," explained that these words had no application to England "governed by equal laws." [2] At Manchester the

is, in the Italian style, such a simplicity, purity, elegance, brightness, which I suppose the word classical implies, that it seems to befit the notion of an angel or saint."— *Newman*, by J. L. May, p. 82.

[1] *British Critic*, vol. 28, p. 473. Cf. *North of England Magazine*, vol. i. p. 169: "We then call upon him, on the day anxiously looked for through the week as the time of rest for wearied limb and anxious mind, to sit on hard oak forms apart from his fellow men, though in the presence of his God."

[2] Faulkner, *Chartism and the Churches*, p. 37.

parson substituted his own text: "My house is a house of prayer, but you have made it a den of thieves." At Bury "the worthy Rector being fully prepared for their visit, gave them a lecture on keeping the peace and obeying the law which from its length as well as from its force, many of them would not exactly relish."[1] In a few instances there was disorder. In most of the churches the Chartist congregations had to listen to critical sermons, but on one occasion they were specially invited to attend the Roman Catholic Cathedral at Norwich, where the preacher, taking as his text "Let him that hath two coats impart to him that hath none," preached an inflammatory sermon on the Reformation and the wrongs done by Protestants to the poor.[2]

In spite of all the reforms that Parliament had made, we can see from the case of Leeds and of Manchester how ill placed the Church was for making religion a vital force in the life of the poor. Leeds in 1843 and Manchester in 1850 lived under ecclesiastical arrangements as anomalous and indefensible as the municipal arrangements under which they lived at the opening of the century. Leeds was a single unwieldy parish, divided into eleven townships, each maintaining its own poor. The population was about 150,000. Distributed among these eleven townships there were twenty-one churches, eighteen of which were served by clergymen who were technically perpetual curates, without a cure of souls: that is, their duties were limited to the celebration of Divine Service on Sundays and holy days. Some of the churches had been built under special Acts of Parliament, and three of these were private property from which the poor were deliberately excluded. In the township of Leeds itself there were ten churches, and a good deal less than half the seats were free.[3] Thus the only clergy who were responsible for the care of the 150,000 persons in the parish, outside the duties of the Sunday, were the clergy of three churches. Nearly all the marriages, funerals, and baptisms were performed at the Parish Church. This was the state of things to which

[1] *Leeds Mercury*, August 10, 1839. [2] *Times*, September 9, 1839.
[3] Bradford was in this respect worse off than Leeds. In 1841 Bradford, with a population of 66,000, had four churches, the Parish Church with no free seats, Christ Church with 60 free seats, St. John the Less with no free seats, and St. James's Church built by John Wood, the factory reformer, with 600 free seats.—John James, *History of Bradford*, p. 104.

Dean Hook put an end in 1844, when he obtained the Leeds Vicarage Act, dividing up his huge parish, depriving his own office of emoluments and prestige, giving Leeds a responsible and resident clergy, and making the floor of every one of the twelve new parish churches free.[1]

The case of Manchester in some respects was still more remarkable. Here the dead hand laid its burden on 400,000 people. In the fifteenth century a rector of Manchester proposed to the parishioners to rebuild the parish church and make it collegiate, appropriating the tithes and other endowments to the maintenance of the new college. This arrangement was carried out ; the church which is now the Cathedral was rebuilt, and a College was formed, consisting of a Warden, Fellows, Chaplains, and others. This College degenerated into a nest of sinecures. In 1830 the Warden, four Fellows, two Chaplains, a Clerk in Orders, and a lay Clerk, drew an income of over £5000 from the property of the College, but repudiated all care of souls in the parish, and all duties outside the Collegiate Church.[2] The people of Manchester had thus to make their own provision ; about fifty-three churches were built and some endowments provided. In 1847, when Manchester was made a bishopric, the first bishop, Prince Lee, found that the town which gave its name to his see, with nearly half a million inhabitants, was without any pastoral supervision, though the Chapter over which he presided lived handsomely on the revenues of the parish. This scandal was extinguished in 1850, when the people of Manchester, led by the Bishop, obtained an Act of Parliament, at a cost of £4000, creating a number of parishes, each of which was to be a rectory, with cure of souls, and making a just distribution of the revenues of the Chapter.

[1] See *Life of Dean Hook*, by Stephens, vol. ii. pp. 167-170. The report of the Statistical Committee of the Leeds Town Council gives some interesting facts about the churches and chapels in Leeds in the year 1839. There were then 9 churches with 13,235 sittings ; 3 Catholic chapels with 1970 sittings ; 17 Methodist chapels with 16,340 sittings ; 6 Independent chapels with 6030 sittings, and 5 belonging to other sects with 3876 sittings. The total population was about 82,000. There were three wards, chiefly inhabited by the working classes with a population of 43,000, and these were the bad wards in respect of streets, housing, and cellar dwellings. In these wards there were 2 churches with 2634 sittings ; 8 Methodist chapels with 6780 sittings ; 2 Catholic chapels with 1070 sittings, and 2 Independent chapels with 980 sittings.

[2] A paragraph headed " Manchester and Leeds Railway, the Poor Man's Church," in the *Bradford Observer* of September 14, 1837, records that the railway wanted to buy some land at Newton Heath for which they offered the clergy £7000, and on arbitration had to give £8724. The clergy asked £24,000.

The Act was contested, and the report of the proceedings in Committee threw some valuable light on the state of Manchester. The counsel for the Bill stated that there were nearly 400,000 people in Manchester, that there were 60,000 sittings in the churches, and that about a third of them were free. The endowments of the churches were in some cases no more than £30 a year, and there were very few in which a house was provided; hence most of the churches were absolutely dependent on pew rents.[1]

Hook's achievement at Leeds shows that the difficulties that faced the Church were not insuperable to a man with a genius for leadership. When he went to Leeds in 1838 the Church was hated by the Dissenters and ignored by everybody else. There were fifty communicants. The parishioners, who elected seven out of the eight churchwardens, used to elect a standing opposition to the Vicar, who appointed the eighth. Hook was vicar for twenty-eight years. When he left, the Church was a power in Leeds as nowhere else in England. The revolution he made in the ecclesiastical system has been described. It was accompanied by a moral revolution, which converted a Church despised and disliked into a Church that inspired affection and respect among all classes. Blomfield had explained that the wishes of the rich Churchmen had to be considered in manufacturing districts. Hook never acted on this principle. He told the squires and the farmers at a great agricultural dinner at Leeds, that one of the first needs of the time was to give the agricultural labourer leisure and education.[2] He took the chair on several occasions at meetings in favour of the Ten Hours Bill, even when the principal speaker was so tempestuous an orator as Oastler.[3] He lost subscriptions for his churches in consequence, for he had just issued his manifesto to the people of Leeds, and the Evangelicals were seeking to stir up opposition among the rich.[4] In his early days at Leeds the Chartists ran a list of candidates at the meeting for electing churchwardens, and carried all of them. The Chartist churchwardens who were thus thrust upon Hook soon learned to respect him: they

---

[1] See Manchester Rectory Division Bill. Report of the Evidence given before the Committee of the House of Commons, Session of 1850. Printed for the Churchwardens of Manchester. See especially pp. 2 and 3.
[2] *Leeds Intelligencer*, August 31, 1839. [3] *Leeds Mercury*, March 14, 1846.
[4] *Life of Dean Hook*, by Stephens, vol. ii. pp. 175 and 177.

worked with him and not against him, and one of them became an ardent churchman.[1] Workmen helped to administer all his organisations, and to provide funds for his schemes. Thirteen churches were built and the parish church rebuilt while he was vicar, but he had no difficulty in raising the money needed for his parishes, and Church rates were never imposed.[2] Two incidents illustrate the confidence and esteem which he inspired among the poorer classes. When the Queen visited Leeds, the Friendly Societies chose him to present their address of welcome; during a strike in the mining industry, the colliers asked for abitration by three arbitrators, one to be named by the employers, one by the men, and the third by the Vicar of Leeds.

Hook's career shows what could be done by a man of character and power. But it illustrates also another aspect of the Church's difficulties. The Church was distracted between the two movements which had brought power and purpose into its life. The Evangelical movement had brought earnestness and devotion; the Tractarian movement had brought a wider and deeper sense of the place of religion in history and civilisation. The great change in the character and spirit of the clergy which is apparent if we contrast 1850 with 1800 is the result largely of these two movements.[3] But the movements were rivals, and bitter rivals, and their quarrels at this time brought out what was bad rather than what was good in each of them: the narrow outlook of the Evangelicals, and the stiff pride of the High Churchmen. The Evangelicals were by this time more occupied in combating the Tractarian theology than in prosecuting the missionary aims that had once inspired them.[4] Their critics said indeed that they had so completely lost their first ardour that Evangelical clergy were rather more apt than

---

[1] *Life of Dean Hook*, by Stephens, vol. ii. p. 121. See *Annual Register*, 1843, p. 53.

[2] Samuel Morley said to the House of Lords Committee on Church Rates in 1859 that Hook " utterly repudiated any of these forced contributions and left Leeds with the sincere respect of Dissenters."

[3] The *Guardian* remarked (November 18, 1846) that the Tractarian revival had filled the nave of St. Paul's to excess, whereas Rowland Hill, the preacher (died 1833), had said that the nave would be the safest place in London for artillery practice on a Sunday morning.

[4] A good illustration of the ferocity of evangelical intolerance is provided by the attacks on Father Mathew's temperance crusade in Ireland. A leading evangelical preacher, the Rev. Hugh Stowell, argued that a sober Catholic Ireland was a greater danger to Protestant England than a drunken Catholic Ireland. See pamphlet of Thomas Spencer (Herbert Spencer's uncle): *The Pillars of the Church.*

others to live away from their churches when those churches were in poor districts.[1] Whether this is true or not, it is probable that now that Evangelical views were fashionable, Evangelical clergy were less eager and devoted than they had been when they were facing unpopularity, and were therefore tested men. The Oxford movement again brought difficulty as well as inspiration, for it taught a view of the Church and its claims that Englishmen do not find it easy to accept.[2] Hook suffered at the hands of both schools. The Evangelicals obstructed his reforms and the Puseyites objected to his teaching. In 1848 some of Pusey's friends built the church of St. Saviour's, Leeds, where the needs of a very poor population were to be served by clergymen living in a community. This was the first expression of the spirit which established settlements later in the century in the poorer districts of every large town. But of the fifteen clergy who were connected with St. Saviour's in the first fourteen years of its life, no less than nine seceded to the Church of Rome. The Church, which had to overtake the neglect of half a century, was thus disabled and distracted by its internal conflicts.

It is curious to turn from the picture of the spiritual plight of the great towns at this time to the energy spent on discussion and argument within the Church. For the Church was full of vitality and movement, rich in thinkers, teachers, men of

[1] " Tell me what sort of a churchman the new rector is to be," said a lady to a friend of hers who was living in the parsonage in the heart of a manufacturing parish, and was expecting to be displaced by the death of the incumbent, " and I will tell you whether you are likely to be disturbed. If he is a Low Churchman he 'll be sure to take a house out of the town."—*British Critic*, vol. 38, p. 369.

[2] The greater the emphasis on the unique character of the Church, the less easy was it to tolerate dissent. " Dissenters are but mushrooms," was a line in a song composed by a High Church poet, which was used with great effect to raise the temperature of a Nonconformist meeting.

Carlyle derided these claims. " O Heavens, what shall we say of Puseyism, in comparison to Twelfth-Century Catholicism? Little or nothing; for indeed it is a matter to strike one dumb.

> The Builder of this Universe was wise,
> He plann'd all souls, all systems, planets, particles :
> The Plan He shap'd all Worlds and Æons by,
> Was—Heavens !—was thy small Nine-and-thirty Articles ?

That certain human souls, living on this practical Earth, should think to save themselves and a ruined world by noisy theoretic demonstrations and laudations of *the* Church, instead of some unnoisy, unconscious, but *practical*, total, heart-and-soul demonstration of *a* Church : this, in the circle of revolving ages, this also was a thing we were to see."—*Past and Present*, p. 161.

saintly life and serious scholarship. Newman, Pusey, Maurice, Robertson, Whateley, were all helping to form the English mind of the next generation. This was the absorbing task of the hour. Dr. Gore has remarked that after the third century, with the rise of Arianism, the emphasis in the history of the Church passes from right living to right thinking, from conduct to orthodoxy.[1] Something like this happened in early Victorian England, and the influence of the Church as a social power suffered in consequence. The ferment of that intellectual life had important results in politics as well as in thought. Maurice had his disciples in public life, and he helped to inspire and influence social reform long after he was dead. The Tractarian movement helped to raise the tone of politics, for Gladstone, teaching a nation to look beyond its rights to a higher law, had inherited its outlook on the life of the world. But in the days when Chartism was spreading over the towns, this intellectual vigour found its expression in the bitter strife of Evangelical and Tractarian : a strife that disabled the Church as a missionary power.[2] " The conviction has been brought home to some of us with terrible force," wrote one of the wisest and noblest men of the age, " that while religious men are disputing on what ground they shall unite, as members of an Evangelical Alliance, as English Churchmen, as Romanists, the great body of Englishmen is becoming bitterly indifferent to us all, and smiles grimly and contemptuously at our controversies." [3] It is significant that when Dr. Scoresby issued his plan for the welfare of factory women, he said of it that " though not necessarily religious, it would act favourably as the pioneer to religion. It would serve to clear the obstacles to their return to the Christian fold of a class of persons now as to large numbers almost entirely estranged." [4] While the party men led by Pusey and Shaftesbury, " theological champions, armed at all points," were filling

[1] *Christ and Society*, p. 96.
[2] " As to the Church, my friend," wrote Dickens in 1855, " I am sick of it. The spectacle presented by it, indecent squabbles of priests of most denominations and the exemplary unfairness and rancours with which they conduct their differences, utterly repel me. . . . Here more Popery, there more Methodism—as many forms of consignment to clerical damnation as there are articles, and all in one for ever quarrelling body."—*Letters*, ii. 21.
[3] F. D. Maurice, *Tracts on Christian Socialism*, viii.
[4] *American Factories and their Female Operatives*, by W. Scoresby, 1845.

the Church with the sound of conflict, the mass of the poor in most of the great towns remained outside it.

When the census of 1851 was taken it was decided to make an effort to ascertain what proportion of the English people attended church and chapel and what provision was made for them. Questions were sent to clergymen of all denominations, and the answers were tabulated and examined. It is clear from the information thus obtained that the Church as well as the Nonconformist bodies had been very active in this period. For whereas five hundred new churches were built in the thirty years between 1801 and 1831, over two thousand were built in the twenty years between 1831 and 1851. In the first thirty years the State gave rather over a million to this purpose, and private benefactors just under two million; in the second period the State gave half a million, and private benefactors five million and a half. Other statistics give the same impression of progress, for large sums had been given for the aid of smaller livings. It was estimated from the returns that just over half the people who went to church or chapel belonged to the Church. The Church provided accommodation for rather over five million people. On Census Sunday some two and a half million persons attended morning service, just under two million afternoon service, and eight hundred and sixty thousand attended evening service.

Returns, obtained by asking ministers to count their flocks, were not likely to give too unfavourable a picture. Bishop Wilberforce, indeed, contended in the House of Lords in an arrogant speech that the figures were worthless: the Church, he argued, had not counted all its worshippers, and other bodies, particularly the Methodists, had erred on the other side.[1] But the figures were generally taken to show that in spite of all the efforts that had been made, none of the Churches had drawn the mass of the working classes to religion. Convocation of Canterbury declared, " It is deeply to be deplored that there are at present large numbers of the poorer population, especially in our great towns, who are habitually absent from the public worship of God and live with little or no sense of true religion."[2] It was agreed that the existing arrangements and resources of the Church were insufficient for its task, and Convocation re-

---

[1] House of Lords, July 15, 1854.   [2] *Times*, July 21, 1854.

commended that clergymen should live together in poor districts " preaching, exhorting, visiting the sick and poor in their own homes, and superintending schools." [1] The novelty of this idea shows how slow the Church, with all its new spirit of devotion, had been to adapt itself to the special conditions of town life created by the Industrial Revolution.

[1] The *Times*, then in the full ardour of that campaign against ecclesiastical abuses of which Trollope gives a picture in *The Warden* (published 1855), observed on this scheme : " Nothing could be more reasonable than these remarks, nor have we anything to add except that in reading them we appear to be reading the description of a collegiate or cathedral establishment engaged in its proper duties."—July 22, 1854.

In the summer of 1854 the clergy in some of the large towns such as Birmingham and Sheffield took to preaching in the streets on Sundays.—*Leeds Intelligencer*, July 15, 1854.

CHAPTER XIII

RELIGION

THE NONCONFORMIST CHURCHES

" One chief cause of the dislike which the labouring population entertain for
religious services is thought to be the maintenance of those distinctions by which
they are separated as a class from the class above them.   Working men, it is contended, cannot enter our religious structures without having pressed upon their
notice some memento of their inferiority.   The existence of pews and the
position of the free seats are, it is said, alone sufficient to deter them from our
churches ;   and religion has thus come to be regarded as a purely middle-class
propriety or luxury."

> Census of 1851, *Religious Worship in England and Wales*, abridged
> from the Official Report made by Horace Mann to George
> Graham, Registrar-General, p. xciv.

About the character of the Methodist revival, the most
important event in eighteenth-century England, there is general
agreement.   It was one of the periodical outbursts of vitality
that have marked the history of Christianity ; for its predecessors we must turn to the great movements associated with
such names as those of St. Benedict, St. Francis, John Wycliffe,
and John Huss.   Its founder created a body of preachers who
resembled the early disciples of St. Francis, alike in their relation
to the religion in power and in their view of their own mission.
Their business was not to teach a new theology,[1] but to bring
ardour and purpose into a Church whose teaching had become
formal and cold, and whose life and conduct reflected and
respected too faithfully the spirit and outlook of the world.
They were not rebels against the authority of this indolent and
comfortable institution ; they were rebels against the easy-going
pagan life of the time, with its neglect of the passionate gospel
which the Christian Church came to life to preach.   The
Church had become more like a school of social manners than
a witness to a militant faith ; there was no note of indignation
or rapture in its pulpits.   The Methodists desired to supply the
fervour that was lacking.   They were not Nonconformists but

---

[1] " In matters of religion I am for as few innovations as possible."—Wesley, *Works*,
vol. vii. p. 512.

revivalists, and they succeeded in reviving both the Established and the Nonconformist Churches. The relation in which they stood to the Church was well illustrated by the rules that Wesley laid down forbidding preachers to hold services in Church hours unless the incumbent was a " notoriously wicked man " or unless he preached Arian or " equally pernicious doctrine." [1]

These early preachers resembled the Franciscans in another respect. They practised an austere simplicity of life; they were to make themselves conspicuous amid the levity of the age by their earnest and solemn behaviour.[2]   A strict discipline was required of them. They were not to use tobacco for " smoaking, chewing, or snuff," except on doctor's orders; they were to fast; they were to avoid spirituous liquors; they were " to converse sparingly and cautiously with women, particularly with young women "; preachers desiring to marry were to consult their brethren, and any member who married an unbeliever was to be expelled. They were bidden expressly not to affect the gentleman, but to remember that a preacher of the Gospel is the servant of all.

Such a crusade, inspired and directed by a man of genius, was bound to produce remarkable results among the classes neglected by the Church. Wesley and his disciples converted whole districts like the mining parts of Cornwall from a life of dissipation and plunder to devout and orderly habits. All over England there were great numbers of ignorant men and women who were now for the first time brought under the influence of religion. Their imagination was captured, and this new ardour took them out of their lives of rough hardship into dreams of sublime duty and happiness.[3]

When Wesley died in 1791 there were 72,000 Wesleyan

---

[1] " Q. In what view may the Methodist preachers be considered ?—A. As messengers sent by the Lord out of the common way. To provoke the regular clergy to jealousy, and to supply the great lack of service towards those who are perishing for want of knowledge, and above all, to reform the nation by spreading scriptural holiness over the land."—Minutes of several conversations between the Rev. John Wesley, M.A., and the preachers in connection with him, concerning the form of discipline established among the preachers and people in the Methodist Societies, 1779.

[2] " Your strictness of life, taking the whole of it together, may likewise be accounted new: I mean your making it a rule to abstain from fashionable diversions, from reading plays, romances, or books of humour, from singing innocent songs, or talking in a gay diverting manner."—Wesley, *Works*, vol. viii. p. 351.

[3] See Dr. Priestley's great tribute, quoted Warner, *The Wesleyan Movement and the Industrial Revolution*, p. 175 : "To you is the civilisation, the industry and sobriety of great numbers of the working classes owing."

Methodist members. This great body of enthusiasm was not yet lost to the Church, for after Wesley's death there was a balance of opinion among the Methodist preachers in favour of drawing back into the established fold.[1] If the Church had been wisely governed at that moment, reunion would have come about. But the Church was cold and narrow-minded, and the Methodists were left to consolidate their power in a special church devoted to Wesley's tradition. Some of its leading preachers were in favour of creating a kind of episcopacy, but this proposal was defeated. The arrangements adopted gave a very definite character to the Methodist Church; in the first place, the separate churches and districts were all kept under strict authority by the central body; in the second place, power and discipline were concentrated in the hands of the ministers who formed the annual Conference.[2]

This concentration of authority provoked periodical discontent and occasional secessions. The Methodist New Connexion Church was founded in 1797 by Methodists who desired to give the lay congregations an active part in the conduct of worship and the choice of ministers; the Primitive Methodist Church was founded in 1812 by Methodists who desired to organise great camp meetings in imitation of the methods employed in America. The Methodist Conference took the same kind of alarm over this development as the Established Church had taken when the early Methodists set the example of open-air preaching, and its hostility to camp preaching led to this secession. In 1834 Joseph Rayner Stephens, at that time a Methodist minister, was suspended for his conduct in accepting the position of Secretary of a Society for promoting the separation of Church and State. His suspension brought discontent in Lancashire to a head, and a rebel minister, Warren, carried large numbers out of the Society. There was a still more serious struggle over the constitution of the Conference in the late forties, which ended in the loss of about 100,000 members.

In spite of these difficulties the Wesleyan Methodist Church grew steadily. In the middle of the century the Methodist New Connexion had some 15,000 members, the Primitive Methodists

---

[1] *History of Methodism*, by Townsend, Workman and Eayrs, vol. i. p. 369 and p. 384.
[2] Wesley had opposed the people having a share in the choice either of stewards or leaders. " We are not republicans and never intend to be."—*Works*, vol. xii. p. 455.

about 100,000, and the Wesleyan Methodists about 350,000. The religious census of 1851 gives the number of sittings in chapels: Methodists of all Churches over two million, Independents a little over one million, Baptists three-quarters of a million.[1]

When a Revivalist movement settles into an established institution there is inevitably a change in its spirit and atmosphere. In some parts of England and Wales Methodism was still a Revivalist movement. Thus the Commission on the Employment of Children in 1843 gave a glowing account of the work done by the Methodists in districts like the Forest of Dean and North Wales, closely resembling the descriptions of Wesley's work in Cornwall. The colliers had been the terror of the surrounding country " for gross ignorance, rudeness, and irreligion, almost without parallel in any Christian community." Churches there were none except on the extreme outskirts; the great area of the Forest being extra-parochial, though very populous, and schools were almost unknown. In this district a striking change had been produced by the work of the Dissenters. " The success of their zeal is everywhere exhibited in the immense number of chapels which have been built within the last thirty years. The money to build them has been drawn from the pockets of the farmers, small tradesmen, and the working orders, by means of penny subscriptions in the chapels, to which even the boys who are earning wages contribute." So in North Wales: " What the established Church has not yet been able to supply, the Dissenters have; chapels have everywhere been built by them, and their efforts, always unsupported and often scoffed at by the clergy, gentry, and influential proprietors, have been attended with signal success." [2]

In many industrial districts, on the other hand, Methodism

[1] Wesleyan Methodists, total sittings 2,194,298, free 1,066,312; Independents, total sittings 1,067,760, free 438,212; Baptists, total sittings 752,393, free 377,571. The numbers given as attending Methodist services on Census Sunday were 856,697 in the morning, 740,712 in the afternoon, and 1,351,990 in the evening. The figures for the Independents were 524,613, 232,285, and 457,162, and for the Baptists, 360,806, 224,268, and 336,116.

[2] The paper on the statistics of a district in Monmouthshire, published in the *Journal of the Royal Statistical Society* for 1840, quoted on p. 152, contains this passage: " In the year 1831, 37 public-houses supplied the wants of the whole parish, but at present there are 38 public-houses and 132 beershops, making a total of 170 places for the sale of intoxicating drinks; besides a number of houses where it is sold without licence under the characteristic name of Bid-Alls. About a month ago a good many men at the Varteg Forge turned over a new leaf and became temperate, when an immediate

was rather one of the settled religions than a new and passionate gospel. Its progress consequently was much slower. In the days of the Chartists there were more Methodist members in South Cornwall than in Manchester, Salford, and Stockport, though those towns contained a larger population than the whole of Cornwall. In Lancashire the Methodist Churches did not increase as fast as the population.[1] In Leeds the increase was much more rapid, but Dawson, the famous minister, was disappointed with the results there as well.[2] Faucher said that you did not see the working classes in the chapels of Manchester and Leeds. The people walking to service along the streets " in silence and with a reserved and formal attitude " belonged exclusively to the middle classes; the operatives loitered at their doors or lounged in street corners until the hour of service was over and the public-house opened its doors.[3]

change took place. These men were not previously much in the habit of going to a place of worship, and the nearest chapel was three-quarters of a mile off. In one week applications were made for ground to erect three places of worship and one school-room, by those very persons who, as drunkards, had rested satisfied without any for 20 years previously ; 25 of these men immediately joined a reading society belonging to the works."

[1] Between 1830 and 1850 the population of Lancashire increased by fifty per cent. The places embraced in the Manchester District in the Reports of the Methodist Conference increased faster than the average, for they included such rapidly growing towns as Manchester, Stockport, Bolton, Rochdale, Oldham, and Blackburn. The Methodist members for those circuits increased by about twenty per cent. In Manchester the figure rose from 6070 to 6767; in Stockport from 1355 to 1653; in Rochdale and Blackburn the figures show a decline. Musgrave (*Origin of Methodism in Bolton*) gives the number of members in 1800 as 1234, and in 1850 as 2196; the population of Bolton had increased in the half-century from 18,000 to 60,000.

The writer of a series of sketches in the *North of England Magazine* confirms this impression of Manchester. " Visit the churches and chapels of this great town ; look around the various congregations, richly and gaily dressed, comfortably seated in easy-cushioned pews, and say how many of the real horny-handed workmen will be found among the group, although the proportion of that class to the rest of our population is so great."—" Characteristics of Manchester," *North of England Magazine*, 1842, vol. i. p. 169.

[2] " William Dawson remarked towards the close of his life, ' an inquiry having been made respecting the work of God at Leeds. . . . Our numbers do not increase in the way we had a right to expect after the erection of our new chapels. Some persons attribute this to one reason, some to another. My opinion is that we have the Reform Bill chiefly to blame for it. It introduced several of our friends into office ; they then began to dabble in politics, attention was soon divided ; municipal business put in its claim for the time and care they formerly gave to the Church.' "— Everett, *Memoirs of William Dawson*, 1842, p. 433.

[3] The chapters of Faucher's work that described Manchester were published separately, annotated by a member of the Manchester *Athenæum*, who often corrected Faucher's impressions out of his more intimate knowledge. He left this statement as it stood.

The editor of the *British Critic* said that this was true of all the large towns. Reviewing the Annual Report of the General Society for Promoting District Visiting, and other publications of the kind, he made a very positive statement on this subject. " The accounts which the various little periodicals before us give of the religious wretchedness of our large towns would be incredible to us if we had not taken great pains to ascertain the real state of the case by personal observation and inquiry. It may be truly said that the whole of our manufacturing population, the whole of the poorer classes, are alienated from the Church. Yet this does not by any means express the sum of their misery. An enormous population ; three-fourths or nine-tenths are neither church people nor of any other religion."[1] This seems to have been the general impression of the time. *The Universe*, established in 1846, as an independent unsectarian journal, referred to this topic in its first issue, observing that the working classes had been to an awful extent estranged from the means of grace and the hope of glory. " Very few of them attend places of worship." [2]

It is clear that Methodism, in losing its first missionary character, had fallen to some extent under the same shadow as the Church, the shadow of respectability. In early days the weavers used to attend chapel with their aprons rolled round their waists [3] and some of them had thought that to drop their aprons would mean that they had conformed to the world. By this time these democratic habits had disappeared. In 1842 the Annual Report of the Wesleyan Methodist Conference regretted that in times of distress the poor neglected chapel " because a want of suitable clothing leaves a meanness in their appearance which is chiefly conspicuous by its being contrasted with that of the more favoured of their brethren. To attend God's house under any circumstances with at least cleanly persons is a paramount duty ; to attend with comfortable and neat clothing is a sacred propriety ; but if it should please God that through straitened circumstances our garments are coarser than those of our brethren, and that they are worn

---

[1] Vol. 28, p. 345 (1840).
[2] It is probable that this was less true of the large industrial villages where class separation was less acute. The state of the large towns naturally attracted more attention.
[3] Benjamin Smith, *Methodism in Macclesfield*, p. 212.

by age, we are not thereby absolved from the general duty."
A witness before the Health of Towns Commission drew the
line between those who could dress for chapel and those who
could not. "The general practice is, on the Sunday evening
for those who are not able to make a decent appearance at a
place of worship to congregate together, pay their halfpenny
or penny, and send for a newspaper from a public-house."[1]

The distinction between the respectable and the common
people was emphasised in chapel as in church, by the distinction
between pews and free seats. This distinction had brought
with it all the dangers that Wesley dreaded, for Wesley had
stood out against the system of pew rents. In Wesley's
London headquarters, the Foundry, "all benches were alike.
No difference was made here between the rich and the poor;
no one was allowed to call any seat his own, first comers sat
down first."[2] In December 1787 Wesley had a difference
with his Committee on this point, and his language shows
what a serious view he took of the threatened change. "The
Committee proposed to me ... that everyone who took a
pew should have it as his own. Thus overturning, at one blow,
the discipline which I had been establishing for fifty years."
Three days later he reports the satisfactory result of the discussion.
"We had another meeting of the Committee, who after a calm
and loving consultation, judged it best that none should claim
any pew of his own, either in the new chapel or in West Street."[3]
But Wesley's principle did not long survive his death. In
1798 the West Street Chapel moved to Great Queen Street, and
pew rents were introduced.[4] In Macclesfield the pew rents of
Cumberland Street Chapel, where five aldermen were seat-
holders, amounted in 1803 to £305.[5] One of the leading
Methodist ministers was distressed as he saw this principle
gaining ground in the arrangements and life of Methodism.
When he went to open Brunswick Street Chapel in Leeds, his
biographer tells us, Dawson was vexed to find a notice on the
circular announcing the services to be held. "The trustees,
wishing to accommodate the respectable friends who may

[1] 1844 Health of Towns Commission, First Report, p. 51.
[2] John Telford, *Two West End Chapels*, p. 7.
[3] *Journal*, Curnock's Standard Edition, vol. 10, pp. 349, 350.
[4] John Telford, *op. cit.* p. 78.
[5] Benjamin Smith, *Methodism in Macclesfield*, p. 212.

attend on this occasion, propose to reserve the entire gallery of the Brunswick St. Chapel for their use.   To facilitate this silver will be taken at the foot of the stairs."[1]   Yet Dawson's biographer tells us that Brunswick Street Chapel with its 3000 sittings became still more respectable later.   " In the generous spirit of the text of mercy, ' The poor have the gospel preached to them,' one thousand free sittings were appropriated for such as were unable to pay for them.   Since then, however, it is to be regretted the number of free seats has been considerably reduced."[2]

Molesworth, the Vicar of Rochdale, who was Bright's antagonist in a famous conflict over Church rates, spoke in one of his pamphlets of " the desire of the builder, the proprietor, and the popular preacher to get good interest for his capital " as an evil common alike to the Church and to Nonconformity. He might have illustrated his argument by the incident in the church at Birkenhead quoted in the previous chapter, or by an incident in the life of the founder of Owens College at Manchester.   " John Owens, the founder of Owens College, formerly attended Mosley Street Chapel and had a large square pew.   When Dr. McColl became so popular and attracted such crowds, the half-empty square pew was regarded with covetous eyes by the deacons, who greedily snapped up every spare inch of sitting room.   Mr. Owens was asked to be so good as to allow part of his pew to be let to others, but he was so offended as to leave the place, and after for a time joining the Unitarians, found his way to St. John's Church."[3]   The system of pew rents was partly due in the case of the Nonconformists to the heavy debts on the chapels.   " Trustees have had to ' farm ' their seats to raise the interest money ; and in fact to avoid utter ruin."[4]

By the middle of the century this tendency was causing deep concern in the best Methodist minds.   A well-known Methodist

---

[1] Everett, *Memoirs of William Dawson*, p. 332.   [2] Everett, *op. cit.* p. 331.
[3] J. T. Slugg, *Manchester Fifty Years Ago*, 1881, p. 141.
[4] Jobson, *Chapel and School Architecture*.   It is probable that chapel building had been too rapid in the twenties.   A study of Axon's *Annals of Manchester* shows that no less than seventeen Methodist chapels were built between 1810 and 1830.   Ten churches and eight Baptist or Independent chapels were built during those years.   In the next twenty years only three Methodist chapels were built.   The Church suffered after 1830 because it had too few churches.   Nonconformists suffered because they had too many chapels.

minister, F. J. Jobson, wrote a series of articles in the *Watchman* in 1849 on " Chapel and School Architecture." These articles were revised and published as a book at the special request of the Methodist Conference. Jobson said that the Church of England was throwing off its pew doors, and was very anxious to make it understood that the establishment was preeminently the poor man's Church, but that Methodism, if carried out in the spirit of its native genius, was far better adapted to befriend the poor, for it had less of class distinction in it. " If, then, it be consistent with itself, in its chapel accommodation, it will make it evident that it provides largely for the poor. It must be confessed that, of late years, this has not been so evident as it might have been. Following the forms and fashions of other communities, it has, in some instances, but scantily supplied the poor with sittings. It has, in others, by drawing-room seats and scarlet curtains separated the congregation too much into distinct sections. Our chapels have been fitted up too much as private dwellings than as places of public worship; and the free sittings, if sufficient, not made readily perceivable nor easily accessible. I could name chapels with expensive architectural frontispieces of stone and with interior ornaments of ' dead white and gold ' where the poor's seats are like sheep pens, in the four corners of the building and behind the pulpit; and where, even then, the seats adjoining are screened off most carefully by high rods and curtains. I am no believer in the doctrine of ' equality ' as it is now expounded by many—I regard it as foolish and contrary to the order of God. . . . But admitting all this, it is not only unbecoming but detrimental to Methodism (and it would be so to any church) thus to appear to neglect the poor."

Other disadvantages followed from this system. It was alleged by some writers that chapels in the poorer parts of the towns decreased as the well-to-do class moved into the new suburbs, and towns divided themselves into respectable and working-class communities.[1] A Wesleyan minister of standing,

---

[1] Compare *Condition of Liverpool, Religious and Social*, by A. Hume, 1860, and *Church of England Home Missionary to the Poor*, 1862, by A. Hume. Hume was a well-known writer on social questions and a Liverpool clergyman. His statements were challenged by H. S. Skeats, the Nonconformist historian. In 1837, a parson, answering some critic who had attacked the sale of livings, retorted that, bad as this was, it was no worse to sell advowsons than to sell chapels. He gave examples of

giving evidence before a Committee of the House of Lords upon Church Rates in 1859, spoke of the practice as if it were not uncommon. " When the middle classes and well-to-do people who have been in the habit of attending the chapel go away into the country or to some suburban residences, it follows, almost as a matter of course, that the seat rents fail, and another chapel is erected in a suburban district, and the congregation is transferred and the chapel ceases to be occupied as it was formerly." [1] The witness said elsewhere that the Methodists had systematised the contributions of the poor, and that they were therefore less dependent on the middle classes than other denominations. But it seems to have been the general view of those who had studied the problem that, as it was put by Horace Mann, the great increase of accommodation in church and chapel in the last twenty years had been for the benefit of the middle classes,[2] and that the poorer classes were worse off in this respect as in others when towns separated into respectable and proletarian quarters.[3]

There was another cause tending to alienate the poor. The Methodist and the Radical movements came into conflict. The attitude to civil government that was proper for Methodists was defined in the " Minutes of Several Conversations with the Rev. J. Wesley and the Preachers in connexion with him," published in 1779. " None of us shall either in writing or conversation speak lightly or irreverently of the Government under which we live. The oracles of God command us to be subject to the higher powers, and that ' Honour the King ' is thus connected with the ' Fear of God.' " Preachers who were melting great audiences of rough miners to tears with descriptions of the tenderness or the solemnities of a religion of which they heard for the first

this practice from advertisements appearing in the *Christian Advocate*, such as this: " The chapel is situate in a populous vicinity, containing 46 pews with accommodation for 207 sittings, which number may be doubled by the creation of galleries ; offering very lucrative advantages in the hands of a well-conducted proprietorship. May be viewed." The writer quoted other advertisements ; one, *e.g.*, of a chapel at Stockport, in which it is pointed out that the chapel could be converted to other uses.—*The Voluntary System*, by S. R. Maitland, 1837, pp. 13 and 14. A chapel in the worst part of Birmingham was bought by the Socialists.—Evidence of Rev. M. A. Collinson, Appendix to First Report Midland Mining Commission, p. 7.

[1] Evidence of the Rev. George Osborne, Questions 1773 and 1779.

[2] *Religious Worship in England and Wales*, abridged from the Official Report made by Horace Mann to George Graham, Registrar-General.

[3] The Irish population were in a different position in this respect. Readers of the newspapers must be struck by the frequency with which they report the deaths of Catholic priests in the typhus epidemics, *e.g. Leeds Mercury*, July 11, 1847.

time, found no difficulty in observing this command. One thing, and one thing only, was in the mind of preacher and congregation. But when the Methodist Church became a great organisation in the midst of a population like that of Manchester or Leeds, in a world where the justice or injustice of institutions was fiercely debated, the situation was more complicated. The Methodist rule against speaking lightly or irreverently of the Government came to be interpreted as implying not merely a negative but a positive duty. On the accession of George the Fourth, the Conference presented an address of congratulation, speaking of " our undeviating attachment to your illustrious House, your sacred Person, and to the unrivalled constitution of our country," an address which provoked a remonstrance from " a well wisher to Methodism," who said the poor had become from necessity politicians, and that Mr. Bunting, the author of this address, " was quitting the cottage for the palace."[1] The Annual Reports of the Conference took as Conservative a view of popular agitation as any clerical justices. The only references to Trade Unions are severe,[2] and the Chartist movement is condemned in the strongest language.[3] The Wesleyan preachers in the Bath district resolved in 1839 that any Methodist who joined himself to the Chartists should be excluded from their body.[4] The Conference of the

[1] See also, for mutual hostility of Methodists and Reformers in 1818-20, *Recollections of My Own Life and Times*, by Thomas Jackson (a leading Wesleyan minister), pp. 172-184.

[2] In 1833 : " In these times of conflict among certain classes of the community, keep at the utmost distance from all associations which are subversive of the principles of true and proper liberty, employing unlawful oaths, and threats and force to acquire new members, and to accomplish purposes which would tend to destroy the very framework of society."

[3] In 1842 : " In the present season of commercial embarrassment and national distress, when infidels and irreligious men are charging all the sufferings of the community upon the selfish policy of rulers, and upon existing institutions said to be ill-constructed. . . ."

In 1849 : " During the agitations of the year, and while disloyal and disaffected men have been endeavouring to allure the humbler classes of our fellow-countrymen in their schemes, and have sought to excite them against their rulers, it has given us unspeakable pleasure to behold your spirit and conduct. . . ."

[4] *Bath Post* quoted by *The Chartist*, May 25, 1839. The impression made on the Chartists by the Methodists was scarcely less favourable than that made by the Church. " Without seeking to give offence to any religious sect," wrote Gammage, " it may safely be asserted that if there is a body of men in England who are in the service and uphold the principles of despotism, that body is the Wesleyan conference. Because Stephens had been guilty of the unpardonable crime of denouncing the laws of the factory for their cruel oppression of the poor, he was soon marked out for persecution, the ground for that persecution being that contrary to his duties as a minister of the gospel, he interfered and mixed himself up with political questions. . . . Had he

Methodist New Connexion condemned the strikes of 1843, speaking of " the political demagogues " by whom the masses were misguided and inflamed, and rejoicing that no members of the Connexion were found among the leaders of or participators in the disturbances of the time.

To understand the conservative character of Methodism, we must remember that it was exposed at this time to a very active attack from the followers of Owen. The Halls of Science resounded with doctrine not less hostile to Methodism than to the industrial order. An energetic campaign was carried on by lectures (Owen himself travelled about from town to town) and by pamphlets. This was essentially an age of controversy, and of angry controversy. Atheists and Christians were in conflict : Protestants and Catholics : Puseyites and Evangelicals : Churchmen and Dissenters : Owenites and all respectable religions. In this atmosphere of controversy it was inevitable that the Owenite campaign [1] should make Methodism politically still more conservative. No Methodist wished to be confused in the public mind with doctrines so aggressive and so hateful : to denounce equality was one way of defending religion.

There were, of course, several ways in which the Methodist and Nonconformist life of the time reflected a more democratic spirit than the Established Church. Ministers were often poor men,[2] and the workman could find a place in the chapel as a local preacher or a class leader. When Dr. Arnold wanted to make the Church a national institution, he proposed two reforms : the first, that the churches should be used for the religious services of all denominations, the second that the

never interfered but on the side of the wealthy, he would never have given offence to that solemn hypocritical conclave." In 1841 the minister at the Horton Lane Chapel, Bradford, published a sermon together with a letter he had addressed to the Bradford candidates at the General Election, in which he said : " We have among us Chartists and Socialists, the one the radical subverters of our constitution, the other the infidel blasphemers of our religion."—*The Dangers and Duties of the Christian Elector*, by the Minister of Horton Lane Chapel, 1841.

[1] There was an immense literature in support of Owenite teaching. This kind of pamphlet was common : " Lycurgus and the Spartans historically considered ; being a rapid sketch of the Life of Lycurgus and of the Laws and Institutions he established at Sparta, illustrating the power of circumstances in forming the human character," by J. N. Bailey.

[2] This was specially true of the Primitive Methodists. The General Minutes of Conference fixed the salary of a minister at 14s. a week for a married man, with a small house, rates and taxes, and 2s. a week for each child. In 1850 the figure was raised to 17s. See also Warner, *op. cit.* p. 248.

Church should imitate the Methodist plan for making use of laymen. The workman who went to chapel might listen to a fellow workman in the pulpit; he would find fellow workmen helping in the affairs of the chapel. But the chapel was none the less a place where "comfortable and neat clothing was a sacred propriety"; where, in other words, the black coat was a badge, where the difference between the workman who had risen to be a bourgeois and the workman who had fallen to be a pauper was as sharp as anywhere else.[1] M. Halévy in his brilliant study has summed up the social significance of the Nonconformity of the time: "Puritan Nonconformity thus tended to become a transitional creed, a stage in the history of an English family. The unskilled labourer becomes in turn a skilled workman, an artisan, the head of a small business, a business man possessed of a modest capital, and as he rises out of the barbarism in which the working class was plunged, he becomes a Nonconformist. If he himself rises still higher on the social ladder, or if his children rise after his death, he or they go over to the Church of England."[2] Thus what happened to Nonconformist religion as it became a settled system, was that it took rather than gave a standard. The spirit of the age put its own bias and character on this missionary religion. Religion did not give its colour to the world: the world gave its colour to religion. Success and failure in the struggle of life looked very much the same inside the chapel as they looked outside it. There, as elsewhere, the institutions of the time seemed to be designed for the man moving up the ladder. This view finds illuminating expression in a question and answer given in the evidence before the Lords Committee on Church Rates. Something had been said about pew rents, as keeping the poor from chapel. Mr. Terrell was under examination. "Has it ever come under your observation," he was asked, "that when a man becomes a religious and moral man he has a competence to pay pew rent?"—"Religion," so he replied, "always tends to give a man the power to pay for his religion, and the will."[3]

[1] Hine, *History of Hitchin*, vol. ii. p. 127, describes the agitation caused among the Congregationalists of that town in 1812 when their minister married a domestic servant.
[2] *England in 1815*, p. 371.
[3] Mr. Hornblower went a little further in *The Skin Game*: "God helps those who help themselves—that is at the bottom of all religion."
Mr. Terrell said, in the course of his evidence: "If I were to tell you the truth,

It is easy to see how this spirit arose. All religious revivals
have laid great emphasis on the duty of work and the wickedness
of idleness. "Laziness," said St. Benedict, "is the enemy of
the soul." Wesley said that an idle man was driven out of the
Methodist societies like a thief or a murderer. Industry was
thus a cardinal virtue. Naturally, then, Methodists made
industrious and successful workmen, tradesmen, managers, and
employers.[1] It was natural for men in this atmosphere to think
that if a man was poor it was the consequence of his own
wickedness. This was a favourite doctrine in the days of
Defoe, and Wesley himself had denounced it. But as Methodism became less and less of a revival, and more and more a
settled religion, the temptation to associate wealth with industry
and poverty with sloth was strong. Methodists who took that
view had accepted the harsh standards that were provoking discontent and giving to religion the complexion and the tone of
business life. Poverty thus looked very much like crime and
wealth very much like virtue. Wesley himself taught that
a man should make what he could by honest means, and spend
the surplus, when his bare needs had been satisfied, on charity
and good works. But he realised that men might yield to the
temptation to make a different use of their acquisitions. "I do
not see how it is possible in the nature of things, for any revival
of religion to continue long. For religion must necessarily
produce both Industry and Frugality. And these cannot but
produce Riches. But as Riches increase, so will Pride, Anger,
and Love of the World in all its branches." [2]

The effect of the conservative and respectable character that
religious organisations had assumed was seen in the growth of
what the Duke of Wellington would have called "fancy
religions." As the orderly ceremonies of church and chapel
left unsatisfied the primitive emotional temperament, which had
been excited to such wild ecstasies by the early Methodist

dissent is rather the religion of the middling classes; the Church takes the high and the
low; the rich and the poor; we take the medium; so that we have not an excess of
poor people among dissenters."

[1] See Warner, *op. cit.* p. 167.

[2] *Arminian Magazine*, 1787, pp. 155-6. The *West Riding Herald* quoted a story
of Wesley, that when he was called on to make a return of his plate in 1766, he replied
that he had two teaspoons at London and two at Bristol. "This is all the plate I
have at present, and I shall not buy any more while so many around me want bread."
The paper made the comment: "Wesley would not know his own religion were he
again on earth."—*West Riding Herald*, December 22, 1837.

preaching, religious agitation took new forms. Thus Joanna Southcott, a fanatic who told the world in 1802 that she was to be the mother of a prophet, found some following in Lancashire, and churches were established in her name. There were independent sects like the Bible Christians and the Sandemanian Baptists. Swedenborg had a number of congregations. More important than the rest of these movements was the response to the teaching of Mormonism, which at one time caused a not inconsiderable emigration to the United States. Mormon leaders came over in 1840 and conducted a vigorous recruiting campaign. They ran a paper at Liverpool, set up branches of the Church in most large towns, and established a shipping agency for emigration. When the religious census was taken in 1851 the Mormons had two hundred and twenty-two places of worship with some thirty thousand sittings, and the commentator on the census figures said of Mormonism that it had " an importance and position with the working classes, which perhaps should draw to it much more than it has yet received of the attention of our public teachers." [1]

A different need was met by the Chartist churches which sprang up in the forties. The earliest of these churches was established in Scotland, but they soon spread to England. This movement was inspired partly by the desire to draw people away from the influence of the religions that taught resignation to the established order. " Were the Chartists to do this," said the Chartist circular, " ecclesiastical tyranny would soon die a natural death, and clerical domination be banished from our land. One great obstacle to the onward progress of the present movement would thus be put out of the way." [2] Some, again, were interested in the project because they wanted to combat the impression, of which great use was made by opponents, that Chartists were infidels. The Chartist leaders included men like Hetherington, Watson, Carlile, Cooper and Holyoake, who were propagandists against Christianity, but Wade and Spencer were Anglican clergymen; Stephens, expelled by the Methodists, remained a Methodist, preaching in chapels of his own, provided by his workmen followers; Lovett was for a short time a Methodist Bible Christian, and he always called himself a

---

[1] *Religious Worship in England and Wales*, p. 52.
[2] See *Chartism and the Churches*, by H. U. Faulkner, p. 42.

Christian ; [1] Solly was a Unitarian minister ; Vincent attended Quaker meetings, and other leaders were Baptists, Congregationalists, and Catholics. A Bible Christian minister, named Schofield, was one of the Chartists who were tried at the Lancaster Assizes.[2] This fact, however, did not deter some critics of the movement from treating Chartist as another name for blasphemer or atheist.

There were thus good reasons for starting the Chartist churches, but it would be a mistake to suppose that their significance began and ended in tactics. They met a fundamental need which was neglected in the conventional teaching of church and chapel. The Chartist churches were taught and served by men who believed, as one of the best known of their preachers put it, that " Christianity should prevail in everyday life, that commerce should be conducted on Christian principles, and not on those of Mammon, and that every other institution ought to be based on the doctrines of Christianity." [3] The Report of the Midland Mining Commission described the great success of this preacher, O'Neill, in Birmingham and the Midlands.[4] It was stated that there was a deep religious feeling in the district (prayer meetings and hymn-singing were common in the pits), and the Chartists had stepped in where the churches had failed. The services were held in halls, schools, or private houses. Sermons were preached ; children were baptized, and the Lord's Supper administered. The congregations were largely composed of Methodists and Baptists, who found in these services the kind of Christian teaching they wanted and missed in their own chapels.

---

[1] When asked by the chaplain, on his admission to prison, what was his religion, he answered that he was of that religion which Christ taught, and which very few in authority practise, if he might judge from their conduct.—*Life and Struggles of William Lovett*, with an Introduction by R. H. Tawney, vol. i. p. 233.

[2] See Faulkner, *op. cit.* pp. 18 and 90.   [3] Midland Mining Commission, pp. 608, etc.

[4] Solly has given an attractive picture of O'Neill in his Chartist novel, *James Woodford.* " It seems he was an out and out Chartist, but he was also a firm believer in Christ and Christianity, and so he thought the two things might be united, and finding some Baptist or Methodist workmen of the same mind with himself, they formed this Christian Chartist Society. When it was first launched, respectable folks looked at them much as you would look at a mad dog. But they worked quietly on, ' instant in season and out of season,' always abounding in good works, and careful to give no offence. If a neighbour or neighbour's child were ill, a ' Christian Chartist ' was sure to be ready to run for the doctor or sit up to nurse all the night long. If help were wanted for a burial, half a dozen Christian Chartists would volunteer to carry the coffin. If a fight had to be stopped, a quarrel prevented, there were Christian Chartists ready to do it."—Vol. ii. p. 89.

Religion has been defined by Professor Whitehead as " what a man does with his solitariness," and in this sense it may be as self-regarding as any other activity. It may take a man no further than his own shadow. For it may take him from his material cares and ambitions to plunge him in meditations in which his own life in a different aspect is still the centre. " Methodism with its eye forever turned on its own navel; asking itself with torturing anxiety of Hope and Fear, ' Am I right? am I wrong? Shall I be saved? shall I not be damned?' —what is this," asked Carlyle, " at bottom, but a new phasis of *Egoism*, stretched out into the Infinite? not always the heavenlier for its infinitude !"[1] Carlyle's description was true of one kind of Methodist. But of course a man may do with his solitariness something nobler than this. The chapels, if they found a home for men and women tormented by such anxieties, found a home also for men and women in whose passionate desire for communion with God " the unseen took shape to common eye." The mystic sought a happiness that had no relation to the popular ideas of heaven and hell. There were thousands of men and women in Manchester and Leeds who found self-respect and contentment in the duties and the dreams of their religion. In this way religion made numbers of men and women happier, more unselfish, more ready to pity the sorrows of their fellow men, more ready to undertake burdens for their relief.[2] The Methodist movement did for eighteenth-century England what Christianity did for the ancient world, giving to men of conscience and compassion a cause for which to live, and blending the idea of the brotherhood of man with the most sublime of the mysteries of religion.

There is, however, a sense in which religion is not what a man does with his solitariness, but what a man does with his gregariousness. Religion gave its colour to the collective imagination of the primitive village watching anxiously the seasons of sowing and harvest. Sometimes in the history of the world it has almost filled the content of that imagination. " In the Middle Ages," says Professor Powicke, " the hold of the Church was due to the fact that it could satisfy the best

---

[1] *Past and Present*, p. 161.
[2] See, for example, the influence of the Quakers in Hitchin, and that of the Unitarians in Liverpool, and of Churchmen like Wood and Rand in Bradford.

cravings of the whole man, his love of beauty, his desire for goodness, his endeavour after truth." [1] Nobody could expect that religion should fill precisely this place in the more developed and complicated society of nineteenth-century England. Professor Unwin put it that the separation of the spheres of politics, religion, science, and industry, was the result of long ages of progress. But you could not say of Churchmen or Methodists or Baptists that they were merely so many men and women worshipping in their own way without any common life or any common influence. " Christianity is first of all a way of life in fellowship." [2] Fellowship takes a man out of his solitariness. These religious bodies were not only bodies of men holding certain beliefs and practising religious observances ; they were bodies of people with a discipline affecting social conduct. The Quakers carried discipline so far as to disown their members for marrying non-Quakers ; a rule enforced until the middle of the century.   These bodies, then, with their rules and taboos about manners and habits, were necessarily a most important influence on the social imagination of the time. What was the nature of that influence ?

A moral revolt is always apt to answer extravagance by extravagance. The Methodist revolt was no exception. It was a revolt against dissolute manners, and it demanded ascetic manners. Wesley was proud, as we have seen, that the Methodists abstained from " reading plays, romances, or books of humour, from singing innocent songs, or talking in a gay diverting manner." He said that to educate a child you must break his will, and when he drew up the rules for his school at Kingswood he said that he allowed no time for play, because he who plays as a boy will play when he is a man.   If a man puts play outside his life, he surrenders tastes and pleasures that are an essential part of human history : the source of much of the beauty, the grace, the power, and the virtue, that distinguish higher from lower forms of character and intelligence.   A man or a society may make that sacrifice for a particular object. And a man who has renounced something, taking stern vows upon himself, at the bidding of conscience, is richer as well as poorer.   An ascetic life touches the imagination of the man who chooses it, for deliberate sacrifice is an act of resolution,

[1] *Legacy of the Middle Ages*, p. 39.   [2] *Christ and Society*, Charles Gore, p. 165.

bringing the satisfaction that comes from living your life at a bracing pitch. But to serve this purpose an ascetic life must be the choice of the man who leads it. When an ascetic life is thrust on others, it deprives them of opportunities for satisfying their imagination in which mankind has found light and inspiration, and puts nothing in their place.

This is what happened at this time to the English people. The sacrifices that a society, its mind fixed on some sublime idea of its duty, might make of its own will, were forced by the rich on the poor. Windham and Sheridan described in their speeches, and Bulwer Lytton and Peacock in their books, the joyless life of the English village, when magistrates and country gentlemen decided that Puritanism was an excellent medicine for the labourers.[1] The new towns lived under this shadow. For the government of the towns was largely in the hands of men who had been brought up under the influence of the Puritan revival : a revival in which, as we have seen, religion and business had drawn together. The movement against cruel sports which ought, as Sheridan wished, to have been combined with a movement for encouraging innocent sports, became a movement against popular amusements of all kinds. It almost looked as if Whitefield's famous dictum that no recreation, considered as such, was innocent, was to govern the life of the new town. There were exceptional people, like Lord Dartmouth, who set aside a field for athletic sports, in order to wean the people of West Bromwich from bull-fighting,[2] but he was almost as exceptional among town landlords as was Boulton, who supported a petition for a playhouse at Birmingham, among the great iron masters.[3]

The influence of this spirit, spread over the life of the time, was manifest in the decline of the theatre. The last half of the eighteenth century has been described by Lecky as the golden age of the English drama : " It saw Garrick, Macklin, and

---

[1] Bulwer Lytton remarked that " the very essence of our laws has been against the social aims of the humble which have been called idleness, and against the amusements of the poor which have been stigmatised as disorder," and that this discrimination illustrated his contention that poverty, elsewhere a misfortune, was treated in England as a crime.

Readers of *Crotchet Castle*, published 1831, will remember Peacock's description of Sir Simon Steeltrap.

[2] 1845 Health of Towns Commission, Second Report, Appendix, p. 7, and 1838 Committee on Education, p. 96.

[3] Ashton, *Iron and Steel in the Industrial Revolution*, p. 225.

Barry in their prime; it witnessed the splendid rise of John Kemble and Mrs. Siddons, as well as the lighter graces of Miss Farren, Mrs. Jordan, and Mrs. Abington, and at a time when the great Shakespearean revival was at its height, it also produced the plays of Goldsmith, Sheridan, Foote, and Home. There was an incontestable improvement in the moral tendency, and still more in the refinement of the theatre, and it was noticed that a coarseness which excited no reprobation under George I. was no longer tolerated on the stage. The revolt of popular feeling against the legislative discouragement of the theatre had now become very marked."[1] This revolt showed itself in the evasion of the Act of 1737,[2] which had confined the legitimate drama to the Haymarket, Covent Garden, and Drury Lane, and also in the money spent by the large towns to obtain a special Act of Parliament to enable them to set up a theatre. In this way theatres were provided between 1767 and 1775 in Edinburgh, Bath, Bristol, York, Hull, Liverpool, Manchester, and Chester. In 1778 a concession was made, and magistrates were allowed to grant licences for special performances for sixty days. Tate Wilkinson, an actor, took companies to the North of England, where good plays were given, either in Theatres Royal set up by special Act of Parliament, or in theatres licensed on this plan. Mrs. Siddons, Mrs. Jordan, and other good actors visited the provinces every year.

If anybody had been told in 1780 that in the next half-century the English people would grow much richer; that the picture given in his book by Tate Wilkinson, of the country gentlemen round Wakefield who supported his theatre there, would seem modest in comparison with the wealth that would spring up round all the new towns; that every industrial town would have a large, comfortable class with leisure; that this accession of wealth would be accompanied by a burst of literary power; he might well have supposed that the theatre would play a great part in the life of this time, and help to guide and inspire the imagination of the great population whose fortunes have been followed in these pages. What would have seemed more natural than that writers who were masters of another literary

---

[1] Lecky, *History of England in the Eighteenth Century*, vol. vii. p. 201.
[2] In 1737 Sir John Barnard had so amended the Bill introduced by Walpole, creating the censorship, as to make it illegal to license any theatre except within the limits of Westminster or in any place where the King happened to be residing.

form, like Scott and Dickens, would turn to the drama, as Fielding and Goldsmith had turned to it in the eighteenth century, and as Galsworthy and Bennett were to turn to it in the twentieth ; that Dickens, who was to do more to draw English people together than any other influence in the time, would write comedies, as he wrote novels, that rich and poor alike could enjoy ? What would have been the surprise of such a person to be told that the theatre would rapidly decline, that in 1853 there would be one theatre in Manchester and no theatre at all in Salford, and that in 1873 Kingsley would be able to write, " Few highly educated men now think it worth while to go to see any play, and that exactly for the same reasons as the Puritans put forward ; and still fewer highly educated men think it worth while to write plays ; finding that since the grosser excitements of the imagination have become forbidden themes, there is really very little to write about." [1]

There were, of course, more causes than one for this remarkable decline. The law was still adverse in certain ways. Down to 1834 dramatic authors had no protection, and provincial theatres could act a piece that had been given in London, without paying the author anything. It was not until 1843 that magistrates were allowed to license theatres. More general reasons are to be found in the rise of the cheap print and rival attractions.[2] But undoubtedly one cause was the influence of the Methodists.[3] That influence was exerted with some success even in the early days of Methodism. In 1764 John Wesley wrote to the Mayor and Corporation of Bristol protesting against the proposal to build a theatre, not merely because " most of the present stage entertainments sap the foundation of all religion," but also because a theatre would be " peculiarly hurtful to a trading city, giving a wrong turn to youth especially, gay, trifling, and directly opposite to the spirit of industry and close application to business." [4] He added that the Corporation of

---

[1] *Plays and Puritans*, p. 69.
[2] See St. John Ervine, *The Organised Theatre*, pp. 111 ff.
[3] Lecky, *op. cit.*, vol. ii. p. 192, and Raumer, *op. cit.*, vol. ii. p. 218.
[4] Wesley himself enjoyed seeing the Westminster boys give their Terence play, and he spoke highly of the morality he found both in Terence and Homer. On the other hand, he said that he could not admire Greek statues, because they were images of heathen gods, and he wrote about the British Museum : " What account will a man give to the Judge of quick and dead for a life spent in collecting all these ? "—*Journal*, December 1780.

Nottingham had been led by these considerations to forbid the building of a new theatre. Wesley was using here an argument that served for men who were not Methodists. Thus Archbishop Cornwallis—not much of a Methodist in his own habits, for his Sunday parties at Lambeth drew down a rebuke from George the Third—opposed the Manchester Playhouse Bill in 1775 on the ground that theatres encouraged idleness in industrial towns. Tate Wilkinson had to encounter strong opposition in the provinces, and he described the outbursts of a clergyman of the Low Church at Hull, who declared that "everyone who entered a playhouse was, with the players, equally certain of eternal damnation."[1] As Methodism spread among the employing class, this influence spread in the industrial towns. Dickens deplored the effect in discouraging the theatre and encouraging less desirable substitutes. Three months before his death he wrote that "the narrow-minded fanatics who decry the theatre and defame its artists are absolutely the advocates of depraved and barbarous amusements. For wherever a good drama and well-regulated theatre decline, some distorted form of theatrical entertainment will inevitably arise in their place."[2] He pointed out that this moral had been urged in *Hard Times*.

The Methodists did with the English Sunday what they did with the English theatre. For the mass of the working classes there was only one day on which they were free from the discipline of mill and workshop. On that day they were refused recreation for mind or body, music or games, beauty of art or nature. They sought diversions where they could find them. The Yorkshire and Lancashire papers are full of complaints that the youth of the large towns spent Sunday gambling in the streets, or in drunkenness and brutal sports, and that the behaviour of the populace was distressing and inconvenient to respectable people.[3] An engineer who had been abroad described the difference in this respect between English and Continental life. He told the Factory Commission that at Mülhausen, where most of the people were Protestant, the workmen went to church in the morning and spent the rest of

[1] *Wandering Patentee*, vol. i. p. 111.   [2] *Letters*, vol. iii. p. 438 (March 1870).
[3] Such statements are frequent in the *Leeds Mercury*, *Bradford Observer*, and other papers. Cf., too, the Report of the Children's Employment Commission, 1843, on the streets of Sheffield.

the day in the country playing games, whereas in England " a man can do nothing but go to a public house on Sunday, and when there you can do nothing but drink." Chadwick, who cited the engineer's evidence, suggested to the Committee on Drunkenness that public gardens should be provided, with free admission after morning service on Sundays.[1] Unhappily Sabbatarian prejudice was too strong, and the English people were left to gloom and drink.

The fate of the Botanical Gardens at Leeds is a good illustration of the strength of this Puritan feeling. The Gardens did not pay, and when the shareholders decided to give them up, it was proposed that the town council should acquire them. The *Leeds Intelligencer* gave strong support to this proposal, suggesting that they should be thrown open on Sundays, as that was the only day when the working classes could enjoy them.[2] This was too bold a plan for respectable Leeds, whose scruples were well represented in a leading article that was published a few months later in the *Leeds Mercury* on the subject of Sabbath observance. " It would be a wretched exchange to draw the poor of England out of their Churches, Chapels, Sunday-schools and quiet homes into public exhibitions and places of amusement on the Lord's Day." [3] The " quiet homes " in which the poor of Leeds were invited to spend their happy Sundays included a good many houses of the kind described by Mr. Robert Baker in his Sanitary Report, where fourteen people lay ill of typhus, without a single bed in the place.

Leeds was not peculiar in this respect. At Liverpool we read, " on Sundays . . . all the public houses are opened, and all the public walks, cemeteries and zoological and botanical gardens, where the people might amuse themselves innocently, are closed." " Have the public a right of going to those gardens on any day ? "—" Not the public generally ; but the cemeteries are opened to the public every day of the week except Sunday." [4] Manchester was under the same cloud. The *North of England Magazine* published a series of sketches

---

[1] Committee on Drunkenness, 1834, pp. 34 and 35. Some Churchmen, of course, agreed with Chadwick, such as Hook, Kingsley, and Clay, the chaplain of the House of Correction at Preston, who was in favour of Sunday cricket.—Select Committee on Public-Houses, 1852-53.

[2] *Leeds Intelligencer*, May 9, 1846.   [3] *Leeds Mercury*, November 14, 1846.

[4] 1834 Committee on Drunkenness, p. 317. Evidence of John Finch the Owenite.

describing the life of that city in 1842, and the shutting of the Zoological Gardens on Sundays was cited as one of the worst injustices inflicted on the mass of the population. The writer quoted a French observer Bruet, who remarked, " The observance of the Sunday in England is rigorously enforced by church and state. There is only one exception : the dram shops. All shops must be closed, all places of innocent amusement or instruction, such as Botanical Gardens or Museums, must be rigorously shut, but the folding doors of the gin palace may open to any man who pushes his foot against them." [1]

Maurice reminded these strict Sabbatarians who were afraid of the counter-attraction of " a few statues and a few gardens," that the Christian religion had made its way in the Roman Empire against theatre and amphitheatre and ample facilities for gratifying every intellectual and every brutal taste.[2] Dickens, in touch with the habits of the poor, saw how important were the instincts which were outraged by this harsh and false view of life, and how grave an injury this intolerance inflicted on taste and character. Writing in 1855 in a mood of deep depression about the English people, he named as one of the chief causes of the moral disappointments of the age, the infinite mischief done by what he called " bringing up the soul and body of the land to be a good child or to go to the beershop." [3]

What effort did the churches that imposed these ascetic habits make themselves to satisfy the imagination of the working classes ? They were confronted with a great population of uneducated men and women, who had lost that contact with nature which is the inspiration of all religion, living in surroundings where nothing bore witness to the gracious or the solemn beauty of the world. The daily struggle for a livelihood was made harsher and more absorbing, because the prestige of power and wealth was unchallenged, and self-respect and poverty seemed incompatible. The mill to-day ; the workhouse to-morrow. To minds caught and held in this inexorable rhythm, religion could only speak by an impressive symbolism, by beauty of building or music. Did the churches that put a ban on the culture of the ancient world, in the name of religion, substitute the culture of the Middle Ages, when religion had

---

[1] The *North of England Magazine*, vol. i. pp. 169 and 200.
[2] Sermon on the Sabbath Day, 1852.   [3] *Letters of Dickens*, vol. i. p. 405.

drawn into its own service, and used for its own dignity, the arts by which the Greeks had given to their drama its solemn power?

The Methodists made one notable contribution. By a happy fortune the two Wesleys were poets and musicians, and singing became an important feature of Methodist services. Wesley published a book of hymns and tunes, "designed chiefly for the use of the people called Methodist," and in his *Journal* he described from time to time the pleasure with which he had noticed the progress of music. In 1787 he found a Sunday School at Bolton, with 800 children, of whom 100 were taught singing. He was disturbed by a tendency in some places to introduce more formal music, and he drew up rules for the guidance of chapels. Anthems were not to be sung; great care was to be taken in training; and the whole congregation was to be exhorted to sing, "not one in ten only." Coleridge said that the hearty congregational singing of English hymns kept the humbler Methodists together,[1] and Horace Mann, when commenting on the figures of the Religious Census, said that the Methodists had discovered a form of service specially suitable for poor people.

With this exception, music played little part in the religious life of the time. Wesley, fearing quarrels over the introduction of organs, said that no organ was to be placed in a chapel until it was proposed in the Conference. One of the fiercest controversies in the Methodist world arose over a conflict at Brunswick Street Chapel, Leeds, in 1828, on this question. A later writer remarked that at this time poor men and women in the Yorkshire towns used to save up their pennies for an oratorio, and yet religious bodies were very slow to satisfy this desire in public worship.[2] Bishop Blomfield deprecated the introduction of cathedral services, the use of surplices, and processions, and when a clergyman wrote describing the ordinary church services as "blank, dismal, oppressive, and dreary," he replied, "If the minister *reads* with devotion and solemnity (not *intones*); if the congregation join in the responses and psalmody; and if sound doctrine and practical exhortations be earnestly and affectionately delivered by the preacher, such epithets as

---

[1] *Table Talk*, p. 90.
[2] Benjamin Gregory, *Sidelights on the Conflicts of Methodism*, p. 63.

you have used are grievously misapplied."[1] Raumer suggested that the utter want of all musical education for the people was a result of the way in which Sunday was observed.[2]

Religion was thus making little use of the arts. The new chapels were bare and ugly;[3] music made its way slowly and with difficulty; there were few imposing ceremonies in church; no rich and noble pageants in the streets, to bring history into the life of Hunslet or Ancoats. Satisfaction was found for the starved dramatic sense of the age in the rhetoric, so common then in church and chapel, which painted the torments of everlasting fire.[4] This stern and forbidding Sunday, with its sanctions of childish terror, its " codes of fearful fantasy," was the gift of religion to a people needing above all things some space in its life in which it could lose itself in noble wonder, in the enjoyment of beauty of form or sound, in submission to ideas that could stir the spirit of fellowship and communion. " The lower classes," said Raumer, " who often have to toil wearily through every other day, find Sunday as it is constantly described, the weariest of all. Often after serving an austere master, they are made to find in the Father of Love, an austerer still."[5]

[1] *Memoir*, p. 325. [2] *Op. cit.*, vol. ii. p. 18.
[3] For architecture, see R. P. Jones, *Nonconformist Church Architecture*, p. 31.
[4] It is significant that the biographer of the famous Methodist preacher, William Dawson, speaking of his power as a pulpit orator, chose his handling of this topic as the best example of his gifts. Dawson told his terrified hearers that a man's torment in hell would be all the fiercer because his parents had prayed for him.—Everett, *op. cit.* p. 393.
[5] Raumer, *op. cit.* vol. ii. p. 16. Compare Lovett's reflections, *Lovett : Life and Struggles*, vol. i. p. 8.

CHAPTER XIV

THE REVOLT

FOR the first quarter of the nineteenth century working-class life was overshadowed by the Combination Acts. These Acts made combination criminal, and in this way gave a wider range to the laws against conspiracy.[1] Their effect in restraining combination is evident from the large number of Trade Unions which came to life after their repeal.[2] But the habit of resistance to misfortune or injustice is strong in the English character, and even while the Combination Acts made organisation dangerous and difficult, Trade Unions were active and daring. They had leaders of courage and ability, like John Gast the shipwright and John Doherty the cotton spinner, and they could often disguise their character under the name of Friendly Societies.

There was another institution to which the working classes looked for help in their difficulties. The London Co-operative & Economic Society was founded by George Mudie in 1821: the London Co-operative Society was founded as a trading society in 1826, with William Lovett as storekeeper. In 1828 the new movement had an excellent organ in the *Co-operator*, established by Dr. William King. By 1832 great progress had been made. There were nearly five hundred co-operative societies in active life: Doherty's paper, the *United Trades Co-operative Journal*, which had been established in 1830, preached the new gospel to a large and growing public; half-yearly congresses were held, and projects establishing villages

---

[1] This aspect of the Combination Acts on which Dicey dwelt (*Relation between Law and Public Opinion in the Nineteenth Century*) has perhaps scarcely received sufficient attention from Mrs. George, who contended, in the *Economic Journal* (*Economic History*, 1927), that the Combination Acts were unimportant.

[2] The Steam Engine Makers Society, the London Shipwrights Association (1824), the Northumberland and Durham Colliers Union (1825), the Journeymen Steam Engine Makers (1826), the Friendly Society of Carpenters and Joiners (1827), are only a few of the many Trade Unions constituted or reconstituted after the repeal of the Combination Acts.—Cole, *History of the British Working-Class Movement*, vol. i. p. 91.

of co-operation were in the air. These societies were partly propagandist and partly practical. Some of them ran shops, others tried to organise production. The earlier ambitions of this movement ended in disappointment, but these experiments led later to the creation and success of the modern co-operative society, pursuing more limited aims but throwing a far-reaching influence on working-class life.

It is not the purpose of these pages to describe the fortunes of the several working-class organisations of the time. Men and women combined to improve their conditions, to raise wages, to shorten hours, or to resist attempts to reduce wages or to lengthen the working day. The history of these different efforts is important, interesting, and instructive. But there are certain movements which possess a wider significance. Hope and discontent assume at times a more sweeping character, revealing a deeper emotion, a stronger tide of feeling and ambition. We look at this or that strike or agitation, and we see men resenting or resisting a particular injustice : we look at the passions which fired the spirit of the Owenite campaign or the Chartist agitation, and we see a revolt against a view of life, a protest against a general system. The discontent discussed in this volume is the discontent that has this universal sound.

In the winter of 1829 the Grand General Union of All the Operative Spinners of the United Kingdom was founded by John Doherty : in the autumn of 1834 the Grand National Moral Union of the Productive Classes, which had grown out of that experiment, passed into history. In those five years the mind of the working-class world was on the march. There is at once an element of grandeur and an element of pathos in the heroic faith that inspired with such passion and hope a million men and women whose power and dreams were so ludicrously mismatched. But the history of that effort to construct a new social order is remarkable for the support it received and the ideas it reflected.

In July 1830, six months after he had founded his General Spinners Union, Doherty launched the National Association for the Protection of Labour with an organ, the *United Trades Co-operative Journal*. There were soon 150 societies collected under its roof. Beginning in the textile industries, the Association spread to the potteries and the mining districts, besides drawing into its circle any number of small societies of mill-wrights and mechanics. In 1831 it had 100,000 members and a new weekly paper, *The Voice of the People*, of which 30,000 copies were sold every week, although its price was sevenpence. When the difficulties in the way of working-class organisation are considered, these figures look sensational. But they look modest and humdrum in the light of the later successes of this extraordinary awakening. The textile industries had given the first movement its start. The builders now took their place with a Builders' Union which, after winning a number of local victories, established itself as the leading union in the country, with a membership of 40,000 or 50,000. At this juncture Robert Owen, who had returned in 1829 from the United States where he had made an unsuccessful social experiment, came into touch with the Trade Union movement. It was a great opportunity for a man with a gospel, for the movement, alive with hope and ambition, was ready to welcome a prophet with open arms. Owen put his idea of a new moral order based on co-operation before the builders, and they accepted it. From a programme that sought to redress grievances, to put down abuses and to improve conditions of employment, they turned to a great scheme for reorganising the building industry by means of a Grand National Guild under the direct control of the Union.

For the next twelve months the new ideas made rapid head-way. The Grand National Consolidated Trades Union, founded in October 1833, soon had half a million members, and it was believed that the Trade Unionists in the country, all told, numbered twice that figure. It embraced, besides the great and powerful organisations, classes like agricultural labourers and women workers for whom combination seemed impossible except under some unusual stimulus of despair or excitement. It looked as if the whole working-class population, bringing its hopes and its dreams and all its institutions from the chapel to the benefit society, had enlisted under a single flag. The Grand National Union was, in fact, the revolt of the classes, for whom the civilisation described in earlier chapters had left un-satisfied certain fundamental instincts of human nature.

Of course the Union was defeated, as any movement whose ambition so far exceeded its power was bound to be defeated. It had against it a Government reposing now on the broad basis of property, large and small, rather than on the narrow basis of eighteenth-century privilege. It had against it a race of employers hard, successful, and combative. In March 1834 Melbourne struck at its weakest point, and being as ruthless in politics as he was gentle in manners, he struck one of those blows which resound through the world and leave their echoes for generations. His victims were agricultural labourers, belonging to the county in which famine and intimidation had brought man's spirit down to the lowest level. Some agricultural labourers at Tolpuddle in Dorset had formed a branch of the Friendly Society of Agricultural Labourers, and had administered the oaths that were part of the ritual commonly followed on such occasions. But the use of this ritual had been made a crime by laws that had been passed in 1797 at the time of the mutiny of the Nore. Six men were prosecuted, and being found guilty, as the *Annual Register* (p. 39) describes it, " of swearing agricultural labourers, and binding them to an observance of the illegal oath, by ceremonies partaking of mingled folly, superstition and ferocity," they were transported for seven years.[1] Melbourne insisted on carrying out this inhuman sentence, in spite of protests and entreaty, showing himself one of those men who can be merciless in cold blood when the hour of anxiety has passed. The effect was immediate. The Grand Union proceeded to abolish the obnoxious oaths, but an organisation so loosely constructed was ill adapted to combat panic. There was naturally more enthusiasm than efficiency at the service of the movement, and it would have needed no ordinary skill to organise this vast mass of hope and faith into an orderly and disciplined army.

The Government had done its work. But the employers scarcely needed such aid. They fought and overcame the movement in detail. Different sets of employers, the builders in Derby, the hosiers in Leicester, the clothiers in Leeds, all in turn offered their work-people the choice of leaving their employment or signing a document renouncing the Union. The Grand Union found itself in charge of a great and straggling battlefield on which these hastily organised workmen were pitted against men made inexorable by their self-confidence and

---

[1] See, for a full account, G. B. Hurst, "The Dorchester Labourers," *English Historical Review*, January 1925.

resolute by those stern qualities that had carried them from poverty to wealth. For a struggle of this kind its resources were hopelessly inadequate. And as difficulty and disappointment came thick upon them, the several leaders inevitably became more and more conscious of each other's shortcomings. The Grand Union stumbled along for a few months with dwindling strength, its last days embittered by all the distressing incidents that mark such defeats. But its failure does not obscure the significance of the birth and life of this movement. In a population whose economic condition, according to the statisticians, was better than that of their fathers and grandfathers, something like a million men and women had left the routine of their lives, made sacrifices, faced dangers and suffered punishment to proclaim to the world that this improved condition left them acutely dissatisfied.

The revolt was inspired by men who had larger ideas than those of the ordinary Trade Union leader. This was true of Doherty, of Owen, and of the men who edited the papers of the cause. The working class was stirred by the belief that society might be radically changed ; that life need not wear so hard and ungenerous a face ; that the poor might have a share in the civilisation of their age. The movement, then, is significant because of its scale, its character, and its ideas. It is remarkable also for something else. Its failure did not mark the end of the revolt. The Owenite revolt was followed by the revolt of Chartism.

The Charter itself was the product of the London Working Men's Association, a body of London Radicals among whom Lovett and Place were the leading figures. Place, Lovett, Hetherington, and other Radicals had been brought together in a campaign against the Newspaper Stamp Duty. This duty, first imposed in the time of Queen Anne, and now standing at the high figure of fourpence, Castlereagh had used in order to strike at Cobbett and his fellow Radicals, for one of the Six Acts (1819) imposed this duty on all periodicals costing less than sixpence. It was hoped that the Whigs would repeal this duty, but they maintained it, and as Radical editors refused to be silenced, there was a stiff struggle between journalists and the law. Between 1830 and 1836, 500 men were sent to prison for selling unstamped papers. The agitation was so far successful that the duty was reduced to a penny in 1836 : it was not abolished till 1855.

In 1836 Place and Lovett co-operated in another enterprise. They formed the London Working Men's Association for discussing political reform. It was this body which drew up the Charter with its six points—manhood suffrage, ballot, annual parliament, equal electorate districts, payment of members, and abolition of the property qualification for Parliament. Missionaries were sent out into the provinces, and this programme gradually drew together the different Radical movements of the time, including the passionate agitation that had been provoked in the north by the new Poor Law. The Charter thus became the rallying flag for a number of different discontents, and much of the energy and spirit that had been collected for the Grand National was now brought into the service of this cause.

The history of the movement is confused and perplexing, because it embraced not merely divergent but mutually hostile schools of reform.[1] We give the name of Chartist to the London artisan who shared Lovett's enthusiasm for education and a cheap press : to the Birmingham politician who supported Attwood's campaign for a reform of the currency : to the handloom weaver or the miner who flocked to the meetings where Oastler denounced the Poor Law, or Feargus O'Connor was spinning one project after another from his active and ill-regulated brain : to the South Wales miner who followed Frost with a pike to Newport and to prison. The leaders of the working classes were sharply divided, and they hated each other with that peculiar bitterness which often makes the controversies of rival reformers the most truculent contro-

---

[1] This was specially true of the relations of the anti-Poor Law agitation and the agitation for the Charter. The Rev. G. S. Bull refused to take part in a great anti-Poor Law demonstration on Hartshead Moor because a resolution was to be proposed in favour of Universal suffrage (*Bradford Observer*, August 18, 1837), and next year he complained that anti-Poor Law meetings were converted into Radical meetings and declared that he would never act again with Radicals (*Halifax Express*, February 3, 1838). On the other side, the Chartists were not less critical of their allies. " In the hands of a red-hot Tory like Earl Stanhope, the nephew and admirer of that base and bloody tool of tyranny, Wm. Pitt," wrote the *Chartist*, " the anti-Poor Law agitation becomes nothing more than a trick of faction, a trick by which the Tories hope to get hold of the places and salaries of the Whigs with the intention of using their power when they get it in a much worse manner than the Whigs ever have or ever can use it. A Government which Lord Stanhope would support would not only rivet the Poor Law upon the country, but it would have a Yeomanry massacre once a month."—*The Chartist*, June 30, 1839.

versies of all. If you could have put into one small room Owen, Place, Lovett, Hetherington, Cobbett, Oastler, and Feargus O'Connor, you would have provided the kind of entertainment offered to the London public by the showman who proposed to exhibit together a mad bull with a cat tied to its tail, a bear and a dog dressed with fireworks. Yet in the ranks of the Chartists each one of these men could count his devoted disciples by the thousand.[1]

The history of the movement reflects these conditions. The London artisan was Radical : he wanted democratic parliaments and popular education. In the North there was quite a different atmosphere. There the new Poor Law, of which Place approved, was detested as a cause and a symbol of the growing degradation of the working classes. Large numbers of hand-loom weavers, a race dying slowly and painfully, found themselves threatened with the loss of the allowances on which they depended, and it looked as if the new law was to complete their personal servitude. The capitalist had given the poor man the factory system : the middle classes had now given him the workhouse. He was to be driven from one to the other by the unfeeling masters of his life. Roebuck had defended the underlying principle of the new law with a declaration that the lot of the pauper must be made less eligible than that of the workman. " There are at present in the North of England," said the *Poor Man's Guardian*, " some 800,000 handloom weavers of whom many thousands cannot earn more than 5s. 6d. per week, out of which they have to pay 2s. for rent and lodging. Now we should like to know from Mr. Roebuck how a pauper is to be

---

[1] Owen on Universal Suffrage : " Were you to have a Parliament chosen next year by universal suffrage and vote by ballot, it would be most probably the least efficient, most turbulent, and worst public assembly that has yet ruled this country."—Letter to *Poor Man's Guardian*, October 31, 1835.

Hetherington on Cobbett : " Cobbett seems to think that if the working classes can get beer and bacon they should rest satisfied, no matter how abject their state of drudgery and subjection to their fellow men."—*Poor Man's Guardian*, September 28, 1833.

" Had this doctrine of Cobbett been propounded by a parson or a Wesleyan swaddler or by any other description of lazy impostor whose credit in the world depends on his power of gulling the multitude, we should have bestowed on it the charity of silence."—*Poor Man's Guardian*, October 3, 1833.

Lovett on Feargus O'Connor : " You may or may not be aware that I regard Feargus O'Connor as the chief marplot in our movement in favour of the Charter ; a man who, by his personal conduct, joined to his malignant influence in the *Northern Star*, has been the blight of Democracy from the first moment he opened his lips as its *professed* advocate."—*History of the Chartist Movement*, by Julius West, p. 204.

made less comfortable than these independent persons. Does he propose the treadmill or the stocks? " [1]

Yet in some respects Lancashire and Yorkshire lived in surroundings less brutalising than those of South Wales. Some of the worst abuses had been checked or reformed in the textile districts, but in South Wales improvement had not begun. Merthyr Tydvil, the centre of a district where a little group of ironmasters had made princely fortunes, had no lighting, water, or drainage. Here the King's writ scarcely ran, for all the laws against truck were disregarded. It is not surprising, therefore, that a miner who slept with fifteen other persons in a room in Merthyr Tydvil and worked for a master who lived in the palace of Cyfarthfa Castle, was often a different kind of Chartist from the London mechanic for whom the injustices of life were less outrageous and who looked to patient and steady education as the true remedy for England's wrongs.

In the summer of 1839 a Convention of some fifty or sixty delegates from the branches met first in London and then in Birmingham to prepare their petition and organise their plan. The petition was presented to Parliament in July, and rejected by 235 votes to 46. From this moment the difficulties to unity became insuperable. Fielden and Attwood wanted the Convention to draw up another petition, but the Convention was led away into a discussion of tactics. How was Parliament to be made to listen? A general strike? This plan, originally proposed by Benbow, a publican, and recommended at one time by Fielden, was in favour for some weeks. A boycott? A run on the banks? Armed violence? The debates reveal all the turns and shifts of men moving among large ideas and yet afraid of each other's shadows. Such is the effect of the presence of a few reckless men in a body that has to devise a plan of action. The disagreements that divided the movement all came to the surface, and Chartism never regained its unity.

The sequel was Frost's miserable rising in South Wales. Frost's men assembled on the 3rd November, intending to enter the little town of Newport in the night. Frost hoped to occupy the town, detain a small force of soldiers which had been sent there as a garrison, and then to march to Monmouth to rescue

[1] November 14, 1835.

Vincent, the well-known Chartist orator, from prison. But his plans miscarried. His men, after wandering about for several hours, arrived in broad daylight, and the soldiers, lodged in a hotel, swept the streets with rifle fire as the rioters entered. This was the only outbreak of violence, for in the North, where provocation was acute, Sir Charles James Napier managed to keep the peace and not merely to keep order. Napier, who was not only a very wise man but also more than half a Chartist himself, took infinite trouble to avoid a conflict, and the general respect in which he was held was a powerful influence on the side of peace.

Chartism never recovered its earlier force. A serious attempt was made to reorganise the movement in 1842, and Lovett managed to arrange a working alliance with the left wing of the Anti-Corn Law League. The Coalition put up Joseph Sturge as a candidate for Nottingham at a by-election, and very nearly won the seat. The effect of the new combination was seen when the complete suffrage petition was presented to the House of Commons, for Villiers, one of the Free Trade leaders, spoke and Cobden voted for it. But the plan for what was called a Complete Suffrage party was wrecked by Feargus O'Connor, who was determined to keep the movement in his own hands. He succeeded in his tactics, made Chartism and the Repeal movement deadly enemies, and, competing with popular leaders like Bright and Cobden, who had all the foresight and judgment that he lacked, he led the Chartists to their final catastrophe. At what point the madness, which was too evident to be disregarded in 1852, overcame him, it would be difficult to decide. The last years of Chartism were occupied with his furious quarrels with other leaders and his wild agrarian schemes, and, when the final Chartist petition was presented to Parliament in 1848, the demonstration which had spread such alarm in anticipation proved in the event a complete fiasco, leaving a legend of ridicule about what had been a great and significant movement. Napoleon III., then a refugee, living in King Street, served as a special constable and was able to reflect on the difference between revolution in London and revolution in Paris.

It is natural that historians, with their imagination caught by the movements that made 1848 so lurid a memory for European government, should think lightly of a revolt that had so sober a career and so slight a casualty list.   Fourteen men were killed in Frost's escapade at Newport and some fifty wounded.[1]   When we remember the slender provision for the maintenance of order (until 1839 neither Manchester nor Birmingham had a properly organised police force, and Bradford, with a population of 66,000, depended in the early forties on six constables), it seems extraordinary that more violence was not attempted, and that the Newport rising is an isolated incident.   But the English workman is and always has been less ready to try violence than the workman of the Continent.[2]   Disinclination for street fighting did not mean that the Chartists were not in earnest, or that they were unready to run personal risks for their cause.   There were not many collisions between Chartists and soldiers, but Chartists and Trade Unionists went to exile or to prison in large numbers whenever excitement ran high.   In the summer of 1842, when there were strikes and riots in Lancashire, Yorkshire, and the Potteries, the executive committee of the National Chartist Association published a manifesto urging the strikers to avoid violence but to hold out until the Charter was won.   This manifesto was treated by the Government as a treasonable proclamation.   After the riots had subsided Special Commissions were held at Liverpool and Stafford.   The Liverpool Commission transported 11 men and imprisoned 115; the Stafford Commission transported 54 and imprisoned 154.

For some ten years of English history the English poor found in these agitations an opportunity of protesting against the place they occupied in the raw industrial settlements spreading over the North and the Midlands.   This is the significance of the campaigns that began with Doherty's great combination and ended when the last Chartist petition died under the derision of the House of Commons.   These campaigns reflect the different experiences of different populations.   The poor in Newport or Merthyr Tydvil, the poor in London or Birmingham, the poor in Bradford or Manchester, might all of them find in the colour and circumstances of their lives something to wound their pride, something to make their poverty a disgrace, but they were not necessarily smarting under the same grievance.

[1] The *Times* suggested that the English middle classes were sterner stuff than the *gros épiciers* who went down before the Paris workmen.—June 8, 1848.
[2] See Cooke-Taylor, *Tour in the Manufacturing Districts of Lancashire, 1842*, on the law-abiding character of the Lancashire poor.

The new Poor Law, as we have seen, seemed a much greater hardship in some districts than in others. The hand-loom weavers had sometimes been compelled by the overseers to send their children to the mill, but they had never suffered the degrading slavery that the village labourer had endured. For the hand-loom weaver, then, the new Poor Law meant the loss of his personal independence. The decline in the discontent in the North was not unconnected with the decline in the numbers of the hand-loom weavers, for their numbers fell from 100,000 in 1842 to 50,000 in 1848 and 30,000 in 1854.[1]

The difficulty of successful agitation among the workmen of the time was described by Place in 1835. " Propose to a working man any great measure affecting the whole body, and he immediately asks himself the question, What am I to get by it, meaning, what at the *instant* am I to have in my hand, or in my pocket, which I should like to have ? To this he replies— nothing. There he sticks ; he does nothing ; he has not the heart to do anything even for his own advantage if that advantage be remote, and he has no desire to stir himself for the advantage of other persons." [2] This difficulty had been overcome in the Owenite campaign ; it was overcome in the Chartist agitation. The men and women who went to a Chartist meeting and listened to O'Brien, or Vincent, or Cooper, or O'Connor, did not merely think of themselves with a shilling or two more in their pockets, they were swept along by the rhetoric which described their place in society, degraded and insulted, their lives spent in the cold and the dark in a world of luxury and wealth. Their indignation was fired by this picture of society as it was : their imagination was touched by a picture of society as it might be. The Chartist rhetoric, that is, moved and excited all those social instincts that were disregarded or flouted in the arrangements of their lives. That is why the special topic mattered little. Vincent wrote to Place : " In Northampton I publicly administered the teetotal pledge. I have proposed the formation of public libraries and lecture rooms. Every appeal to the intellect and virtue of the masses is most cordially responded to." [3] Chartism was not a precise

---

[1] Slosson, *Decline of the Chartist Movement*, p. 131.   [2] Wallas, *Life of Place*, p. 370.
[3] Wallas, *Life of Place*, p. 379.   The Chartists of Wakefield, *e.g.*, sent their good wishes to the Duke of Newcastle when he started a society to put down prize-fighting.— *Leeds Mercury*, September 18, 1847.

logical demand for a particular reform : it was a protest as incoherent as the life that had provoked it. We may say of these men
and women that their burning sense of wrong made them follow
any leader who promised them a radical change : whether he
talked like Owen or Cobbett, like Oastler or O'Connor :
whether he appealed to the ambitions of the Trade Unionist or
the memories of the peasant : whether he offered to go forward
or to go back, to build a golden future or recall a glittering past.

To regard Chartism as an episode, as an effort that failed, a
flash in the pan, something to which you can give date of birth
and death, is to misread the history of the time. The chief
feature of that history is the growth and prevalence of discontent. No doubt that discontent was due to different causes
and fed from different sources : the discomforts of the change
from the life of the peasant or the artisan to that of the factory
worker ; the pressure from time to time of mass unemployment
unrelieved by any remedy ; the special hardships of the new
Poor Law. But if its general character is to be described, it was
discontent excited by the philosophy of life, of which the new
town was the symbol and the expression. " The political
economists in Church and State," said the *Crisis*, " are the real
high priests of the realm. They have set up the golden calf.
. . . Impious, dissatisfied people, say they, you men without
property, mob and scum of the earth, with minds born to inferiority and hands made for our service. Why if you are still
discontented do you not seek to accumulate wealth and so
become respectable like ourselves ? " [1]

Joseph Toynbee tried to teach his generation that the " comforts of those who live by their labour did not by any means
depend upon the mere money and amount of their wages." [2]
Chartism illustrated this truth. The discontent of which it was
a symbol was provoked by an inequality that condemned the
mass of the poor to a life without leisure or grace, without
enjoyment or education, making them

> " A savage horde among the civilised,
> A servile band among the lordly free." [3]

The workmen's newspapers and manifestoes show how conscious they were of the want of sympathy and colour in their

[1] June 1, 1833.   [2] Quoted in Normanby's speech, July 26, 1844.
[3] *Excursion*, book ix. 310.

surroundings ; of the sharp division that was drawn between those who could enjoy life, and those who had to bear its burdens.[1] For amid the triumphs of nature or of art, the masterpieces of God or man, there was nothing that seemed to belong to them, or to speak to them of a harmony that could subdue the spirit of strife and care. The *Pioneer*, a workman's paper, contrasted the bleak poverty of these towns with the full life of the ancient democracies, remarking that the oratorios in the Catholic churches had to satisfy and educate all the tastes and interests for which such lavish provision was made in Greece and Rome.[2] The restrictions which made Sunday a day of gloom, only relieved by drunkenness, were bitterly resented in their papers. " The atrocious Bill for Sabbath coercion," which was pressed on the reformed Parliament by Sir Andrew Agnew, was described in the *Pioneer* in the same tone and language as the factory system.[3] " It would in short make the veriest wretch in the most infanticidal of our factories hate the Lord's Day more than he does the overlooker and the billy roller, and drive every rational man in the country to rebellion or the madhouse." [4]

The stern life of the new town offered so strong a provocation that it could make rebels out of the men whom Place de-

[1] " The poor starved eye has no green spot to look upon ; the weary sameness of its range is in some loom or lathe or vice or swift-revolving mechanism ; midst dust and grease and smoke, and all the rudiments of nausea. Is this an atmosphere for free-born souls ? And yet they tell us we must love our country. To love a thing we never see, save when necessity, hard pinching want makes our thin shanks go tramp the road for provender ; and then our free-born neighbours call us vagabonds."— *Pioneer*, December 7, 1833.

" You might invite us now and then to have a concert, to take an airing in your barouche, to see the works of art and splendid exhibitions."—*Pioneer*, November 16, 1833.

[2] " For the complete popular enjoyment of works of art by the people, with the exception of that which for a particular purpose is allowed in the Catholic churches, we must look back to the democracies of antiquity."—Quoted in *Pioneer*, September 28, 1833.

Cleave's Gazette quoted from Harriet Martineau : " Where are the public grounds in which the poor of our large towns may take the air and exercise themselves in games ? Where are the theatres, the museums, the newsrooms to which the poor may resort without an expense unsuited to their means ? "—March 30, 1839.

[3] " Now the evidence of our senses proves to us the condition of the people of the present day, cursed with all the horrors of poverty in the midst of an abundance, and deprived of the shadow of freedom. Witness the atrocious Bill for Sabbath Coercion ! Witness the horrible Factory System ! Witness the Standing Army of redcoats, and *armed blue* soldiery, deceitfully called Police ! ! Witness the tread-mills and the yoking of paupers to drag carts and gravel as beasts of burden. . . ."—*The Working Man's Friend*, April 6, 1833.

[4] Compare *Poor Man's Guardian*, April 6, 1833 : " Let us go to hell in our own way,

scribed as short-sighted and selfish, thinking only of their immediate gain. The workman was swept into one movement after another, as his imagination was captured first by this gospel, then by that. Any man who could promise with golden tongue to lead him out of his hard and desolate world became his leader. "Every appeal," said Vincent, " to the intellect and virtue of the masses is most cordially responded to." The rulers of this new society had forgotten that if you wish to satisfy a people you must satisfy its imagination: the leaders of the revolt knew that if you want to rouse a people you must rouse its imagination. The Chartist movement, like Owen's movement, was imagination in action. And when Chartism flickered out this force was not lost. It went into different movements like the movement for education, the movement for public health, the Trade Union movements, the movement for temperance, and the later movements for the franchise. Long after the great project of 1848 had collapsed amid the relief and ridicule of London, the virtue of the Chartist movement was by these means building up the self-respect of the English workman. In this sense, as in some others, Chartism deserved the phrase Mill applied to it, the victory of the vanquished.[1]

and leave the Agnews and Percevals to do the same, or to go to Bedlam or the devil if they please."
Hood wrote an Ode to Sir Andrew Agnew, ending:
" do not further search
To make a Sunday Workhouse of the Church."

[1] Quoted by James Bonar, "John Stuart Mill the Reformer," *Indian Journal of Economics*, April 1930.

CHAPTER XV

THE DUEL OF LANDLORD AND MANUFACTURER

1838-1847

It looked in the thirties as though English politics would be dominated for half a century by a passionate quarrel between rich and poor. This quarrel had broken out before 1832, and the Reform Bill seemed only to have made it more violent. As the *Chartist* put it : " The first use which a class always makes of its representation is to shift its burden upon somebody else's shoulders." [1] The advent of the middle class to power was no exception to the rule. What was the gift of the Reform Parliament to the poor ? The east wind of the new Poor Law.

If we look at the history of England between 1840 and 1890, we see that the conflict which seemed so imminent died away. There was less class war in the fifties than in the thirties. For this change there were two reasons : the class war was pacified by the influence of a general civilising movement, which modified the sharp consequences of the Industrial Revolution, and it was distracted by another conflict between the landlord and the manufacturer which determined the course of politics for the next ten years. [2] The two agitations in which this quarrel found its outlet are the agitation for the Repeal of the Corn Laws and the agitation for the Ten Hours Bill.

The history of the Corn Laws in Parliament begins or four purposes with the passing of the Corn Law of 1815, prohibiting

---

[1] March 31, 1839. Cf. Mill, who favoured the extension of the suffrage " to keep the middle classes in that salutary awe, without which, no doubt, these classes would be just like any other oligarchy."—*Reorganisation of the Reform Party*, quoted by Neff, *Carlyle and Mill*, p. 216.

[2] The common view of this struggle is roughly correct, but it must be remembered that there were many persons who were both for Repeal of the Corn Laws and for the Ten Hours Bill. Some of the leading manufacturers supported the Ten Hours Bill, such as Fielden, Kay of Bury, Kenworthy of Blackburn, Wood, Walker, and Rand of Bradford. Some leading landowners like Howick and Fitzwilliam and Holland supported Repeal.

importation when the price was below 80s. a quarter.   In 1828 Wellington set up a sliding scale beginning with a duty of 36s. 8d. at 50s., decreasing to 16s. 8d. at 68s., and 1s. at 73s.   In 1841 the Whigs proposed a fixed duty at 8s., but the dissolution of that year brought in Peel who carried a new sliding scale beginning with a 20s. duty at 51s., decreasing to 12s. at 60s., and 1s. at 73s., Russell and Melbourne being beaten in their efforts to substitute a fixed duty.   So far the official policies of the Liberal and Conservative parties were Protection, by a fixed duty in the first case and by a sliding duty in the second, but all the time, of course, there had been an important body of opinion in Parliament in favour of dropping Protection altogether.   In the Lords men like Fitzwilliam, Brougham, Durham, and Holland had voted in favour of this policy in 1839 : in the Commons, Villiers made annual motions for Repeal, being supported in 1842 by 90 votes, in 1843 by 125, and in 1844 by 124.

In 1845 came the shock of the Irish Potato Famine.   Peel, faced with a starving population and embarrassed by the failure of the English harvest, saw that it was impossible to maintain the law that kept food out of the country.   But if that law was suspended, could it be reimposed ?   While Peel was hesitating, Lord John Russell wrote his famous letter to the electors of the city of London announcing his conversion to Repeal.   In December Peel proposed to his Cabinet to modify the Corn Law, and resigned office because two of his colleagues, Stanley and Buccleuch, dissented.   Russell was asked to form a government, but he soon abandoned the task, nominally because Howick would not join him if Palmerston went to the Foreign Office, really because he was not prepared for a battle with the Lords over Protection.   Peel returned to office, introduced a Bill providing for the admission of corn at 1s. duty after February 1, 1849, and carried it through Parliament in the summer of 1846.[1]

The organisation which had got rid of the Corn Laws with the help of famine had gained a victory as rapid as it was sensational, for it was only in September 1838 that the Anti-Corn Law League was established.   The League is famous in history, not

---

[1] The second reading passed by a majority of 88 on March 27; the third, by a majority of 98 on May 15.   In the first of these divisions the majority consisted of 202 Liberals and 102 Conservatives, the minority of 8 Liberals and 208 Conservatives.

merely because of its achievement, but because of its leaders,
two men who were particularly powerful in combination.
Cobden was a man with a large reflective mind and an unrivalled
gift for argument and exposition.   Bright, a more combative
man, often, in his earlier career, bitter, rasping, and unfair,
became a consummate master of a simple eloquence which was
always telling and often beautiful.

To understand the effects of this agitation on the temper and
imagination of the time, we must note certain facts about it.
The Anti-Corn Law League was organised and financed by a
rich class with a remarkable capacity for propaganda and
organisation acquired in the world of business.   It was able to
employ expert writers and speakers all over the country.   By
1842 the League had spent a hundred thousand pounds : in
1843 it raised fifty thousand pounds : in 1844 it raised nearly a
hundred thousand pounds and was spending a thousand pounds
a week.[1]   At a meeting of the League in Manchester in 1845,
£60,000 was subscribed in an hour and a half.   Such were the
resources at the command of this agitation.   They were put to
most effective use.   At a time when there was a rage for
periodical literature, the League distributed nine million carefully argued tracts by means of a staff of eight hundred persons.
The League had its organ called at first the *Circular* and afterwards the *League*.   Meetings were held incessantly all over the
country, and the League paid the Chartists the compliment of
arranging conventions from time to time in the principal towns.
Towards the end of the agitation the League discovered another
weapon.   The Reform Act of 1832 gave the county vote to
the 40s. freeholder.   The League set up an office to facilitate
the purchase of freeholds in the county constituencies by free-
traders from the neighbouring towns, in the West Riding and
Lancashire.   If Repeal had not come in 1846, the same plan
would have been applied in Middlesex and Surrey.

This agitation, led and financed by rich men, was so conducted as to draw poor men into its orbit.   It was essentially
popular in character.   The Repeal of the Corn Laws was
demanded in the interests of English industry, which suffered
because exchange was impeded for the sake of English landowners.   Under certain conditions a contest over the Corn

[1] Morley, *Cobden*, vol. i. p. 312.

Laws would have been a contest between industry and agriculture, between the townsman and the peasant. But the agrarian history of England, with the dispossession of the peasant and the degradation of the labourer, made it impossible for the struggle to assume such a complexion in English politics. No man, knowing the history of the English village for the last half century, could persuade himself that the Corn Laws had brought anything but hunger to the mass of the village population. The poor, as the *Times* put it, deserted the landlords in this struggle, but then the landlords had first deserted the poor. Thus the campaign became a campaign against a rich class. The Repealers asserted more than once that they had concentrated on one question and put every other issue on one side. It would be truer to say that they had concentrated on one class, for the columns of the *League* were filled with the crimes of landlords and with denunciations of the game laws and other abuses of feudal power. The Repeal agitation was in certain aspects an agitation for an object of great importance to the industrial capitalists, and the subscription lists to its funds show how widely this truth was recognised. But it was at the same time an agitation pressing day after day the wrongs of the poor, and denouncing the selfishness of the rich.

The agitation was fiercely polemical. Even Cobden who preferred argument to invective, gave the discussion the kind of tonic that politics demanded at this time in such a passage as that in which he compared the landlords to the German nobles.[1] " They had heard of the Union of Hanse Towns. Why did they unite ? To put down aristocratic plunderers ; and they would say to the aristocrats of England, Why do you plunder the bee-hives of Lancashire and Yorkshire ? "[2] The *Times* pointed out that one great difficulty about the public health agitation was that it never became violent and therefore never became interesting. The movement for the Repeal of the Corn Laws was a fighting movement organised by a combative class. The *League* boasted in its farewell number that it was the only agitation in English history which had been founded

---

[1] See a fine letter by Cobden given in Morley's *Life*, in which he regretted that the conditions of a popular agitation sometimes forced him to be more violent than he wished to be.—Vol. i. p. 211.

[2] *Bradford Observer*, February 28, 1839.

and conducted exclusively by the middle classes. It had at its back men who were indignant about a general injustice, and not less indignant about a particular injustice of which they thought themselves the victims. A movement, alive in this way with public and private anger, interested the English people from the first.

The agitation for the Repeal of the Corn Laws was thus an important force in distracting the class quarrel that had found its expression in Chartism, for it was in one aspect at any rate a quarrel with the rich on behalf of the poor. And it was a quarrel on an issue on which the workmen originally agreed with the Repealers. For the working classes were by tradition free traders on this question. The Corn Bill of 1815 had excited the most violent opposition. " The Repeal of the Corn Laws " was inscribed together with " Universal Suffrage " and "Annual Parliaments" on the flags that were carried to Peterloo. The early Chartist movement was not hostile to the Repeal movement : it was merely sceptical of its prospects and sus-picious of its promoters. The *Chartist* wrote strongly in favour of Free Trade in February 1839 as the only way of saving England from the fate of Holland. In March the paper criticised the Corn Law repealers as thirty or forty gentlemen representing themselves and their own breeches' pockets, un-likely to make an impression on the selfishness of the landlords. In the same month it argued that the stubborn resistance of the House of Lords ought to convince the middle classes that Repeal was only to be obtained by combining with the Chartists. " Put a pike in a fishpond and he will eat up every roach and dace first, avoiding the perch because he has a sharp back fin which cuts his mouth : but when the roach and dace are all gone, and hunger presses, he attacks the perch and despite the fin back he soon makes an end of them." [1] The Corn lords were the pike, the middle classes were the perch, and the working classes, the roach and dace, were already swallowed. A Free Trade paper, the *Morning Chronicle*, proposed an arrangement with the Chartists, who were to be offered household suffrage, but the *Chartist* rejected any idea of such a compromise. In 1842, as we have seen, there was an attempt to bring the move-ments together in the establishment of the complete Suffrage

[1] March 23, 1839.

party. Lovett was one of its promoters. Proceedings began with a private conference at which Joseph Sturge and John Bright met some of the Chartists. A public conference at Birmingham in April 1842, at which Vincent, Bronterre O'Brien, John Bright and Henry Solly were among the speakers, resolved to enter on a crusade. Sturge stood at a by-election at Nottingham in May 1842 as the candidate of this party, and was only just defeated by John Walter. But the movement was destroyed by the sinister hand of Feargus O'Connor, under whose influence the Chartist movement and the Repeal movement were forced into a violent quarrel. It was a quarrel in which Chartism suffered much more than Repeal. Feargus O'Connor could make a loud noise, but when it came to a contest the League could make a louder.

We must now turn to the agitation for the Ten Hours Bill. The history of the agitation goes back to the first Factory Act passed in 1802 by the elder Peel. This Act limited the hours for apprentice children to twelve a day for six days of the week. In 1819 Peel succeeded in putting another Act on the Statute Book. This Act, much more modest than he wished, forbade the employment of children under nine in cotton mills and limited the hours of children between nine and sixteen to twelve, exclusive of meal hours. In 1831 John Cam Hobhouse carried a Bill extending the twelve hours' day to all persons under eighteen. In 1831 Michael Sadler, a Tory M.P., introduced a Bill limiting hours in all mills for persons under eighteen to ten. At the election of 1832 Sadler lost his seat and Ashley took his place as parliamentary leader of the cause, occupying in this agitation the place Villiers occupied in the Repeal agitation. In 1833 he introduced a Bill on Sadler's lines, but the Whig Government amended it, improving it in one important respect, for inspection was introduced, but weakening it on its main principle, for whereas the hours for children under thirteen were to be limited to nine, the hours for persons between thirteen and eighteen were to be limited to twelve.

From this time the factory struggle was as much a struggle for a ten hours' day for all persons under eighteen as the struggle for amending the Corn Laws was a struggle for repealing them. You might amend the factory system without passing a Ten

Hours Bill. The factory system was indeed amended and improved in detail before the Ten Hours Bill was passed. But, so far as popular agitation was concerned, the factory question was the ten hours question and no other. The Ten Hours Bill raised, in one sense, a complicated issue. It had become clear by this time that it was impossible so to organise the working arrangements of the mill as to combine a twelve hours' day for adults with a ten hours' day for persons under eighteen. A ten hours' day for persons under eighteen meant that the day for persons over eighteen would also be a ten hours' day. Parliament was therefore being asked to limit the hours for adults and not merely the hours for children, to limit the hours for the whole mill, not for one set of workers. This is what the workmen understood by factory reform.

In Parliament there were people like Roebuck who were against all restrictions. There were, at the same time, people like Fielden who were in favour of restricting the hours of adult labour directly and definitely by law. Such men were few. The great majority of members could be divided into two classes. One class would have liked to restrict the hours of persons under eighteen, but preferred to leave such persons unprotected rather than run the risk of injuring industry by restricting the hours of adults. The second class did not want to run the risk of injuring industry by restricting the hours of adults, but preferred to take the risk involved in that reduction, rather than leave children under eighteen working twelve hours a day. The Ten Hours Bill became law when a number of persons like Lord John Russell and Macaulay passed from the first of these classes to the second. This happened when the Whigs were no longer in office and Peel had become Prime Minister.

The great debates in Parliament took place in the years 1844, 1846, and 1847. Peel's Government introduced a Factory Bill in 1844, making a number of detailed improvements in the law. Ashley tried to insert a ten hours clause in the Government Bill. Opinion was so nicely balanced that Ashley succeeded with one of his amendments by a majority of nine votes, though when the same issue came before the House on a different clause he was defeated by seven votes. Parliament thus threw the Government Bill into confusion. The Government therefore introduced a second Bill, with a plain warning that this time they would resign if the House of Commons reduced the hours of labour. A great many members who would have liked to support Ashley were not prepared to turn the Government out, and as a consequence of this threat he was beaten, when he tried to amend their second Bill, by 297 votes to 159. This year he was supported for the first time by the leading Whigs. The relation of the parties in the House to the parties in the press was curious. The Conservative press in the industrial towns was strongly in favour of the Ten Hours Bill : the Liberal press, with the exception of the *Bradford Observer*, was strongly opposed to it. Peel said that he would resign rather than let the House of Commons pass the Bill which the Conservative press wanted, while leading Liberals like Lord John Russell, Sir George Grey, and Macaulay gave strong support to the Bill of which the Liberal press believed, with Peel, that it would be disastrous to industry. The *Leeds Mercury*, the *Universe*, and the *Nonconformist* were angry with Russell and Grey, while the Conservative press was dissatisfied with Peel.

In January 1846 Ashley resigned his seat. He had been converted to Repeal, and he was too conscientious to sit and vote as a Free Trader, having been elected as a Protectionist.[1] Before resigning he introduced a Ten Hours Bill, and this Bill, in Fielden's charge, came up for second reading on May 22, a week after Peel's Bill for the gradual Abolition of the Corn Laws had passed its third reading. The Bill was now defeated by ten votes, the opponents (205) consisting of 81 Liberals, 73 Peelites, and 51 Protectionists ; the supporters, of 71 Liberals, 117 Protectionists, and 7 Peelites.[2] On June 25 Peel's Government fell, and Russell succeeded him as Prime Minister. Conditions were therefore much more favourable, for though the House of Commons had not changed, the new Prime Minister was a friend and not an opponent. Ashley was still out of the House. Fielden introduced his Bill on January 26, 1847, and its second reading was carried on February 17 by 195 votes to 87. The

---

[1] The *League* and John Bright both treated Ashley very ungenerously on this occasion, the *League* taunting him with his late conversion, and Bright making a personal attack upon him in his absence. Other Free Traders were more magnanimous, and there was a serious proposal in Bradford to adopt Ashley as a Free Trade candidate. Cobden was in favour of it. See *Bradford Observer*, April 9, 1846.

[2] These figures are given in the *Ten Hours Advocate*, p. 93.

Whig leaders wanted to make the Bill an Eleven Hours Bill, thinking that the risk of industrial loss would be diminished, and knowing that many millowners in the North, like Sir Titus Salt and Marshall of Leeds, had adopted an eleven hours' day.[1]   But Peel, though he thought it dangerous to reduce hours at all, preferred ten hours to eleven ; for he thought that if Parliament made the smaller change the workmen would continue to agitate for the larger.   He and his friends therefore took no part on this issue, and the proposal to substitute eleven for ten was defeated on March 17 by 144 to 66.   Russell's Government accepted the decision of the House and gave the Bill the fullest support, overcoming Bright's efforts to kill it by obstruction by promising Government time.   In consequence, the Bill became law without difficulty.   Brougham and Clarendon attacked the Bill in the Lords, but they were beaten by 53 to 11.

The organisation which conducted the campaign outside Parliament was a Central Short Time Committee (with branches in all the different towns), made up of trade unionists, of whom the most famous was John Doherty, and supporters from other classes, of whom the most important were Fielden, Wood, and Oastler, and the Rev. G. S. Bull.   The Committee was poor in comparison with the League, which could draw on the help of manufacturers whose public spirit was encouraged by the prospect of commercial advantage.   In this case the chief support came from manufacturers who stood to lose, if Peel and Cobden were correct in their estimate of the consequences of the Bill, for the sixpences and threepences of the mill workers were supplemented by large subscriptions from manufacturers like Fielden and John Wood, the Bradford worsted spinner, who is said to have spent in all forty thousand pounds. The movement had an organ for a few months in the *Ten Hours Advocate*, which was started in September 1846, a weekly paper which makes dull reading when compared with the lively pages of the *League*.   But the agitation itself was as polemical as the agitation against the Corn Laws.   This was not true of Ashley's part in it.   His sense of personal responsibility, his

---

[1] The reduction at Salt's mills was celebrated by a banquet at Bradford.   There were a number of similar experiments at this time, most of them pronounced successful (*e.g.* at Huddersfield), but it was reported that an experiment at Preston had been unfavourable.—*Leeds Mercury*, April 4, 1846, April 11, 1846 ; *Leeds Intelligencer*, March 21, 1846.

feeling for the dignity of public life, and his dread of exciting popular passion governed his conduct on the platform as everywhere else.   Several of his allies were of a different temper, and their rhetoric was as vehement as that of any of the League speakers.   The Protectionist papers argued at the time of the Chartist riots that the wildest Chartist orators were less to blame for the violence of class feeling than the orators of the League.[1]   Oastler was a match for any of them.   When he spoke of teaching children to put needles into the machines they were tending, the *Manchester Guardian* remarked that so reckless a speaker ought to be placed under restraint either by his friends or by the law.[2]

As a result of these two agitations England rang from one end to the other with denunciations of the rich by the rich.   Feargus O'Connor or Bronterre O'Brien could not say harsher things than the landlords were saying of the manufacturers and the manufacturers of the landlords.   How did a Leaguer describe the life of the agricultural labourer ?   " What ! six shillings a week for wages, and the morning's sun, and the singing of birds, and sportive lambs, and winding streams, and the mountain breeze, and a little wholesome labour—six shillings a week, and all this !   And nothing to do with your six shillings a week, but merely to pay your rent, buy your food, clothe yourselves and your families, and lay by something for old age !   Happy people ! " [3]   *Punch*, commenting on the unfortunate remark of the Duke of Norfolk that curry powder was very soothing in an ill-filled stomach, and on discussions that were proceeding about different kinds of diet, suggested that the landlords should hold a competition in peasants instead of in fat cattle.   The catalogue might read like this : " No. 1. A short-legged Norfolk labourer.   Fed on boiling water and curry powder. Walked thirty miles to the Exhibition.   Bred in the Norwich workhouse.   First prize."   " No. 2. A Hampshire labourer. Supported entirely on starch.   Brought in a cab half a mile to the Exhibition by Dr. Buckland.   Second prize. . . ." [4]   Then

---

[1] Cf. the *Leeds Intelligencer*, January 5, 1839, on the prosecution of Stephens, and the *Liverpool Courier*, March 5, 1843, on the Chartist trials.

[2] *Manchester Guardian*, September 24 and 28, 1836.   Oastler might have replied that he made this speech in answer to magistrates who said they would not carry out the Factory Acts.

[3] Morley's *Cobden*, vol. i. p. 210.

[4] Quoted by the *League*, January 3, 1846.   *Punch*, like the *Times*, helped both

what about the mill worker ? On this subject Mr. Ferrand, the member for Bingley, had the sharpest tongue. Indeed, the House of Commons was perpetually engaged in personal controversies of which he was the centre. Here is an account that he gave to the House of Commons of the conditions of life of the textile workpeople. " The poor weavers who are perhaps only receiving 3s. 6d. or 4s. a week, are constantly mulcted in this manner by these overlookers, who have their own wages paid out of what they can deduct from these plundered wretches, and a percentage on the amount. Then, again, mark what follows : they have not even the small amount paid in money—it is paid in goods—in rotten corn—in ' cheap flour ' : and when the poor man carries it home to his wife and family, after in vain endeavouring to induce his master to pay him his wages in money, he finds the flour which he had received as wages in the previous week still unconsumed, the quality being so bad, that the stomachs of his sickly children had been unable to retain it." [1]

These descriptions were, of course, denounced as false, but so far as the theme of this chapter is concerned, whether they were true or false does not matter. They are cited to show that the worst that could be said of the rich by the poor was being said by the rich of one another. Inevitably the strength of class passion was distracted.

The Chartists might say that if the workman would listen to them he would obtain blessings in comparison with which the Repeal of the Corn Laws and the Ten Hours Bill would seem trifling gains. Some of the Chartists following Feargus O'Connor were even against Repeal. But when Ebenezer Elliott said that he was for the Charter but did not want to be starved first, he spoke for great numbers of working men and women. In such minds the revolutionary movement was short-circuited. The battle that Feargus O'Connor was fighting in which the poor were invited to struggle with the rich, ceased to be the central spectacle of politics. It was much more exciting to watch rich men fighting with rich men, pelting each other with the wrongs of the poor.

agitations, and the *Ten Hours Advocate* quoted a remonstrance addressed to John Bright in its columns.

[1] House of Commons, February 14, 1842.

These agitations were important for another reason. A description has been attempted in earlier chapters of the forces and influences that tended to alienate the poor both from the Established and the Nonconformist Churches. The Chartist movement scared most of the religious leaders. These two agitations provided an opportunity for bringing the Churches into touch with the feelings and desires of the poor. The Nonconformists threw themselves into the Repeal movement. At one League meeting no less than seven hundred Nonconformist clergy sat on the platform. An issue had arisen, unlike that of Chartism, on which Nonconformists could take the side of the poor without disturbing the unity or peace of their organisation. This agitation helped to give Nonconformity its hold on the village labourers. In the final struggle in the House of Lords, Bishops Thirlwall and Wilberforce made two of the best speeches on behalf of Repeal, and the bishops voted for Repeal by 15 to 9,[1] but in the main the Church had been either neutral or hostile.[2]

The Nonconformists threw themselves into the Repeal agitation; the Church took up the Ten Hours Bill. In the thirties all the Churches were cold to this cause. Bull, the Bradford parson, speaking at Manchester in April 1833, said that out of seventy clergy in Manchester only two had come out as public advocates of this reform. " It cannot be because they are slow to speak, for I have myself heard the eloquence of your Stowells, your Newtons, and your McColls." [3]   In the forties the *Burnley Bee*, a newspaper started to oppose the Bill, complained of the leading part taken by the Church in the agitation. The Vicars of Leeds, Bradford, Wakefield, Huddersfield, Dewsbury, and of many smaller towns, acted as Chairmen regularly at meetings for the Ten Hours Bill; another Lancashire Vicar, Canon Wray, took the same part at Manchester; the Vicar of Leigh prepared a petition at his own expense. The Church paper, the *Guardian*, gave strong support to the Bill. " We must have a time to eat and a time to sleep ; a time to rise up and a time to sit down ; " a time," as it has been eloquently

---

[1] House of Lords, May 25, 1846. The *League*, in praising Wilberforce's speech, remarked that the bishop remembered the soldiers guarding his father's house in 1815, when his father had provoked popular fury by voting for the Corn Bill.

[2] Cobden, House of Commons, April 18, 1842.

[3] Alfred, *History of the Factory Movement*, vol. ii. p. 25.

said, " to live in and a time to die in " ; a time to shape life into immortality :

Continuo has leges, aeternaque foedera nobis
Imposuit natura ;

Nature will avenge herself for the robbery if she is defrauded by oppression and cupidity." [1] The Nonconformists were less active. Kydd names in his history a few Nonconformist ministers, including the famous William Dawson, and he mentions that one of them, a Baptist, gave offence to some of the principal members of his congregation.[2] This is not surprising, for the strongest opponent of the Bill in the press was the *Leeds Mercury*, the ablest spokesman of Nonconformist politics, and the *Nonconformist* also followed John Bright. " The Ten Hours Bill, founded upon a vicious principle, would curtail the rights of labour without permanently increasing its comforts. It would cost the poor man too much—it would ultimately repay him nothing." [3] The *Watchman*, the Wesleyan Methodist paper, was neutral, both on the Ten Hours Bill and the Repeal of the Corn Laws, holding that the one question of supreme importance was that of "infusing as much as possible of the old Protestant spirit—the spirit of our Reformers—into the next Representative Assembly of our land." [4] Thus these two agitations, by bringing the Nonconformists and the Established Church into politics on the side of the poor, in one or other of their quarrels with the rich, helped to soften the impression that the life and circumstances of the Churches made on the imagination of the working classes. The Nonconformist clergy befriended the poor against the landowner ; the Church clergy befriended the poor against the manufacturer.

The life and career of these agitations affected profoundly the class war of the forties. The success that followed them gave a new tone to working life from the fifties. The Repeal of the Corn Laws removed a sense of injustice in a dramatic manner, and helped to produce a great expansion of trade, which eased the hardships of town life. The passing of the Ten Hours Act was even more important as an influence on the imagination of the poor. There were many who said that it was wrong to make food dearer for the poor, and the Repeal of the Corn Laws

[1] May 6, 1846.
[2] Alfred, *op. cit.*, vol. ii. pp. 224 and 230.
[3] May 27, 1846.
[4] June 3, 1846.

signified the success of that contention.[1]   The passing of the Ten Hours Act signified the success of a contention that had a harder battle to fight: the contention that the workman had a right to a share in the culture and leisure enjoyed by other classes.   The Factory agitation, starting as a crusade for the protection of children, had ended as a successful campaign for the right of the working classes to a larger life.

---

[1] The immediate effect of Repeal was to prevent a rise in the price of bread, not to reduce the price. The fall in prices did not come till the seventies.—Venn, *Foundation of Agricultural Economics*, p. 316.

CHAPTER XVI

THE BATTLE FOR PUBLIC HEALTH

"I have carried you to some of the towns and cities of the country most distinguished by its special characteristics; I have mentioned places which supply a large portion of the fuel that feeds our chimneys and furnaces—which forge the iron and steel that first shape and then waft along our countless manufactures—which weave the fabrics that on the banks of the Volga meet and outsell the products of all the looms of Asia and clothe the furthest tropics. Then let it not be said, or if it has been said hitherto, let it be said no longer, that the hives of this vast industry and the sources of these innumerable supplies of comfort and civilisation to all mankind—the homes of the men who do and make these things—should be pre-eminently the seats of filth, of disease, of degradation in its worst shapes and forms."

LORD MORPETH, House of Commons, February 10, 1848.

"I am obliged to remember the negro huts in the West Indies, many hundreds of which I have visited in other days, and I feel bound to admit that before the Emancipation Act, the greatest outcry would have been raised against any proprietor who would have lodged his slaves in such residences as those I have lately seen within a walk of your Lordships' House."

LORD NORMANBY, House of Lords, July 26, 1844.

THE general arrangement of English local government to-day follows certain definite principles. Over every area there is some local responsible authority with duties imposed and powers bestowed by Parliament. These authorities are grouped in a hierarchy from the parish meeting to the county council, the powers exercised by a county borough differing from those exercised by a non-county borough, and the duties of an urban district council differing from those of a rural council. Above this system of local authorities we find some central department such as the Ministry of Health or the Board of Education, with certain limited powers of inspection and control. The local and central authorities are connected also in another manner, for the local authorities subject to this kind of pressure are stimulated by direct help from the central government in the form of grants in aid. In the year 1920 these grants amounted to some forty-five millions. English local government differs from American local government in giving more power to the central authorities, whilst it differs from local government on the Continent in giving greater freedom to the local authority.[1]

When statesmen and thinkers set out to attack the evils described in an earlier chapter, scarcely any of this machinery existed. There was no Local Government Board or Ministry of Health. In the towns there were no local authorities with effective powers, and in the country there were rarely authorities with any powers at all.[2] Grants in aid for local services were unknown.

The campaign began in 1838. Edwin Chadwick, the man who took the first step, may be regarded as the chief benefactor of his age if you look at the power and courage with which he brought abuses to light, and as its evil genius if you dwell on the fate of any plan of reform that fell into his hands. This unpopular man used in this case for his purpose an unpopular institution. In 1838 the Poor Law Commission published a report calling attention to the vast burden thrown on the rates by sickness and epidemics, the result of sanitary conditions. The report contained some striking evidence about Whitechapel and Bethnal Green, given by three doctors, all of them famous either then or later—Southwood Smith, Arnott, and Kay. Chadwick suggested privately to Bishop Blomfield that he should ask in the House of Lords for a similar return for the whole of England. The request was granted. Chadwick set to work, and in 1842 the Poor Law Commission published his justly celebrated Report on the Sanitary Condition of the Labouring Population of Great Britain.

When Blomfield moved in the Lords, R. A. Slaney, one of the most useful and active of members, moved in the House of Commons, proposing the appointment of a Select Committee. This Committee, known as the Health of Towns Committee,

---

[1] Those who are interested in the development of the distinctive principles of English local government should study the paper read by Mr. Tom Taylor, chiefly known as the editor of *Punch*, for many years an able civil servant, to the Sanitary Science Congress in 1857. The struggle over centralisation was then proceeding, and Taylor's exposition of the relations of central to local government was singularly successful as a forecast.

[2] Lord Morpeth showed in his speech, House of Commons, May 5, 1848, that thirteen years after the passing of the Municipal Corporations Act there were only 95 towns in England in which the elected town council had any power to control sewage or paving, either by itself or jointly with Commissioners, and that there were 276 towns with a population of over 5000 inhabitants that were left so far as sanitation, streets, and water were concerned, to complete anarchy.

reported in June 1840. It recommended a general Building Act, a general Sewage Act, and the creation of a Board of Health in every town, with instructions to look after the water supply, burial grounds, open spaces, lodging-houses, and slums. Southwood Smith, who like Chadwick had been Bentham's private secretary, gave evidence before this Committee, and took steps to interest the new Home Secretary, Lord Normanby, in the cause of sanitary reform. A visit to the slums of East London made Normanby as ardent for reform as Southwood Smith himself, and he promptly introduced two Bills in the House of Lords, one for the regulation of buildings, and the other for the regulation of drainage, of a drastic and revolutionary character.[1] The second Bill was split up in committee into two Bills, the Drainage of Buildings Bill and the Borough Improvement Bill. These three Bills gave town councils the power to take land compulsorily, with an appeal to the Department of Woods and Forests, and provided for the appointment of surveyors and assistant surveyors by town councils and J.P.'s. The surveyor had to be notified before a building was begun. Houses were not to be built back to back, or below the level of the ground if without an area: no cellar was to be used as a dwelling without a window and fireplace and open area: houses were not to be built in close alleys, and streets were to be thirty feet wide when there was a carriage-way, and twenty feet wide in other cases. No house was to be built until the site was drained, and drains were to be constructed for houses already built. New streets were to be levelled under the direction of the Commissioners of Sewers.

There was little reported debate in the House of Lords. The only active opponent was Lyndhurst, who said on May 4, 1841, that he had not been on the select committee which examined the Bills, and that the discussion in the House of Lords had been inadequate. Normanby retorted that it was Lyndhurst's own fault that he had not attended the debates. One member proposed to exclude Birmingham, but for the most part the Bills received strong support. The Mayor and Burgesses of Leeds sent a petition in favour of the Drainage Bill.[2] Lord Ellenborough wished that the Bill had been more drastic. " They saw beside great wealth the greatest possible misery with no

---

[1] January 29, 1841.　　　　　　　　　　[2] February 12, 1841.

sort of connection between the classes so distinguished."[1] Normanby urged that the Bill should be passed as soon as possible, " because the profits derived from building tenements for the residence of the poor were so great that many speculators were at present employed in creating houses of an indifferent description."[2] On another occasion he pointed out that if the Bill which he was now moving had been passed thirty years earlier, " many of the present evils would not only not have attained their present alarming state but would never have existed at all."[1]

The Bills passed the Lords, but in May the Whig Government fell, and in the Election that followed they were defeated. Melbourne was succeeded by Peel as Prime Minister, a change for the better ; Normanby was succeeded by Sir James Graham as Home Secretary, a change for the worse.

Next year Normanby introduced his Bills again in the Lords (February 7, 1842), this time as a private member. Lord Salisbury offered some opposition, though he said he would withdraw it if Normanby would agree to send his Bills to a select committee, but Wellington gave Normanby his support and the Bills were read a third time in February. When the Bills were introduced in the House of Commons by Fox Maule on February 23, 1842, a debate followed, in the course of which Sir James Graham said that he objected to allowing town councils to mortgage the borough rate for improvements without limit, and that he intended to introduce a Bill himself. Still the Bills went to a select committee which took evidence from London, Liverpool, Manchester, and Leeds. As a result of this evidence the clause forbidding back-to-back houses disappeared.

This particular clause was supported by one witness only, a London engineer. The Liverpool witness said that the Liverpool town council had considered the proposal and rejected it on the ground of expense. The Manchester witnesses said that the clause would raise the cost of the cheapest house from £96 to £119, and of the third-class house, generally occupied by skilled artisans, from £141 to £179. The labouring classes lived in the main in back-to-back houses, covering sixteen superficial yards, for which they paid a rent of two to three shillings, the landlord paying all the rates and making repairs inside and out. Working men with large families took the double house,

---

[1] February 12, 1841.   [2] April 1, 1841.

being enabled to pay the rent by the earnings of their children and the rent they received from lodgers. The Town Clerk of Leeds was also opposed to the clause, contending that it would drive the working class into lodgings, but he held that it should be made compulsory to provide an open space of thirty or forty square yards at the end of every four or five cottages. House property was the favourite investment of small men in Leeds, and there were 1200 freeholders who had bought houses out of their savings. This evidence was too much for the Committee, and the proposal was abandoned.[1]

Normanby's Bills were reported to the House of Commons, but they were postponed in return for the promise of a Government Bill in the following year. Peel's Government decided, however, in 1843, not to introduce a Bill but to set up a Commission on the Health of Towns. This Commission, of which the Duke of Buccleuch was Chairman, contained among its members two active members of Parliament, R. A. Slaney and Lord Lincoln, and two distinguished men of science, Lyon Playfair and H. T. De la Beche. The Commission issued its first Report in the summer of 1844, and its second in the spring of 1845. The education of public opinion thus continued, and the local legislation of the next few years shows that the new ideas were making progress outside Parliament. Birkenhead, Nottingham, and Liverpool, all took action in the spirit of Normanby's proposals. The Birkenhead Improvement Com-

---

[1] Two years after Normanby's Committee had been warned by the Chairman of the Sewerage and Paving Committee of the Manchester Commissioners of Police that the cost was prohibitive, this reform was effected by a local Act, for Heron, the Town Clerk of Manchester, told the Sanitary Commission in 1869 that a local Act of 1844, requiring that every house should have a privy and ash-pit behind it, had put an end to the practice of building back-to-back houses. " The consequence of that legislation has been that in Manchester, since 1844, the building of back-to-back houses, which is one of the most crying nuisances that can be imagined, has been illegal " (Sanitary Commission, First Report, 1869, Heron's evidence, p. 144). In Bradford an attempt to bring about this reform by a similar method made in the early sixties was defeated by the speculative builders (*ibid.*, J. Rayner's evidence, p. 122, and Cudworth, *Historical Notes of Corporation of Bradford*, p. 145). Mr. Joseph Priestley has given a description of the Bradford back-to-back houses in *The Good Companions*: " the product of an ingenious architectural scheme that crammed four dwelling-houses into the space of two and enabled some past citizens to drive a carriage and pair and take their wives and daughters to the Paris Exhibition in 1867." The proposal to forbid the building of these houses by a general law was revived by Sir Benjamin Hall when President of the Board of Health in 1855. Hall said that he had received communications on the subject from Sunderland, Leicester, Coventry, and other places, and that some of the largest towns in the kingdom were in favour of this reform (House of Commons, January 23, 1855). But nothing came of the proposal, and these houses were not made illegal until 1909.

missioners obtained an Act in 1843,[1] which set aside a large area for a park for public recreation, forbade the building of houses in close courts, regulated the size of rooms and the number of windows, compelled owners of houses to supply privies, and provided that streets should be twenty-four feet wide where there was a carriage-way, and eighteen where there was not. At Nottingham an Inclosure Act of 1845, enclosing 1069 acres, set apart 130 for recreation, and laid down strict rules for the development of the rest of the area. The streets were to be thirty-six feet wide, alleys and courts twenty feet, and buildings were not to be higher than the width of the streets. Each house was to have a separate privy, and a yard or garden thirty feet long. No dwelling-house was to adjoin another building on more than two sides; no room without a fireplace or proper ventilation was to be used as a workshop or bedroom; every house was to have three bedrooms of certain fixed dimensions. Cesspools were never to be within ten feet of a house.[2] Liverpool, having obtained an Act in 1842, proceeded to amend it by a much more drastic Act in 1846.[3] This Act made regulations about houses, courts, and cellars; provided for "effectually sewering and draining the borough," laid it down that no cellars under any house in a court were to be let as dwellings, that no houses were to be erected without drains, and that every new street should be at least thirty feet wide. An interesting feature of this Act was the clause providing for the appointment of a duly qualified medical practitioner as Medical Officer of Health. The first doctor to hold the office was W. H. Duncan, Physician to the Liverpool Infirmary, who had already laid the foundations of his fame as a sanitary reformer and a great public servant.

In 1844 the Health of Towns Commission published its first Report. This Report was largely the work of Chadwick. Fifty large towns had been surveyed. In forty-two the drainage, and in thirty-one the water supply, was decidedly bad; there were only six in which the water supply was good, and scarcely

---

[1] 6 and 7 Vict. cap. xiii., Local.

[2] 8 and 9 Vict. cap. vii., Private. The Nottingham Act broke down in some respects in practice, owing to overcrowding in the new houses, but the effect of these regulations was seen in the death-rate of this district in 1872, 20·9 per 1000 as compared with a death-rate of 31·2 in the old town. See Report on Sanitary Condition of Nottingham by Edward Seaton, M.O.H., 1873, in Nottingham Library.

[3] 9 and 10 Vict. cap. cxxvii., Local.

one in which the drainage was good. Next year the Commissioners made their recommendations. It was essential, they argued, that the responsibility now divided between different local bodies for paving, draining, cleansing the streets, and supplying water should be concentrated in the hands of a single authority : that those authorities should have additional powers and their districts be made co-extensive with the natural areas for drainage. But their most novel suggestion was the proposal that the Crown should have power to inspect and supervise the work of the local authorities. The *Times* had attacked Normanby's Bill in February 1841 as " the reckless and wanton invasion of property and liberty," but from this time onwards it was a powerful and steadfast friend to the cause of public health.[1] It gave a warm support to the report of the Commissioners, and a general support to the Bill based on its Report introduced by Lord Lincoln in 1845. Lincoln explained that the Government did not propose to proceed with the Bill that year, but had introduced it to give the opportunity for discussion in the recess.

Lincoln's Bill made the Home Office the central department, and gave the Home Secretary power to appoint inspectors whose duty it would be to hold local inquiries and prepare plans for boundaries mapping out England into districts. Local authorities were to be elected for these areas by ratepayers with a property qualification, but in corporate towns a certain number of Commissioners were to be elected from the town council, and a certain number from the borough magistrates. The Bill excited some opposition from the local authorities.[2] It received a general but discriminating support from the Health of Towns Association, an educational and propagandist body formed by Southwood Smith, of which Normanby, Ashley, Tooke, and Joseph Toynbee were active members. Next year politics were thrown into confusion by the crisis over the Repeal of the Corn Laws. The Conservative party was broken up; Peel resigned in June 1846, and Lincoln's Bill made no further progress. Parliament, however, passed two useful

[1] Delane became editor in May 1841.
[2] The *Times* on September 4 published an extract from the *Morning Advertiser* to the effect that Manchester was opposed to the Bill and was calling on the parochial and corporate bodies to join in resistance. The *Manchester Guardian* disliked the proposal to set up new local authorities instead of using those already in existence.

measures : one, the Baths and Wash-houses Act,[1] which authorised borough councils to establish baths and wash-houses out
of the rates; the other the Nuisance Removal Act. The second
was passed as a temporary Act, but it was afterwards made
permanent.

On Peel's fall, Lord John Russell became Prime Minister for
the first time. Events had thus brought back the Whigs to
power, and though Normanby had left politics to become
Ambassador in Paris, it was known that sanitary reform would
be one of their principal measures. The *Leeds Intelligencer*
published an enthusiastic article on the prospects of reform.
" This species of legislation on so vast and comprehensive a
scale is novel and as grand as it is novel. We know of nothing
which so much marks the kind of enlightened relations that are
springing up in society as this interference by the State on behalf
of the health and physical well-being of our industrial classes.
Hitherto public cleanliness in our great towns and cities has been
an aristocratic appendage and an elegant luxury. The legislation
announced last session and about to be executed in this, has laid
down the principle that the health, cleanliness, and purity of the
poor man's street and dwelling just as much as the rich man's
are to be a primary concern of the State. This is true democracy. Let restless, shallow-headed Brights chatter as they
will about democratic reforms." [2]

Unhappily these hopes were in part disappointed, for the
Reform movement took at one point a wrong turn, and the cause
of public health suffered in consequence.

It is not surprising that a study of the conditions revealed in
the Reports of the Health of Towns Commission had impressed
politicians with the negligence of the local authorities. The
government of the towns was largely in the hands of men with
limited horizons : men chiefly concerned for economy and un-
inspired by large or generous ambitions. This class predominated among electors and elected. In some cases the
obstacles to reform were even more serious, for it happened
sometimes that the men who were put in charge of the health
of the town were themselves interested in the maintenance of

---

[1] 9 and 10 Vict. cap. 74. See *Bolton Chronicle* of July 5, 1848, for an illustration
of the great usefulness of this Act. Maximum charges were fixed, 1d. for a cold bath,
2d. for a hot bath, and 1d. an hour for the use of the wash-house.
[2] December 26, 1846.

abuses.[1]   But Parliament was itself a good deal to blame.   The Municipal Corporations Act was an unimaginative measure little calculated to fire ambition or public spirit, and withholding power that the local authorities needed for effective action. The blame that now fell on the town councils was in some cases due to the select bodies that survived in the form of Improvement Commissioners, and there was some truth in the contention of the town councils that they had never had a fair chance.   It was clearly desirable, therefore, that the statesman who wished to introduce some measure of control or guidance from the centre should avoid any unnecessary collision with local sentiment.

Lord Lincoln had proposed, in his 1845 Bill, that the Home Office should act as a central department.   The Health of Towns Association had objected, in an unfortunate moment, that the Home Office had a great deal on its hands already and that this new task needed a new authority.   In this suggestion there lurked a danger.   For sanitary reformers were tempted to look for a precedent to the Poor Law Commission.[2]   In that case, they reflected, a special body exercising special powers had rescued a nation from scandals that had grown up under the lax administration of local authorities.   The old Poor Law authorities had been negligent, incompetent, and sometimes corrupt : they had been put on one side by a board of energetic men armed by Parliament with exceptional means of interference. The sanitary authorities where they existed were negligent, incompetent, and sometimes corrupt.   Why should not the same remedy be applied ?   The *Leeds Intelligencer* had suggested in December 1846 that Parliament should set up a Ministry of Health.   Lord Morpeth, the Commissioner of Woods and Forests in the new Government, the Minister in charge of this reform, proposed instead to set up a Board resembling the Poor Law Commission in its structure and also in its relation to Parliament.   This Board was not to be an ordinary Department under the care and orders of a Minister responsible to Parliament, but a body of Commissioners, of equal authority, with a Minister sitting at the table as an ordinary member.

[1] See speech of W. J. Fox, House of Commons, March 10, 1859.
[2] Normanby had suggested this model in an otherwise admirable speech in the House of Lords on July 26, 1844.

In the Bill as introduced on March 30, 1847, this body was given large powers both of initiating and superintending sanitary reform. It could hold a local inquiry, define a district and set up a public health authority for that district. The boundaries of a town could be extended if necessary. In the corporate towns the town council would act as the local authority: in non-corporate towns local Commissioners would be appointed, partly by the Crown and partly by the ratepayers. These local bodies would appoint local surveyors and inspectors of nuisances: they would look after the streets, drainage, building regulations, nuisances like those of smoke, slaughter-houses, and cemeteries: they would have the power to construct waterworks and gas-works. For the expenses of permanent works they would have power to borrow money and recover the principal and interest by moderate instalments, not from the owner but from the occupier. " In this manner we hope we shall remove what we consider to be the chief obstacle to improvements in towns, which is the opposition of owners to what they consider the serious expense attending them." [1] The Board was to have a general superintending power.

Lincoln criticised the scheme on the ground that it gave too much power to the central authority, and that town councils, being political in character, could not safely be given control over surrounding areas. Hume and Brotherton were favourable, but Morpeth soon found that he could not hope to hold his own against all the powerful interests that were threatened, or thought themselves to be threatened, by his Bill. The land-owners, whose opposition he had hoped to disarm, resisted his Bill from first to last.[2] Their spokesmen complained that land-owners in the neighbourhood might have to pay for draining a town. Morpeth said that the landowners were not affected. Brotherton administered a sharp rebuke. " Hon. members

---

[1] Morpeth, House of Commons, March 30, 1847.

[2] The *Times* called the Bill " the object of singular Protectionist aversion."—July 3, 1847. Dickens composed a petition for such objectors. " The taxation for the purpose of draining and ameliorating such would fall most unjustly and oppressively on your memorialists, whose manor house, lawns, pleasure grounds, arable lands, and pasture grounds could neither directly nor indirectly derive any benefit whatever from the purpose for which such hereditaments and tenements would be rated in pursuance of the powers of the Public Health Act.—Crotch, *Charles Dickens as Social Reformer*, p. 103.

connected with those districts were very sensitive ; but he could tell them that in the suburbs of large towns, landowners had derived great advantages from the industry of their neighbours, and he knew cases where landowners had their income advanced from £5000 to £20,000 a year, without doing a single thing to promote the welfare of the inhabitants by whom they were so much benefited." [1]   The various vested interests, water companies, gas companies, burial companies, and others, offered so effective a resistance that many of the clauses relating to these subjects were completely remodelled.[2]   The more general fears of property and business found an appropriate representative in Hudson, the railway king, member of Parliament for Sunderland and Lord Mayor of York.   More than once he drew upon himself the fire of the *Times*.   " The Honourable Member for Sunderland, to do him justice, is a perfectly consistent legislator. From one simple rule he has never deviated since the day when his splendid promises prevailed with the electors of that borough. He denounces everything whatever except railways . . . railways are both medicine and meat. . . . In the present increase of private speculation, conducted, of course, on the most private principles, it becomes the more necessary for the State to provide that the interests of the public shall not be thrust into a corner. Railways are made to pay, and Mr. Hudson himself understands how to carry out that principle with the most offensive rigour." [3] Morpeth hoped at first to save his Bill by making large concessions.   He began by dropping London.[4]   He limited the Bill to corporate towns, allowing non-corporate towns to come

[1] House of Commons, June 18, 1847.

[2] In 1842 a deputation had waited on Graham to object to Normanby's Bill, which included " gentlemen who had invested money in burial grounds, who described the hardships the Bill would inflict on Dissenters."—*Times*, December 23, 1842.   In Morpeth's original Bill the local Boards were given power to construct waterworks and gas-works, but clauses were inserted to compel them to contract with any existing companies.

[3] July 2, 1847.   The *Times* had called attention more than once to the disturbance caused by railway extension, and had demanded that the railway companies should be compelled to re-house the poor who were evicted.   See *Times*, November 11, 1845. For an illustration of such disturbances, see Inquiry into the Condition of the Poor of Newcastle-upon-Tyne, published by the *Newcastle Chronicle*, 1850, pp. 23 and 48.

[4] " Our metropolis," said the *Times* in a bitter comment, " the greatest and wealthiest in the world, consigns to pestilential air and bad drainage more than a moiety of its two million inhabitants, and offers far less means of useful instruction and innocent recreation than many a third-class capital."—July 22, 1847.

After dropping London, the Government set up a Royal Commission of Inquiry for the Metropolis in the autumn of 1847.   This Commission recommended the consolidation of the several Sewers Commissions into one body with additional statutory

under the Act on petition; he agreed that all local Commissioners should be elected by the ratepayers and none by the Crown; he took the sting, and, as some critics said, the virtue, out of the clauses about gas and water. Yet he had in the summer to abandon his Bill. But the year was not wasted, for several Acts were passed, consolidating clauses generally found in local Improvement Bills, in order to cheapen and simplify local legislation. A town authority, wishing to obtain powers for providing gas, water, and other improvements, could incorporate all or any of these clauses in its own Act, thereby saving itself trouble and expense.[1]

Morpeth returned to his task early in the following year, introducing his new Bill on February 10, 1848. The Bill differed in some respects from its predecessor, but the creation of a central board on the model of the Poor Law Commission was the most important feature of the new Bill as it had been of the old. London was excluded. Boundaries were not enlarged to suit the natural areas of drainage, but the ratepayers in districts outside the towns were in such cases to elect representatives to sit with town councils. In non-corporate towns ratepayers were to elect local boards. Certain duties were to be obligatory. Local boards were to compel owners or occupiers to provide house drains, to see that there was a sufficient supply of water, to appoint a surveyor and inspector of nuisances. Other duties were permissive. The local authority might make by-laws about the removal of filth : they might alter sewers, pave streets, provide places for public recreation, and appoint an officer of health. " If this bill will not do," said the *Times*, " what will ? . . . Unless objectors are prepared with some positive measures of their own, we really think they had better hold their peace and have done with it." [2] The objectors were not disposed to follow this advice.

The feature of the Bill which provoked the most general criticism was the proposal to establish a central authority with

powers. An Act was passed on these lines in 1848, a separate Act being passed for the City of London in the same session.—Simon, *English Sanitary Institutions*, p. 206.

[1] *E.g.* 10 and 11 Vict. cap. 15 (gasworks), cap. 17 (waterworks), and cap. 34 (paving, draining, cleansing, lighting and improving). Such use of model clauses was recommended by Hume. The first of such Acts, nine of which related to public health, was passed in 1845. See Redlich and Hirst, *Local Government in England*, p. 139.

[2] February 11, 1848.

the power both of initiating and superintending reform.   This was represented as a French principle foreign to English tradition and obnoxious to English sentiment.   These objections were pressed in Parliament by a member who was under no suspicion of speaking for any vested interest, Urquhart, an interesting and romantic figure in the politics of the time, and they were pressed outside Parliament by the historian Toulmin Smith.   The *Times* replied to these arguments that centralisation and government patronage were evils, but that in this case the alternative was worse.   " A town of manufacturers and speculators is apt to leave the poor to shift for themselves, to stew in cellars and garrets, nor are landlords and farmers [1] apt to care much for cottages. . . . Something of a central authority is necessary to wrestle with the selfishness of wealth." [2]

But whatever the virtues or defects of central authorities, it is clear that the particular form of centralisation adopted, the setting up of a central board composed on the provocative model of the Poor Law Commission, was a lamentable blunder. It roused the determined opposition of town councils.   The Bill did not spare their dignity, and it brought their delegates to London in hot haste to denounce it as intolerable tyranny.   The hostility to the Bill found its most uncompromising expression in the *Leeds Mercury*, which went so far as to withdraw its support from Lord Morpeth when he appeared as a candidate for the West Riding in the autumn of the year.   " What populous and enlightened towns," it wrote, " like Bradford, Halifax, Huddersfield, Wakefield, and a score of others in the manufacturing district round us want, is simple and efficient means for attending to their own sanitary regulation." [3]   In the

---

[1] " There is one difficulty which suggests itself to me, and that is that in the rural districts the farmers who are most interested in the district and the roads are generally the people most opposed to all sanitary improvements."—Tom Taylor's Evidence, Royal Sanitary Commission, 1869, First Report, p. 16.

[2] The *Times*, May 9, 1848.

[3] March 4, 1848.   At this very time the news columns of the paper reported that in Bradford, one of these " populous and enlightened towns," butchers were in the habit of slaughtering sheep and calves in the doorways of their shops.   On August 17 Doctor McTurk wrote a long letter to the *Bradford Observer* describing the dreadful state of the streets of Bradford and the imminent danger of cholera.   In October of that year the streets surveyor reported to the Town Council that there existed in all directions masses of filth from which the most foul stenches were constantly expelled, producing disease and wretchedness on every hand.—*Bradford Observer*, October 12. In the next twelve months there were 420 deaths from cholera in Bradford.—Cudworth, *op. cit.* p. 118.

same article the editor referred to Leeds as " this borough in which so much has been done and projected for the public health." [1] Nor was the *Leeds Mercury* concerned only for the rights and dignities of the large towns. " We disapprove of opposition on behalf of existing corporate towns only : it would abandon every non-corporate place to the mercy of the framers of the Bill."

But even the opposition of the town councils to the Bill revealed the existence of a local demand for some sort of reform. A great deal had been done by the propaganda of bodies like the Health of Towns Association, by the pressure of parsons and doctors, and in some towns by working-class associations, to create alarm and indignation about the state of the towns. Hence even the town councils, whether from conviction or fear, did not adopt a purely destructive tone. The Bradford town council, for example, rejected a proposal to send an angry petition merely condemning the Bill, adopting instead a petition which, whilst hostile to the scheme of the Bill, admitted the need of strong measures.[2] The Mayor of Leeds published an alternative scheme which would have given a central board certain limited powers of inspection. The Mayor of Bolton, while denouncing the Government proposals, proceeded to obtain and to publish a detailed report on the condition of Bolton from the Secretary of the Mechanics Institute, which was full of the most dreadful revelations. All these authorities, in fact, though thrown into violent opposition by Morpeth's proposal, recognised the necessity for action.

The strength of the demand for reform is shown also by a study of the local press. In each of the protesting towns important local papers defended the Bill, some in its most drastic form, some urging certain modifications. Thus the *Manchester Guardian*, while agreeing with the Manchester town council that the new authority was given too detailed a control, held strongly that some control was needed. The spokesman of the Manchester town council had argued that the new Bill did nothing for Manchester that was not already done under the

---

[1] In Leeds the author of the important statistical Report published by the first town council in 1839, addressed an Oddfellows meeting in support of Morpeth's Bill, at which he said that he hoped this would be the last occasion in which he would have to expose the disgraceful state of Leeds.

[2] *Bradford Observer*, March 9, 1848.

Manchester Improvement Act. The *Manchester Guardian* commented dryly that "In practice the effect would be the making of private drains the general rule, not as now the rather rare exception." The news columns of the paper gave, indeed, ample justification for the tone of the leading articles. On September 13, the Public Accountant reported that nearly one-third of the ash-pits in the borough were in a condition dangerous to health in consequence of a reduction of the scavenging force. A few weeks later, the chairman of one of the committees of the town council explained that he was going to save the rates £4000 a year by reverting to the old practice of hand-sweeping in the streets, though, as the *Manchester Guardian* pointed out, the condition of the Manchester streets when that method was in force had been notorious. The *Birmingham Journal* too, in spite of the opposition of the town council, gave the strongest support to the Bill, arguing that the expense of all the necessary sanitary provision for the poorer classes would be defrayed by a rate not exceeding 4d. per week per house, but that unless the superintending power of the central authority was preserved, the Bill would be inoperative.[1] The *Leeds Intelligencer* was so much impressed by the filth and squalor of the streets of Leeds, that it welcomed the proposal to give a central body far-reaching powers. The *Bradford Observer*, though supporting the petition of the town council, made it clear that it would prefer the Bill with its imperfections to no Bill at all, and when the opponents of the Bill were hopeful of defeating it, the *Observer* rallied to its defence, pointing to the Bradford death-rate. The average age of death at Pateley Bridge was thirty-six, and at Bradford it was twenty, but the middle classes lived as long in Bradford as in Pateley Bridge. It was the Bradford poor who made this startling difference. The defeat of the Bill would mean "That the poor victims of our dirty lanes and false patriotism would be left to fester and die."[2] The *Bolton Chronicle*, too, published a whole series of articles on the revelations of the report on the state of the town: "For abundant dirt, for lack of drainage, for crowded and disgusting homes, for the numbers sweltering amidst noxious airs and poisonous gases, for pestilential nuisances, for defective sewerage and complete absence of all sanitary arrangements, properly so-called, we can justly claim, if we do

[1] February 12 and May 20, 1848.   [2] April 17, 1848.

not bear away, the palm. There may be other towns as bad in these respects, but can anybody point us out a worse ? " [1]

Morpeth's Bill, then, in its early form, though it provoked organised opposition from town councils, received a considerable amount of local support. The next stage in the proceedings was described twenty years later by one of the actors. Several representatives of local authorities met in London to put their objections to the Bill, and as a result of negotiations Morpeth allowed the Town Clerk of Manchester together with Brotherton and Beckett, M.P. for Leeds, to confer with the draughtsmen of the Bill and to help to remodel it. [2] In this process the general superintending power of the new department disappeared. Lord Lincoln, who had criticised the Bill as giving too great a control to the central authority, argued justly that this concession went too far in the other direction. The *Manchester Guardian* also regretted the disappearance of this provision, reminding the rulers of Manchester in a sharp sentence that the proposal to create a central authority was not a spontaneous fantasy of Lord Morpeth's imagination. " The measure brought forward has been rendered necessary and has been imposed on the Government through the inability or the unwillingness of the local authorities to accomplish the desired end by placing our towns in a tolerable sanitary state. Had these shown themselves capable of accomplishing the work, it would no doubt have been willingly left to them by the legislature." [3] The *Leeds Intelligencer* was not less distressed, denouncing what it called the mutilation of the Bill, and arguing that in places like Leeds which had a bad local Improvement Act, little or nothing would be done. [4] Even after these large concessions had been made, the Bill struggled with great difficulty on to the Statute Book. Disraeli said that it owed its success to Morpeth's great personal popularity. [5]

[1] July 1, 1848.
[2] First Report of Royal Sanitary Commission, 1869, Heron's evidence, p. 130. The Mayor of Leeds published a letter in the *Leeds Mercury* of March 11, 1848, proposing an alternative scheme. Let the Government pass a model Bill and allow a certain proportion of the inhabitants to ask for the Bill to be adopted. If the Bill were adopted, the same proportion of inhabitants might have the right to complain to a central authority that the Act was not properly carried out. The Central Board would thus constitute the Board of Advice and Appeal.
[3] May 20, 1848.   [4] April 15 and July 15, 1848.
[5] House of Commons, August 30, 1848. Disraeli spoke of " those qualities which

The Public Health Act of 1848 [1] set up for five years a Central Board of Health, consisting of three members, one of them *ex-officio* the Commissioner of Woods and Forests. It provided also for the creation of local Boards of Health, who were to be endowed with certain powers and charged with certain duties. In a municipal borough the Board of Health was to be the town council, elsewhere it was to be a special Board elected by the ratepayers on the same plan as the Boards of Guardians. A town council might adopt the Act, in which case it could exercise these powers without the expense of a special local Act. But the Central Board, in certain circumstances, might take action in places where the Act was not adopted. If the death-rate in any place exceeded 23 per 1000, or if 10 per cent. of the inhabitants asked for it, the Central Board might hold an inquiry and create a local Board of Health district and a local Board of Health. In such a case the Act might be forced on a local authority that did not want it. A town council might be converted into a Board of Health against its will.

An Act which gave just so much power and no more was ill-contrived for its purpose, and it was made worse by the choice of the Board to execute it. It is difficult to understand how Ministers, painfully aware as they must have been of the atmosphere of resentment and suspicion in which the Act was received, came to choose the most hated man in England as a member of the Board. For Chadwick, who would have been excellent if you wanted to make a popular law odious, was expected in this case to make an obnoxious law attractive. Whatever chance the Act had of success was thrown away, when the Government announced that the new Board would consist of Lord Morpeth, Lord Ashley, and Edwin Chadwick.

The defects of the Act became very plain during the lifetime of the Board. The Act enabled the Board to force the hand of a reluctant local authority but not to compel that authority to take any effective action. It was indeed less likely, rather than more likely, that a sullen authority would carry out a measure thrust upon it. The Central Board had no power of super-

---

have rendered him deservedly one of the most popular men in this House and in this country."

[1] 11 and 12 Vict. cap. 63.

intendence or inspection, and the local authority was in no mood to take guidance from an authority whose powers it resented.[1] If a local authority chose to neglect its duty it could defy the Board of Health.   The extreme case was that of New-castle.   An outbreak of cholera in Newcastle led the Govern-ment to send a Commission of Enquiry in January 1854.   This Commission reported that the filthy condition of that town (of which Palmerston once said that the account of it made a civilised man shudder) was due to nuisances which the Corpora-tion had the power but not the will to suppress, and that there were some members of the town council to whom these nuisances were a source of profit.[2]   The Board of Health was powerless.

The defects of the Board were also apparent.   After making an admirable report on the water supply and the burial arrange-ments of London, both of them in a scandalous condition, they proceeded to recommend that the duty and power of burying the dead and providing drainage and water for the metropolis should be assigned to the central authority.   A Bill designed on this extraordinary basis was passed in 1850, but it was of course unworkable, and it was repealed in 1852.[3]   The *Times*, reviewing this ambitious scheme when the Board fell, reminded Chadwick that the Jupiter of antiquity had been a modest person, for he had been content with the sky, leaving the sea to Neptune and the infernal regions to Pluto.[4]   Such proposals justified the suspicion with which local authorities had watched the creation of this Board.   Its reports proved the neces-sity of reforms, but its proposals embarrassed their execution.

The Board lasted six years, and, as has been seen, it made many of the mistakes to be expected from Chadwick's want of judgment and want of tact.   But its career marks an important stage in the history of public health.   The Act was adopted in

---

[1] One of the inspectors under the Act told the Royal Sanitary Commission in 1869 that in cases of which he had had experience the Act had remained a dead-letter when it had been forced upon any local authority.—First Report, p. 41.

[2] See the speech of Sir Benjamin Hall, the President of the Board of Health, House of Commons, January 23, 1855.   He attempted to turn the feeling excited by this report to account, and he inserted a clause in his Nuisance Removal Bill giving the magistrates power to proceed against a negligent local authority.   The Town Clerk of Manchester protested against this provision, arguing that any such power should be given to a central authority rather than to the magistrates.   The clause was dropped, and it was not till 1866 that power was taken to coerce the recalcitrant authority.—Select Committee, Public Health and Nuisance Bills, 1854-55.

[3] Simon, *op. cit.* p. 220.   [4] August 1, 1854.

some 200 places. A separate local Act would have cost each of these places about £2000.[1] These places included several of the growing industrial towns where sanitary measures were specially needed, such as Bolton, Bradford, Hartlepool, Merthyr Tydvil, Preston, Sunderland, Wakefield, Wigan, and Wolverhampton. The Report of the Board reviewing its career showed that at Preston, Lancaster, Wigan, and other places the Board had given help and expert advice about water and drainage, and that it had sanctioned applications to mortgage the rates for improvements for sums amounting altogether to over a million. Incidentally also the Act was the cause of improvements in towns where it was not adopted, for Leeds and Birmingham and other large towns, wishing to keep out the Board, promoted Bills of their own. Birmingham spent £10,000 in this way rather than accept the general Act. Newcastle also adopted an Act, but treated its own Act with as little respect as if it had been Chadwick's.[2]

The Board also deserves credit for two Housing Acts passed in 1851,[3] one of them described by Dickens as the best measure ever passed in Parliament. This Act made compulsory the licensing and inspection of all common lodging-houses. The other Act, which empowered local authorities to raise a rate and build lodging-houses, was a dead-letter from the first. Shaftesbury carried both Bills through Parliament, and he brought before the House of Lords the hardships and overcrowding caused by improvement and railway schemes. A Committee was appointed at his instance, but nothing came of its recommendations.

The Board lasted till 1854, when the House of Commons got rid of it. The Government tried to save the Board by dropping Chadwick and putting the Board under the Home Office. These concessions did not avail, and the Board was extinguished by 74 votes to 65. The place of this anomalous department

[1] The applications for the Public Health Act were 19 in 1849, 66 in 1850, 36 in 1851, 57 in 1852, 20 in 1853, and 9 in 1854. Sir Benjamin Hall argued that the declining figures showed that there was something wrong with the Act.—January 23, 1855.
[2] Royal Sanitary Commission, 1869, First Report, Rawlinson's evidence, p. 41, and Hall's speech, House of Commons, January 23, 1855: " In the words of the Town Surveyor, the Local Acts have been a dead-letter altogether." There were three Local Acts, 1837, 1846, and 1853. See An Inquiry into the Condition of the Poor of Newcastle-upon-Tyne, published by the *Newcastle Chronicle*, 1850, pp. 60-68.
[3] 14 and 15 Vict. caps. 28 and 34.

was taken by a Board of Ministers with a paid president.[1] This new department retained until 1858 the powers vested in the old Board, but it was now in the hands of Sir Benjamin Hall, a reformer but a keen critic of Chadwick, who was under no suspicion of wishing to limit or discourage local autonomy. Hall put an end to a bad method of employing his staff, which had added to the unpopularity of his predecessors. He made the engineers employed by the department its full-time servants, removed altogether from private practice.

The long struggle to make her town life healthy and decent, in which England has been engaged ever since the Industrial Revolution, took a definite character at this time. The Improvement Commissioners set up by eighteenth-century practice had tried to make town life healthy and decent for the richer classes. In the thirties Chadwick inaugurated a new and more ambitious effort, the effort to make town life healthy and tolerable for all classes. However unhappy his plans, he deserves the utmost credit for that bold initiative.

We can see to-day that of all the tasks set to the English people at that time none was more pressing than this. Unfortunately other tasks and other interests attracted the main strength of the wealth, the statesmanship, and the energy of the nation. For England was as mad about railways in the forties as she had been, in Boulton's phrase, about steam mills in the twenties. When few of her towns had sewers or water, paved or lighted streets, Railway Bills were passed through Parliament authorising the raising of over three hundred million pounds.[2] The *Times*, which fought a gallant battle against this waste of power, remarked that Macaulay's New Zealander would find that England had brought herself to the verge of bankruptcy by building viaducts at a moment when three hundred streets in a rich district of the metropolis were without a sewer.[3]

---

[1] " When Mr. Chadwick had succeeded in getting the Poor Law Board into as much discredit as the Board of Health suffers from now, the remedy was found in making the Poor Law Board a parliamentary department and placing at its head a person of sense and moderation. Responsibility being direct and undivided, all difficulty ceased and the voice of complaint, once so frequent, is now seldom heard. Why should not we apply to the department which Mr. Chadwick has just ruined the same remedy as to the one he ruined last? Give the Board of Health back to the Commissioner of Works, make him responsible for its actions, and give him the power of directing that action without which such responsibility would be unjust."—*Times*, July 11, 1854.

[2] *Times*, November 19, 1848.

[3] November 17, 1847. Sir E. T. Cook remarked in his Life of that famous editor,

Bradford, with 100,000 people, started to attack her disgraceful squalor by spending something like £3000 a year.[1] Property owners still preferred dirt to expenditure. The *Times* warned these economists that they would lose in the end : " The rates paid by the rich are regulated by the sickness to which they abandon the poor.   Twenty pounds expended in the sewerage of a blind alley would save fifty pounds to be otherwise raised by the overseers of the poor." [2]   There were moments when the scare of cholera brought this argument home, but in normal times it made little impression.   The scale of values represented by the large investment in railways and the reluctance to spend anything on the English town, meant that the average rich man believed in the remedy of the Industrial Revolution, and held that if enterprise were encouraged, this new town population could be safely left to itself.   As late as 1848, it was argued in the House of Commons that property was in danger from the proposal to allow a town council to make a park.[3]

The politics of the age reflected this atmosphere.   Mr. Temperley has said that as you watch Gladstone making up the nation's accounts as neatly as a grocer, you can see the spirit of the age fashioning greatness in its pattern.[4]   This age produced half a dozen of the most eloquent and the most persuasive speakers that have ever engaged in English politics.   Nobody who studied the masterpieces of this art, whether he turned to Palmerston or Cobden, to Peel or Bright, to Gladstone or Disraeli, would have any idea of the battle that was raging at this time between health and disease, between life and death, in the English towns.   Other questions filled the minds of the great orators who could make what seemed important to them-

that Delane deliberately sacrificed a great deal of advertisement revenue when he attacked the disastrous railway speculation of the time.

[1] *Bradford Observer*, January 15, 1848.

[2] November 17, 1848.   " The great plague of London will be revived and naturalised for the sake of saving half as many pounds as are found readily forthcoming for a German mine or French railway."—*Times*, September 14, 1848.

[3] See *Bradford Observer*, May 25, 1848.   It is interesting to see from an elaborate Report prepared by Goschen when President of the Poor Law Board in 1870, that the local rates went up between 1815 and 1868 from eight or nine millions to sixteen or seventeen ;   that five and a half millions of this increase represented expenditure for improvements under the legislation of the forties and later ; that the amount levied for rates had increased in Lancashire by 184 per cent., and in the West Riding by 64 per cent., whilst, on the other hand, the rateable value of Lancashire had increased by 247 per cent., and that of the West Riding by 146 per cent.

[4] *Victorian Age in Politics*, p. 67.

selves seem important to the nation.[1] A public man, conscious of power and principle, setting out on a career in politics, would dream in the flights of his ambition of the office of Chancellor of the Exchequer, or Secretary of State for Foreign Affairs ; the offices concerned with the English towns were regarded as the lesser duties of Government, departments which a man would enter by one door and leave by another for some more attractive or distinguished appointment. "It was of course to be expected," said the *Times*, "that the tenacious spirit of ' protection ' would fight every inch of ground, and surrender no vested interest even in the foulest filth without a struggle. But we are not to be persuaded that stench and smoke could have preserved that which corn and sugar lost, if they had but been attacked with half the same determination."[2] The attack on dirt, disease, and death was carried on in an atmosphere in which men were thinking all the time of other things. Governments with the Health of Towns Reports before them never dreamed of making grants for public health. The utmost they would do was to lend money at 5 per cent., repayable first in thirty and then in twenty years.[3]

Two orators at different times did for the English towns what Peel and Cobden did for Free Trade. One was cholera, the other was the cotton famine. The Town Improvements of the forties followed the cholera scare : in the sixties the Government met the distress into which the cotton famine threw Lancashire by granting loans for Public Works at $3\frac{1}{2}$ per cent., under two Acts passed in 1862 and 1863, and Villiers the President of the Poor Law Board issued an admirable circular, calling attention to the great need of improvements in the Lancashire towns, the want of sewers and drains, of parks and gardens, and of good supplies of water. In two years nearly two millions were spent on these purposes.[4]

[1] We get a good illustration of the position Public Health occupied in the estimation of statesmen as a political question of the time in the correspondence between Cobden and Peel in June 1846, reviewing the situation, in which the subject is never mentioned. —Morley, *Life of Cobden*, vol. i. p. 390, etc. Although the *Annual Register* devoted to the proceedings of Parliament 259 pages in 1847 and 194 pages in 1848, the debates on the Public Health Bills are ignored.   [2] November 17, 1847.

[3] The amount of money borrowed in ten years between 1848 and 1858 was just under three millions.—Tom Taylor's evidence, Royal Sanitary Commission, 1869, First Report, p. 25.

[4] Bolton and Oldham supplied themselves with public parks ; Blackburn, Accrington, Stockport, and other towns made great improvements. See Sanitary Commission, First Report, Rawlinson's evidence.

Pushing gallantly against great difficulties, a few men like Chadwick, Slaney, Bishop Blomfield, Normanby, Lincoln, Ashley, Morpeth, Toynbee, and Hume, with the powerful help of Delane and Dickens, taught the nation, however slowly, the lesson of the Chartist agitation.   The Acts that they put on the Statute Book between 1845 and 1854 showed that Parliament had become aware of a problem to which the statesmen of the thirties had been blind.   In the thirties the English town was a raw settlement, where men and women lived as men and women live on a gold-field.   Twenty years later some of these towns were busy paving and draining their neglected streets, and a few of them were building libraries and making public parks.

CHAPTER XVII

THE BEGINNINGS OF POPULAR CULTURE

THE School Inspectors' Reports are depressing reading, and it might seem that the ordinary boys and girls, with their short school life, had little chance of carrying away the ability to read any kind of literature with enjoyment. And yet a passion for reading was a marked feature of the late thirties and the forties, and a flood of cheap periodical literature was produced specially adapted to the tastes of the working classes.

In 1836, a witness before the Select Committee on Arts and Principles of Design (p. 50), described how his firm, with their steam printing machines, produced the *Penny Magazine*, the *Saturday Magazine*, and *Chambers's Journal*. "And every Saturday," he said, " I have the satisfaction of reflecting that 360,000 copies of these useful publications are issued to the public, diffusing science and taste and good feeling, without one sentence of an immoral tendency in the whole." *Chambers's Edinburgh Journal*, as it was at first called, was the earliest, and certainly the best, of these cheap weekly periodicals. It was started by William and Robert Chambers, the well-known educational publishers and writers, in February 1832, and aimed at satisfying what they called the " universal appetite for instruction." " The people of Great Britain and Ireland," said the opening article, " have never yet been properly cared for, in the way of presenting knowledge, under its most cheering and captivating aspect, to their immediate observation." The paper, which cost only $1\frac{1}{2}$d., consisted of eight big pages containing simple, but not patronising, articles on literary, historical, or scientific subjects, accounts of foreign countries being specially prominent; and every week there was one short story. " I shall make a point," wrote the editor, " of giving them every week, if I can find room, a nice amusing tale, either original, or selected from the best modern authors—no ordinary trash about

314

Italian castles, and daggers, and ghosts in the blue chamber, and similar nonsense, but something really good."

Success was immediate. *Chambers's Journal* penetrated all over the kingdom; a circulation of 30,000 was attained at once, and in a few years it reached 80,000. *Chambers's Journal* was followed eight weeks later by the *Penny Magazine*, published by the Society for the Diffusion of Useful Knowledge, in the hope that it would "tend to fix the mind upon calmer, and, it may be, purer subjects of thought than the violence of party discussion, or the stimulating details of crime and suffering." Unlike *Chambers's*, it published illustrations, but no fiction was allowed. It contained eight pages, of a smaller and more convenient size than *Chambers's Journal*, giving miscellaneous and improving information. Thus a typical number, for April 1, 1837, had illustrated articles on Weymouth, and on Mackerel Fishery, a description of the fair at Nijni Novgorod, and an account of "The Daring and Ferocity of the Weasel." The *Saturday Magazine* was a similar production issued by the S.P.C.K., and included a certain amount of religious matter, whereas the *Penny Magazine* was secular.

In the forties these three periodicals had to struggle against a growing appetite for " trash about Italian castles, and daggers, and ghosts in the blue chamber, and similar nonsense "; the *Saturday Magazine* and the *Penny Magazine* went under; *Chambers's Journal* survived.

The chief competitor of *Chambers's Journal* as a periodical for the family circle was the *Family Herald*, established at the end of 1842 and priced at a penny. William Lovett, in 1849, estimated that about 125,000 of the *Family Herald* were sold weekly, while *Chambers's Journal* and *Eliza Cook's Journal* had circulations of some 65,000 and 55,000 respectively.[1]

The *Family Herald* contained many romantic tales about abbesses' secrets, or aristocrats whose carriages broke down in lonely spots, mixed with moral stories of modern young ladies who missed their chances of matrimony through losing their temper with servants or " aspiring to expensive amusements." It also lived up to its second title, " Useful Information and Amusement for the Million," publishing, in addition to such items as "Mems. for Mothers," " Amusing Anecdotes," and so forth, many short

---

[1] Select Committee on Public Libraries, 1849, p. 178.

biographical sketches of famous men like Confucius, Sir Isaac Newton, or Priestley, and also long articles on somewhat abstruse problems such as " Why there are Black Men in the World, and What is the Meaning of Africa?" Long extracts were also given from the 1843 Children's Employment Commission Report, a feature one can hardly imagine appearing in a modern paper of the kind. By 1848 it had rather changed its character, and much space was devoted to articles on Etiquette of Her Majesty's Drawing Room, whilst in the Answers to Correspondents, which have become an important feature of the paper, Albert K. is assured that he has a right to quarter his paternal and maternal arms, and change his motto also, but that he must apply to the Heralds' College.

Eliza Cook's Journal, a paper started in 1849, was of a very serious and instructive character, and every week printed a moral poem by the founder and editor, the well-known authoress of " The Old Armchair." She had professed herself in the opening number as anxious to give her " feeble aid to the gigantic struggle for intellectual elevation now going on." Sympathy with the poor and the oppressed was the characteristic note of the *Journal* ; two verses of one of the poems called " Thank God for Summer " will illustrate this :

> " Oh, Ice-toothed King, I loved you once—but now
>   I never see you come without a pang
> Of hopeless pity shadowing my brow,
>   To think how naked flesh must feel your fang.
>   .   .   .   .   .
> And when fair Flora sends her butterfly,
>   Painted and spangled, as her herald mummer,
> ' Now for warm holidays,' my heart will cry,
>   ' The poor will suffer less ! '   Thank God for Summer."

Even the fiction was of a didactic character, and dealt for the most part with modern characters. Thus the erring vagrant girl who starts the story by refusing to be seduced by a famous judge, fresh from a meeting to strengthen the criminal law, ends it, not, as one might expect, as the hero's wife, but as the superintendent of the female side of his model Vagrants' Lodging House. In another story, the Squire, who begins with a thoughtless declaration that he would think no more of shooting a poacher than a thief, ends by abandoning game-preserving altogether, after an affray in which an under-keeper shoots his poacher brother.

Another paper appealing to the ordinary working man, that realised and reflected the growing taste for fiction, was *Cleave's Penny Gazette of Variety and Amusement,* which started in 1837 as *Cleave's London Satirist and Gazette of Variety.* It had a wide circulation, being very popular, amongst other places, in the Potteries. John Cleave, the Chartist, was one of the original members of the London Working Men's Association, and had been closely associated with Hetherington in the battle for an unstamped press. Before the reduction of the duty he published *Cleave's Weekly Police Gazette and Journal of News, Politics and Literature,* one of the many advanced 2d. papers published in defiance of the law. The reduction of the stamp duty from 4d. to 1d. in 1836 had the paradoxical effect of making it harder for the cheap papers to continue their existence, since it was made more difficult to evade the 1d. tax than it had been to evade the 4d. tax. Cleave, who had been forced to raise the price of his *Police Gazette* from 2d. to 3½d., found it impossible to run a regular stamped newspaper. He therefore started a paper of a different character, calling it the *Penny Gazette.* His avowed aim, since he could no longer preach politics, was to place in the hands of the working class " a paper which while it ministers to their amusement, shall set them a-thinking, by mixing up the graver matters of personal and universal interest, with the lighter and more ephemeral gaieties of the passing moment."

Cleave's Gazette claimed in 1841 (September 18) to have been one of the first " of the now numerous progeny of periodical *broadsheets* to which the intellectual requirements of the millions, and their juster appreciation of the real truth that ' Knowledge is Power' gave birth." The paper announced its intention of keeping free of politics, but it contained vigorous cartoons satirising the Whigs, the Tories, Royalty, and the current abuses of the time, and reproduced addresses to the Working Men's Association and accounts of the Dorchester Labourers, as well as more general articles advocating Temperance, the opening of Museums on Sundays, and similar topics, interspersed with varied information about gardening, household matters, natural history, and anecdotes about the domestic habits of Milton or canine attachment.   Fiction was a regular feature, often in the form of extracts from Dickens, or sketches written in the style of Pickwick, so common at the time.   After 1841, in response to suggestions, the paper increased the space devoted to fiction and published many romances of "thrilling interest," dealing with the kind of themes that Mrs. Radcliffe had made popular in her novels, and Jane Austen had satirised in *Northanger Abbey*.   Knights, robbers, monks, countesses, play their parts; travellers are forced to take refuge from darkness or storms in ruined castles, where they find Florinda di Castro, once the brightest star of the Spanish court, now a bandit's bride, or it may be some "unfortunate being born to wealth" who now "lies rotting and withering" in a cell, or it may be simply a severed hand with a brilliant ring on it, and a miniature which evokes from the traveller the exclamation, "Almighty Heavens, my sister !" Similar tales were also a feature of the *Penny Satirist*, a paper started in 1837, and said to have been subsidised by the Anti-Corn Law League,[1] and of a lower class, scurrilous weekly, called *Bell's Penny Despatch, Sporting and Police Gazette, and Newspaper of Romance, and Penny Sunday Chronicle*.[2]

But all these purveyors of fiction were eclipsed by an enterprising publisher and bookseller, Edward Lloyd, better known as the founder of *Lloyd's Newspaper*, who realised the commercial importance of the taste for bloodcurdling or sentimental fiction, which cheap methods of printing now made it possible to satisfy.   Lloyd's *Companion to the Penny Sunday Times and People's Police Gazette*, a weekly paper, price 1d., which first appeared in September 1841, contained practically nothing but thrilling tales, and instead of the political cartoon of papers of its type, it printed a coarsely executed illustration of one of the more exciting incidents in a story, unless there chanced to be some murder or explosion to serve for a suitable subject.   So successful was this venture, that in 1843 Lloyd published a *Weekly Penny Miscellany*, a paper of a smaller size, containing sixteen close-packed pages of tales and romances, some short, some serials, without any illustrations.   This *Miscellany* in its turn was so successful, and the piles of manu-

[1] Thomas Frost, *Forty Years' Recollections*, 1880, p. 84.
[2] *Bell's Penny Despatch*, in August 1842, began to devote a large number of its columns to a translation of *Voltaire's Philosophical Dictionary*.

scripts offered the editor grew so high, that in the same year he started a similar paper, containing another sixteen pages of the same wares, called *Lloyd's Penny Atlas and Weekly Register of Novel Entertainment*.[1] In addition to these periodicals, Lloyd's issued in penny parts a great number of novels and romances some of which had already appeared in the periodicals. An amusing account is given by Thomas Frost in his *Forty Years' Recollections* of his attempts to join the ranks of Lloyd's writers. Thinking that he had produced something better than *Varney the Vampire*, with its morbid unreality, or *Ada the Betrayed*, with its sickly sentimentality, he presented himself and his manuscript to the famous office, where the manager explained that as their public was very different from the public reached by three-volume novels, " we sometimes distrust our own judgement, and place the manuscript in the hands of an illiterate person—a servant or machine-boy, for instance. If they pronounce favourably upon it we think it will do." In this case the verdict was unfavourable, but Frost found a rival house to publish his story.

What Frost calls the " Salisbury Square School of Fiction," [2] was looked at askance by educated persons, to whom its highfalutin style and absurd plots were repugnant. " The penny stamp upon newspapers," said a witness before the Committee on Libraries in 1849,[3] " makes the cost of a good thing dear, and adds facility to the cheap people to circulate trash to an extent which is almost incredible ; the rubbish issued every Saturday is very great indeed." Many critics thought the " rubbish " " replete with moral contamination." William Lovett, who can hardly be pictured as absorbed in such tales as *Alice Home, or the Revenge of the Blighted One*,[4] speaking from hearsay, described Lloyd's productions, in their earlier days, as having an " immoral and anti-social character." [5] Lloyd's own accounts of his aims and achievements are very different. " We shall make it our study," he explained in the preface to the first volume of his *Penny Miscellany*, " to maintain the high majesty

[1] Lloyd was said to pay his authors 10s. per instalment.—Frost, *op. cit.* p. 85.
[2] From Lloyd's office in Salisbury Square. [3] Pp. 85 and 86.
[4] The headings of one of the chapters will illustrate the character of this and other interminable stories : " Chapter LXXXV. The Strange Odour in the Old House.—The Finding of the Gamester's Body.—A Critical Moment.—Sir Charles Home's Insensibility."
[5] Committee on Public Libraries, 1849, p. 180.

of virtue over the turbulence of vice, and to make our pages, while they glow with the romantic and the chivalrous, so replete with true nobility of sentiment, that we shall, as hitherto, find our way, and maintain our place, among the young and pure of heart." " We must likewise," he announced, " in some degree, claim for ourselves the merit, if we may be allowed the term, of laying before a large and intelligent class of readers, at a charge comparatively insignificant, those same pleasures of the imagination which have hitherto, to a great extent, only graced the polished leisure of the wealthy ; at the same time that we have done so, we have found with unmingled satisfaction that correct tastes, glowing fancies, and an admirable perception of the poetical and the beautiful, are as well to be found by the humblest firesides as in the lordly mansions of the great and the noble." " We have ever found," wrote the editor of the *Penny Atlas*,[1] " in our intercourse with our readers, that those fictions in which the innocent, although environed by snares, and nearly brought to destruction by the wicked and designing, ultimately triumphed, and proved the goodness of right over might, were welcomed and read with delight. Can there be a more convincing proof of the ennobling power of Romance, if it be directed in the proper channel ? " The formula for the stories is well described : " We paint temptation—we paint virtue—we describe how it is oppressed and borne down by the wicked, and then we show how, like a spring of tempered steel, the rebound of its energies places it on a higher pinnacle of excellence than it before affected, while the wild turbulence of vice has brought forth nothing but evil fruits and deep vexation of spirit."

Lloyd, in the preface to the 1846 volume of his *Miscellany*, noted the death of the *Penny Magazine*, which its editor, Charles Knight, had apparently attributed to the popularity of Lloyd's publications. He alluded with contempt to other futile attempts to share with himself " the field he has so honourably won," but a serious competitor for public favour was G. W. M. Reynolds, founder of *Reynolds' Newspaper*, a prolific writer, whose publications were apt to be more concerned with " the turbulence of vice " than with the " high majesty of virtue." His most popular work, said to be a

[1] See preface to first volume.

favourite in that low grade of society which frequented the Ragged Schools, was the *Mysteries of London*, a book of a sententiously virtuous tone, which, in its own words, " raked amidst the filth and loathsomeness of society " with, it seems, a special eye to the sins of the titled. A hoary voluptuary of a marquis is described with great gusto, dying in the midst of his harem, and high-born villains, low-born miscreants, wicked old hags, and ladies with forms " modelled to the most exquisite and voluptuous symmetry," jostle each other in a bewildering kaleidoscope. Two short quotations from successive pages will illustrate its character :

"Having thus expressed his appalling menaces, the Resurrection Man hurried from the apartment. Lady Ravensworth pressed her hands to her brow murmuring, ' O heavens ! I shall go mad—I shall go mad ! ' "

But she found a friend in need :

" ' The corpse of the murdered woman must not be allowed to remain in that pond,' said Eliza in a low but emphatic tone. ' I have divined your thoughts, madam,' observed the valet. ' To-night I will bury it— painful and horrible though that duty be.' "

Thomas Frost defended the Salisbury Square School of Fiction, and argued in his *Recollections* that it served a good purpose in its day. " It was the connecting link between the Monmouth Street ballads and ' last dying speeches,' lives of highwaymen, and terrific legends of diabolism which consti- tuted the favourite reading of the masses fifty years ago, and the more wholesome refined literature enjoyed by them at the present day." Popular taste followed the taste of other classes. Scott made mediaeval chivalry romantic and fascinating to the educated ; the uneducated wanted also to have barons and castles and monasteries brought into the monotony and the gloom of their daily life. It is not surprising or regrettable that men and women working in a mill and living in Ancoats or Hunslet turned eagerly to the pages of *The Smuggler King, or the Foundling of the Wreck*, or *The Black Phantom of the Castle*. A crude imaginative tale, like a crude imaginative play, helped to take them out of their world, and thus satisfied an instinct for which mankind has needed satisfaction in all ages, an instinct satisfied sometimes by noble literature, sometimes by coarse or violent literature. The workman who liked to read about the wicked marquis and the noble lady had the same taste as the middle classes, who enjoyed the books of which Sir George Trevelyan gives an entertaining account in his *Life of Macaulay*. Macaulay studied the novels of Mrs. Meeke, with heroes in a low rank of life, who turned out to be the sons of dukes, and of Mrs. Kitty Cuthbertson, who wrote *The Forest of Montalbano* and *Santo Sebastiano, or the Young Protector*. Macaulay counted the number of fainting fits in this last work, and discovered that they came to twenty-seven. Eleven of them went to the credit of " Julia de Clifford." Lord St. Orville only had one, but he seems to have made up in quality for what he lacked in quantity. " One of the sweetest smiles that ever animated the face of mortal now diffused itself over the countenance of Lord St. Orville, as he fell at the feet of Julia in a death-like swoon." [1]

All classes wanted exciting and sentimental literature, and writers who could supply it found readers everywhere. The spread of popular fiction may, indeed, be counted among the civilising influences of the time. One great writer had emerged whose popularity showed that if the poor swallowed bad art eagerly, they had a relish for great art when it was offered to them. *Cleave's Gazette* published long extracts from *Nicholas Nickleby*, and thus the workman in Ancoats and Sydney Smith in his elegant library were enjoying the same masterpieces.[2]

Fiction was not, of course, the only reading of the working classes. The men at Birmingham, of whom a lecturer said that they got up at five and worked till eight for book money, before going to their day's work, did not get out of bed in the early hours in order to buy the *Mysteries of London*. More serious culture was pursued and encouraged.[3] In practically every town of any size an intelligent workman who wanted to improve and educate himself would find by the forties a Mechanics' Institution, or some similar society. In England, in 1850, it was estimated that there were 700 of these societies with 107,000 members. The libraries connected with them contained over

---

[1] *Life and Letters of Macaulay*, vol. i. p. 96.

[2] " I stood out against Mr. Dickens as long as I could," wrote Sydney Smith, " but he has conquered me."—Forster's *Life of Dickens*, vol. i. p. 153. A great deal of spurious Dickens was produced at this time. Dickens was said to have threatened an injunction at first, but to have admitted afterwards that they were a good advertisement for him.—H. R. Fox Bourne, *English Newspapers*, vol. ii. p. 120.

[3] For whole subject see A. E. Dobbs, *Education and Social Movements*.

THE BEGINNINGS OF POPULAR CULTURE 323

690,000 books.[1] But though the figures sound impressive, these institutions caused much searching of heart. They had failed to fulfil the expectations of their founders. Their rate of mortality was high, though their birth-rate was also high, and even in those that were comfortably established the membership was apt to fluctuate with alarming rapidity. To understand their position, it is necessary to glance back at their origins.

These institutions were started by Brougham and Birkbeck [2] at a time when, as a writer described it, " there still prevailed in many quarters a strong jealousy of any political discussion by the people, and still more of any society which proposed to assemble periodically several hundreds of the labouring classes." [3] Hence their founders, in their desire to conciliate opposition, banned political or religious discussion or books, and forbade newspapers. Even so, the *St. James' Chronicle* could say of the London Mechanics' Institution in 1825, " A scheme more completely adapted for the destruction of this empire could not have been invented by the author of evil himself than that which the depraved ambition of some men, the vanity of others, and the supineness of a third and more important class, has so nearly perfected." [4] Even their advocates felt a certain need for apology : " I am at a loss," said Sir Benjamin Heywood, President of the Manchester Mechanics' Institution, in 1827, " to see how we are disturbing the proper station of the working classes, and giving them an undue elevation ; we do not alter their relative position ; a spirit of intellectual activity, unequalled in any age or country, now prevails amongst us, and, if the superstructure be renewed and strengthened, it does not seem fitting that the foundation should be neglected." [5]

Mechanics' Institutions were established in the hope of popularising scientific knowledge, and incidentally making the workman better at his work. The latter motive at first received the chief emphasis. At Manchester, for example, the preamble declared that " This society was formed for the purpose of enabling Mechanics and Artizans of whatever trade they may be,

[1] J. W. Hudson, *History of Adult Education*, 1851, p. vi.
[2] The London Mechanics' Institution was started in December 1823, the institutions at Manchester, Newcastle, and Leeds in 1824, at Birmingham and Liverpool in 1825.
[3] *Report on State of Mechanics' Institutions,* Thomas Coates, published by Society for Diffusion of Useful Knowledge, 1841, p. 24.
[4] *A Short History of Birkbeck College,* C. Delisle Burns, 1924, p. 27.
[5] *Addresses at the Manchester Mechanics' Institution,* 1843, p. 33.

to become acquainted with such branches of science as are of practical application in the exercise of that trade, that they may possess a more thorough knowledge of their business, acquire a greater degree of skill in the practice of it, and be qualified to make improvements and even new inventions in the Arts which they respectively profess." [1] It was a time when there seemed no limit to the possibilities of scientific and mechanical discoveries, and it was hoped that the new institutions might benefit not only their members but science itself by " uniting and concentrating the scattered rays of genius, which might otherwise be dissipated and lost to the scientific world." [2]

Mechanics' Institutions had the difficult task of providing instruction for students on very different levels of book learning. Many members could not even read or write. Hence the Institutions had not only to spread scientific truths, but to act as glorified evening elementary schools as well, with classes for reading, writing, and arithmetic. They provided courses of lectures, classes of various kinds, and libraries, with reading-rooms often attached to them.[3] But when the first excitement and enthusiasm had worn off, numbers dwindled in an alarming manner. The cult of the lecture soon languished. " After the first novelty of listening to lectures is over, the workmen can rarely be induced to attend them," wrote a disillusioned observer in 1839.[4] It was discovered that the topic of the steam engine roused no enthusiasm in manufacturing districts.[5] " The jaded artisan," explained John Cleave in 1842, " needs some relaxation after the severe privations and enervating toils of the day, and however much he may desire scientific lore, will turn with disgust from the necessary instruction, if presented in a mere dry and detailed form, ungarnished by a palatable admixture of the lighter mental food of general literature." [6] A correspondent of the *Poor Man's Guardian* [7] put it more bluntly : " Many of us are already saturated with as much of what is called science as we can carry."

The art of popular lecturing was in its infancy, and, as a successful lecturer on non-scientific subjects to Mechanics' Institutions

[1] Hudson, *op. cit.* p. 56.   [2] *Ibid.* p. 55.
[3] Quarterly subscriptions were usually required, varying from 2s. 6d. to 5s., or more.
[4] Report on State of Mechanics' Institutions, 1841, p. 14.
[5] Committee on Public Libraries, 1849, p. 158.
[6] *Cleave's Gazette*, March 19, 1842.   [7] December 19, 1835.

expressed it in 1849, " A man must have a very happy talent for lecturing if he succeeds in making scientific lectures popular." [1] Let us imagine a workman, eager to know the secrets of the new balloons, attending Mr. Tatum's first lecture on *Aerostation* at the London Mechanics' Institution. This is what he would be told at the outset. " Before the principles of *Aerostation* could be properly comprehended, a knowledge of *Pneumatics* was requisite ; and he had a right to presume, from the lectures which had been delivered on that subject, that the Members were acquainted with the nature and properties of *air*. A knowledge of *hydrostatics* is also essential to the study of a science which treats of bodies floating in a certain medium, by displacing a quantity of the fluid in which they float, equal in weight to the floating body. Besides this, it is necessary to know that *air* is a *gravitating medium*, and, therefore, not only *Pneumatics*, but *Hydrostatics* must be understood ; so far, at least, as relates to the *specific gravities* of bodies. Chemistry also is necessary. . . ." [2] It is not surprising that the workman was shy of the lecture-room, and that when he went there he preferred the lectures given by local men in language which he could understand.

In the places where numbers kept up, it was noticed that the members were no longer, as at first was the case, predominantly workmen ; clerks and small craftsmen took their place.[3] Enthusiasts could account for this by explaining that, thanks to the opportunities for improvement, members rose in the social scale, and the institution rose with them,[4] but this was not the usual view. Hudson has an interesting description of the way in which middle-aged professional men, and heads of firms, invaded the Athenæums, ousting the young clerks for whom they were intended. The clerks, in their turn, anxious to avoid the society of " the governor," joined the Mechanics' Institutions, where " the warehouseman, the packer, the carter, and the mill-hand shun the society of the clerk and the foreman, and . . . in turn quit the Institution which was established expressly for them." [5]

---

[1] Committee on Public Libraries, 1849, p. 154. Dr. Birkbeck, of course, had this talent.
[2] *London Mechanics' Register*, 1827, vol. iii. p. 252.
[3] The Report on the State of Mechanics' Institutions in 1841 (p. 19) gives a table of forty-five institutions with 9905 members, of whom only 4396 were mechanics.
[4] 1849 Committee on Libraries, p. 155.   [5] Hudson, *op. cit.* p. vii.

Apart from the class difficulty, the Mechanics' Institutions suffered in the thirties and the forties from the competition of Socialist and Chartist meetings and Halls.[1]   Under Owen's inspiration, Halls of Science sprang up in different towns.   The translator of Faucher's book described, in 1844, the Hall of Science at Manchester, raised exclusively by the savings of mechanics and artisans, at a cost of £7000, containing the finest and most spacious lecture-hall in the town.   Here the disciples of Owen had a day and Sunday school, conducted oratorios and festivals, and organised rural excursions and "cheap and innocent recreation" for the working classes.[2]   They were opposed vigorously by the evangelical section of the religious public, but they did not allow fermented liquor, and were generally admitted to have done much to refine the habits of the working classes.   He added that the large sums of money that they raised showed that they belonged to the wealthier portions of the working classes.[3]

An interesting description of the kind of entertainment provided at such Halls was given by John Finch, the Owenite iron merchant of Liverpool, who had visited two London societies.[4] Successful dance meetings were held fortnightly, at which two hours were devoted to dancing, half an hour to a lecture, and from one to one and a half hours to music and singing.   At one of these working-class balls at which he had recently been present there were as many as 400 persons, some three-quarters of them being of the working class.   They paid 1s. for entrance and 6d. for tea or coffee.   This particular London society

---

[1] Cf. Lovett's account of the founding of the London Working Men's Association in 1836.   Workmen must cease to depend on others, they must educate themselves. One of the objects was "to form a library of reference and useful information, to maintain a place where they can associate for mental improvement. . . ."   Also cf. his address to the Working Men's Association : " Let us, then, in the absence of means to hire a better place of meeting—meet at each other's houses.   Let us be punctual in our attendance, as best contributing to our union and improvement; and, as an essential requisite, seek to obtain a select library of books, choosing those at first which will best inform of our political and social rights.   Let us blend, as far as our means will enable us, study with recreation. . . . "—*Life and Struggles of William Lovett*, 1920 edition, pp. 92 and 95.

[2] " They were among the first to introduce tea-parties at a low rate of admission."

[3] *Manchester in 1844*, by M. Léon Faucher, translated 1844, p. 25.   This Hall of Science was afterwards bought by the subscribers to the Public Library for £1200 in 1850, and it was handed over with its stock of books to the Corporation, becoming the first Manchester Free Library.   It was taken down in 1877.—See Axon's *Annals of Manchester*.

[4] 1834 Committee on Drunkenness, pp. 321 ff.

enjoyed the name of " The Institution of the Intelligent and Well-disposed of the Working Classes for the removal of Ignorance and Poverty by means of Education and Employment." Mr. Finch explained that dances were not the only activities of these societies. On other evenings of the week they held meetings for moral and scientific improvement, specially for the study of the science of society or of human happiness. He had attempted to introduce something of the kind at Liverpool, but had failed.

Even those who were not drawn directly into the Owenite or Chartist movements objected to the restrictions on newspapers and on discussion. A mass of periodical political publications were being turned out, written to attract and interest the workman.[1] If he wished to read them or to discuss exciting new ideas such as the points of the Charter, it was useless to go to the Mechanics' Institutions. These establishments indeed suffered from both sides ; on the one hand, the keenest spirits were attracted away by Chartism ; on the other hand, in spite of precautions, they were regarded by many persons as hotbeds of subversive thought, and rival institutions, connected with the Church, sprang up in many places to provide the advantages without the dangers.[2] Considerable efforts were made to increase the attractions of Mechanics' Institutions ; the ban on newspapers was gradually lifted ;[3] the character of the lectures was altered ; the arts encroached on the sciences ; " Light literature, criticism, music, and the drama " took the place of the systematic study of chemistry, hydrostatics, and optics. It is interesting to glance at some of the subjects offered by lecturers in 1841. Half a page taken at random will show the great

---

[1] " Almost every large town has its *Trades Herald, Workman's Advocate, Workers' Guardian*, or some other equally zealous and useful publication, all strenuously advocating the necessity of duly rewarding labour, and of improvement in the condition of the working classes."—*Voice of the People*, June 18, 1831.

[2] See Report on Mechanics' Institutions, 1841, p. 15, on Church Mechanics' Institutions : " As these societies depend principally upon honorary members for support, the subscription to them is usually very small (only 1s. a quarter), and the workmen have all the advantages of a Mechanics' Institution at a very cheap rate. But, on the other hand, this rivalry divides the small funds, which united are seldom adequate to the efficient support of a single institution." Hook established Church popular libraries in Leeds, twenty-eight in all, with reading-rooms, open at a subscription of 1d. or 2d. a week.—*Leeds Intelligencer*, January 19 and April 20, 1839. Hook was in favour of an amalgamation between the two sets of institutions.—See his essay in *Meliora*, edited by Viscount Ingestre, 1853.

[3] They were admitted, after a struggle, in Manchester in 1840, in Newcastle not till 1847.

variety.[1] Fourteen lecturers among them offer the following subjects : " Physiology ; Language ; Detection of Arsenic ; Zoology ; Wood Engraving—America ; Chemistry ; Physiology ; City of Rome—Turkey, etc. ; The Writings of Dickens; Astronomy ; Geography—Society Prejudice — Laughter— Female Affection—Bacon, etc. ; The Irish and Ireland ; Artificial Supply of Water."   Classes were made more varied : " The working-mechanics who generally prefer the sterner studies have given place to others who attend the dancing, and the essay and discussion classes, as more congenial to their tastes." [2]

Attempts were also made to improve the libraries at Mechanics' Institutions.   These libraries, whose totals of books often sounded very imposing, suffered from being composed largely of gifts.   A lecturer who had made a special study of the subject described them vividly : " Many of the books are gift books, turned out of people's shelves, and are never used, and old magazines of different kinds, so that, out of 1000 volumes, perhaps there may be only 400 or 500 useful ones.   The rest are, many of them, only annual registers and old religious magazines, that are never taken down from the shelves." [3] Samuel Smiles, who was well acquainted with the Yorkshire Institutions, said much the same thing: "Many of the books in mechanics' institutions are very unattractive ; many of those books, for instance, which are given by way of presents, are books which nobody would think of reading now-a-days ; a large proportion of them are dull, heavy books." [4]   He remarked truly that to make a library successful there must be money for buying fresh books.   Fiction was now made an important feature of the libraries,[5] and it was even complained of the various Manchester Mechanics' Institutions in 1849 that they were " in the hands of a party who buy amusing books, and those who are really disposed to improve themselves have no voice." [6]   In the Nottingham Mechanics' Institution in 1849-50, a third of the library of 5000 volumes consisted of

---

[1] Report on Mechanics' Institutions, p. 110.   [2] Hudson, *op. cit.* p. 98.
[3] 1849 Committee on Public Libraries, p. 79.   [4] *Ibid.* p. 127.
[5] The important and flourishing Sheffield Mechanics' Library, founded in 1823, refused to admit novels and plays.   The Committee evidently found it difficult to be consistent, for, whilst refusing Shakespeare, they accepted Sophocles and Euripides, and Bulwer was admitted and Scott cast out.—See Hudson, *op. cit.* pp. 159 and 160.
[6] 1849 Committee on Public Libraries, p. 78.

fiction, and two-thirds of the books issued were poetry or novels.[1]

Many libraries suffered from the survival of the original ban on theological and political works. At Nottingham this induced many workmen to set up their own libraries at public-houses. These little private libraries, containing many novels and some political works, originated in ten men clubbing together and buying Howitt's *History of Priestcraft*.[2] In some of the colliery districts, too, the miners were said to form similar village libraries instead of joining Mechanics' Institutions.[3] Mr. Dawson, the lecturer, who had a wide acquaintance with manufacturing towns, did not think that the ban on theology was much of a grievance : " the working classes prefer historical and political works; they do not trouble theological works much." Froissart's *Chronicles* he mentioned as being in great demand, and also Coxe's *Revolutions of Europe*. But he deprecated the great mass of rubbish issued every Saturday, and said rather bitterly, " For the last many years in England everybody has been educating the people, but they have forgotten to find them any books."[4] Rational recreation, "substituting . . . intellectual for sensual pleasures," had from early days been one of the objects of Mechanics' Institutions, and attempts had been made to organise excursions, like the one to the Liverpool Zoological Gardens, where " one of our party read to us the descriptive account of the animals, as we stood round the respective enclosures." [5] This lighter side was now considerably developed. Cheap concerts too were introduced. In Manchester they began in 1837, and for seven years paid their way. Sometimes a spirit of frivolity crept in. " Our members," wrote one sad correspondent in 1841, " appear far more anxious now to get up a ball on Easter Tuesday than to assist in the formation of classes." [6]

In Manchester, where the change in the social grade of the members was especially marked, three Lyceums were started in 1838, to attract the working classes, with news-rooms, libraries, lectures, classes, and " rational and innocent evening recrea-

[1] Hudson, *op. cit.* p. 148.
[2] 1849 Committee on Public Libraries, p. 80.
[3] *Ibid.* p. 157.   [4] *Ibid.* pp. 80, 81, and 85.
[5] *Addresses at Manchester Mechanics' Institution*, by Sir B. Heywood, p. 66.
[6] Report on Mechanics' Institutions, p. 76.

tions." The charge was only 2s. a quarter, and women were encouraged to join and were admitted for 1s. 6d. a quarter. At first these establishments met with considerable success; the Ancoats Lyceum had a membership of 735, the Salford Lyceum had 1500 members, and that at Chorlton 530 members.[1] But as the forties went on, " general depression and apparent decay " set in, and in 1850 " the managers of the existing Lyceums complain that the young men who should attend their classes, are to be found in casinos and public-houses licensed for musical performances." The truth was that most workmen preferred lighter forms of recreation, and the growth of places for entertainment proved disastrous to the establishments which combined moral improvement and pleasure.

Mechanics' Institutions, then, useful though they were, failed to accomplish all that was expected of them. Their founders had overestimated the zeal for knowledge in the working classes. They pictured all workmen, or at any rate all skilled workmen, as craving for instruction, like the Birmingham men of whom a successful lecturer at Mechanics' Institutions spoke in 1849. " I have known men rise at five and work till eight for book money, and then go to their day's work." He could pick out, he said, five or six working men as amongst the most intelligent and best-read persons in Birmingham. " They are men who have wrestled it out." [2] But the cold fact is that the passion for knowledge is not widely distributed in any class, and when sacrifices must be made to satisfy it, the distribution is narrower still. Before the Ten Hours Act, too, many factory workers must have been physically debarred from attending lectures or classes. That, considering the circumstances, a remarkable desire for knowledge existed, was shown not only in the attendance, such as it was, at the Mechanics' Institutions, but in the numbers of small so-called Mutual Improvement Societies that sprang up, some of them mushroom growths that soon died away, others developing into organised societies.[3] A few working men would meet regularly in the

[1] See, for Lyceums, Hudson, *op. cit.* pp. 135 ff. The list of lectures given at the Ancoats Lyceum during 1841 shows that there were 7 on Organisation and Animal Mechanism; 1 on the Eye; 3 on the Steam Engine; 4 on the Writings and Character of Shakespeare; 2 on the Opium Trade and War with China; 3 on Peace, War, and Capital Punishment; 2 on the Character and Writings of Byron; 2 on the Influence of Parents on their Offspring.   [2] 1849 Committee on Libraries, pp. 82 and 83.

[3] See, for these Mutual Improvement Societies, an interesting article in *Eliza Cook's*

evenings " to improve themselves by mutual intercourse," and this sometimes led to the starting of regular classes. The Leeds Mutual Improvement Society, started by four young men in 1844, went through a stage when " reading, writing, grammar, and arithmetic, were taught and learned amidst rakes, and hoes, and broken flowerpots " in an old garden house. By 1850 it was giving classes on subjects including Discussion, Chemistry, and French to eighty members, in extensive premises in a back yard off Kirkgate.[1] There was a special crop of these informal and unpretentious gatherings in the northern counties in 1849 and 1850, largely, no doubt, as the result of the Ten Hours Act.[2] Even lectures of the right kind, given by the right kind of man, could be a success, as was shown by the case of Mr. Richardson, a self-educated teacher, who for fifteen years, in 1850, had gone round as a peripatetic lecturer on Science to the scattered northern villages, where " the toiling mining population of Durham and Northumberland proceed over the hills in rain, sleet, and frost, that they may learn the great truths which civilization has made manifest." He lectured on Electricity, Pneumatics, etc., " travelling day by day, by cart, by rail and by coach far from the great towns and public highways, with his extensive and beautiful electrical apparatus, valued at £500." " Somewhat provincial in his dialect, perfect as a manipulator, and correct in his statements, he never fails to interest and instruct." [3]

The original hope that Mechanics' Institutions, once established with help from benevolent persons, would become self-supporting, soon vanished. The system of quarterly subscriptions, even when fixed at the low rate of 3s., as at Birmingham, was unpopular with workmen. If the sum was raised the numbers fell off. There were no endowments from pious founders and benefactors ; living benefactors were essential and were often generous, but in addition there was a constant

Journal, May 19, 1849. The Preston Temperance Advocate, June 1837, describes the " Academies " in Preston where eighteen or twenty men would rent a two-roomed cottage for 1s. 9d. or 3s. a week, and use the top room for learning to read and write, the bottom room for social meetings.

[1] Hudson, op. cit. p. 95. Cf. the Portsea Dockyard Mechanics, who started classes amongst themselves.—Ibid. p. 154.

[2] Hudson, op. cit. p. 191. Cf. the formation of libraries in almost every large village in Derbyshire and thereabouts (see 1849 Committee on Public Libraries, p. 86). See also evidence of Samuel Smiles, ibid. p. 126.

[3] Hudson, op. cit. p. 200.

campaign to raise funds by means of bazaars, exhibitions, and soirées.   Though the museums of stuffed natural-history specimens or models of machinery usually became neglected dust traps, instead of producing the intellectual elevation expected from them, a great appetite existed for temporary exhibitions.   At Liverpool three exhibitions between 1840 and 1844 raised £5000 for the Mechanics' Institution.   Patent ice, cartoons, dissolving views, a panorama, evening concerts, and a diving-bell were among the attractions.   It is clear that much of the energy that should have been spent on spreading education was devoted to these campaigns for raising funds.

It was complained that whilst working-class energy was spent liberally on efforts to make a success of " provident societies, trade societies, temperance societies, and the various political clubs that from time to time agitate the country, there is no evidence to show any of this spirit of proselytism in favour of Mechanics' Institutions." [1]   John Cleave answered that ill success was attributable, " not to the apathy of Working Men—but to their utter and just repugnance to institutions supported in a great measure by patronage and conducted by patronage." [2]   When we read in Hudson that " The lawned Divine, and the ermined Duke feel a pleasure in presiding over the festivals of the artizan and the day labourer," [3] it is easy to understand that many artisans and day labourers preferred the small informal societies which they had created themselves, where the improvement was done by themselves and not by their betters.   But when these small societies grew to any size, problems of finance became as acute as in the case of Mechanics' Institutions, and even Lovett's National Hall depended on " donations from benevolent individuals."   Much gratuitous work was done, but premises had to be rented or maintained, teachers and lecturers of advanced subjects had to be paid, and the fees that could be charged without discouraging membership seldom covered the cost.   How narrow was the margin even where the membership was satisfactory and enthusiastic was shown by the position of the Ancoats Lyceum in its flourishing days in 1841, when the income had exceeded the expenditure, but the Directors were warned that should they " take an injudicious step, such as

---

[1] Report on Mechanics' Institutions, p. 22.
[2] *Cleave's Penny Gazette*, March 19, 1842.   [3] Hudson, *op. cit.* p. v.

engaging a Lecturer who should prove a failure, for three nights, at two guineas per night, this, with the expense of printing, would exhaust the surplus, and leave no attractions for the remainder of the quarter. . . ."[1]

In 1841 (March 11) it was proposed in the House of Commons by Mr. Gillon that grants should be given to Mechanics' Institutions. He pointed out that Oxford and Cambridge received public money, and claimed the same privilege for advanced education for working men.[2] Peel, then in opposition, blessed the project, but when he came into office he found the difficulties too formidable. The episode of the Hullah classes was a warning that any attempt to help adult education would involve the Government that made it in all the quarrels that had raged so fiercely over the education of children.

Hullah was a musician with a genius for teaching music and inspiring others with his own enthusiasm, whose powers Dr. Kay determined to utilise for English education. Under the auspices of the Committee of Council for Education, though without any financial help from them, Hullah started a singing school for schoolmasters at Exeter Hall in 1841, employing an adaptation of M. Wilhem's methods which he had studied in France. The success was extraordinary ; the classes were thrown open to the public, and in addition to the schoolmasters and mistresses, Sunday-school teachers, mechanics, and shopkeepers trooped in.[3] In 1842 over 3000 persons were attending the classes held by Mr. Hullah and his assistants, and it was estimated that 50,000 school children in London were being taught on his method by teachers who had been trained in it. At the request of the pupils, three other classes were formed for teaching writing, arithmetic, and linear drawing, on the synthetic method. But though Hullah generously not only gave his own services for nothing, but paid his assistants, the classes were not self-supporting. The fees charged were low, but probably as much as the pupils could pay ; for sixty lessons school teachers paid 15s., mechanics and workpeople 8s. or 10s., and the well-to-do 30s. To start the classes, subscriptions had been raised from Dr. Kay, Lord Wharncliffe, and others.

<hr>

[1] Report on Mechanics' Institutions, p. 48.

[2] Dr. Hook took the same view. See his essay in *Meliora*.

[3] See H. Holman, *English National Education*, p. 80, and Frank Smith, *Life of Kay-Shuttleworth*, pp. 128 ff.

In 1842 (July 12) Lord Wharncliffe presented to the House of Lords a petition from 1600 of the pupils, asking for a grant from Parliament. Financial help could not be given out of the regular grant for education, since that was all earmarked for particular purposes. Wharncliffe was entirely favourable to the proposal, and announced that he wished to secure from Parliament an acknowledgment of its duty to help these classes. On the same day Peel presented a similar appeal in the House of Commons, giving it a similar blessing, though he demurred to building premises for the classes. All looked well, for the Whigs would certainly offer no opposition. But on July 25 the hopes of a grant were shattered. The Bishop of London presented a petition from Mr. Turner, who claimed to have anticipated Mr. Hullah in his methods. The Bishop, after administering a rebuke to Lord Wharncliffe for his excessively friendly language about Dissenters (see p. 191), announced that though he had been one of the original subscribers to the project, the recent developments in Exeter Hall had alarmed him. Classes were being established in different subjects without provision for religious instruction. In this way you might even establish a normal school where no religion was taught. Wharncliffe could only answer that jealousy of these classes was unreasonable, and he could not understand it. But Church opposition had done its work. A few days later Peel informed Palmerston, who asked a question about the grant (July 29), that though his own feelings were in favour of a subsidy, the subject was "not yet sufficiently matured" to take action. Needless to say, maturity never arrived, and the classes were reduced to a smaller scale in smaller premises, whilst any subsidy required came out of the pocket of the enthusiastic Dr. Kay. Adult education had to wait for half a century for aid from Parliament.

CHAPTER XVIII

THE BEGINNINGS OF COMMON ENJOYMENT

THE society that was created by the influence of the economists and the Puritans was described by three observers, each of them interesting because education or experience had given him a background against which to set this civilisation. One was Dr. Arnold, a student of classical history, steeped in its spirit and lessons; another was a German, named Raumer, Professor of History at Berlin University, who visited England in 1835; the third, a Frenchman named Léon Faucher, who visited England ten years later.[1]

All three observers agreed that the poor man in England had certain advantages over the poor man on the Continent, and that he had a share in the benefits brought by the agrarian and industrial revolutions. " The English workmen and mechanics eat, drink, and are clothed better than any others," wrote Raumer.[2] Dr. Arnold pointed out that " Earthenware has succeeded to wood or pewter; their wives and children can dress better and cheaper, and cheap publications are more numerous."[3] But they were all struck by the social incoherence of these towns, their cold unhappiness, the class division of interests and pleasures, the concentration on a limited and limiting purpose. Faucher pointed out that the industrial towns of France, such as Rouen and Lyons, were not specialised populations; the law in Rouen, the Church in Lyons, made their mark on the life and manners of the community. " But at Manchester industry has found no previous occupant, and knows nothing but itself. Everything is alike, and everything is new.

---

[1] For Dr. Arnold, see the *Englishman's Register* and *Letters to the Sheffield Courant.* For Raumer, *England in 1835*, translated by Austin and Lloyd. For Faucher, *Etudes sur l'Angleterre*, 1845, and *Manchester in 1844.*

[2] *England in 1835*, vol. iii. p. 158. Manchester consumed 2 lbs. of butcher's meat a week per head of the population in 1836; see *Transactions of Manchester Statistical Society*, 1925-26, and Morpeth's speech, House of Commons, March 31, 1847.

[3] *Letters to the Sheffield Courant.*

There is nothing but masters and operatives."[1]   Raumer wrote, after visiting Leeds and Sheffield: "We therefore rarely trace any comprehensive plan, any attention to general convenience, or to beauty and architectonic art.   Capital is employed solely in the creation of new capital.   What is not calculated to promote this end is regarded as useless and superfluous.   It is with a far different view that the west side of London has been enlarged."[2]   Arnold described this concentration in a letter to the *Sheffield Courant*.   "Our great manufacturing towns have risen solely with a view to this relation of employers and employed.   The very name shows this, that they are places where men have assembled together, not for the purposes of social life, but to make calicoes or hardware or broadcloth.   A man sets up a factory and *wants hands*; I beseech you, sir, to observe the very expressions that are used, for they are all significant.   What he wants of his fellow creatures is the loan of their hands; of their heads and hearts he thinks nothing."[3]

The absence of amenities made a great impression on observers who could compare English life with the life of the Continent.   Faucher remarked that the city authorities at Liverpool had prohibited cheap theatres, with the consequence that the poor had to amuse themselves in the tavern or at religious and political meetings, according to their taste.   " If the people of Manchester want to go out on a Sunday," he asked, " where must they go ?   There are no public promenades, no avenues, no public gardens, and no public common . . . everything in the suburbs is closed against them; everything is private property; in the midst of the beautiful scenery of England the operatives are like the Israelites of old, with the promised land before them, but forbidden to enter into it."[4]   Arnold described the separation of taste and feeling between

---

[1] Cf. Peel, speaking on ecclesiastical reforms : " It was unnecessary for him to enlarge upon the benefits to be derived from the presence of an active and pious minister amidst a crowded population, especially where the society was so constituted as to leave hardly any intermediate grades between the employers of labour and the labourers."—House of Commons, May 5, 1843, *Annual Register*.

Cf. also the *Times*, October 17, 1847: ". . . So long as our different ranks of society remain apart, so long as there is no common pursuit to bring them together, no common study to harmonise their sympathies, and to harmonise their affections, so long must England continue to be a nation of castes, classes, and factions."

[2] Vol. iii. p. 142.   [3] November 11, 1831.

[4] *Manchester in 1844*, p. 56.

classes in England, due to the want of galleries and theatres, parks and gardens, as "the peculiar curse of our state of society." He argued that the contrasts between rich and poor were stronger in England than on the Continent. "The most hurried view of the state of things on the Continent must be struck at once with the great difference in this respect between the rest of Europe and ourselves. Abroad, the rich and poor approach one another more nearly in their habits, manners, and in many of their favourite amusements. The richer classes live more simply; the poor have opportunities afforded them of gaining a taste for the more refined pleasures. Nothing has given me more delight than to see the crowds of persons of every condition, who frequent the great botanical gardens at Paris; . . . after what I had seen at the botanical gardens I was not surprised to learn that the people in the late Revolution generally respected the works of art, and that such things were looked upon as national property, which every man had a common interest in protecting." [1]

If English life had kept this bleak and unsympathetic character unchanged, the distractions that drew off the strength of the class conflict of the thirties would not have had more than a temporary effect. But there was a slow and gradual improvement, due partly to the Chartist movement, partly to the teaching of humanists and reformers, which brought amenities into social life and helped to modify the sharp separation of classes that distinguished the England of the thirties. The Chartists, wishing to strike at the monstrous inequality of the age, pressed for the suffrage, because they thought that the provision of political rights would do for the working classes what it had done for the middle classes. They failed, but the instinct for creating a society out of this chaos was prompting other

---

[1] *Englishman's Register*, June 4, 1831. Cf. Godolphin Osborne in *Meliora* in article proposing to open village reading clubs on Sundays : "We saw enough in the Great Exhibition this year to satisfy us that the most bold and unabashed of the lower classes are highly susceptible of moral atmosphere. Place them where all speaks of order, where all around appeals to their better nature, and though they want refinement, they at once prove that the materials for its production are within them."

Cf. also Rev. Orville Dewey (U.S.A.) in *The Old World and the New*, quoted by Sir B. Heywood in *Addresses at the Manchester Mechanics' Institution*, p. 95 : "In seven months upon the Continent of Europe, though living amidst crowds, though living in taverns, in hotels, in public-houses, I have not seen four intoxicated persons ! But I have seen in parks, and gardens, and places of public assembly, millions of persons, exhilarated by music, by spectacles, by scenery, flowers, and fragrance, cheerful without rudeness, and gay without excess."

movements which gained power and emphasis from their agitation. Some of these movements were primarily within the working-class world ; others were movements in which all classes co-operated. Between them they lifted the English town out of its first barbarism.

We get a vivid idea of the importance and meaning of the new movements, if we note that the place of the great civic or religious pageants of the past was taken by a new form of festival. Holidays were rare, but Whit Monday, at least, was kept as a day of rejoicing. Thus, to take a typical Lancashire town, at Blackburn on Whit Monday, 1844, no less than sixteen societies marched in a procession through the town, and the *Blackburn Standard* remarks that though four thousand persons took part, only one person was taken to the police station at the end of the day.[1]

These societies covered a number of needs and interests. They were mainly sick and burial clubs, but, like the old Roman sick and burial clubs, they provided a form of social life, a world in which poor men and women had common affairs to administer and common recreations to enjoy. Such societies were, of course, not new, for they were common in some form from about 1740, and Rose had passed an Act in 1793 for their encouragement. But they developed rapidly at this time, and in 1846 a Registry of Friendly Societies was established. Some of these societies were merely collecting societies, for helping thrift and insurance, in which the members took no part, but the large Orders had a very active social life.[2] The friendly societies, by their social festivities, served in some degree the purpose served by old guild festivals. They provided the dull life of Lancashire with some colour and pageant. They were blamed by critics for pursuing social entertainment, when they should have been concentrating on thrift, but this was an essential part of their life and function. They set up a society in which the poor man could exercise and develop his taste for fellowship. Men whose lives were spent under the

---

[1] The following were the societies : the Royal Veteran Society, the Ancient Order of Foresters, the United Catholic Brethren, the United Catholic Sisters, the Female Gardeners, the Loyal Order of Female Druids, the Royal Order of Shepherdesses, the Royal Order of Shepherds, the Independent Order of Mechanics, the Independent Order of Rechabites, the Blackburn New Borough Benevolent Society, the Loyal Order of Oddfellows. See *Blackburn Standard*, May 21, 1844.

[2] See G. D. H. Cole's *Short History of the Working-Class Movement*, vol. ii. chap. 2.

discipline of the mill felt all the need for such an institution especially strongly, and Professor Clapham thinks it is not unlikely that no less than two-thirds of the men of Lancashire belonged to some friendly society in 1847.[1]

The dignity of each member of a society depends on the observance throughout that society of a recognised standard of behaviour. In the friendly society all ruled, and all obeyed ; the most important of all forms of equality, equality of manners and bearing, was jealously guarded. Hence the importance that was attached to ritual and ceremonies at lodge meetings. The regulations of the Independent Order of Oddfellows imposed fines for such offences as eating, or reading newspapers or books in the lodge room, for swearing, or singing an indecent song, for leaving the room when a song was singing, or for neglecting to address the Chair.[2] An elaborate code of manners was thus practised, and membership of a lodge represented a basis and habit of self-respect. The Laws and Regulations of the Independent Order of Oddfellows were published with a preface setting out the "nature and advantages of Odd Fellowship." The Lodge is described as " a useful school of morality, where from various humours, tempers, customs, and circumstances in life, a considerable portion of useful knowledge may be acquired, relative to men and things ; where talent of every description may emerge from the clouds of obscurity, and expand itself by a proper exertion, where bashfulness and diffidence may gradually wear off, and a modesty of assurance succeed ; where good manners and politeness may be copied from good examples and improved by practice." [3]

Though the workmen had no votes for Parliament and rarely had votes for Town Council or Board of Guardians, there must have been great numbers of working men taking part in the management of trade unions, co-operative societies, temperance societies, and friendly societies by the middle of the century. In this way scope was found for instincts and sympathies for which their occupations gave no opportunity. Men were taking decisions, assuming responsibilities, meeting and con-

---

[1] J. H. Clapham, *An Economic History of Modern Britain*, p. 590.
[2] Cf. the rules of the Club of Diana and Antinous. Dill, *Roman Society from Nero to Marcus Aurelius*, p. 279.
[3] The Oddfellows had libraries in many towns. See 1849 Committee on Public Libraries, p. 81.

sidering other points of view, expressing and developing their own ideas and sharing in significant ritual and ceremony. But meanwhile, the governing world was relaxing the rigours and softening the distinctions of the first industrial age. The change is seen in the mitigation of the Poor Law ; a process of which Dickens observed that it showed that no society could enforce the strict logic of 1834. " I am convinced that its philosophers would sink any Government, any cause, any doctrine, even the most righteous. There is a sense and humanity in the mass in the long run that will not bear them ; and they will wreck their friends always, as they wrecked them in the working of the Poor Law Bill." [1]

The change is seen also in the religious life of the time. " There is no Church, and never was there one," said Landor, " in which the Ministers of religion have so little intercourse with the people as the English. Sunday is the only day that brings them together and not in contact. No feelings are interchanged, or sorrows or joys or hopes communicated. Unpreceded by inquiry or advice, command and denunciation follow the roll call of the day." [2]   So Landor wrote in 1836. The Church was still very defective as a moral force to combat the barbarism of the times in the forties, but there had been a great improvement.[3]   Maurice and Kingsley were creating a new conscience in the Christian Socialist movement. Parsons were taking part in movements for reform like the Ten Hours agitation. Hook was urging Leeds to buy Woodhouse Moor ; Prince Lee, the new Bishop, was pressing for a Free Library in Manchester. It is difficult to imagine parsons like Hay or Ethelstone sending the remonstrance which the clergy of the Ripon diocese sent to Lord Londonderry for fighting a duel.[4]   It is still more difficult to imagine them speaking or writing of the wrongs of the poor with the generous sympathy that inspired the pages of the High Church review, the *British Critic*, in the forties.[5]   In the Nonconformist world, too, the

---

[1] Forster, *Life of Dickens*, vol. ii. p. 235.

[2] *Letters of a Conservative*, Letter 6. Bulwer Lytton, of course, gave the same impression.

[3] The Report on the Census in 1851 remarked on the change. The earlier apathy had disappeared, and clergy and ministers were now foremost in schemes for reform.

[4] *Leeds Mercury*, September 14, 1839.

[5] " . . . The poor have been deprived of their games, their amusements, and their mirth. An inventive age has multiplied to excess the toys and recreations of the

failure of religion to meet the needs of the poorest classes had come to be recognised.[1] The rich Methodists of Manchester built a chapel in the slums of Ancoats, the famous Unitarian minister, J. H. Thom, founded the Domestic Mission in Liverpool, and the Methodist Conference published Jobson's book pressing for a different spirit in chapel life.

The same change is seen in the history of education. Peel said that education had had to make its way against three obstacles : the first, the fear that to educate the poor would imperil existing institutions ; the second, indifference ; the third, religious dissensions.[2] It was an evil day for England when this religious quarrel broke out, but the England engaged in such a quarrel had travelled some distance from the time when Clarissa Harlowe had deprecated a " lettered education," because it " too generally sets people above those servile offices by which the business of the world is carried on." [3] *Clarissa Harlowe* was written in 1740, but in 1817 a Wesleyan Sunday-school in Bradford had to defend itself against critics, who argued that " education would make the lower orders of society less disposed to submit to the constituted authorities and to act in a subordinate capacity," [4] and we know from Hook that every sermon on behalf of a charity school in the twenties had to meet this objection. It would have been difficult to imagine a speaker on popular education in those days saying, as Gladstone said in 1843, " This is the fundamental question—whether education is a system for giving to a man the means of pursuing his temporal calling, or whether, without excluding that purpose, it is likewise a system for operating upon the mind and

---

wealthy ; while the poor are not to be won and beguiled from sensual indulgence, and are only to be preached to and terrified with tracts and treadmills, sermons and six months' imprisonment, into an austere and servile morality."—*British Critic*, quoted by *Times*, November 4, 1842.

[1] See Hurst, *History of Methodism*, vol. iii. p. 1438, for beginning of Wesleyan Town Missions.

[2] " I call on persons of all religious persuasions to look back at what has been the cause of the delay on the subject of education. Originally the cause was fear ; from a fear that general instruction would be dangerous to the institutions of the country. That passed away. It was succeeded by a great indifference as to this most important question—an indifference from which the Dissenting body were the first to be awakened. They set the example of activity in the cause of education. They were followed by others ; and if it was late yet there was certainly a great activity in the promotion of education. But now the cause of the delay has been different. The cause now is to be found in our religious dissensions."—House of Commons, April 22, 1847.

[3] *Clarissa Harlowe*, vol. iv. p. 148 (Sixth Edition).

[4] Scruton's *Old Bradford*, p. 103.

character of the man himself." [1]   Gladstone was asking about popular education a question that belongs to all education : no responsible man would have declared in public that there were classes in society for whom education was unsuitable.

Another sign and result of the change was the campaign for public libraries and museums.   There were libraries connected with the Mechanics' Institutions, and some millowners like the Ashtons, the Strutts, the Marshalls, and the Gregs, had established libraries for their workpeople in early days.   In the forties the practice spread, and there are several references in the *Leeds Intelligencer* and other papers to mills that provided libraries and playgrounds.   Peter Ainsworth and John Bright had libraries for their workpeople.[2]   But there were no public free libraries when Ewart, who occupies in this crusade the place of honour that Brougham holds in the crusade for adult education, began his campaign in 1845.   He proposed (March 6) that town councils should be allowed to impose a rate to establish museums of art, and he pointed out that with railway transport it would be easy to send casts from town to town.   The debate showed how much this kind of provision was needed, and how strong were the obstacles.   One supporter said that the power Ewart wished to give to the towns was possessed by municipal institutions everywhere else in the world.   Mark Philips said that it was essential that the museums should be open under conditions that enabled the working classes to use them.   " The great drawback in the improvement of the operative class was that there was no public institution in existence which they could call their own.   They enjoyed no such advantages as operatives on the continent."   The fear of allowing towns to spend public money was so strong that the Bill was only allowed to pass when its operation had been limited to towns with 10,000 inhabitants.   The rate sanctioned was $\frac{1}{2}$d., and the charge for admission was not to be more than 1d.   The demand that museums should be opened

---

[1] *Liverpool Courier*, January 11, 1843.

[2] Peter Ainsworth had a dining-room and library for his quarrymen.—*Bolton Chronicle*, January 17, 1846.   Peter Ainsworth, supported by John Fletcher, the well-known coal owner, also started a movement to establish an Athenæum at Bolton. —*Bolton Chronicle*, November 14 and December 12, 1846.   The Brights had a library and newsroom.—See *Ten Hours Advocate*, p. 184.   A cotton factory at Bollington, near Macclesfield, had a library, playground, and baths.—*Bradford Observer*, February 26, 1846.

on Sundays was rejected. In 1850 Ewart introduced a Bill to enable town councils to establish libraries and museums.[1] He proposed to abolish the restriction of the Act to towns with 10,000 inhabitants, and to make admission free. There was strong opposition on the ground of extravagance, led by Sibthorp. Ewart stated that Warrington had established a library under the Act of 1845, and that there had been public meetings in Sheffield and Birmingham to demand the Bill. Brotherton, Bright, and W. J. Fox supported him, and in the division Cobden, Hume, and Sir George Grey voted for the Bill, Disraeli and Lord John Manners voting against. In the end Ewart had to accept a compromise, by which the Act was not to be adopted by any town, unless two-thirds of the ratepayers had given their consent.[2]

In spite of handicaps the movement spread. Warrington opened a public library in 1848 ; Salford in 1849 ; Manchester in 1852 ; Bolton and Liverpool in 1853 ; Sheffield, St. Helens, Birkenhead, and Preston before 1860. In Manchester a committee of working men was formed to collect a fund for buying books, and £800 was raised by 20,000 subscribers of the working classes for this object, the total sum subscribed being over £10,000. At Salford, a number of scientific gentlemen formed themselves into a committee to push the library, and Ewart, encouraged by this example, made provision in his Act for the co-optation of such persons for the management of free libraries and museums. Chadwick, the Borough Treasurer of Salford, who gave these facts in a paper, pointed out the great difference between limited libraries and the free public libraries that were open till nine o'clock in the evening. The annual circulation in the latter averaged seven times the number of volumes in the libraries.

The progress of the movement for public parks was another sign of the same spirit. Far-sighted men like Slaney had seen from the first how much town life must suffer from the loss of playgrounds, and he obtained the appointment of the committee

---

[1] See debates on March 13, and April 10.

[2] The Act authorised a ½d. rate, but the money was to be spent only on maintaining museums and libraries, not in buying books. The *Times*, commenting on a later debate on a Bill introduced by Ewart in 1854, described the opposition of the landowners: " Mr. Henley lifted up his voice in defence of the ratepayers, poor souls, who, for a rental of £100 a year, might by the Bill be made to pay 8s. 4d. for so utterly useless an object as a free library."—April 7, 1854.

in 1833 to consider the provision of the question of remedies.[1] One proposal made by this committee was adopted by the Whigs in 1841, when a grant of £10,000 was made for encouraging the provision of public walks and parks. The chief leader of the movement in the House of Commons was James Silk Buckingham, better known as a temperance reformer. Buckingham, who started life as a sailor, had been expelled from India for exposing abuses. He was elected for Sheffield in 1832, and sat in the House of Commons for five years. He sought and obtained redress from the Indian Government for his treatment at their hands, but in his public projects he was less fortunate. For three years in succession he introduced Bills to " facilitate the formation of and establishment of Public Walks, Playgrounds, Baths and Places of healthy Recreation and Amusement." He proposed that a public meeting, convened at the request of fifty ratepayers, should have the power to decide by a majority of two-thirds of the ratepayers present to establish places for recreation, and a committee elected for the purpose was to have the power to borrow up to 10s. per head per inhabitant, and to levy a rate of not more than 3d. in the pound to provide interest and to pay off the borrowed money in twenty years' time. Fundamental rules were laid down for the guidance of the local committees, including one " that the Play Grounds be adapted for Gymnastic Exercises, Cricket, Archery, and other healthy sports, but that all conflicts of a personally irritating nature, such as Wrestling, Cudgelling and Boxing be prohibited, as well as all Games in which cruelty to Animals is involved." Buckingham was curiously sanguine when he introduced his first Public Walks Bill, together with a kindred Bill for providing Literary and Scientific Institutes and Museums. He expected, he said, no objection, and declared that " in the course of a very few years, if these Bills should pass into a law we shall see as many public walks, gardens, and pleasure grounds in the neighbourhood of all our towns, as are now to be found on the Continent of Europe." But this was not to be. Apathy proved as effective as regular opposition. If one of his Bills managed to reach the Report stage, consideration of the Report was deferred again and again, and the session came to an end without further progress.

[1] See p. 106.

It was not until 1847 that local authorities were allowed to use the rates for making a public park without special leave from Parliament. One of the clauses in the Towns Improvement Clauses Act of that year included this provision, and next year it was embodied in the Public Health Act. It is not surprising, therefore, that little progress was made until the forties. The earliest park seems to have been Preston Moor Park (200 acres), which the Corporation laid out in 1833-35.[1] Joseph Strutt's famous gift to Derby of the " Arboretum " was made about 1840, costing him £10,000.[2] There were eleven acres of it " tastefully laid out in grass intersected by broad gravel walks, and planted with a great variety of trees, shrubs, and flowers botanically arranged." The public were admitted free on Sundays, except during service time, and on Wednesdays ; on other days the charge was 6d. In 1845 it was said to be much frequented, and to have " already produced a perceptible effect in improving the appearance and demeanour of the working classes, and it has doubtless conferred an equal benefit upon their health." [3] At Leeds an effort was made in the late thirties. A society of shareholders was started called the Leeds Zoological and Botanical Society, for the purpose of providing recreation for the people, but the scheme, we read, was " smitten with an early blight," and though over £4000 was spent in the purchase of land at Headingley, and a Zoological and Botanical Gardens with a bear pit was opened in 1840 (charge 6d.), it proved a failure, and villas ultimately covered the site. The proposal that the town council should buy the gardens and throw them open on Sundays was unfortunately rejected. The town did not own a public park till 1855, when it bought Woodhouse Moor. Leeds was put to shame by Birkenhead, which obtained an Act, as early as 1843, setting aside for recreation not less than seventy acres and authorising the Commissioners to appropriate part of the park for baths.[4] Apparently the town obtained a much larger park, for at a meeting of the Birkenhead Commissioners in September 1843, it was stated that a park of 226 acres had been reserved for recreation.[5]

---

[1] Some of the freemen objected to this. See 1840 Committee on Freemen, p. 199.
[2] *Manchester Courier*, August 26, 1846.
[3] Second Report of Health of Towns Commission, 1845, Appendix, part ii. p. 274.
[4] 6 and 7 Vict. cap. cxiii.
[5] *Liverpool Courier*, September 13, 1843.

In Manchester there was an active movement in the forties. Workmen's committees were formed for raising funds, and they collected £800 from small subscribers. Peel gave £1000,[1] and Mark Philips and other public men gave large sums. The Mayor went to London to ask for help from the Government grant of 1841, but when he was told that the Government could only give £3000, he held at first that it would be undignified to take so small a subsidy.[2] Ultimately the grant was accepted. Local effort produced in all about £30,000, and three parks were bought; Peel's Park in Salford (32 acres), and Philips' (31 acres) and Queen's Parks (30 acres) in Manchester. The cost of the sites was about £25,000, and the town council estimated the annual expenditure on their upkeep at £650. The opening in 1846 was a great ceremony, attended by the mayors and corporate officials of neighbouring towns. The most notable speech at the banquet was made by one of the secretaries, who pointed to the example set by continental cities in planning their towns. " We spend at present in Manchester, from the profits of the gas service, a sum of £30,000 a year in widening old streets and we ought to take care now that we do not leave the necessity thirty years hence for that expenditure for widening what are now the new streets of Manchester." The example of Manchester stimulated similar movements in other Lancashire towns. At Oldham, £1400 was raised at a public meeting, Fielden giving £100 and the workmen of Mather and Platt £60.[3] Other towns obtained parks in the fifties: Rochdale in 1853, Blackburn in 1855, and Stockport in 1856. Halifax at the same time received the People's Park from Sir Francis Crossley, a princely benefactor of the town where he had made his fortune.[4]

---

[1] " Considering Manchester to be the metropolis of a district to the industry of which I and my family are under very deep obligations."—*Manchester Courier*, August 26, 1846.

[2] *Manchester Guardian*, April 12, 1845. For a full review of the history of the movement and the proceedings at the opening, see *Manchester Courier*, August 26, 1846.

[3] See *Manchester Guardian*, November 4, 1846, and *Halifax Guardian*, December 26, 1846. The Vicar of Oldham spoke in favour, and urged that Parliament should authorise the town councils to make parks at the expense of the rates.

[4] London was well provided, so far as the West End went, with Hyde Park, St. James' Park, Green Park, Kensington Gardens, and for the North-West, Regent's Park.

The 1833 Committee on Public Walks reported that Hyde Park and Green Park were open to all; St. James' Park and Kensington Gardens " to all persons well-behaved and properly dressed." Hyde Park, originally a royal hunting area, had been a place of

If we study the local history of the new towns, we find that private benefactions for public amenities become much more common in the forties and fifties, and a new tradition is created. This was one result of the movement for public parks and libraries. In this respect a change came over social life. One reason for the melancholy condition of the English town was the tradition of private luxury which had become so powerful in the eighteenth century. Bishop Berkeley, writing in 1721, had dwelt on the strong contrast between ancient Greece and eighteenth-century England in this respect.[1] Private splendour was as much a mark of the early industrial age as public meanness;[2] the elegance of the great house as the gracelessness of the new town. The great house symbolised the pride the great lord took in his place in the national life. The mansion, with its libraries, galleries, parks, reflected the atmosphere of authority, of history, of taste and manners, of a life active, spacious, and delightful. A German observer noticed that Englishmen made more of their country house than of their town house. Now this attractive country life, with its beauty, culture, pleasure, and state, was open to all who made their way into the

public resort since the early seventeenth century. St. James' Park, originally the grounds of St. James' Palace, was thrown open by Charles II., who also formed the Green Park by the purchase of fields between St. James' Park and Hyde Park. Regent's Park was made out of Crown land during the regency after 1811, when the last lease of the ground fell in. It was laid out by Nash, who built the terraces round. The Broad Walk was not opened till 1838.

The 1833 Committee recommended the formation of parks for the East, South, and North. Attention was paid to this recommendation. Primrose Hill was secured in 1842 for the public by a payment of £20,236 from the land revenues of the Crown. Victoria Park, for the East End, 265 acres, was finished in 1849. The money, £129,683, came from the sale of York House, and from the current income of the land revenues of the Crown. Battersea Park, for the South, 319 acres, was still being made in 1854; £200,000 of costs came from Public Works Commissioners, the rest from Parliament. One-half of the land purchased was to be sold for building land towards the costs. The inhabitants of Finsbury Borough asked in vain for a park to the North. In 1848 they pointed out that there were open fields between Highbury, Holloway, and the Green Lanes suitable for a 300 acre park. In 1853 they again drew attention to the subject. See Returns relating to Metropolitan Parks, 1854.

[1] "Those noble arts of architecture, sculpture, and painting, do not only adorn the public, but have also an influence on the minds and manners of men, filling them with great ideas, and spiriting them up to an emulation of worthy actions. For this cause they were cultivated and encouraged by the Greek cities, who vied with each other in building and adorning their temples, theatres, porticos, and the like public works, at the same time that they discouraged private luxury; the very reverse of our conduct."—Essay towards preventing the ruin of Great Britain, *Works* (1820), vol. iii. p. 78.

[2] Cf. Morley, *Life of Gladstone*, vol. iii. p. 471, on the building of Eaton, Eastnor, and other great palaces in the early years of the century; and Lecky, *History of England in the Eighteenth Century*, vol. vii. p. 209.

aristocracy; to the men whom success in business, their own or their fathers', brought into this world. The governing class drew into its orbit almost all those who acquired wealth, setting the standard, mode and plan of life. Hence the uninvested wealth of the Industrial Revolution was largely used for creating new territorial families with mansions and estates in the country.[1] The Midland Mining Commission, reporting on the South Staffordshire coalfield, where the population had almost doubled between 1821 and 1841, remarked on the parsimony of the landlords who had been enriched by this development.[2] One large landlord, whose property, according to the Rural Dean of Birmingham, had increased from forty to one hundred fold, gave £20, and refused a site for a church.[3] In other places, notably Lancashire and Yorkshire, rich men built churches and chapels, though Kydd, referring to the building of St. John's Church in Bradford by John Wood in 1837, speaks of his munificence as if it were at that time unusual.[4] The movement for parks and libraries first taught the English manufacturer and merchant to use their wealth in the spirit of the rich citizens of the Roman Empire.

Another sign of the times was the introduction of the Saturday half-holiday for clerks and the agitation for the earlier closing of shops. In 1844 the Manchester merchants decided to make Saturday a half-holiday for all their employees, and this event was celebrated by a soirée in the Town Hall. This was followed by the publication of special guides to the surrounding country such as the " Half Holiday Handbook," of which the

---

[1] The age suffered, of course, from the large proportion of wealth that went into investment; when investment was more difficult and dangerous, men who made money put it into making their towns or their surroundings beautiful. Compare G. M. Trevelyan, *History of England*, p. 371; Hobson, *Wealth and Life*, p. 162.

[2] " Yet amidst these evidences of overflowing wealth and abundance, if we enter the houses of God, few and far between, we might fancy ourselves in some poor far-distant colony, where the simple inhabitants were struggling with the first hardships and difficulties of taming the wilderness around them, and had been able as yet only to construct the tasteless, bare, poverty-stricken edifices which are a standing disgrace to many parts of the country."—Midland Mining Commission, First Report, 1843, cxxvii.

[3] *Ibid.* cxxxi.

[4] " When in possession of riches sufficient to enable him to change from an active Yorkshire manufacturer to the position of a country squire (which change, sanctioned by usage, is the natural desire of many enterprising Englishmen), he built in his native town a substantial, handsome church, parsonage, and schools, the former of which he endowed with an annual stipend of £350."—*History of the Factory Movement*, vol. ii. p. 280.

compiler said : " It is published with a view to supplying a source to which the numerous class—now by means of that generous boon of the Manchester Merchant Princes, the half-holiday—enfranchised from labour and confinement may resort for a guide to excursions and rambles." A movement for early closing of shops seems to have spread all over England at this time. A monthly review, the *General Advertiser*, was founded in 1846, which called itself " A journal of Literature, Science, and Art, and the advocate of an abridgment of the hours of business in all trades with a view to the physical, intellectual, and moral improvement of the Industrial Classes." This paper reported that nearly every town of importance in the kingdom had associations for abridging the hours of business.[1] The Liverpool Market Committee gave orders for closing at seven. In this agitation all parties combined : Cobden and Manners, Hook and Baines, the Dean of Manchester and the great Non-conformist leader, Dr. Vaughan. It was demanded that shops should close at seven in the winter and eight in the summer.

But the most striking and important manifestation of the new spirit was the success of the Ten Hours Bill. The Bill won its way against the prestige and power of the ablest and most experienced statesmen in public life. Peel, like Cobden, believed that to pass the Ten Hours Bill was to invite industrial disaster. Nobody who heard his speeches could think the danger illusory. He enjoyed greater credit than any other man in public life. He had been familiar from childhood with industrial problems ; he had extricated the finances of the nation from the muddle left to him by his predecessors ; he had taken part in the reform of the factories ; he had shown on the income tax that he had larger views than the capitalists, and on the Corn Laws that he had larger views than the landlords ; his skill and courage were unrivalled among men who had taken part in government ; of all debaters, free alike from Bright's bitterness and Brougham's pedantry, he was the most persuasive, giving invariably the impression that he was anxious to answer a hard argument rather than to evade it. When he told his country-men that the Ten Hours Bill was a public danger, no man of

---

[1] See also *Bradford Observer*, November 12, 1846, and Inquiry into Condition of Poor of Newcastle-upon-Tyne, 1850, p. 51.

sense thought that he was saying what he did not believe, or that he believed what he was saying for frivolous reasons.

The House of Commons in 1847 decided to take the risk that Peel thought so menacing. And for what ? To banish from English life a terrible formula, the phrase so long remembered in the mills of Lancashire, that the workman's life was eating, drinking, working, and sleeping. It was believed by the opponents of the Ten Hours Bill that this melancholy formula drove the wheels of Lancashire's industries and gave the English people their proud place in the world.[1] The English people decided that they would risk the loss of that position rather than let that formula oppress their civilisation any longer. It was a momentous choice, and the future of England turned on the answer. If this formula was to continue to rule her life, the English town could not hope to escape from the gloom that darkened the thirties. " Schools and libraries are of small use without time to study," so ran the manifesto of the Short Time Central Committee in 1844. " Parks are well for those only who can have time to perambulate them, and baths are of little use to such dirty people as do not leave work till eight o'clock at night. We protest that it is a mere burlesque upon philanthropy to make provision for these benefits, with a continuance of twelve hours' labour and fifteen hours' occupation for every manufacturing operative above thirteen years of age." [2] Every step taken towards civilising town life meant only another contrast between rich and poor, if the workman was to be shut up in the mill, while the well-to-do enjoyed themselves in the park and the library. The Ten Hours Bill was in this sense the most important event of the first half of the century. The English people were trying to create a larger and more generous life for the English town. The Ten Hours Act meant that the workman was not to be shut out of it.

The passing of the Ten Hours Act was followed by a great

[1] The phrase was used by Windham as early as 1800 : " They appear to act on the opinion that the common people have nothing to do with any amusement ; but ought only to eat, to sleep, and to work."—Speech in defence of bull-baiting, April 18, 1800. *Speeches*, vol. i. p. 339. It was used by Graham in Parliament, March 3, 1847, and was constantly repeated in the Press. On April 1, 1847, the *Universe* had this passage : " It is certainly painful to the reflective mind, conscious of the capabilities and destiny of the human soul, that the great bulk of the people not only of this country, but of all the most favoured countries, 'have only to work, to sleep, to eat, and to die,' but certainly that is a far preferable state than to starve and perish of want and disease."

[2] *Halifax Guardian*, February 7, 1846.

increase of concert rooms and dancing saloons in all the manufacturing towns of Lancashire and Yorkshire. Cooke-Taylor, when he made a tour of Lancashire in 1842, was struck by the good order of public-houses where music was allowed, and he had regretted that magistrates as a rule refused to license houses where concerts were held.[1] " I have gone into some of the concert rooms attached to favoured public-houses which they (the operatives of Manchester) frequent, and I have never been in a more orderly and better behaved company. The music was well selected, the songs perfectly unobjectionable ; the conversation in some intervals between the pieces not only decorous, but to some degree refined, and the quantity of liquor consumed by each individual very trifling." [2] Witnesses before the House of Lords Committee on the Sale of Beer (1849-50) and the Select Committee on Public-Houses (1852-53) described the places of amusement that had sprung up in Manchester after the Ten Hours Act.[3] At these resorts young people could enjoy the delights of " singing in character, dancing of various kinds, clog and grotesque dancing, juggling and tumbling by performers specially engaged." These variety entertainments approached as closely to theatrical performances as the law would permit. We find a pathetic picture in the Report on the Irish Poor in 1836 of an earlier effort of the people of Ancoats to organise such amusements for themselves. " Recently a wretched theatre has been established in an unroofed and ruined building at Ancoats. In this theatre a company of clerks and mechanics enact the most horrid melodrama of murder and crime. The properties and dresses are of the most meagre and ragged description, and the whole adventure greatly below those common to the lowest kind of strolling players. Yet to this mischievous excitement the youth of both sexes resort from the surrounding neighbourhood in crowds, especially on Saturday evening, when as they leave their work at 4 o'clock and are then paid, they have both more leisure and more money." [4]

---

[1] Outside London the magistrates had no control over these places of amusement unless they were connected with public-houses.

[2] Cooke-Taylor, *Tour in Manufacturing Districts*, p. 131.

[3] See specially evidence of Chief Constable of Manchester before the First, and of J. W. Hudson before the Second Committee.

[4] Report on Irish Poor, 1836, p. 58.

In these concert rooms the usual custom was to charge an entrance fee of 2d., for which a check was given entitling the holder to twopennyworth of refreshments. In Manchester, where there were three large resorts of this kind, it was estimated that 25,000 mill hands from the town and the neighbourhood attended them in the week. "It is almost the sole public amusement of the artisans and the working mill hands." They were sometimes denounced as encouraging drunkenness, but the books of the Casino, the largest of these establishments in Manchester, showed that its patrons preferred non-alcoholic refreshments : in one month, in exchange for the twopenny tokens, 180 gallons of ale and porter were given out, as against 1500 gallons of ginger beer and 160 gallons of coffee. In the course of the year at the Casino, 12,000 checks were never presented at all. The Chief Constable of Manchester, no enthusiast for these places, said of another of them where young people were "entertained with singing, dancing, and music," that "if drunkenness occurs, the landlord turns them out immediately." On Sunday nights the resorts connected with licensed houses were closed, but the second largest entertainment house in Manchester, the Victoria Saloon, which was kept by a beerhouse keeper, was open on Sunday evenings and was frequented by factory lads and girls who listened to "what they call sacred polkas."

In Bolton, where there were eight or nine of these resorts offering the attractions of "songs and scenic representations, and conjurors and tumblers," the magistrates, who took an unfavourable view of the development, had a drastic way of keeping the young away from temptation. "Where they are of the proper age we generally whip them." The licensed houses which kept these saloons were threatened with a loss of their licence if they admitted any one under the age of eighteen. In Liverpool, on the other hand, the Borough magistrates welcomed the connection of these entertainments with the existing licensed houses, for they hoped that the seafaring population, by going to concert houses in order to procure drink, would gradually become accustomed to a better form of amusement, and would begin to sing and to dance instead of drinking.[1] The Clerk to the Magistrates gave particulars of ten "Singing Houses" which he had visited, the largest with an audience of 500, the

[1] Committee on Public-Houses, 1852-53, p. 61.

smallest with an audience of seven. The majority of these places he described as well conducted, but a less favourable picture of them was given by a clergyman of the Liverpool Domestic Mission (Reverend Francis Bishop), who described them as demoralising, low and gross.[1] This clergyman gave a curious account of a Sunday evening concert at one of these places, where, to the accompaniment of a twelve-stopped organ, four performers, three men (one " decent but shabby genteel," the others " dirty and ill clad "), and a woman with a loud but faded voice, out of all control, sang a programme consisting of the Old Hundredth Psalm, the Hallelujah Chorus, Bishop Ken's Evening Hymn, and the Jubilate Deo, to a " select drunken company."

Several witnesses condemned these saloons as an unqualified evil. They said that they were haunted by prostitutes, and that boys and girls listened to indecent songs and watched indecent performances. This was sometimes the case. But a more balanced judgment would have found good reason for welcoming this development. One of the witnesses (Mr. Thomas Beggs) spoke with a large experience, for he had been a worker, a foreman, an employer, Secretary of the Health of Towns Association and Secretary of the National Temperance Association.[2] He deplored the indecency and vulgarity that were common in the casinos that he had visited in Leeds, Manchester, and Bolton, but he said that, none the less, concerts and casinos were evidence of an improving taste. When he was a boy in Leeds the working classes had no amusements except skittles and quoits in public-houses; the proportion of the workmen who would prefer better amusements was growing. Another good witness, J. W. Hudson, well known for his connection with Mechanics' Institutions, an active member of the Association for the better Regulation of Public-Houses in Manchester, said that the people of Lancashire and Yorkshire, and especially of Leeds, were more moral than in the past, and that the brutality once so evident at Bolton and Oldham seemed to have passed away. The same tendency was reported by witnesses familiar with the social life of Manchester, Bolton, Birmingham, and Leeds. It was generally agreed that, as the

[1] *Ibid.* pp. 226 ff.
[2] Committee on Public-Houses, 1852-53, pp. 321 ff.

Superintendent of Police at Birmingham put it, the taste for drama was growing and that for brutal sports was on the wane. But the movement for raising the tone of popular amusement had to make its way against the narrow spirit of the time. At Birmingham, for example, first-rate music was offered to the public in the Town Hall at the price of sixpence and threepence, but the religious people were said to object to giving any but sacred music.[1]

A study of the local papers in the thirties and forties shows in various ways how great was the strain of life under the new conditions without leisure, playing fields, or amenities of any kind. Towns pass laws to forbid children from playing with tops in the streets; complaints are made that kites are being flown to the inconvenience of the passers-by; boys and young men are fined for running races on turnpike roads. This last practice was said to be common round some of the Yorkshire towns, and the magistrates imposed heavy fines in order to suppress it.[2]

We get some idea of the difference that the new amenities made if we turn to the evidence given before the Committee on Public-Houses in 1853. A Rational Recreation Association had been started at Leeds; popular concerts were given at the Town Hall,[3] and the Botanical Gardens had now been thrown open on Sundays. Drunkenness had decreased and manners improved. At Manchester the parks were crowded on Sundays, and the Zoological Gardens were well attended by persons who before had spent Sunday dog-fighting or playing at pitch-and-toss in the beerhouses. At Liverpool, steamers took crowds across the river on Sundays, and Sunday had become less drunken. The Committee, reporting on such evidence, remarked: "Your committee cannot conclude this portion of their Report without calling attention to the fact of how few places of rational enjoyment are open to the great mass of the population on Sunday, which serve as a counter attraction to the public-house. They have it in evidence that wherever such opportunities have been provided, they have

---

[1] " It had not fair play because the greater number of religious people took an objection to anything but sacred music being produced, or some such objection as that."— Evidence of Thomas Beggs. Select Committee on Public-Houses, 1852-53, p. 326.

[2] *Leeds Mercury*, March 21, 1846.

[3] The local newspapers report the growth of popular music after the passing of the Ten Hours Act. See, *e.g.*, *Leeds Intelligencer*, for music at Leeds and Halifax, January 21, 1854, and March 18, 1854. See also evidence of Smith and Stevens about Birmingham before Committee on Public-Houses.

been eagerly seized upon, and have led to the decrease of intemperance." [1]

A chapter of local history given to the first Conference of the National Association for the Promotion of Social Science in 1857 showed what could be done by such improvements to draw one of the new industrial towns out of its morass. A speaker who had taken an active part in public work at Macclesfield explained that in the year 1847-48 the death-rate in that town was 42 per thousand, and that one undrained district of seven streets was responsible for this high rate, as well as for the crime of the town. The Public Health Act was adopted and this district was cleansed and reformed, with the result that the death-rate had fallen to 26 per thousand. These improvements were followed by others. Baths and wash-houses were installed, and a public park bought in which as many as forty cricket matches were sometimes played on a single Saturday afternoon when the mills closed. This park was filled every evening in the summer. The opening of the park had been followed by a remarkable decrease of crime. [2]

Wordsworth, describing mediaeval society, made towns the nurseries of civilised custom :

> " Around those Churches, gathered Towns
> Safe from the feudal Castle's haughty frowns ;
> Peaceful abodes, where Justice might uphold
> Her scales with even hand, and culture mould
> The heart to pity." [3]

As he looked at the life of his own age, he gave the town a very different character :

> " there indeed
> Love cannot be nor does it thrive with ease
> Among the close and overcrowded haunts
> Of cities, where the human heart is sick
> And the eye feeds it not and cannot feed. " [4]

---

[1] Select Committee on Public-Houses, 1854, xiv.

[2] *Transactions of the National Association for the Promotion of Social Science*, vol. i. p. 403, Paper by J. O. May : " The question might fairly be asked, what would become of the large masses of people who congregate in the park on a summer's evening after work if they had no such place of resort ? The answer is in some measure suggested by a reference to the police records of the past. Since the opening of the park, cases of ' drunkenness and disorderly conduct' have decreased in the borough 23 per cent., as compared with the preceding three years. ' Making use of obscene and profane language ' has decreased 60 per cent. Gambling has decreased 58 per cent. ; and summary charges of every class have decreased 26 per cent."—P. 407.

[3] *Poems of the Imagination*, suggested during a tour,1833. [4] *Prelude*, xii. 201.

Culture was taught to mould the heart to pity, and light and happiness were brought into the disconsolate life of these over-crowded haunts by the efforts of men and women, such as this citizen of Macclesfield, whose influence on their civilisation was as important as that of the statesmen who struggled over the Corn Laws. But in comparison they are as little known to fame as the monk whose patient labour saved for the world the Histories of Tacitus.

CHAPTER XIX

CONCLUSION

" Hitherto it is questionable if all the mechanical inventions yet made have lightened the day's toil of any human being. They have enabled a greater population to live the same life of drudgery and imprisonment, and an increased number of manufacturers and others to make fortunes. They have increased the comforts of the middle classes. But they have not yet begun to effect those great changes in human destiny, which it is in their nature and in their futurity to accomplish." MILL, *Political Economy* (Third Edition), ii. 322.

THE English people began, a century ago, to make a new society out of a rapidly growing population which had left peasant life and peasant surroundings, to find work in the new industries and homes in the new towns. This book is a survey of their first experiment in that task ; an experiment guided by a particular view of human nature. The rulers of these towns believed that a society of men getting on, trying to get on, thinking always of getting on, and sacrificing everything to getting on, would be a happy and stable society. If they had been asked where they had learnt this truth, they would have said from life, or, if the authority of books was wanted, they might have quoted Pope's lines :

> " Thus God and Nature linked the general frame,
> And bade Self-love and Social be the same " ;

or they might have talked of Adam Smith's " invisible hand," or they might have turned to the pages of Bentham on the pursuit of happiness. If, as might well be the case, they were religious by temperament and outlook, they might have said that the Puritan of the seventeenth century, who argued that " godliness hath the promises of this life as well as of the life to come," [1] was not exceptional in his own age or in any other.

Now the virtues that received special recognition in this philosophy, industry, sobriety, thrift, self-control, are never perhaps more important than in times of rapid change. Nor will any one who recalls the manners and habits that drove Wesley to travel

[1] R. H. Tawney, *Religion and the Rise of Capitalism*, p. 267.

from one end of England to the other preaching repentance, wonder that the early nineteenth century was tempted to think that if those virtues were encouraged and rewarded, the English people need trouble about little else.   But on this plan pursuits and enjoyments that have interested man at different times in his history, and helped to develop his tastes and character, were put on one side.   Beauty was allowed no place in industry, in religion or in city life.

The experiment failed.   Though individuals made fortunes, and poor men became deacons, aldermen, members of Parliament, and country gentlemen, this method did not produce a stable society.   Discontent was widespread and acute.   It was discovered that there was something wanting in this philosophy, and a series of reforms passed through Parliament making town life more attractive.

Why had the experiment failed ?   An attempt has been made in this book to answer that question by showing what life was like when it was believed that regard to the interests of private profit was all the guidance that men needed for the government of societies.   In this chapter an attempt will be made to explain why revolt against this principle took a more passionate form than a revolt against a particular injustice.

We get some light on this subject if we turn to Mill's famous criticism of Bentham.   No educated mind will question the immense benefits that Bentham conferred on the English people. Lord Acton, speaking of the intuition that started him on the task of disentangling the injustices of the law, said that " the day on which that gleam lighted up the clear hard mind of Jeremy Bentham is memorable in the political calendar beyond the entire administration of many statesmen."   Bentham's services to the reform of law and justice, as the master of Romilly, Mackintosh, and Peel, are only part of his great services to progress. But it happens that those deficiencies in his nature and philosophy on which Mill dwelt in this description have a close bearing on the social life of the new towns.

Mill showed that Bentham had a false and defective view of the qualities and forces that inspire and determine conduct ; that " his springs of action " left out such essential motives as the love of beauty and the sense of personal dignity ; that he never thought of man as a being capable of pursuing spiritual perfection as an end. From this misleading view of human nature Bentham constructed a world which Mill described as a collection of persons each pursuing his separate interest or pleasure, in which the law, religion, and public opinion, imposing their several sanctions, serve to prevent more jostling than is unavoidable.

This conception, limited enough in its original form, was not likely to become less limited in the hands of the men who applied it to the new settlements calling for guidance and leadership. The energetic man of business, when told that the best way for him to help the poor of Manchester and Leeds was to make haste to get richer, was not likely to ask himself whether so simple and encouraging a gospel contained the whole truth about something so complicated as a human society, to throw his mind back over history, to recall what had been said on such subjects by Plato or Cicero or St. Augustine or Shakespeare. Nor did it get any less limited in the hands of leaders of morals and manners, who thought that a workman spending a quiet Sunday morning in the public park when he ought to be in a chapel in a black coat was a spectacle so offensive to God that it would bring down on the nation the Divine displeasure.

This philosophy, applied to industry and social life, provoked two agitations, an agitation in the world of literature and an agitation in the world of politics. All that Bentham had forgotten crowded into the pages of Shelley and Wordsworth, Coleridge and Southey, Carlyle and Dickens, Peacock and Disraeli : pages gentle or stern, lucid or confused, pensive or ironical, playing with fancies or thundering with passion. To understand why the Chartist was a figure in history more complex than a man demanding a higher wage, or resenting a particular grievance, we must remember how deeply men and women may be stirred by emotions which they can neither describe nor interpret. The incoherent anger of Manchester and Leeds reflected what those writers had discerned, however unsuccessful they might be in devising remedies : the sickness of a society in which essential instincts were left unsatisfied. The ordinary man would not have put his case as it was put by Wordsworth, or Maurice, or Carlyle, but the error in the ruling philosophy of the time that provoked those writers was the injustice in life that provoked those rebels. Men and women knew that they were the victims of wrong, and that something was false in their world.

The experiment now tried in Manchester and Leeds was not, of course, new in history. The Roman Republic had its great age of acquisition. Dr. Heitland shows in *Agricola* how the early form of domestic slavery changed under the stimulus of the opportunities brought by war and conquest into the hideous system which still dominates our imagination. The crude gospel of gain, pursued without regard to humanity or the welfare of the State, set up the slavery of plantation and mine. The elder Cato, the stern Puritan, the expert in scientific management, told the farmer to sell off his slaves when they grew old with his old iron, and to remember that when a slave was not sleeping he ought to be working. This gospel, pushed ruthlessly in politics, in war, in government, and in industry, nearly brought Roman civilisation to an end. The Italian war, the slave war, the civil wars were the penalties paid by the Roman people for that error.

The Roman Empire rescued the world from this disorder. Its spirit is foreshadowed or reflected in the works of a line of great writers. Cicero composed his sermon describing the universal calamities that had followed the worship of wealth and wilful power : Virgil and Horace made contempt for money the characteristic of the true Roman. In these pages we find moralists and poets looking at their age and its evils and perils as Wordsworth and Carlyle looked at the evils of the age of Bentham. " Love of men cannot be bought by cash payments," said Carlyle, " and without love men cannot endure to be together." Horace, who had seen a world in which soldiers and politicians gained their power by creating mercenary armies or a mercenary electorate, had drawn the same moral from the catastrophe which so nearly extinguished the Roman genius for government.

> " Miraris, cum tu argento post omnia ponas,
> Si nemo praestet quem non merearis amorem ? " [1]

Horace saw, too, that in a society which treated wealth as the measure of a man's worth, discontent was inevitable.

> " At bona pars hominum decepta cupidine falso,
> 'Nil satis est' inquit; 'quia tanti, quantum habeas, sis.'

---

[1] " Can you wonder, when you put money above all else, that nobody pays you the love you do not earn ? "—*Sat.*, I. i. 86.

Quid facias illi ? Jubeas miserum esse, libenter
Quatenus id facit : " [1]

You may pass Lucullus to-day, but Crassus will be richer than you to-morrow. Where is it to end ?

If we want to find the new spirit at its best, we see it in the criticisms passed on Cato by Plutarch. " For my part I look upon it as a sign of a mean and ungenerous disposition to use servants like beasts of burden and to turn them off or sell them in old age ; as if there were no communication to be maintained between man and man any more than interest or necessity required." [2] In this sentence Plutarch put his finger on the central problem. The Roman Empire succeeded in controlling and composing rivalries of men, races, and classes, that had threatened to destroy civilisation, by creating a new order, inspired by the Greek tradition. For the municipal civilisation which spread over the Empire brought back the amenities and the sympathies on which a Greek community relied. The basis of this new social life was the Greek city, with its rejection of the view that a society is a collection of men pursuing separate interests, animated by selfish motives, and kept from discord only by law and other sanctions ; and its use of common enjoyments to create and foster the kind of communication between man and man which makes a stable State.

We are thus brought back to the comparison with which we started. In all ages the service of man's needs has occupied great numbers of men and women in hard, distasteful, and monotonous toil. The ancient world offered one consolation for that toil, the world of the Industrial Revolution another. The ancient world sought to make that lot tolerable by the play of life and laughter and beauty in its cities. The poor man, sharing the delight of admiration and the comforts of fellowship, could imagine, for the hour he passed beneath some noble portico, or on the ringing benches of circus or theatre, that drudgery was only part of his life ; for when the city gave its mind to religion or festival, he stood beside his neighbour, a

---

[1] " But a good many people, misled by blind desire, say, ' You cannot have enough for you get your status from what you have.' What can you do to a man who talks thus ? Bid him be miserable, since that is his whim."—*Sat.*, i. i. 61.

[2] Plutarch, *Marcus Cato*, v. Plutarch's readers will remember that he went on to deprecate such treatment of animals as well.

man among men, lost like his fellows in contemplation or enjoyment.   The new age offered the prizes of wealth and rank to those who excelled in that toil, but it treated delights, that had once made the hardships of common life less rigid and monotonous, as the rewards of rare success.   The arts, instead of helping the complaining and miserable to forget themselves and their wrongs, were employed to give a new lustre to good fortune, to declare the glory of sudden wealth.   Leisure was the exclusive privilege of those for whom work was interesting, giving to those engaged in it a bracing sense of power.

Now ancient civilisation, at its best, was disfigured by injustices that would have outraged the conscience of the age of Bentham, and by cruelties that would have revolted its sense of pity.   The critic of the Roman Empire, as an experiment in making a stable and contented society, might have pointed to Christianity and similar religions, spreading in the great towns the voice of a misery which was bitterly resented.   He might have pointed, too, to the efforts of philosophers to satisfy their consciences by a more direct encounter with those facts of poverty and slavery which civilisation sought to mask beneath its smiling amenities ; some explaining them in terms of science, others denying that such hardship could touch the soul, others, again, taking the heaviest burdens on their own backs to prove how light such burdens were when carried by men who had learnt the difference between true happiness and false.   He could thus have shown that the failures of these efforts were as striking as their successes.   Yet there was a truth behind those efforts that this new age, rich as it was in knowledge where ancient civilisation was ignorant, had still to grasp.

It is obvious that for the majority of human beings a great part of life is occupied with the hard struggle for material security, or material success.   The rulers of Manchester or Leeds believed that man could find his happiness in that struggle, clothing it with ambition or piety, giving the look of romance to its dramatic episodes, and making success or failure in that struggle the mark of success or failure in the whole art of life.   They held that you could treat the desire to grow rich as the object of universal ambition, and that if the path to its attainment was thrown open, the poor man plodding at his task might dream of his future with all the happiness that

Fielding attributed to the young barrister dreaming of the woolsack. Such a plan of life assumed that this struggle called out all man's faculties; that it symbolised somehow the whole of his history, and that it left unemployed and unsatisfied no important element in his nature.

No man can reflect on his own experience without seeing that there is a kind of happiness which is outside that struggle. The happiness that comes to a man when he follows a play or listens to music, when he stands beneath a noble building or looks out over a golden landscape, bears no relation to his own ambitions or his own success. At that moment he escapes from himself into a peace and beauty that belong to a larger world; he re-enters the life of a world which lived before him, and will live after him. The man who can never so escape is like the man described by Lucretius, who dashes from his home to the country, and from the country to his home, restless and weary, a sick man who knows not the cause of his complaint.[1]

To make a society out of men who are sick is to make a sick society. Between the spirit of Athens and that of a gold-field, between a number of persons whose bond of union is their enjoyment of art, religion, beauty, and amusement, and the same number of persons whose bond of union is that each of them hopes to become a rich man, there is a difference that affects the depths and not merely the surface of social life. Man who started on his upward path led by wonder, learning from nature, blending toil with ceremony, with religion, with dance and play, cannot be shut inside the narrow circle devised by the old economists without mortal strain. That is why, when society is sick from this cause, humanists, who are concerned for man's spiritual interest, have attacked, not merely the abuses of their age, but its fundamental philosophy. That is why Cicero, looking at Rome's age of plunder, said that the worst of all constitutions was that in which the richest men were counted the best.[2] That is why Mill, looking at the age of the Industrial Revolution, declared that " the best state for human nature is that in which, while no one is poor, no one

[1] Lucretius, iii. 1060.
[2] " Nec ulla deformior species est civitatis quam illa in quâ opulentissimi optimi putantur."—*De Republica*, i. 51.

desires to be richer, nor has any reason to fear being thrust back, by the efforts of others to push themselves forward."[1]

For the humanists saw that the progress of man has been due to his capacity for disinterested enjoyment and generous pleasure, and that he has succeeded in making societies, just because he could find some other bond between men than the bonds understood by Cato. The pursuit of knowledge and ideas, the search for beauty and feeling in culture and religion, the emotions of pride and pity excited by a common litera-ture and history, these have spread the deeper spirit of fellow-ship. The ties which unite societies, crossing the barriers of class, of race, and of time, are created by the sympathies that have civilised the habits and the mind of man.[2] "So that if the invention of the ship," wrote Bacon, in a famous passage, "was thought so noble, which carrieth riches and com-modities from place to place, and consociateth the most remote regions in participation of their fruits, how much more are letters to be magnified, which as ships pass through the vast seas of time, and make ages so distant to participate of the wisdom, illuminations, and inventions, the one of the other?"[3]

Dr. Bridges, describing the birth of man's mind from his response to the beauty of nature, drew a picture of the wolf hunting all his life after nightfall, under starlit skies, without the first inklings of wonder.[4] Yet even the wolf, as he steals across the silence of Mount Olympus, may turn to gaze on the vast peace that lies over the enchanted world described in *Endymion*, the world of bird and beast, of sea and mountain, sleeping in the silver moonlight. The men and women who now lived in blind streets had lived, themselves or their fathers, beneath the open spaces of heaven. In the high moments of his history man has answered the beauty of nature with the beauty of cities, but for these exiles the dreams of mind and hand were as faint and distant as the mountains and the forests whence those dreams had come. No public grace adorned their towns; religion was too often a stern

[1] *Principles of Political Economy*, bk. iv. chap. 6.
[2] See Galsworthy's description of the place of beauty in social life in *Castles in Spain*.
[3] *Advancement of Learning*, viii. 6.
[4] *Testament of Beauty*, 319.

and selfish fantasy; music and painting were strangers, at home among the elegant rich, but doubtful of their welcome in this raw confusion; ships brought the riches of the East across the Indian Ocean, but those other ships which " pass through the vast seas of time " never spread their splendid sails.   Science herself, the goddess of the age, kept her gifts for the fortunate.   For though man's power and knowledge had made a new world since Odysseus fretted for his home in Calypso's cavern, the spinner, guiding the myriad wheels that clothed the distant East, was condemned to spend his life longing, like Homer's ploughman, for the hour of sunset and supper.   But the spirit of wonder which had created art and religion, music and letters, gardens and playing fields, was not dead in the toiling men and women shut within these sullen streets.   That spirit could not live at peace in treadmill cities where the daylight never broke upon the beauty and the wisdom of the world.

TABLE OF DATES

PRIME MINISTER

1837. MELBOURNE. New Parliament. Conservatives, 310; Liberals, etc., 348.
Anti-Poor Law riots at Bradford.
Birmingham Political Union revived.

1838. MELBOURNE. Poor Law Commission Report on Epidemics.
People's Charter published.
Anti-Corn Law League established.
Anti-Poor Law riots at Dewsbury, Huddersfield, and Todmorden.
Manchester incorporated.

1839. MELBOURNE. Harvey's motion for recreation allotments.
Lord John Russell's educational scheme announced.
Chartist Convention meets in London.
Bedchamber incident.
Chartist Convention moves to Birmingham.
Education Committee of Privy Council established.
First Chartist Petition.
Chartist Convention dissolved.
Newport rising.
Police Act for Sunday closing in London.
Birmingham incorporated.

1840. MELBOURNE. Report of Select Committee on Health of Towns.
Pakington's Beerhouse Licensing Act.

1841. MELBOURNE. Proposal for grant to Mechanics' Institutions.
Normanby's Public Health Bill.
General Election.
National Charter Association founded.
New Parliament. Conservatives, 367; Liberals, etc., 286.

(Sept.) PEEL. Lovett's National Association founded.

1842. PEEL. Normanby reintroduces Public Health Bill.
Mines Report.
Complete Suffrage movement and petition.
Second Chartist petition.
Report on Sanitary Condition of Labouring Population.
Proposal for grant to Hullah's classes.
Mines Act.
Peel imposes income-tax (first time since 1816).
Strikes and riots in industrial districts.

1843. PEEL. Second Report of Children's Employment Commission.
Factory Bill with educational clauses introduced and dropped.
Voluntaryist campaign started.
Select Committee on Allotments.

PRIME MINISTER

1843. PEEL. Ashley's Allotment Bill.
Worsley's Return of Acreage of Waste Land.
Sheffield incorporated.
Magistrates empowered to license theatres.
Birkenhead Public Park.

1844 PEEL. Factory Act.
First Report of Health of Towns Commission.
Worsley's General Inclosure Bill.
Cowper's Field Gardens Bill.
Select Committee on Inclosure.
Half-holiday established by Manchester merchants.
Anti-Corn Law League spends £1000 a week on agitation.
Leeds Vicarage Act.

1845. PEEL. Second Report of Health of Towns Commission.
Lincoln's Public Health Bill.
Cowper's Field Gardens Bill.
Museums Act.
Nottingham Inclosure Act.
General Inclosure Act.
Inclosure Commission established.
Maynooth Grant Act.
Andover Workhouse scandal.
Peel resigns and Russell fails to form a Ministry.
Newman joins Church of Rome.
Disraeli publishes *Sybil*.

1846. PEEL. Repeal of Corn Laws carried.
(June) RUSSELL. Baths and Washhouses Act.
Important Liverpool Health Act.
Educational Minutes establishing pupil teacher system published.
Registry of Friendly Societies.
Opening of Manchester parks.

1847. RUSSELL. Morpeth's Public Health Bill introduced and attacked.
Ten Hours Bill passed.
General Election.
New Parliament. Peelites, 105; Protectionists, 226; Liberals, 325.
Poor Law Commission dissolved.
Poor Law Board established.
Towns Improvement Clauses Act.
Manchester bishopric established.
Bradford incorporated.

1848. RUSSELL. Third Chartist petition.
Morpeth's Public Health Act.
Board of Health established.

	PRIME MINISTER	
1848.	RUSSELL.	Sunday morning closing made compulsory. Public library at Warrington. Maurice and Kingsley start Christian Socialist movement.
1849.	RUSSELL.	Select Committee on Public Libraries. Public library at Salford. Internal Methodist crisis.
1850.	RUSSELL.	Death of Peel. Public Libraries Act. Manchester Rectory Act. Papal Bull creating Roman Catholic bishops in England causes commotion.
1851.	RUSSELL.	The Great Exhibition. Owens College opened at Manchester.
1852.	RUSSELL.	General Election.
(Feb.)	DERBY.	Death of Duke of Wellington. New Parliament. Liberals, 315; Conservatives, 299; Peelites, 40.
(Dec.)	ABERDEEN.	Public library at Manchester.
1853.	ABERDEEN.	Gladstone's first Budget. Advertisement duty repealed. Public libraries at Liverpool and Bolton. Public park at Rochdale.
1854.	ABERDEEN.	Board of Health dissolved. New Board with Sir B. Hall as President. Dickens publishes *Hard Times*. Crimean War.

INDEX

DATE DUE
